Beyond the Threshold

Beyond the Threshold

Afterlife Beliefs and Experiences
in World Religions

Christopher M. Moreman

ROWMAN & LITTLEFIELD PUBLISHERS, INC.
Lanham • Boulder • New York • Toronto • Plymouth, UK

ROWMAN & LITTLEFIELD PUBLISHERS, INC.

Published in the United States of America
by Rowman & Littlefield Publishers, Inc.
A wholly owned subsidiary of The Rowman & Littlefield Publishing Group, Inc.
4501 Forbes Boulevard, Suite 200, Lanham, Maryland 20706
www.rowmanlittlefield.com

Estover Road
Plymouth PL6 7PY
United Kingdom

Copyright © 2008 by Rowman & Littlefield Publishers, Inc.
First paperback edition 2010

British Library Cataloguing in Publication Information Available

Library of Congress Cataloging-in-Publication Data:

The hardback edition of this book was previously cataloged by the Library of Congress as
follows:

Moreman, Christopher M., 1974–
  Beyond the threshold : afterlife beliefs and experiences in world religions / Christopher
Moreman.
       p. cm.
  1. Future life. I. Title.
  BL535.M68 2008
  202'.3—dc22   2008016699

ISBN: 978-0-7425-6228-8 (cloth : alk. paper)
ISBN: 978-0-7425-6229-5 (pbk. : alk. paper)
ISBN: 978-0-7425-6552-4 (electronic)

Printed in the United States of America

♾™ The paper used in this publication meets the minimum requirements of American
National Standard for Information Sciences—Permanence of Paper for Printed Library
Materials, ANSI/NISO Z39.48-1992.

For my cousin, Richard Leger,
who found out for himself
the answers to all of these questions
far too soon for the rest of us.

Contents

Acknowledgments

There are many people to whom I must credit for assistance with the production of this text, which has followed a long road from dissertation to book. I would like to begin by expressing my gratitude to those professors who read and commented on the work in progress. Foremost among these is my supervisor, Professor Paul Badham, who guided me through the doctoral stage and managed the difficulties of communication at a distance. Thanks are also due the following who read chapters in their own individual areas of specialization: Professor Dan Cohn-Sherbok, Dr. Gary Bunt, Dr. Ismail Hacinebioglu, Dr. Maya Warrier, Dr. Wendy Dossett, Professor Xinzhong Yao, and Dr. John Palmer. Dr. Denise Cush deserves credit for acting as the external reviewer of the thesis.

I would like to thank Drs. Michael Thalbourne and Lance Storm for asking me to contribute a chapter to their collection, *The Survival of Human Consciousness: Essays on the Possibility of Life After Death*, and to the editors at Mac-Farland & Company, Inc., for permitting me to include a revised version of this chapter as the conclusion to my book.

I must also acknowledge the support of both the Society for Psychical Research and Concordia University's Institute for Canadian Jewish Studies as they both provided financial assistance during my research. Dr. Norm Ravvin, Chair of Canadian Jewish Studies, was of great help. The Parapsychology Foundation also generously awarded me the D. Scott Rogo Award toward revising the thesis into a book.

I would like to thank the following for additional comments at various stages of writing: Dr. Vanessa Sasson, Dr. Ciaran O'Keefe, and David Fiore.

I owe gratitude to Sarah Stanton and Brian Romer, Elaine McGarraugh, and the rest of the editorial staff at Rowman & Littlefield for following this book through its final stages.

Dr. Deena Rymhs continues to offer her ongoing support and inspiration, for which I am ever grateful.

~

Introduction

Death. The word itself invokes fear. As human beings, every person experiences life in all of its myriad aspects daily. Death lies beyond the pale of this experience, but remains ever present all the same. As every person lives, death lies constantly at some unknown point in the future. Western society, for the most part, has become a death-denying culture. The miracles of science and medicine are expected to cure all ills, and death is no exception. Certainly, modern advances have extended the average human life span by decades. Still, death is unavoidable, and yet we try to ignore it, or perhaps to pretend it will not happen to us. Elisabeth Kübler-Ross, the perennial expert on death and dying in the modern West, says, "in our unconscious, death is never possible for ourselves."[1] It defies the imagination to conceive of an ending to life and to itself, though the knowledge that death awaits every person is sure.

With death as an eventual certainty, fear then revolves around the state beyond that threshold between this world and whatever lies beyond. Hamlet's "undiscovered country from whose bourn no traveller returns,"[2] looms we know not when. The knowledge of an impending ambush leading to some obscure fate colors our time on this earth, whether we are conscious of it or not. Decisions of what to spend one's time on cannot be made without the perspective that one does not have time to do everything in a single lifetime. As such, humans are possessed of an over-arching pursuit of meaning in everything one does in one's life. The manner in which one views death, and what lies beyond, influences one's value judgments and plays an important role in determining where one finds meaning. John Hick points out that, "the two mysteries [of life and death] are inextricably bound together. If we wish to think realistically about life we cannot avoid also thinking about death."[3] People's daily decisions will undoubtedly be based, to some extent, upon their vision of what lies beyond death. To believe a certain proposition, as Hick says, "is, primarily, to possess (or be possessed by) a set of tendencies, liabilities, or dispositions to act in ways appropriate to the truth of that proposition in situations to which the proposition is seen to be relevant."[4] If life is a journey, the question of which forks one might take depends on whether one believes that it is a journey leading to some form of afterlife or one that simply leads nowhere.

Speculation is rife as to what the state beyond death might be like, and since time immemorial, humans have tried to come to grips with the possibilities. Religion has been a bastion of eschatological thought for millennia, and continues to be a major source for hope and comfort to the dying and bereaved. Every major world religion includes some thought on the state of the individual after bodily death, often as a central component of faith. In instances where the orthodox religion prefers to avoid such discussion, most obviously with such thinkers as Confucius or the Buddha, the popular mind forces the topic upon them. In fact, most religions have officially encouraged their adherents to focus more on how to live life in this world and less on the world to come. Still, people demand to know the fate of their parents and friends, and the ultimate fate to which they too will eventually succumb.

In an increasingly secular and materialistic world, religious ideology and discussion of the supernatural in general have come to be viewed in many circles with utter contempt. In 1844, Karl Marx referred to religion as "the opium of the people,"[5] and Richard Dawkins over a century later called religious teachings, "viruses of the mind."[6] Materialism denies any form of a life after death, arguing vehemently against all notions that seem to contradict present scientific theory, or that cannot be somehow tested in a strict laboratory setting. Corliss Lamont sums up the mechanistic attitude toward death in opposition to what he calls "*The Illusion of Immortality*":

biologically speaking, natural death is not in the least mysterious, but is as understandable as birth itself. Both occurrences are part of a biological process that provides for a perpetual fountain of youth. Remarkable as human bodies are, Nature eventually discards them for fresh ones; and it ought not to be surprising if, remarkable as human personalities are, Nature adopts the same policy towards them.[7]

Regardless of scientific skepticism, or perhaps due to the hollowness of it, billions of people worldwide embrace established religions and hold strong beliefs in such abstract concepts as a life after death, in whatever form those ideas might take. The philosopher C. J. Ducasse surmised that there is no a priori reason to disregard the possibility of some form of survival beyond bodily death:

> that persistence of consciousness in some form after death is both theoretically and empirically possible: *theoretically possible* since analysis of the supposition of such persistence finds no contradiction implicit in it; and *empirically possible* since that supposition is not inconsistent with any definitely known empirical fact.[8]

In the tradition of Mircea Eliade, this book will investigate both the belief systems of the major world religions on life after death, and the individual experiences that appear in this variety of cultural contexts.

The first part of this book will examine in detail the beliefs in death and what lies beyond, that are found in the various major world religions; the theoretical possibilities as described by Ducasse. Of the myriad religions of the world, space constraints allow for a discussion of only some. In this volume, I focus on the so-called "major world religions" of Judaism, Christianity, Islam, Hinduism, Buddhism, Taoism, and Confucianism. One could make an argument for the inclusion of other schools as well, including Sikhism, Jainism, and Shintoism. The religions I have chosen to focus on, however, represent the standard in terms of surveys of world religions. These represent the spiritual traditions of great swaths of humankind and have had tremendous impact on world history. The Abrahamic monotheisms of Judaism, Christianity, and Islam are all related in some ways, but the differences are as important as the similarities, especially considering the present world stage. Hinduism represents the vast range of spiritual traditions of India extending back thousands of years and represents a significant portion of the world's population both today and throughout history. Buddhism, originally sprouting in India, has moved on to become a major spiritual and philosophical factor in most of Asia. Finally, the religions of China remain important despite Communist suppression of religious identity as traditional concepts and rituals have been retained against a nominal atheism and continue to form an essential component of the fabric of Chinese culture. With the religions chosen for this book, then, I am aiming to cover a vast proportion of global belief while capturing a degree of diversity. Religions like Sikhism and Jainism represent significant populations in their own rights, and Shintoism deserves attention as the traditional religion of Japan. For that matter, the disparate African traditions would require a volume of their own. For the time being, however, these are traditions that will have to be explored in another volume.

In the present book, I will trace the evolution of the chosen schools of thought through an historical analysis of each religion individually. Additionally, the chapters are specifically organized in an attempt to show some chronological coherence, both in the text and in the religious traditions themselves, especially where the development of a given religion was clearly dependent upon an older faith. In addition to relating the beliefs of each religious tradition, I have also made an effort to incorporate folkloric material as well in order to illustrate both the orthodox religious traditions and the lived experience of each for those who ascribe to one faith or another. The wealth of information covered in this volume is immense and I have made every effort to be concise, while still covering the material in detail.

The first chapter will discuss the ancient religions of the Mediterranean region and the Middle East, as a kind of background for further discussion. Egyptian, Mesopotamian, Greek, and Roman views of death will receive specific attention. The ideas expressed by these ancient cultures have had an immense impact upon the modern philosophies of the West and clearly relate to the development of all Western religions. At the same time, extending the discussion into the ancient West can help to further a comparative conversation with the religions of the East. While the ancient civilizations covered in this first section have all died, their philosophies remain alive to the present day because of this very impact. Understanding them is essential to understanding what has come after.

My three subsequent chapters cover the great monotheistic religions of Judaism, Christianity, and Islam. These faiths share a very close relationship, each building upon the prophecies and teachings of the last, stemming from their common origins in the deserts of the Middle East. Judaism was the first of the three to become established, born as a contemporary of those religions discussed in the first chapter. The prophetic tradition of Moses, Judaism survives in a variety of forms into the present day. Christianity grew directly out of the Jewish faith, Jesus himself having been born a Jew. Acknowledged by his followers as the prophesied Messiah, this contention was rejected by the mainstream of Judaism and thus a schism erupted that launched a new religion that would be more influential than any throughout the formation of the Western world. Finally, Islam was revealed through the Prophet Muhammad, the last in a line of prophets including Jesus, Moses, and Abraham, several centuries after the death of Jesus, providing a uniquely Arabic belief system that has grown to become one of the largest religions in the world today.[9]

Following these, the subsequent three chapters concern themselves with Eastern religions. Beginning with Hinduism, the religion of India, from which Buddhism was a later outgrowth, and then closing with the three great religions of China. Hinduism stakes the claim as the oldest surviving religion in the world, having a history that extends back thousands of years before Christ. Hinduism should not be seen as a monolithic tradition that has remained relatively unchanged for all of this time. Instead, it should more accurately be seen as a catchall term for the variety of spiritualities that exist and have existed in South Asia for centuries. Among the philosophies of India, Buddhism appeared as a means to democratize religious experience, bringing it from the hands of the priestly classes to an ever-widening availability as it evolved. The religions of China take up the final chapter of the first section of my work and present us with a composite of beliefs, which are usually reduced to three main traditions. The indigenous traditions of Confucianism and Taoism have become interwoven with a new form of Buddhism that was forced to adapt in many ways to the Chinese worldview. Alongside these three Chinese religions there is also a strong current of folk belief that unites them all.

In outlining the evolution of these divergent belief systems, I will eventually lead into a comparative discourse of them all. Where a survey of world religions is useful in the pursuit of knowledge, the analysis of the ideas is of greater interest theoretically. I have therefore reserved a concluding chapter for an in-depth discussion comparing and contrasting the different belief systems. Similarities and differences will both be discussed with an eye to finding some common ground. As death is a universal human experience, one might expect to find similarities in the beliefs attendant to it. The first section, outlining the beliefs of these great traditions, is necessary before a deeper examination of the human experience of death can be accomplished.

While the detailed theologies that have been developed over centuries contain obvious differences—reincarnation versus resurrection, for instance—certain other beliefs transcend geography and history, appearing in vastly different cultures throughout time. One example might be the existence of some spirit, soul, or other ethereal substance logically distinct from the body, that, while in constant interaction with the body throughout normal daily life, is believed to both leave the body temporarily in certain circumstances and then permanently at death to exist in some other form separate from the body. While the former speculations may rely solely on faith, the latter beliefs are founded upon legitimate experiences. Human experience is to some extent a product of cultural expectation, but just as importantly (if not more so) human experience dictates the parameters for cultural belief. As such, all of the world's religions, despite the intricate workings of their individual eschatologies, incorporate some elements of cross-cultural human experience. While mainstream religion tends to ignore these phenomena, it is just such experiences (what Alan Segal labels "Religiously Interpreted States of Consciousness or RISCs"[10]) that have continued to force debate on issues of what lies beyond death. In dealing with each religious tradition, an effort will be made to illustrate the types of experiences found that might be seen as indicative of an afterlife and supporting the beliefs of the faithful. It is here that I rely on folklore as a collection of what might be considered unofficial cultural knowledge, as opposed to the orthodox official cultural knowledge.

The second half of my study will then delve into these experiences themselves—the empirical possibilities alluded to by Ducasse earlier—critically and in specific detail in order to evaluate their worth as empirical evidence for an afterlife, and to determine their weight in terms of constructors or constructions of belief. Empiricism, it must be remembered, refers to the importance of human experience as a determinant for the reality of a given phenomenon. In this second half of the book, I am specifically examining aspects of human experience. Often, experiences relating to an afterlife are considered strange if not impossible, and so are all too often completely ignored. This simply fails to do justice to the range of human experience that surrounds the ultimate human reality of death. In the event that some experiences related to an afterlife are universal human experiences, then it is important to see how such experiences affect religious belief systems, if at all. This examination will contribute further to the project at hand in working through the relationship of experience to certain beliefs.

Scientific research into the area of anomalous experience began in earnest in the late nineteenth century when a group of Cambridge scholars came together to form the Society for Psychical Research with the express intent to examine the possibility of the survival of the human person beyond death. These "psychical researchers" conducted exhaustive, and controversial, studies of purported evidence from spirit mediums, case studies of apparitions, and other as yet unexplained human experiences. More recently, such research has evolved into controlled laboratory experimentation with the birth of the relatively young science of parapsychology. While mainstream scientists often revile the subject matter of such research, parapsychologists continue to uncover data that are increasingly troublesome for the tenability of a purely materialistic paradigm. Any challenge to a purely materialistic worldview is of direct consequence for the religions of world, relying as they universally do on the reality of some nonmaterial form of reality. While the kinds of research going on examine such diverse areas as telepathy, the power of prayer, and the ability to spy a remote location through the use of clairvoyance, those phenomena directly related to the question of human survival can be divided into four categories, each of which will get special treatment in this book.

That people have reported seeing ghosts throughout history is undeniable. Spirits reportedly appear in private dreams as well as to groups of people who are totally awake. Stories of haunted houses, as well as recognized apparitions, are very common in every culture and can be found within every religious tradition however much adherents are enjoined to ignore them. Attempts to communicate with spirits, and with the dead in general, have been carried out since well before recorded history. Spirit mediums and shamans have been known to visit the spirit world and have an affinity for speaking with the dead, bringing solace and comfort to family and friends left behind, and providing strange insights into the alleged world beyond. Similarly, shamans, as well as mystics of every faith, describe the sensation of leaving their bodies in a spiritual form and being able to travel wide distances in this discarnate state. In some cases, dreams themselves are thought to involve such out-of-body travel. There is also the matter of similar experiences occurring at or near the moment of death, in which the individual not only feels the separation of the self from the body but seems to travel to the next world and then return to tell the tale in what are known as near-death experiences. Finally, there are also those rare (for modern Western religions, in any event) instances where people claim to remember having been born in a past life. Such memories require an acceptance of some form of belief in reincarnation if they are to be taken at face value, but other possibilities will be discussed as well. And so, I will devote a chapter each to apparitions and hauntings; mediumistic communications; out-of-body and near-death experiences; and past-life memories. In these chapters, an effort will be made to discuss objectively just what has been discovered in relation to these strange phenomena from a scientific standpoint. That humans have these experiences cannot be denied. What remains is, first, to determine how such experiences might fit into the various religious worldviews, and, second, to determine whether any of these experiences can actually be seen to provide sustainable evidence for what may happen after individual death.

In the end, I will attempt to draw the details presented in both parts of my text together and form a synthesis of some kind. The cross-cultural experiences of contact with the spirit world investigated by psychic research can be seen as a core element to belief in life after death. Every world religion encounters these experiences and antecedent beliefs and deals with them accordingly. As beliefs have evolved, they have diverged along differing lines to form distinct schools of thought dependent upon a great amount of faith. Still, scientific investigation can perhaps provide some support to the notion that there are core experiences at the root of all such beliefs. I will make some effort to formulate a hypothesis for life after death that involves evidence from empirical investigation and will incorporate the complexities of thought composed by the various religions over centuries of consideration upon this topic. Obviously, all such discussion remains at the level of speculation, but I hope through the analysis of scientific investigation and centuries of philosophical thought on the topic that some synthesis might be formed that will bring us closer to an understanding of what lies beyond the threshold of death while we remain in the world of the living.

Notes

1. Elisabeth Kübler-Ross, *On Death and Dying* (New York: Touchstone, 1969), p. 16.

2. William Shakespeare, "The Tragedy of Hamlet, Prince of Denmark," in *The Complete Works*, eds. Stanley Wells, et al. (Oxford: Clarenden, 1988), Act 3, Scene 1, line 81–82, p. 670.

3. John Hick, *Death and Eternal Life* (London: Collins, 1976), p. 22.

4. John Hick, *Faith and Knowledge* (London: MacMillan, 1967), p. 247.

5. Karl Marx, "Contribution to the Critique of Hegel's Philosophy of Right," in *On Religion*, eds. Karl Marx and Friedrich Engels (New York: Shocken, 1964), pp. 41–43.

6. Richard Dawkins, "Viruses of the Mind," in *Dennett and His Critics: Demystifying Mind*, ed. Bo Dalhbom (Cambridge, Mass.: Blackwell, 1993).

7. Corliss Lamont, *The Illusion of Immortality* (New York: Philosophical Library, 1959), p. 73.

8. C. J. Ducasse, *A Critical Examination of the Belief in a Life After Death* (LaSalle, Ill.: C.C. Thomas, 1961), p. 132.

9. Alan Segal's recent study of afterlife beliefs in Western thought is critical to mention in connection with the first four chapters of my own work as his is vastly more encyclopedic than my present book. Segal's text, *Life After Death* (New York: Doubleday, 2004), provides lengthy detail into not only the histories of afterlife beliefs in the monotheistic traditions and their antecedents, as I do here, but provides a wealth of information on the histories of each tradition in general.

10. Segal, *Life After Death*, pp. 322–350.

PART ONE

AN OVERVIEW OF BELIEFS
IN AN AFTERLIFE FROM
MAJOR WORLD RELIGIONS

CHAPTER ONE

~

Ancient Conceptions

A suitable place to begin a detailed examination of the beliefs surrounding life after death in the world's religions might be in what are often considered the origins of Western thought, the Ancient Near East. Among the myriad civilizations to have called this part of the world home, only a small handful have become well-known through their fundamental impact on the progress of history. When looking at cultures long since passed, one must rely upon surviving written records and whatever assumptions can be made based on the archaeological evidence, particularly for our present purposes funerary evidence. We can only assume that whatever is gleaned from such scanty sources is insufficient to form a complete picture of the true beliefs of the people, yet with this knowledge in hand, I will attempt to formulate as clear a picture as possible.

Mesopotamia

Ancient Mesopotamia, situated roughly where Iraq is today, straddled the Tigris and Euphrates rivers (Mesopotamia itself meaning "between rivers") and was home to a number of civilizations in early times. Sumerians, Akkadians, Babylonians, and others successively came into predominance in this area. The wide array of groups who occupied this area were not uniform in their beliefs and cultures, and so evidence of "notions of death and afterlife is unevenly scattered over 2,500 years of history."[1] This scattering of materials from various civilizations occupying the same locale over such an extensive period of time makes it extremely difficult to ascertain the precise beliefs of any one group versus another, or even to know when changes in belief systems may have occurred. W. G. Lambert notes yet another difficulty as, "A 'theology' of a subject is presumably a systematic descriptive account of the relevant religious views and outlooks. As such, an account of the subject under consideration cannot be expected in cuneiform texts, since the ancients were not given to producing descriptive accounts of this kind."[2] What follows, therefore, is piecemeal, pointing to some Mesopotamian ideas of death and beyond.

While these ancients may not have formulated much in the way of detailed religious thought, the literature they did leave contains some valuable mythic and epic narratives. Though there is no specific theology carved in stone, so to speak, one can construct a system of beliefs by looking at these myths. Typically, the Mesopotamian view of life and death is described as very dark and nihilistic. Humans were created to work for the gods, and their sole purpose was, "to provide [the gods] with food, drink, clothes and places to live—the temples and sanctuaries, the 'homes' of the gods. This is the predominant human function; anything else, including their own needs, is secondary."[3] To ensure that humans would be obedient servants, the gods placed the yoke of death upon them to keep them in check. With this fact firmly in mind, to the average Mesopotamian, "the inevitability of death was accepted as an indisputable and irremedial [sic] fact of everyday occurrence, and what lay beyond the grave was so obscure as to be hardly a matter of very serious conjecture."[4]

So humans lived day to day, knowing death awaited them, but unaware of when it would strike. "But death was not the absolute end. Man had a soul (*etimmu*), inherited from the slain god whose body was used in the creation of man."[5] Still, the picture of the afterlife gave humans nothing to look forward to. Once a person died, the *etimmu* would leave the body and travel down to a somber underworld, referred to as the "land of no return," where life was a dim and distant shadow of life on Earth. As the goddess Ishtar descended into the underworld, she described the goal of her journey thus:

> To the house of shadows, the dwelling of Irkalla,
> To the house without exit for him who enters therein,
> To the road, whence there is no turning,
> To the house without light for him who enters therein,
> The place where dust is their nourishment, clay their food.[6]

In the most famous piece of Mesopotamian literature, *The Epic of Gilgamesh*, dating as far back as the third millennium BCE, it is this bleak view of the afterlife that drives the protagonist, Gilgamesh, to literally travel to the ends of the Earth to discover the secret of eternal life. He is spurred to action after the death of his closest friend, Enkidu. While Enkidu is lying upon his deathbed in the throes of a serious illness, he wakes from a dream in which he claims to have had a glimpse of the underworld into which he is about to venture. He recounts being led into the underworld by a monster and bearing witness to the fates of kings, priests, and sages who have become servants to the goddess of the dead, Ereshkigal.

> In the house of ashes, where I entered,
> I saw [the mighty], their crowns fallen to the dirt.
> I heard about crowned kings who ruled the land from days of old,
> Worldly images of Anu and Enlil, waiting table with roast meats,
> Serving baked good, filling glasses with water from cool steins.[7]

While this vision certainly portrays a dismal afterlife, the epic as a whole might be seen as actually discouraging a fear of death. Gilgamesh grieves for his friend on the grand scale of ancient heroes before setting off on his quest. He launches on a journey to find Utnapishtim, known to be the only human ever to have been granted immortality by the gods due to his role in saving humans from the great deluge. The journey is long but he finally reaches the island upon which Utnapishtim and his wife are said to dwell forever. However, it is not everlasting life that Gilgamesh finds there, but the assurance that death is as natural and unavoidable as is sleep. "The sleeping and the dead, how like brothers they are!"[8] Just as man cannot remain awake forever, he must one day rest eternally. Finally, Utnapishtim challenges Gilgamesh to remain awake for six days and seven nights, for if he could do that, then he might become immortal. Gilgamesh fails, however, and falls asleep almost immediately. Upon waking, he is sent back to his home to rule and to live until his eventual and unavoidable death.

An alternate version of Enkidu's death appears at the end of the epic, in a tablet that does not fit chronologically with the others. In this poem, Enkidu becomes trapped in the underworld while on an adventure and Gilgamesh prays to several gods for his return. One of the deities consents and Enkidu rises, ghost-like from the ground. He then describes a netherworld in some ways similar to that described previously, however he provides details of how different people "live" in the underworld. Bearing offspring is revealed to be of central importance to one's fate in the netherworld, as those with more sons are described in much brighter terms, those with seven sons claimed to be "like a man close to the gods."[9] This emphasis on children, combined with references to libations made at the grave, indicates some form of ancestral worship, at least to the extent that those who receive libations and remembrance beyond the grave lead a much happier existence than those who have no such favors from the living. At the other end of the spectrum, however, Gilgamesh inquires of his friend: "The one whose spirit has no one left alive to love him: have you seen him?" And Enkidu's ghost replies: "I have. The left-overs of the pot, the scraps of bread thrown in the gutter [what no dead dog will eat] he eats."[10] Without descendents to remember you in death leaves you in eternal despair.

J. S. Cooper describes how this ancestral worship was considered a kind of double-edged blade. The living were expected to leave behind many children, especially sons. These sons were expected to honor the memories of their fathers through ritual acts. In turn, those among the dead who were not offered libations or given proper burial might become angry and return to harass the living.

> The effects of the ghosts of the unburied or untended dead on the living are truly calamitous. In addition to haunting the living while asleep or awake, which can be unsettling in the extreme, they are the cause of numerous physical and psychological maladies. But if properly cared for, ghosts can be invoked for protection . . .
>
> Thus the carrot and the stick. The same ghost who, untended, can disrupt and ruin a person's life can, when properly cared for, be a valuable assistant against other malefactors.[11]

And so, in order not to incite the wrath of an unfriendly ghost, it was up to the surviving family members to pay tribute to them in death. Not only would such offerings ensure that no harm would come from the dead, but it might also entreat them to offer protection from such things as illness and the resentment of less fortunate spirits. The efforts of Gilgamesh to gain the return of his friend, even in ghostly form, seems to indicate the difficulty of this process but it also suggests that such efforts might meet with success and that the living and dead might still encounter each other.

All in all, the general outlook focused squarely on living life and contributing to the community through procreation with a continued reverence for past generations. The afterlife was not discussed in any great detail, though it was evidently thought to be a relatively bleak existence. Those who had living progeny to keep their memories alive in the land of the living might have some form of happiness.

Egypt

The Mesopotamian outlook on death and the hereafter can be equated to the basic foundation of other Near Eastern views. The Egyptians, who existed as contemporaries of many Mesopotamian cultures, certainly recognized a similar belief early on, though over time they developed a much more complex system.

Unlike the Mesopotamians, who avoided discussion of the topic, the Egyptians came to display a kind of obsession with death. The wealth of information they left on the subject is confusing, however, and in places contradictory.

> So far as they can be reconstructed, the earliest Egyptian beliefs concerning existence after death resembled the two traditions that are amply documented throughout the world: the dwelling place of the dead was either underground or else in the sky—more precisely, among the stars. After death, souls made their way to the stars and shared in their eternity . . .
> The subterranean localisation of the other world was a predominant belief in the Neolithic cultures. Already as early as the pre-dynastic period . . . certain religious traditions bound up with agriculture found expression in the mythico-ritual Osirian complex.[12]

To a certain extent, one can find here a view corresponding with some of the Mesopotamian beliefs discussed previously. The addition of Osiris is something new, however, as is the concept of finding one's place amongst the stars. In the Egyptian view, these divergent concepts are represented each by a specific god: Osiris symbolizing a chthonic force of rebirth and renewal, and Ra, god of the Sun, surging forth through the sky cyclically with the light of a new day.

In his position as Sun God, Ra was closely associated with the pharaoh, the light of the people. Ra and the pharaoh were not only symbolic of each other, but the pharaoh was believed to be the physical embodiment of the god himself. In this way, the pharaoh was considered to be a god and was thus immortal. "[H]is death meant no more than his translation to heaven. The continuity from one incarnate god to another incarnate god, and hence the continuity of the cosmic order, was insured."[13] When the pharaoh's earthly body died, he lived on in the heavens as a star and a new pharaoh came to power as a new incarnation of the divine power of Ra. According to the *Egyptian Book of the Dead*: "My soul is the God, my soul is eternity."[14] The multitude of stars appeared as minor suns illuminating the night sky, each one the lasting impression of a former earthly pharaoh. Still, the living pharaoh embodied the greatest light of Ra, the sun. Despite the equation of the pharaoh with the stars, there remained also a great concern for the preservation of the physical body after death.

For several thousand years, Egyptians went to great lengths to preserve the corpse through an elaborate process of mummification. This was a practice at first limited to the pharaoh but eventually extended to include almost everyone. The abstract concept of an immortal aspect of the pharaoh existing without a physical body escaped the early Egyptian imagination, as they believed that the continued existence of the body was essential to the continued existence of the celestial form.[15] As Mircea Eliade, commenting specifically on the *Pyramid Texts* (circa 2350 BCE), states: "Here, certainly, there are two different ideologies that are not yet adequately integrated."[16] The idea of mummification was based on the notion that the spirit, *ka*, needed time to form a spiritual body and so the physical body would provide the home for the *ka* until the spiritual body was ready and it could leave.[17] Jan Assmann describes how the dismemberment and re-memberment of the body in mummification served as a transitioning ritual across the liminal space between life and death.[18]

The Egyptians believed that a person was actually made up of various aspects, each with its own individual postmortem existence. For its part, the body comprised the home of the physical being and the mummification ensured the survival of those earthly aspects. The *ka* is that part that consists of the personality of the individual and is the aspect that travels to the hereafter. A third aspect, the *ba*, forms the middle ground between the other two forms. The *ba* is the ghost or shade of the person and remains closely attached to the body and its tomb. In this way, it was possible to conceive of the dead as both residing with the stars, but also remaining within the tomb where they had been laid to rest.

Having briefly considered the beliefs connected with the Sun God and the pharaoh, it remains to discuss the myth of Osiris and the importance it has for concepts of life and death. In the story, Osiris is murdered by his brother, Set, and dismembered. His wife, Isis, gathers his various parts and unites them all with the notable exception of his phallus, which had been cast into the Nile and eaten by a fish. After praying for him to be restored to life, Osiris rises to take his place as king of the underworld. In his death and rebirth, he becomes a symbol for regenerative growth. The phallus, as an emblem of fertility, was thought to have made the Nile fertile when it was cast into it. Osiris' death and rebirth became easily associated with the yearly rejuvenation of the vegetation along the Nile banks. Osiris, then, was seen as a giver of life and a lord of the dead, tying the natural order together from birth to death in an ongoing cycle.

These ideas all intermingled to form a complex view of life after death. The *ka* of the dead was thought to leave the body and tomb behind and enter the subterranean realm of Osiris. Once appearing before the Lord of the Dead, the spirits of the dead would see their own virtues, in the spiritualized form of their heart, weighed against a feather. Failure of this test of merit would see them devoured by the Eater of the Dead, the crocodile-headed god, Attim. To be thus devoured resulted in total annihilation, the so-called "second death" most feared by Egyptians. On the other hand, if the test was passed, the individual would be allowed to travel further through the underworld with the solitary hope of "arrival at the resurrection point on the eastern horizon, where the deceased will enter a cosmic permanency, sharing in the daily rebirth of the sun god Re or Ra."[19] In this way, the dead become part of the collective heavenly procession with the sun across the sky, compared to the individually marked stars of the pharaohs.

An alternate version of events has the Egyptian soul being allowed entrance into a realm known as the Field of Rushes, which is a heavenly place not unlike the Nile valley itself, thus allowing every person the chance to continue to enjoy life at its best.[20]

The *Pyramid Texts* were inscribed in the tombs of kings to ensure that the soul of the pharaoh would have the tools both to travel to the underworld and to pass any challenges and judgments therein. Once these texts were democratized and popularized, they, along with the later *Coffin Texts* and *Egyptian Book of the Dead*, formed the necessary foundation of incantations and rituals needed to ensure the well-being of the dead and to ward off the dreaded second death of total annihilation. The Egyptians loved life, living in the splendor of the fruitful Nile valley, and they hoped for more of the same in the afterlife. Jan Zandee, among others, described the Egyptians as a people who feared death, and who considered it "the enemy of the good life on earth."[21] This statement is now recognized as not entirely accurate, and must be seen in relation to the fear of total obliteration, of a second-death, in the event that the necessary rituals were not carried out. With these fail-safes appropriately taken care of, the dying had little worry of what lay beyond.

In terms of the relationship between the living and the dead, the Egyptians left slightly more information than did the Mesopotamians. The dead, in the form of the *ba*, were thought to remain by the grave. As such, communication between the living and the dead was possible at the grave site, though unlike the kind of face-to-face encounter described in the *Epic of Gilgamesh*, the Egyptians wrote letters to the dead that were then left at the tomb.[22] At other times, relatives would visit the tomb to share offerings of meals with them, talking amongst themselves, but never in conversation with the dead. In the same way as their Near Eastern neighbors, however, they were expected to make these gestures as matters of respect for the dead and to ensure that they would be remembered by the living.[23]

Like the Greeks (to be discussed next) and Mesopotamians, from earliest times the Egyptians blamed their unhappy dead for causing all manner of problems, from bad temper and marital discord to serious illness and obstetrical disaster. The reasons for their unhappiness were the same as in Greece and Mesopotamia as well: they had not been buried properly, they had been murdered, or they had died too early.[24] These are themes that we will see repeated in other cultures as well.

Proper burial and respect for the grave were as important to the Egyptians as they were for the Mesopotamians. The ghostly *ba* were known to frighten away

would-be grave robbers by manifesting about the grave, and might also haunt people who neglected their dutiful respect of the dead.[25] Indeed, the ancient Egyptians
recognized that the dead did sometimes appear to the living. The survival of the
dead "belonged to the data of actual experience,"[26] as demonstrated by the appearance of the dead in dreams, or even the occasional waking apparition. More
than simply appearing to the living, sometimes the dead would even molest them
physically. At least one legend tells of a dead man constructing a golem-like clay
facsimile of himself, called a *shabti*, that he can send to the world of the living in
order to extract revenge against his king for breaking promises made before the
man's death.[27] Yet another ghostly aspect, the *akh*, had the ability to possess the living to wreak further havoc.[28] There are even reports of ghosts attempting to
forcibly engage in sexual relations with the living.[29] The *ba* was typically depicted
in Egyptian texts as a bird with a human head. The association of spirits of the dead
with birds is a common one across cultures, though one may see this description as
simply stylistic in this context given that the writing of the Egyptians appears in
the form of picture symbols. In any event, the notion that apparitions of the dead
might appear to the living, either at the gravesite or in the act of haunting specific
individuals, was well known to the Egyptians from an early time. Additionally,
there were some magicians who were capable of directly communicating with the
spirits of the dead, normally with the intention of discovering the reason for its dis-
pleasure with the living.[30] Much like mediums in other cultures, these individuals
typically adopted so-called "familiar spirits" through whom wider contact with the
deceased was made possible.

In short, the ancient Egyptians, for all their concern for the dead, reveal little about their beliefs of the afterlife per se. An obvious concern for the physical continuance of the body is evident from the earliest times. Ritual performance was necessary to ensure that the spirit of the dead would not be lost but
would continue in association with the sun after an arduous journey through the
underworld. Except for the Field of Rushes being equated with life by the Nile,
we have no idea what the heavenly aspects of this fate might have been, though
it was certainly seen as highly desirable if for no other reason than to be in the
company of gods. The pharaohs also had a similar fate to look forward to,
though their passage through the underworld to become one with the stars was
all but guaranteed both by their station in life as incarnations of the Sun God
as well as the extensive availability of pyramid texts to aid them in the afterlife.

Greco-Roman

Unlike the previously mentioned civilizations, the Greeks were profuse writers
of myth, religion, and philosophy, providing an abundant supply of information

concerning not only beliefs in life after death but experiences therewith as well. Helen North has helpfully delineated a short list of beliefs known in earliest Greek history.[31] Obviously, not all of these beliefs were held by everyone, but many would have at least been familiar throughout the ancient Greek world. Beginning with a discussion of these beliefs, the chapter will then move on to look at later developments in Greek (and Roman) thinking about death.

(1) Something of the human personality—an aspect called the *psyche*, or later, *daemon*—was thought to survive the death of the body. There are actually three aspects of the soul described: the *psyche*, *thymos*, and *noos*. The *thymos* is the conscious, feeling soul, and the *noos* is the action and seat of intelligent seeing. They belong to the body and perish with it. The *psyche* alone survives: in the living person it is simply the life that can be lost; in death it is the pallid, strengthless shade.[32]

(2) The surviving aspect resided in some specific location. This location was variously held to be either within the tomb, somewhere beneath the earth, or even far away at the edge of the known world.

(3) The existence of the spirit, or shade, was thought to be a dim one. Spirits retained a recognizable semblance of their earthly appearance but were mere shadows of their former selves.

(4) The realm of the dead was ruled by Hades, the brother of Zeus, and his wife, Persephone. This land was known as Tartarus, though it was also called the House of Hades, sometimes shortened to simply Hades. The famous King Minos dwelt there and took the role of judge, settling disputes amongst the dead, though sometimes he was considered to have judged the dead themselves. The Isles of the Blessed are distinct from Hades, and are reserved only for certain special heroes and are ruled by either Kronos or Rhadamanthys, both among the Titan generation of godlike beings.

(5) Funeral rites of some kind or another were mandatory for the dead's passage to the underworld, if even brief or symbolic. If these were not performed, the gods, let alone the dead themselves, became angered.

(6) For those who believed that the shade remained in residence near the grave, it was thought possible to communicate with these spirits through the offering of food and libations.

These features of ancient Greek belief in the state of humans after death are drawn mainly from surviving poems that had been passed down orally until finally written down around the eighth century BCE. The main sources for modern understanding are the epic poems, the *Iliad* and *Odyssey*, ascribed to the fabled figure, Homer, and the shorter poems of the equally mysterious Hesiod. The afterlife described by these poets is a dark and dreary one, similar to that of the Mesopotamians. Hesiod's *Theogony* provides the following poetic description of Tartarus, the underworld:

> And there, in order, are the ends and springs
> Of gloomy earth and misty Tartarus,
> And of the barren sea and starry heaven,
> Murky and awful, loathed by the very gods.
> There is the yawning mouth of hell . . .[33]

Death features prominently in both of Homer's epics as well, but perhaps the best description of the underworld appears in the *Odyssey*.[34] Here, the hero, Odysseus, travels, as did Gilgamesh, to the ends of the Earth in order to perform a detailed necromantic ritual aimed at summoning the ghost of the blind prophet, Teiresias, in order to secure from him valued information. Once the ritual is complete, all manner of spirits emerge from the depths of Hades, clamoring for a chance to speak of their fate. Teiresias himself describes the underworld simply as, "the joyless region."[35] The great hero of the *Iliad*, Achilles, appears to Odysseus as a shade and laments his fate in death despite his lordly status among the living:

> Better, I say, to break sod as a farm hand
> For some poor country man, on iron rations,
> Than lord it over all the exhausted dead.[36]

Most of the throngs of dead are consigned to the same fate as vague shades in a dark underworld with no indication of judgment for one's deeds. There are at least some, however, whose sins have been deemed so heinous that they are tortured endlessly in Tartarus. Odysseus sees examples of those who have been so judged. Tantalus, known in Greek mythology for feeding his son to the gods, is seen punished by being forever plagued by hunger and thirst, surrounded by water and fruit-laden branches, though unable to reach either of them. Likewise, Sisyphus is seen forced to push a stone up a hill only to see it fall back to the bottom and begin again as punishment for his betrayal of the gods.[37]

From these early ideas of what amounts to a cult of the dead and the notion of a vast underworld of shades, later poets elaborated and expanded the picture of the afterlife. The Greek tragedians formed an important part of Greek religion, as theater was often incorporated into religious rituals when not a form of ritual in itself. Thus, the ideas portrayed in their plays are reflective of the evolution of Greek thought. As ever, though, the reader must be aware of the confluence of religious conviction and artistic license; herein lays a fruit of cultural evolution. Helen North aptly warns: "A word of caution: Each treats the material with great freedom. There was no dogma to which he was obliged to conform, and because beliefs varied so widely (although actual rites seem to have been quite uniform), each writer could select what would enhance his poetic or philosophical purpose."[38]

And so, elaborations began to appear and the Greek concepts on life after death began to move away from their earlier origins. Homer's epics form the basis for future considerations, but changes are obvious. Quickly, a multitude of competing belief systems began to appear, stemming not only from drama but also from more sophisticated philosophical thinking. Some systems, such as those displayed in the Greek tragedies, which relied heavily on the ancient myths, tended to stay closer to Homer than others. The Pythagoreans offered the philosophy of reincarnation and Plato even suggested that Homer should be censored in the perfect world of his *Republic*. The effect was that, over time, the Homeric concept of a bleak afterlife was abandoned in lieu of one where there was hope for personal transcendence and reward after death, as well as punishment and damnation for evil. In addition, interaction with the dead became more and more frequent and much more personal.

Possibly the most important innovation made by the Greek tragedians, especially for our present purposes, is in their treatment of the dead themselves, rather than any serious new philosophical implications for the afterlife. Sarah Iles Johnston discusses this idea at some length, pointing out that in later Greek literature, specifically the tragedies, it was possible to summon aid from the dead much more simply than it was in Homer.[39] The most obvious example is the summoning of the dead king, Darius, in Aeschylus' *Persians*. It was not only dramatically appropriate for the poet's purposes, but it also set a new standard when, in the words of H. D. Broadhead: "Darius' ghost should rise majestically from the tomb in response only to libations and prayers, and that he should not require blood-offerings, as did Homer's 'strengthless heads of the dead.'"[40] While the *Odyssey* left the suggestion that the dead could be summoned through complicated and practically impossible feats, such dramas as these describe the possibility of contact between the living and the dead as much more attainable. Certainly, the other ancient civilizations of the Near East also believed in their ability to communicate with the dead to some extent, but they did not expect to receive straightforward answers from them, and certainly did not describe their appearance as blatantly as did the Greek tragedians.

The Greek Oracles of the Dead, in which devotees would follow the instructions of priests in order to encounter deceased loved ones either in dreams or awake in a darkened setting, catered directly to this developing belief. Appearances of the dead occurred so frequently in the tragedies that a device known as Charon's Steps, after the mythical boatman of the dead, was created. The device consisted of a passage under the stage, leading from backstage to the chorus, where a trapdoor would enable the actor to rise up from the underworld. Ghosts appear in each of *The Eumenides, Alcestes, Hecuba, Polyxena,* and of course *The Persians,* sometimes summoned, but sometimes coming of their own accord. Still, while the Greek tragedians allow for easier access to those beyond the grave, all is not perfect in the land of the dead. Darius points out that, "[l]eaving Hades is especially difficult, and the gods of the underworld are better at taking than releasing."[41] And, again, he advises those still on Earth to, "[l]end your souls to pleasure a day at a time, despite the difficulties, since wealth is of no use to the dead."[42]

For a brighter view of the afterlife, we must turn to the enigmatic mystery cults of, among others, Orphism and Eleusis. Little is known about these cults, aside from the fact that they have roots dating as far back as the works of Homer. Although the Eleusinian mysteries and the Orphic cults are the best known of the mystery religions, there were a number of similar cults in the ancient Greek world. While the differences between these cults may have been quite profound, they shared the common elements of obscurity, and the belief in man's immortal soul and future life in a way quite opposed to that gleaned in Homer. The second *Homeric Hymn to Demeter* tells the tale of the sanctioned kidnap of Demeter's daughter, Persephone, by the Lord of the Underworld, Hades. In the hymn, the link is drawn between Demeter, goddess of fertility and the harvest, and her daughter who ends up spending part of the year in the depths of the underworld and the remaining part above ground with her mother. A cycle of death and rebirth, exemplified by the cycles of the harvest, is thus illustrated and one can see the obvious similarity to the cult of Osiris in Egypt.

The Orphic mysteries enjoyed an equally long following, dating to the time of Homer and extending well into the Roman period. While the Eleusinian mysteries focused on the goddess as a symbol of birth and rebirth, Orphism worshipped, somewhat ambiguously, both the archer and Sun God Apollo, and the earthy and effeminate Dionysus.

> The Dionysiac sectaries accounted for man's inner struggle: they perceived that he is both pulled by the baser motives of the flesh and prompted by the nobler aspirations of the soul. Their aim then was to purify the soul from the defilement of its corporeal home that in purity it might enjoy its proper life. This end might not be quickly accomplished: many rounds of life and death were needed before purification could be complete.[43]

In the mystery religions, the need for purification is important. In the world, there is good and there is evil; the body is the locus of evil while the soul houses the purest good. The goal of every life, then, is to draw one's self away from the base bodily desires toward the nobler objectives of the soul, or higher mind. To quote Empedocles: "He [Zeus; God; the divine intellect] is mind alone, holy and beyond description."[44] And for Empedocles, Love was the means of achieving this higher union in a constant cycle of union and compartmentalization.[45] Initiates to the mysteries would be almost guaranteed salvation as they were vouchsafed the secrets by which to purify themselves before death. The souls of the purified dead would then leave Earth and Hades behind to exist in a higher place or to become one with the divine intellect. The uninitiated would be condemned to the eternal suffering of a Homeric underworld, or worse.

Alternately, successive incarnations would have the opportunity to improve and draw closer and closer to purity with each successive incarnation. The Pythagoreans stressed the need for "recollection" in order to remember the deeds and sufferings of a previous incarnation in order to learn from past mistakes.[46] Pythagoras himself claimed to remember a long succession of past lives, including one as the Trojan hero, Euphorbus.[47] And so, there existed a tradition of reward and punishment also involving reincarnation through successive lives, which grew alongside the tradition of Homer. At first, these mystery religions were little more than tiny, individual cults, but the appealing notions of eternal life in heavenly bliss won out over the earlier view of a dark and shadowy eternity. By the time of Christ, people from across the Near East were making pilgrimages to places like Eleusis in order to be initiated.

Plato's philosophy on life after death represents some of the most sophisticated thought to come out of ancient Greece, conveyed through the voice of Socrates in a number of dialogues. These dialogues display a certain inconsistency, which may be accounted for by a philosophy that only evolved as their author matured. Alternatively, it may be that Plato simply refused to commit to one set of beliefs in favor of the freedom to adjust according to the specific argument. In any case, there are some ideas that come through solidly enough that we can discern a framework for what might be considered Platonic thought, bearing a striking similarity to the Orphic mysteries.

The *Phaedo* emphasizes the diametrical opposition of body and mind (or soul, which is essentially equated with mind for Plato). Mind is equated with the divine, while the mortal flesh of the body is looked down upon as base. The body is but a vehicle and a servant to the higher mind. Says Socrates: "Then if you see a man resentful that he is going to die, isn't this proof enough for you that he's no lover of wisdom after all, but what we may call a lover of the body?"[48] Wisdom comes from a higher mind, a divine source, and it is the mind which should dominate the body as the gods dominate humankind. One must only listen to hear the guiding principle emanating both from within and without;

Socrates had his *daemon* and looked to his dreams to discover his purpose, which came to him from the divine source.

While his logical argument for the immortality of the soul has little value by way of evidence, Plato relies heavily on tradition in asserting the belief that the divine element, the soul or mind, continues to exist beyond the death of the body. Socrates cites the "ancient doctrine" of Orphism when describing how the souls of the dead exist in Hades.[49] He describes various scenes, all of which basically tell the same story of how the souls of the dead are judged in the underworld. Those that have led exceptionally good lives, like Menelaus, travel up to a heavenly place called the Isles of the Blessed. Those who have been exceptionally evil, such as Tantalus and Sisyphus, are sent into Tartarus to suffer eternally. All others are sent to various levels of purgation where they are prepared for a new life of learning.

Philosophy is the goal of life, specifically to know the higher philosophy and to live the good life of a lover of wisdom. Plato alternates between giving the dead the opportunity to decide their own fate in the next life based upon what they have learned as of yet,[50] or to be a victim of a doctrine much like the Indian system of *karma*, in which a man is obliged to, "undergo the same treatment as he himself meted out to his victim, and to conclude his earthly existence by encountering a similar fate."[51] Even still, the evil man is doomed by his ignorance to pick a life in which he will suffer, so the choice, when it is given, is indeed a loaded one.

Plato recounts the story of Er, who woke from the dead on his own funeral pyre to describe what he experienced beyond the threshold of death. What Er reports is a world quite unlike that described by either Enkidu or Homer. Er describes meeting other souls in a festival-like atmosphere where the dead camp in tents, embracing old friends, and telling stories of their experiences. There are judges as well, who tell Er that he must go back and tell people what he has seen. These judges divide the souls up and force them to either ascend to a heavenly realm of joy or descend into a painful hell. Er does not describe what these realms might be like, though he witnesses the bright and shining souls returning from heaven as well as the filthy, weeping souls returning from hell. In both cases, they are prepared for another life on earth after this brief period of purgatory with the hopes that they will eventually achieve a higher state of mind that will release them from the cycle.[52]

Plato is also concerned with people who fear death. In order that no person should fear death in any way, he goes so far as to suggest that certain parts of Homer's works ought to be edited to prevent their fostering a fear of death in the Guardian class of his Utopian *Republic*. On more rational grounds, Socrates speaks the following:

There is good hope that death is a blessing, for it is one of two things: either the dead are nothing and have no perception of anything, or it is, as we are told, a change and a relocating for the soul from here to another place. If it is complete lack of perception, like a dreamless sleep, then death would be a great advantage . . . [for who doesn't love an uninterrupted sleep?] . . . If death is like this I say it is an advantage, for all eternity would then seem to be no more than a single night. If, on the other hand, death is a change from here to another place, and what we are told is true and all who have died are there, what greater blessing could there be, gentlemen of the jury?[53]

And so, Plato reveals a systematic belief in the existence of the human soul beyond the death of its body, in some distant location, which serves as a purgation before reincarnation into a new life. The overall purpose of this process is for humanity to achieve a love of wisdom and eventually go on to join the divine in heavenly bliss. There has been some contention among scholars as to whether Plato believed in the existence of the *individual* after death, which is not necessarily the same as the existence of one's soul.[54] Considering his emphasis on the individual in life and the descriptions of separate, individual souls in his arguments, it is hard to believe that he could have meant anything else. However, one must remember that the Greeks placed much less importance on individual survival than do modern Western religions. Still, Plato does mention instances of the dead nurturing hatreds beyond the grave. This alone is enough to suggest that Plato is describing the existence of individual souls, at least in the purgatory between lives. When the soul is reborn, it has no memory as it is forced to march the Plains of Forgetfulness, and thus begins a new life with a clean slate. On the other hand, though we are told little of the Isles of the Blessed, one might assume, especially when we recognize the Orphic influences at work in Plato's ideology, that it is a place of total union between all things and the divine intellect.

The Neoplatonists emphasized the idea of unification of the individual soul with the higher divinity. "Soul extends from the Divine Mind down to the last shadow of reality in bodies, where it is found in Nature."[55] Plotinus argues from experience as his own mystical experiences of union with the absolute suggest that the individual soul is also a part of a greater whole and will, in the end, be reunited with that whole. He had the transcendent feeling of leaving his body and merging, albeit temporarily, with the divine. This paradox is characteristic of mystic philosophy and, to some extent, defies simple rules of logic. It must be understood that every soul is *both* an individual and *also* part of the One. In union with the One, the individual soul is not annihilated but instead becomes more whole by reuniting with distant aspects.

At the other extreme of belief, there were those who concerned themselves so wholly with this world that they rejected the idea of any other world at all. Aristotle is somewhat sympathetic to the Platonic notion with his ideas of dividing man into two parts, one passive and one active, with the latter dominating the former. In a similar fashion to Plato, Aristotle argues that the body be considered passive and under the control of a higher intelligence. Where Aristotle differs, however, and where the tendency to focus on this world over any other comes from, is in the locus of the self. Aristotle believed that the individual resided with the passive body, and that the active aspect was a higher power. "Aristotle certainly regarded the active soul as similar to God if not identical with Him. But it could have no memory, no individuality, and therefore no conscious life apart from the human body accompanying its earthly existence."[56]

Therefore, when a person died, they were truly dead. An immortal aspect existed but it did not retain any sense of the individual. This idea, however, is not as nihilistic as it may seem. It is simply a form of the Platonic doctrine of reunion with the absolute expressed in a more extreme form. The thing that animates *is* the divine. When a person dies, *that* part lives on. The individuality of the self resides in the body and so it is that part that dies with the body.

The Stoics were one group of thinkers that took Aristotle's doctrine of the passive and active parts of man and adapted it by removing divinity from man's active aspect and simply renaming it, "the mind." They argued that since everything is matter, both the passive and active aspects, the body and the mind, must also be matter. They simply explained that the mind was made of finer matter than was the body and could thus interpenetrate the body. This finer mind-matter thus interpenetrated all physical bodies, creating a kind of world-mind. So, if everything is matter and it is all motivated by the same great machine, the Stoics devoted their attention to living in this world rather than speculating on another one.

The paragon of materialism in the ancient world, Epicurus, went further still with these ideas. Like the Stoics, he believed that all things were composed of atoms and that there was no other aspect of man. The difference here, however, is that Epicureans held that there was no separate mind-matter and no world-mind interpenetrating all things. Atoms were the essential building blocks of all things, including individual minds. Thus, when one's body died and decomposed, so too did one's mind. Immortality did not exist in the form of a world-mind, let alone any divine union. Instead, the only form of continued existence was a vicarious one lived by the indestructible atoms, which would eternally disconnect from one another at the death of the person and then reform into something else. And so was born the Epicurean philosophy of pleasure seeking and pain avoidance during one's only life. One may be reminded of the Mesopotamian philosophy of eat, drink, and be merry, but rather than a bleak afterlife to look forward to, the Epicureans proposed that there was no afterlife.

Despite these emerging materialistic philosophies, encounters with the dead are not uncommon in ancient works. Beginning with what is already familiar from the discussion of Mesopotamia and Egypt, apparitions are a very common occurrence in the ancient Greek world. They appear in the works of Homer and then continue to do so right through into the Roman period. The variety of apparitions seen is remarkable, and one reason for this is that in many cases the Greeks did not differentiate between apparitions of gods, demons, or spirits of the dead. The source of confusion comes from the translation of the two primary Greek words referring to apparitions: *eidolon* and *daemon*. The former is often translated as spirit but might equally refer to any image, or hallucination, that appears before a person. The latter is even more ambiguous, sometimes referring to the appearance of gods, dead heroes, or even the souls of the dead in general. This confusion continues into the Roman period with the Latin equivalent of *manes*, which maintains the broadest definition of apparitions. Because of this, to distinguish what kind of apparition one is dealing with one must look carefully at the context in which the words appear. There is always the conceived possibility that a particular vision might be a god in disguise, throwing into question even the appearance of a dead friend, who may simply be a god in another form.

A typical manifestation may appear in the form of a dream. E. R. Dodds delineates three types of dreams as described in antiquity:[57] 1) symbolic—like a riddle in need of interpretation, as most dreams are thought to be even today; 2) visions—more specifically, precognitive dreams; 3) oracles—in which a respected person, perhaps even a god, appears to reveal advice or information. It is this latter class that is of interest here.

For instance, note the following passage from Homer's *Iliad*:

> No sooner had sleep caught [Achilles] . . . than the ghost of stricken Patroclus drifted up . . . He was like the man to the life, every feature, the same tall build and the fine eyes and voice and the very robes that used to clothe his body.[58]

Concerning such nocturnal visitations, the classicist Frederic Myers pointed out that, "[d]reams of departed friends are likely to be the first phenomenon which inspires mankind with the idea that they can hold converse with a spiritual world."[59] As the result of dreamtime appearances, many people, even today, are convinced of the continuing existence of their beloved after death.

The Asclepian Oracles of the Dead provided individuals with a place where, in addition to the healings normally ascribed to the god Asclepius, they could reunite with loved ones to ask questions or merely to be reassured as to their continued existence. The oracles worked by a method of incubation. This involved resident priests who would help induce clients into an altered state of consciousness in which they would remain for some time, often through the night. It was in this altered state that the visions would appear. Sometimes the god Asclepius himself would appear to introduce the departed spirit in the dream, sometimes he was thought to appear in some other form, perhaps even that of the summoned spirit. There are several examples in the literature of the use of these oracles and we may begin with an interesting excerpt from Plutarch:

> [Pausanias had summoned a girl from town in order to seduce her.] When the girl arrived she asked the attendants at his door to take away his light, and, as she moved in silence through the darkness toward the bed on which Pausanias lay sleeping, she accidentally stumbled and upset the lampstand. Pausanias, awakened by the noise, snatched the dagger which he kept by his side and, mistaking the girl for an intruder who meant him harm, struck her to the ground, where she died from her injuries. Thereafter Kleonike [the girl] allowed Pausanias no peace, visiting him at night as a phantom in his dreams and cursing him in a rhyme which ran:
>
> > *Your day of reckoning draws near*
> > *With punishment for lust severe.*
>
> . . . driven to distraction by the ghost of Kleonike, Pausanias had recourse to the oracle of the dead at Herakleia, where he called up her spirit and pleaded for absolution of her wrath. Kleonike, when she appeared, told Pausanias that a speedy end to his troubles awaited him in Sparta, hinting it seems at his forthcoming death. Such is the tale that many writers tell.[60]

There are also some cases of the Oracles of the Dead—the most famous being at Ephyra—at which it is uncertain if the pilgrims saw the apparitions in the form of dreams or in an awakened state.[61] In most cases, pilgrims were coming simply to deal with the grief of having lost a loved one. They came for no other reason than to see their mother, or child, or lover just one more time. In these cases, there is no evidence that they saw anything other than a fulfilled wish, especially in those instances where the apparitions appeared within a dream. Spiros Mousselimis, in his study of the oracle at Ephyra, argues that a locally grown hallucinogen may have been responsible for the visions.[62]

There are some examples that do lend themselves more readily as evidence of something other than simple wish-fulfilling dreams. Herodotus provides us with one such example in his *Histories*. The story tells of how Periander sought out an Oracle of the Dead in order to ask his dead wife, Melissa, about the location of a lost object. Melissa orders him to appease her with clothes, as she was not buried in the proper attire. After he burns clothing in her honor, she again appears to him and gives him the exact location of the lost object.[63] This story harks back to the notion of a cult of the dead, combining both the need for respect and proper burial of the dead and the divinatory nature of communications from the dead. Similarly, Dodds finds four stories of apparitions recorded in the Epidaurian temple record. One, as an example, concerns a missing sum of money. Here, the deceased appeared in a dream, introduced by Asclepius, and then instructed the pilgrim as to where and from whom he could find the money.[64]

At least Hesiod, Thales, Pythagoras, Empedocles, and Plato, among others, all accepted the existence of disembodied spirits. They all accepted that a person's soul would leave the body after death and continue in some form of individual existence, at least for a time. Within such belief systems, it is very likely that souls might appear to the living. On the other hand, there were those ardent doubters who rejected any notion of an afterlife. Much like today, the overall atmosphere was one of skepticism, though the idea of ghosts was an accepted one. Materialists contended that the relationship between apparitions and the dream state was the solution to the question of what ghosts were constituted.[65] Others recognized that many apparitions often appeared in the full waking state as well, thus making the previous thesis untenable. Instead, they resorted to the idea that since all things were physical, perhaps images might be floating about in space like a filmy mass waiting to land in someone's eyes.[66] Of course, there was always the possibility that these things were merely hallucinations and misinterpretations, though others were doubtless convinced of the veracity of their visions when the spirits conveyed information otherwise unknown to the living, as in the previous examples.

In addition to those ancient instances where information was transferred from the dead, there are also some important cases of so-called crisis-apparitions in the literature. In such cases, a living person bears witness to the ghost of someone they thought to be alive, only to later confirm that the individual in question had died at the time of the sighting. The Elder Pliny, for instance, relates the story of a man named Corfidius who became aware of his own brother's death upon being visited by his apparition quite by surprise.[67]

We also find many examples of hauntings in the ancient texts. The most common motivation usually attributed to the return of spirits of the dead is an improper burial, just as it was for the other ancient Near Eastern cultures. Special care must be taken to ensure that the dead are treated with respect and that they are duly buried. The ghost of Elpenor demands a proper burial from Odysseus, a demand that he dutifully complies with in order to avoid a spectral wrath.[68] This was also the request made by Patroclus to Achilles when he appeared in the dream mentioned previously. In later texts, it also becomes important to not only respect the dead but to respect the living as ghosts might often come back to haunt those who had wronged them in life as well as in death. Plato warns that would-be murderers should best beware, "full of fear and loathing at his own violent sufferings," for, "to the full limit of his powers he visits his own anguish on the perpetrator of the crime."[69] Haunted houses are documented alongside haunted persons. The Roman comic playwright, Plautus, in his play, *Mostellaria* (ca. 200–194 BCE), describes what may be, according to Debbie Felton,[70] the earliest haunted house story in Greek or Roman literature. And Plutarch relates the story of a young man (perhaps ironically) named Damon who was treacherously murdered while anointing himself with oil in a bath house: "For a long time after, so our fathers say, ghostly figures were seen about the place and moaning noises heard. Because of this they walled up the entrance to the baths, and even now those who live nearby believe that the place is haunted by apparitions and disturbing cries."[71]

Communication with the dead was thought possible from the earliest times, as witnessed by Homer's description of Odysseus' ritualistic summoning of the spirit of Teiresias and its evolution into the more simplistic summoning of Darius in Greek tragedy. The gradual simplification of access to the dead made it possible for some to offer their services as necromancers who could, for a small fee, summon up the dead to help or harm others. Johnston notes, "[a] passage in Plato's *Republic* [364 b5–c5] mentions experts who travel from door to door offering to inscribe curse tablets (*katadesmoi*) and send ghosts against victims (*epagogoi*) for a fee, which, in concert with the passage from the *Laws* just mentioned [933 d1–e5], assures us that there was in fact a thriving business in manipulating the dead."[72]

In addition, there were also so-called "belly-talkers" (*engastrimuthoi*), who claimed to have a daemon resident in their bellies that could communicate through their lips when in a trance.[73] Later, theurgists sought communication with higher beings through trance mediumship. Similarly, there are the famous Oracles of Apollo where, unlike the Oracles of the Dead already discussed, visitors could expect to receive answers from the gods, speaking through the mouth of a woman, the *Pythia*. While the first few examples deal with direct contact between the living and the dead, the latter tend to focus more and more on divine beings rather than deceased individuals, at least as intermediaries if not complete replacements. The dead were identified with divinity, and so communications from the dead would not have been discouraged, per se. On the other hand, the prevailing view among the general populace was that spirits of the dead required offerings and respect, and that the only ones who remained earthbound were of the most dangerous kind. Combining this view with the practice of certain necromancers of conjuring curses from the dead described by Plato, one can readily understand the level of suspicion surrounding communication with the spirits of the dead. It was considered safer to receive communications from gods and nonhuman daemons than to summon up generally irate spirits.

From another perspective, the ancient Greeks also believed it was possible for the soul to leave the body during life and travel outside the body. Plotinus was mentioned previously for his mystical ecstasy, but the experience was known to others as well. By way of example, Pliny the Elder describes one Hermotimus of Clazomenae, who was accustomed to having his soul leave his body and roam about, reporting back to him what it had seen on its journeys. This detailed account goes on to describe how Hermotimus' body would remain in a half-conscious state while his soul was away on these forays. Unfortunately, the distracted Hermotimus was ill prepared when some enemies captured his body while the soul was traveling and burned him alive.[74] In any event, the soul was thought capable of leaving the body during life, with only death severing the tie between them.

From this discussion a clear progression of ideas can be drawn. The earliest civilizations, Mesopotamian, Egyptian, and Greek, held certain fundamental beliefs in common, especially those relating to experiences of contact with the dead. Commonly, the average person was believed to enter into a dark and dismal realm in which one became but a shadow of one's former self. Heroes and kings, most noticeably in the Egyptian system, were given a special place in the afterlife. As ideas developed, richer notions of the individual's fate after death appeared. In most cases, ideas of an eventual paradise were not fully developed, while those of hellish punishments were devised for the particularly evil. Notions of reincarnation dealt more fully with the distribution of rewards and punishments. In any event, contact with the dead through mediumistic communications as well as actual sightings maintained the belief that humans have some aspect that survives the death of the body.

Notes

1. J. S. Cooper, "The Fate of Mankind: Death and Afterlife in Ancient Mesopotamia," in *Death and Afterlife: Perspectives of World Religions*, ed. Hiroshi Obayashi (New York: Greenwood, 1992), p. 20.

2. W. G. Lambert, "The Theology of Death," in *Death in Mesopotamia: Papers Read at the XXVIe rencontre assyriologique internationale*, ed. B. Alster (Copenhagen: Akademisk forlag, 1980), p. 53.

3. Jon Davies, *Death, Burial and Rebirth in the Religions of Antiquity* (London: Routledge, 1999), p. 52.

4. Edwin Oliver James, *Myth and Ritual in the Ancient Near East* (London: Thames and Hudson, 1958), p. 220.

5. Lambert, "The Theology of Death," p. 58.

6. Morris Jastrow, "Descent of the Goddess Ishtar into the Lower World," *The Civilization of Babylonia and Assyria* (1915; repr., New York: Benjamin Blom, 1971), p. 454.

7. John Gardner and John Maier, *Gilgamesh* (New York: Vintage, 1985), p. 178.

8. Gardner and Maier, *Gilgamesh*, p. 224.

9. Gardner and Maier, *Gilgamesh*, p. 266.

10. Gardner and Maier, *Gilgamesh*, p. 270.

11. Cooper, "The Fate of Mankind," pp. 28–29.

12. Mircea Eliade, *A History of Religious Ideas*, vol. 1, trans. W. R. Trask (Chicago: University of Chicago Press, 1978), pp. 94–95.

13. Eliade, *A History of Religious Ideas*, p. 86.

14. E. A. W. Budge, *The Egyptian Book of the Dead* (New York: Dover, 1967), p. 180, plate 28, line 15.

15. H. Frankfort, *Ancient Egyptian Religion: An Interpretation* (New York: Harper & Row, 1961), pp. 92–93.

16. Eliade, *A History of Religious Ideas*, p. 95.

17. E. A. W. Budge, *Egyptian Religion: Egyptian Ideas of the Future Life* (London: Routledge & Kegan Paul, 1979), p. 168.

18. Jan Assmann, *Death and Salvation in Ancient Egypt*, trans. David Lorton (Ithaca, NY: Cornell University Press, 2005), pp. 23–38.

19. Davies, *Death, Burial and Rebirth*, pp. 31–32.

20. R. O. Faulkner, *The Ancient Egyptian Book of the Dead* (London: The British Museum, 1985), pp. 112–113.

21. Jan Zandee, *Death as an Enemy: According to Ancient Egyptian Conceptions*, trans. W. F. Klasens (Leiden: E. J. Brill, 1960), p. 2.

22. Frankfort, *Ancient Egyptian Religion*, p. 89.

23. See Assmann, *Death and Salvation*, pp. 330–348, for examples of some of the spells employed to summon the dead in order to receive offerings.

24. Sarah Iles Johnston, *Restless Dead: Encounters Between the Living and the Dead in Ancient Greece* (Berkeley, CA: University of California Press, 1999), p. 90.

25. W. J. Murnane, "Taking it With You: The Problem of Death and Afterlife in Ancient Egypt," in *Death and Afterlife: Perspectives of World Religions*, ed. Hiroshi Obayashi (New York: Greenwood, 1992), p. 40.

26. Frankfort, *Ancient Egyptian Religion*, p. 89.

27. M. Idel, *Golem: Jewish Magical and Mystical Traditions on the Artificial Anthropoid* (Albany, NY: 1990), pp. 3–4 cited in Assmann, *Death and Salvation*, p. 111.

28. Geraldine Pinch, *Magic in Ancient Egypt* (Austin: University of Texas, 1994), p. 45.

29. Davies, *Death, Burial and Rebirth*, p. 32. This phenomenon is found in many other cultures and can readily be equated with the normal human experience of night emission or perhaps sleep paralysis.

30. Pinch, *Magic in Ancient Egypt*, p. 46.

31. H. F. North, "Death and Afterlife in Greek Tragedy and Plato," in *Death and Afterlife: Perspectives of World Religions*, ed. Hiroshi Obayashi (New York: Greenwood, 1992), pp. 49–50.

32. K. Corrigan, "Body and Soul in Ancient Religious Experience," in *Classical Mediterranean Spirituality*, ed. A. H. Armstrong (New York: Crossroad, 1986), p. 361.

33. Hesiod, *Theogony*, in *Hesiod and Theognis*, trans. Dorothea Walker (London: Penguin, 1973), p. 47.

34. Homer, *The Odyssey*, trans. Robert Fitzgerald (New York: Vintage Classics, 1990), Book 11, pp. 185–206.

35. *Odyssey*, Book 11, p. 188.

36. *Odyssey*, Book 11, p. 201.

37. *Odyssey*, Book 11, pp. 204–205.

38. North, "Death and Afterlife," pp. 50–51.

39. Johnston, *Restless Dead*, pp. 30–35.

40. H. D. Broadhead, ed., *The Persae of Aeschylus* (Cambridge, UK: Cambridge University Press, 1960), p. 306.

41. Aeschylus, *Persians*, trans. E. Hall (Warminster, UK: Aris & Phillips, 1996), line 685, p. 79.

42. *Persians*, line 840, p. 89.

43. C. H. Moore, *Ancient Beliefs in the Immortality of the Soul* (New York: Cooper Square, 1963), pp. 8–9.

44. Corrigan, "Body and Soul," p. 278.

45. D. O'Brien, *Empedocles' Cosmic Cycle* (Cambridge, UK: Cambridge University Press, 1969).

46. E. R. Dodds, *The Greeks and the Irrational* (Berkeley, CA: University of California Press, 1959), p. 152.

47. Diogenes Laertius, "The Life of Pythagoras," in *The Lives and Opinions of Eminent Philosophers*, trans. C. D. Yonge (London: Henry G. Bohn, 1853), Books VIII, V.

48. Plato, *Phaedo*, trans. D. Gallop (Oxford: Clarenden, 1975), p. 13.

49. Plato, *Phaedo*, p. 16.

50. Plato, "Phaedrus," A. Nehamas and P. Woodruff, trans. in Plato, *Complete Works*, ed. J. M. Cooper (Indianapolis: Hackett, 1997), pp. 526–527.

51. Plato, "Laws," *Complete Works*, trans. T. J. Saunders, p. 1529.

52. Plato, "Republic," *Complete Works*, trans. G. M. A. Grube, Book 10.

53. Plato, "Apology," *Complete Works*, trans. G. M. A. Grube, p. 35.

54. Moore, *Ancient Beliefs*, p. 27.

55. F. M. Schroeder, "The Self in Ancient Religious Experience," in *Classical Mediterranean Spirituality*, ed. A. H. Armstrong (New York: Crossroad, 1986), p. 380.

56. Moore, *Ancient Beliefs*, pp. 35–36.

57. Dodds, *The Greeks and the Irrational*, p. 107.

58. Homer, *Iliad*, trans. R. Fagles (London: Penguin, 1990), lines 72–79, p. 561.

59. F. W. H. Myers, *Essays Classical* (London: MacMillan, 1883), p. 14.

60. Plutarch, *Life of Kimon*, trans. A. Blamire (London: Institute of Classical Studies, University of London, 1989), 6:4–7, pp. 38–39.

61. Spiros G. Mousselimis, *The Ancient Underworld and the Oracle for Necromancy at Ephyra* (Ioannina, Greece: 1989).

62. Mousselimis, *The Ancient Underworld*, p. 53.

63. Herodotus, *The Histories*, trans. A. de Selincourt (Harmondsworth, UK: Penguin, 1972), 5:92, p. 377.

64. E. R. Dodds, "Supernormal Phenomena in Classical Antiquity," in *The Ancient Concept of Progress: And Other Essays on Greek Literature and Belief* (Oxford: Clarenden, 1973), p. 169.

65. D. Felton, *Haunted Greece and Rome: Ghost Stories From Classical Antiquity* (Austin: University of Texas Press, 1999), p. 21.

66. As per, Lucretius, for example: *On the Nature of the Universe*, trans. R. E. Latham (London: Penguin, 1994), p. xiii.

67. Pliny the Elder, *Natural History*, vol. II, Books III–VII, trans. H. Rackham (London: William Heinemann, 1947), Book VII. LII. 177, p. 625.

68. *Odyssey*, Book 11, p. 187.

69. Plato, "Laws," *Complete Works*, pp. 1523–1524.

70. Felton, *Haunted Greece and Rome*, p. 50.

71. Plutarch, *Life of Kimon*, 1:8, p. 25.

72. Johnston, *Restless Dead*, p. 119.

73. Much of the rest of the information on trance mediums in ancient Greece can be found in Dodds, "Supernormal Phenomena," pp. 156–210, and Dodds, *The Greeks and the Irrational*, pp. 283–311.

74. Pliny the Elder, *Natural History* (1947), VII. LII. 174, p. 623.

CHAPTER TWO

~

Judaism

While most of the ancient schools of Mediterranean thought have seen their adherents disappear with the passing centuries, leaving only echoes in the sophistications of modern thought, one in particular has evolved and survived through to the present time. The history of Judaism is a long and complicated one, spanning a period of well over two thousand years, though traditional myth and legend extend as far as four thousand years and more. From pre-biblical times, the beliefs of the Jews have evolved and adapted to integrate a number of ideas, often seeming to come into conflict with one another. These differences have led to a wide spectrum of differing forms of Judaism, though they all remain linked through certain key beliefs and their use of the same sacred scriptures. In modern times, perhaps as a result of attempts to divest Judaism of any semblance of superstition, the Jewish faith has often been characterized as a "here and now" religion. Simcha Paull Raphael, in his excellent *Jewish Views of the Afterlife*, notes: "As an inadvertent result, both Jews and non-Jews have come to believe that Judaism does not have any conception of a life after death."[1] Certainly, Jews are encouraged to take each day as it comes and to live each day not with a view to reward in the next life but with eyes firmly set on living in the proper way today. Rabbi Joshua Liebman, writing in 1946, urges Jews to accept death as a friend of life: "I often feel that death is not the enemy of life, but its friend, for it is the knowledge that our years are limited which makes them so precious. It is the truth that time is but lent to us which makes us, at our best, look upon our years as a trust handed into our temporary keeping."[2]

The psychologist Victor Frankl describes in moving detail how the horrors of life in a Nazi concentration camp forced one to completely alter the way one looked at life, suggesting perhaps another source of the modern focus on taking one day at a time.

> What was really needed was a fundamental change in our attitude toward life. We had to learn ourselves and furthermore, we had to teach the despairing men, that *it did not really matter what we expected from life, but rather what life expected from us.* We needed to stop asking about the meaning of life, and instead to think of ourselves as those who were being questioned by life—daily and hourly. Our answer must consist, not in talk and meditation, but in right action and in right conduct. Life ultimately means taking the responsibility to find the right answer to its problems and to fulfill the tasks which it constantly sets for each individual.[3] [emphasis in original]

Despite the pragmatic outlook taken by many modern Jews, eschatology has been a central part of Judaism from the very beginning. A review of the historical development of these ideas will illustrate that even if such beliefs are little discussed in Judaism today, they remain central to the Jewish way of life and have been overwhelmingly influential not only within the development of Judaism but also in the formation of the other great monotheisms to be discussed in later chapters.

The earliest Jewish ideas of life after death are drawn from the Jewish Bible, or *Tanakh*, consisting of three sections known as the Prophets, the Writings, and the *Torah*, the latter being considered the first five books of Moses. Together, these form what Christians (with some debate over some books) refer to as the Old Testament. There is actually very little mention of life after death in the Jewish Bible, which is likely one reason for the modern ignorance of such matters. What meager reference there is, however, paints a fairly clear picture of what the ancient Israelites believed awaited them after their deaths. What we find is a fate very similar to the bleak underworld of Mesopotamia and the Hades of ancient Greece.[4] *Sheol*, as the biblical Jews called the underworld, is described as, "[a] land of thick darkness, as darkness itself; a land of the shadow of death, without any order, and where the light is as darkness,"[5] and elsewhere, "the nether-most pit, in dark places, in the deeps."[6] Those that went down to this dark pit in death became mere shadows of their former selves. The hapless author of one of the Psalms laments: "I am counted with them that go down into the pit; I am become as a man that hath no help."[7] And again, in Job— *Eyov* in the Hebrew—the life and death of a person are summed up as follows: "He cometh forth like a flower, and withereth; he fleeth also as a shadow, and continueth not."[8] There is no sense of reward for the meritorious, or any sense of a truly individual existence whatsoever. *Sheol* remains the dark abode of all those who die, regardless of station and deed. Exceptions occur very rarely, and an individual of nearly divine stature might escape the fate of *Sheol*, as, for example, Enoch who did not die but was instead taken up to walk with God.[9] With the exception of certain very special individuals, the dead are a multitude who throng the nether regions with a dull purposelessness. C. H. Moore points out how the dead might gain some brief pleasure vicariously through a limited involvement with the world of the living. "The most for which man can hope is that his shade may be aware of what is done in the world of the living."[10] Certainly, this is not much of a future to look forward to at the end of one's life.

The dead were thought to maintain a certain amount of contact with the world above. In biblical times, it appears that the dead were sometimes conjured to communicate with the living. Despite the clear admonition in Deuteronomy (*Devarim*) of necromancy as an "abomination,"[11] the practice was obviously fairly common in the ancient Middle East. The story of King Saul's encounter with the Witch of En-dor provides a perfect example of the kind of mediumistic phenomena prohibited in the Bible.[12] In this story, Saul, who had himself made an edict against necromancy, chooses to consult a medium to summon the spirit of Samuel for advice. The medium sees the spirit approach, and although invisible to Saul, he soon recognizes Samuel by his description and then falls to the ground in awe at the voice of Samuel speaking to him, perhaps through the mouth of the witch herself. The ghost of Samuel then foresees the future and reveals that Saul and his war efforts are doomed.

Immediately, we can see the close parallels between the earliest ancient belief systems. An anonymous and powerless existence awaits every person in the dark, gloomy world beneath our feet. Still, while powerless below the surface, the dead could be summoned, through certain rituals, to share their supernormal knowledge of worldly affairs with the living.

Aside from entreating such favors as advice and divination, the living were also expected to pay the dead a certain amount of respect. Burial rituals, for instance, were considered extremely important. Leaving a person unburied was considered the most abhorrent of punishments. "The fear with which deprivation of burial was viewed [among the Hebrews] points to a belief, common among the Babylonians and Greeks, that the soul could not rest if its body remained unburied."[13] The possibility also exists that such care for the body indicated an early conception of the buried body as the locus of the spirit after death, and *Sheol* thus equated with the grave itself. Simple burial was not always enough, as many were buried with other objects, perhaps intended to help the dead in the grave—evidence of a materialistic view of the afterlife. Archaeological evidence shows that people in early biblical times gave food to the dead and made small offerings at graves.[14] Whether all of these offerings were made out of respect for the deceased or were intended to curry favor with their spirits is unknown.

The monotheism of the Bible forbade the practice of necromancy as a form of idolatry and denied any form of ancestral worship. If people were performing rituals and providing sacrifices directed toward the dead, they were obviously shirking their responsibilities to *Yahweh*, the Creator. The scriptures of the Jewish Bible were considered to come straight from the Divine. In order for a belief to be officially maintained by the faithful, it would have to be found within the scripture. In the post-biblical rabbinic period, beliefs were refined and began to develop a specifically Judaic flavor. Whatever ties the living had to the dead in terms of divination and communication were suppressed.

Judaism eventually felt the influence of two disparate foreign philosophies. The emerging Greek concept of the immortality of the soul as distinct and separate from the body was increasingly popular, especially when compared to the dreary collective of *Sheol*. On the other hand, the belief in physical resurrection, attributed to the Persian prophet Zarathushtra, began to take hold in the Jewish mind as well, appealing to the traditional belief in the importance of bodily existence. In both cases, the idea of reward or punishment after death for one's deeds during life was a new one. As these ideas infiltrated the Jewish mind, there was a great political pressure on the people that required just such radical ideas to preserve the faith.

Under Greek rule, particularly during the reign of Antiochus Epiphanes in the mid-second century BCE, the Jewish people were being punished for their religious beliefs and were offered rewards to give up their faith to take up pagan practices. Many Jewish people made the change under threat of death. The rabbis then took to interpreting life and death in a new way, both to bring solace to the suffering faithful and to save the faith itself.

> Because of suffering inflicted upon the Jewish people, they were forced to change their beliefs. Those who kept to the old traditions were being tortured, while those who converted to Greek ways were rewarded. This caused a shift as divine reward could not be given to both peoples. Thus, it was said that those who remained loyal to the Torah would rise again one day to enjoy eternal life.[15]

So, where in the earlier worldview, life itself was a reward from God, when life became a hell on earth, the idea of a "World to Come" became necessary in order to find some solace from the fact that some were being rewarded for leaving the faith while those who remained true to God were suffering mightily. And so, these foreign ideas were combined one with the other and added to the uniquely Jewish notion of a Messiah, a savior who would come to emancipate the Jewish people, to form what would become the traditional eschatological scheme of Judaism.

The transition to such a view was not an easy one. Several schools of thought developed, each arguing toward its own ends. Most notably, three main schools of Jewish thought appear in the records. The Sadducees, who formed the upper class clergy, argued for a more traditional approach, regarding death as the ultimate conclusion of one's days. Since they came from the upper classes of Jewish society, they did not feel the same need for future rewards, as they were secure enough that they could still regard life as the ultimate reward.[16] It was a group known as the Pharisees, on the other hand, who argued in favor of feeding the hopes of the masses for divine retribution in the afterlife. This notion, having the backing of the majority of the population, not surprisingly became the main line of thought. The third group, the Essenes, represented the mystical school and were concerned with a monastic way of life, taking a position somewhere in between the two main alternatives. Of this group, Philo is the most famous, attempting in his works to integrate harmoniously the more esoteric Platonic philosophies with the theology of the Hebrew Bible.[17] As is typically the case with mystics, Philo and the Essenes remained relatively obscure in the grand scheme of Judaic development in early times. "Though Philo's writings were highly influential in non-Jewish circles, he was totally unknown to Jews until the Renaissance [and the writings of Moses Maimonides, discussed later]."[18]

By the end of the second century CE, *Talmudic* rabbis, who recorded evolving interpretations of the *Tanakh* in accordance with changing circumstances, in the texts called *Talmud*, went so far as to make the Pharisee position a part of the Jewish canon. Jews were obliged to believe in a resurrection of the Jewish people that would take place after the coming of the Messiah. This was likely a reaction to avert the spreading Hellenization of the Israelites. Resurrection, versus the simple immortality of the soul conceptualized by Plato, appealed to the Jewish people for several reasons, as outlined by Raphael:

> Resurrection held the promise that events would continue in the land of the living, with the righteous victorious. Second, resurrection promised a revival of the Jewish people as a community. It was insufficient that individuals would receive their reward alone, particularly in the context of a religion that saw its relationship with God as communal and therefore demanded national reward. Third, body and soul were viewed as an integrated whole in this lifetime and hence in the future, too.[19]

The *Talmudic* rabbis found references in the scriptures of the *Tanakh* to support their position on resurrection, despite the lack of any detailed mention of life after death. Many of the passages cited allude only vaguely to resurrection.

Deuteronomy quotes: "I kill, and I make alive; I have wounded, and I heal."[20] Of course, as the order of the words in this passage is confusing, the author may simply be referring to the initial creation of life rather than an actual resurrection. Others are more easily understandable, such as the following from Isaiah: "Thy dead shall live, my dead bodies shall arise—awake and sing, ye that dwell in the dust—for Thy dew is as the dew of light, and the earth shall bring to life the shades."[21] This latter passage is more certain in its message of the dead rising from the earth, but one cannot be certain that the author intended a physical rising up or a spiritual one. Perhaps the clearest, and most often cited, passage referring to resurrection is Ezekiel 37. The prophet is vouchsafed a vision of a valley of dry bones, the remnants of the people of Israel. He is instructed to prophesy over the bones thus:

'Thus saith the L-rd GOD unto these bones: Behold, I will cause breath to enter into you, and ye shall live. And I will lay sinews upon you, and will bring up flesh upon you, and cover you with skin, and put breath in you, and ye shall live; and ye shall know that I am Hashem.' So I prophesied as I was commanded; and as I prophesied, there was a noise, and behold a commotion, and the bones came together, bone to its bone. And I beheld, and, lo, there were sinews upon them, and flesh came up, and skin covered them above; but there was no breath in them. Then said He unto me: 'Prophesy unto the breath, prophesy, son of man, and say to the breath: Thus saith the L-rd GOD: Come from the four winds, O breath, and breathe upon these slain, that they may live.' So I prophesied as He commanded me, and the breath came into them, and they lived, and stood up upon their feet, an exceeding great host.[22]

The vivid imagery of this passage convinced many of the biblical merit of the doctrine of resurrection. Some have argued, however, that the passage is simply a poetically worded allegory about the state of the nation of Israel, which through a collective faith in God could rise from dry lifelessness to form a great army marching into the Holy Land. In addition, the passage does not favor *individual* resurrection, but instead insists on the resurrection of *a nation*.[23] Still, it is these passages upon which the authority of resurrection came to rest. One further passage possibly relating to a resurrection, though certainly pertaining to the afterlife, is found in Daniel 12:2. "And many of them that sleep in the dust of the earth shall awake, some to everlasting life, and some to reproaches and everlasting abhorrence."[24] Here, not only do we have the confusion as to whether a physical or spiritual awakening is intended, but more importantly, we discover that first of all, not all of the dead will reawaken and second, of those that do, some will be rewarded and others punished.

Thus, the common early belief in a collective underworld of nameless shades was transformed by the Jews in a manner similar to what we have already seen in the Greek world. The souls of the righteous were brought up to heaven, and the contemptuous went down to the punishment of a place called *Gehenna*. While this dualistic notion of reward and punishment appeared in some of Plato's work, it also appeared in the teachings of Zoroaster, whose details of a fiery pit seem to align more closely to the notion of *Gehenna*. Not all rabbis have accepted the existence of *Gehenna*, but the prevalent position became that it was a pit in the depths of the earth, or a bleak and distant valley, similar to *Sheol* in its dreariness but different in its geography and intent, as will be described.[25] Many today believe punishment in *Gehenna* to be a temporary fate, if it is even accepted as a possibility at all. It was at least accepted amongst the rabbis that the righteous would be rewarded in the end and that the wicked would somehow be punished; however, the details surrounding these basic tenets were hotly debated.

> Some sages argued that the righteous and the wicked would go to their respective places only after resurrection and final judgement. Others maintained that the departed would assume their assigned locations immediately following death. Some asserted that the soul would remain with the body for a brief period (three days, seven days, twelve months, etc.) and then ascend. Others declared that after death the soul returns to a heavenly "treasury" and waits there until the period of resurrection.[26]

While resurrection per se is alluded to only vaguely in the *Tanakh*, the concept appears more and more frequently in the Apocryphal and pseudepigraphical literature. Though these texts have not been incorporated into the Jewish biblical canon, they reflect rabbinical thinking at the time.[27] No more obvious statement can be made than is found in II Macabees 7:9: "You, you fiend are making us depart from present life, but the King of the universe will resurrect us, who die for the sake of His laws, to a new eternal life."[28] Further, the Dead Sea Scrolls list resurrection among the powers of God, and broaden the scope of resurrection to include all of mankind regardless of deed or faith.[29] So, it is during this short period that discussion of the doctrine of resurrection led to a broadening of the idea. From the national resurrection in Ezekiel through to the selective one based upon deeds represented later in Daniel and II Macabees, resurrection became democratized and a fact of life for all humankind. As for the fate of non-Jews, the rabbis of the second century differed sharply in their opinions. The minority view argued that gentiles do not have any place in the world to come. The position as stated by another sage, Rabbi Joshua be Hananiah, prevailed: "*Righteous* gentiles have a place in the world to come."[30]

The doctrine of resurrection preserved the ancient concept of the importance of the physical body in order to have a life after death. While the Jews never went to the extremes seen in ancient Egypt when it came to preserving the bodily remains, proper care and burial of the dead body was always important. The cadaver itself was thought to remain sensitive to its surroundings. The dying were thought to be actually able to feel the worms devouring their decaying flesh as their soul hovered nearby, waiting for an opportunity to reenter the body up until the decaying process had begun. While the rabbis acknowledged this belief, they discouraged the "superstitious" practice of providing food for the dead at the grave. The practice carried on amongst the people, however. There were many who believed that at the time of resurrection, the individual would be raised in the same clothes they had been buried in, encouraging many to bury their loved ones in the best clothes available.[31] The *luz*, a small bone at the base of the spine, was thought to be the kernel around which the resurrected body would be built. This was the only part of the body thought to survive decomposition. For this reason, cremation was impossible lest the resurrection of the person be hindered.[32] Even the paradise of the eventual world to come had been conceived of as a sensual place, with the three main pleasures being Shabbat, sunshine, and sexual intercourse.[33]

Important to our present discussion is the fact that the soul was thought to hover about the body for a few days before departing to await the resurrection. It was never agreed upon as to where the soul went during this interim period. Some say it travels to paradise or *Gehenna*, others that it simply enters a kind of torpor. Whatever its ultimate fate, it seems obvious from the rabbinic literature that the souls of the dead remained accessible to the world of the living at least for a time. In much the same way as the encounter with the witch of En-dor, communication with the dead carried on despite the rabbis' promotion of the biblical prohibitions. Repercussions from the dead were feared throughout this period, and even later, just as they were in ancient times. It became custom for the living to ask forgiveness, in front of witnesses, from the dead in order to avert any spiritual harassment. Complaints from the dead were not unheard of, with the most frequent concerning disrespect not only while living but also after death, particularly when the grave was disturbed or the dead were buried in insufficient clothing.[34]

But positive encounters with the dead were reported as well. The *Talmud* describes the tale of Rav Nahman appearing, soon after his death, in the dreams of his friend Raba. The sole purpose of his visit was to console his friend, who had been mourning him at length, as he describes the moment of his death as harmless, "like pulling a hair out of milk."[35] There is also the tale of Rabbi Akiba ben Joseph's encounter with the dead man, tormented by Sisyphian labor until his still living son should behave piously. In this story, the rabbi takes the man's suffering to heart and goes in search of the living son. Upon finding the boy, he teaches him the *Torah*, training him to become a reader at the synagogue, and thus saves the dead man from further torment.[36]

And then there are completely chance encounters with the spirits of the dead. The story is told of a man who accidentally overheard two spirits talking in a cemetery one night.[37] They spoke to each other of the best time to plant crops for the upcoming year and the man followed their instructions. His success was such that he returned to the cemetery the following year to eavesdrop once more. Again, they discussed the best time for planting and the man again followed their advice. Soon after this, the spirits discovered that they had been spied upon and when the man returned, they refused to speak for fear of being overheard once more.

Dreams are also a constant source of spiritual encounters and divine communication in Judaism. Not only in death but also during sleep, the soul was thought to leave the body, demonstrating the influence of Plato's dualistic ideas. It became a common practice to thank God upon waking for allowing the soul to reunite with the body. These nocturnal out-of-body experiences were taken as important portents. Numbers 12:6 reads in part: "if there be a prophet among you, I the Lord do make Myself known unto him in a vision, I do speak with him in a dream."[38] Sometimes divine communication would come from an angel, Baal Hahalomoth, the dispenser of dreams, or the dreaming soul might encounter the spirits of the dead who would give information to them. Joshua Trachtenberg enumerates a number of examples of dream encounters:

> Reports of the dead appearing in dreams are numerous. The teacher and father-in-law of Eliezer b. Nathan, R. Eliakim b. Joseph, visited him one night to correct a misconception which had led to an erroneous ritual decision; R. Meir of Rothenburg once helped an earnest student, who had never met him in life, to unravel a badly snarled Talmudic passage; Rashi disclosed to his grandson Samuel the correct pronunciation of the Tetragrammaton; according to popular legend, on the third night after he had been tortured to death, R. Ammon of Mainz appeared in a dream to his teacher, R. Kalonymos b. Meshullam, and dictated the solemn *Unetanneh Tokef* which he had composed while writhing in pain. These are a few of the more notable visitations. Visions of the lot that deceased ancestors are enjoying, whether in Paradise or *Gehinnom*, disclosures of hidden treasure, exhortations to repay debts contracted by the visitant, such is the burden of most dreams about the dead.[39]

One prevalent fear was that of the body's susceptibility to attack while the soul was away. Specifically, demons were thought capable of entering a sleeping body and taking control of it. The demons, themselves being evil beings, were sometimes the souls of people who had been terribly evil in life. They were thought to populate desolate and dangerous regions such as deserts and ruins. In some cases, possession occurs when the demon or evil spirit, called *Dybbuk*, enters the body of a living person, whether asleep or awake. In most cases, a serious change in personality is evident and it is often this that signals that possession has occurred. The possessed individual actually begins to act as though they were a different person. A rabbi is necessary to exorcise the possessing entity in these cases, and force it from the victim.[40] The beliefs of the victim are crucial to the success or failure of the exorcism. That is to say, the more confidence the victim has in the efficacy of the rituals, or the stronger one's faith in God, the more likely the exorcism is to be successful.

In addition to dreamtime visitations, there are also reports of deathbed visions. Many have witnessed the Angel of Death at their deathbed. Further, the angel was often accompanied by attendants or spirits of the dead. The *Talmud* records the story of Rabbi Yohanan ben Zakkai who proclaimed to those about him that he saw the deceased King Hezekiah of Judah coming to greet him as he lay on his deathbed.[41] In addition to the visions of specific beings such as these, there are also reports of a life review in which the dying person literally sees his life flash before his eyes, or they are shown the good and bad they have done throughout life.[42]

Martha Himmelfarb examines the genre of tales of those who had been vouchsafed a view of heaven and hell and points out a number of trends that seem to form a lineage of belief from the Orphic Greeks through Judaism to Christianity, and possibly back to Judaism again.[43] Due to a paucity of actual descriptions of heaven, Himmelfarb focuses almost exclusively on journeys to hell, or those parts of otherworldly journeys specifically relating to hell. From such Jewish sources as the *Darkhei Teshuvah* and *Gedulat Moshe*, both medieval texts, as well as older Christian apocalyptic texts, certain features of punishment and torment appear consistently. Namely, *Gehenna* is described as a dark, smoky place flowing with rivers of fire.[44] Sinners are hung painfully from hooks depending upon the nature of their transgressions. Slanderers are hung by their tongues, while adulterers are hung from their genitals, for example. There are also instances where various beasts torment the sinners while they hang, unable to protect themselves. Women who have had abortions or committed infanticide are seen with beasts suckling at their breasts. Finally, there are punishments similar to those found in the ancient Greek myths, denoted as "tantalising punishments" by Himmelfarb, an example of which might be the torture of one who broke his fast too early being hung inches above a body of water though unable to drink and being within view of a ripe fruit tree but unable to reach it.[45] Thus, these horrible physical punishments, whether seen as temporary or eternal, can be contrasted with the enjoyment of the simple pleasures of life in the "World to Come" as described previously.

The Jewish view of life after death remained relatively unchanged over the next several hundred years until religious philosophers began to move away from a strictly physical view of the resurrection and to place an increasing emphasis on the spiritual side of things. Moses Maimonides (d. 1204) is recognized as the single most important thinker in Judaism during the Middle Ages, and is considered one of the most respected Jewish thinkers to this day. Maimonides encouraged a dualistic view of humankind, like Philo before him, arguing for a more Platonic understanding of life after death. The body and the soul were considered separate entities, in fact, even considered irreconcilably different. "Matter is matter, spirit is spirit, and ne'er the twain shall meet is the dictum of the Maimonidean view."[46] With the death of the body, the soul was thought to leave the body only to be resurrected in an allegorical sense, rising up into the light of Heaven in a new spiritual body. For the most part, Maimonides seems to completely ignore the notion of physical resurrection in his own philosophy, while still acknowledging its place as a dogma.[47] Many scholars have debated what appears to be a contradiction in the works of Maimonides concerning this issue of resurrection. Only one of his works, *Treatise on Resurrection*, engages with the topic. The apparent contradiction comes from the fact that while in his other works Maimonides is focused completely on the spiritual reality of the afterlife, in the *Treatise* he argues wholeheartedly in favor of the physical resurrection urged by the rabbis. At least one scholar solves the contradiction by arguing that Maimonides was not in fact the author of this paradoxical work.[48] Whether or not Maimonides did in fact write the *Treatise* is of little import when we consider the effect upon later eras. From the Middle Ages and the time of Maimonides to the eighteenth century, the doctrine of spiritual immortality overtook that of bodily resurrection and became the central belief in Jewish thought. Maimonides encouraged an understanding of the *Tanakh* that involved allegory rather than a literal reading, thus encouraging the evolution of beliefs. Still, many of the rabbinical laws remain firmly held in the philosophy of Maimonides. Of particular interest here are the continuing enforcement of laws condemning idolatry and its association with cults of the dead. From his writing one can be certain that many people still practiced the same kinds of rituals to placate and communicate with the dead as they had done in previous centuries, despite Maimonides' admonition of these rites as "stupid practices."[49] The very fact that he felt the need to attack them asserts that they existed as a constant threat to Judaism.

With an increasingly spiritual view of the afterlife came an increase in ghost stories during the Middle Ages as well. In a change from antiquity, ghosts in this time are described with more character. Ghosts are said to converse with one another, pursue their studies, hold councils to judge spiritual disputes, and even congregate in ghostly services at night in the synagogue.[50] Despite the varied colorful descriptions, certain central themes continue to appear just as they had in more ancient tales. For instance, many ghosts continue to appear simply to comfort their friends and family. There is a story of an undertaker who encountered one of his "clients" on the steps of the synagogue one morning. The spirit simply told him he had appeared in order to reassure his friends that he had arrived into Paradise.[51]

Respect for the dead and the place of burial remained an important practice. Another story tells of a man who decided to build a musical instrument from the wood of another fellow's coffin. The dead man appeared in a dream demanding respect and warning the living man not to use that wood for his creation. The man persisted regardless and built the instrument as he had planned. Soon, he became gravely ill. His son then smashed the instrument, which appeased the spirit and made his father well again.[52]

Further emphasis on the divergence of spirit and body in Jewish thought stems from the mystical school of *Kabbalah* that came into prominence around the time of Maimonides, having been passed down through oral tradition for centuries before. One of the main mystical texts of this esoteric movement, the *Zohar*, has been described as containing "some of Judaism's most sophisticated teachings on the afterlife."[53] A complex system is constructed in this text that envisions numerous worlds, or levels of reality, interlocking one with the other. Various angels and demons control the different levels, some of whom are responsible for the state of humans as beings in the flesh. The soul is believed to come from God and to eventually be destined to reunite with Him. In the meantime, souls will transmigrate from one body to the next always learning until they can finally leave the cycle of life and simply return to God. The Kabbalists went even further than Maimonides, or Philo before him, in attempting to integrate Neoplatonic and Jewish ideas by introducing the notion of reincarnation and also gathering together a number of folkloric and often superstitious beliefs found among the common people to create an esoteric system of extreme complexity.

> Apart from basic ideas concerning reward and punishment, life after death, the Messiah, redemption, and resurrection, there is hardly a commonly held belief among the Jews regarding eschatological details. This lacuna provided an obvious opportunity for free play for the imaginative, the visionary and the superstitious, and so became the field in which the kabbalists left their mark: for they dealt extensively with just these concepts.[54]

There are a great many examples of supernatural phenomena in the Kabbalistic literature that applies directly to the topic of life after death, much of it growing out of the kind of folklore that had been circulating through oral tradition for ages. Deathbed visions are common with the *Zohar* repeatedly mentioning "angelic beings, visionary guides, deceased relatives, and even some rather unfriendly demonic-looking characters."[55] The Angel of Death found in the rabbinic literature also commonly appears. More typical of mystics around the world, the Kabbalists report the ability of the soul to leave the body to travel among the various levels of reality, encountering other beings. Ecclesiastes 12:6–7 says: "Before the silver cord is snapped asunder, and the golden bowl is shattered, and the pitcher is broken at the fountain, and the wheel falleth shattered, into the pit; And the dust returneth to the earth as it was, and the spirit returneth unto God who gave it."[56] This passage has been interpreted by Kabbalists to infer a silver cord connecting the so-called astral body of the soul to the physical body here on Earth. It was believed that once this cord was severed the soul would not be able to return to the body and only then was the body truly dead. The concept of an "astral body" can also be found in the *zel* and *zelem* of the multifaceted soul conceived by the Kabbalists.[57]

As there are multiple worlds conceived of in Kabbalah, so too are there multiple souls. After death, some aspects remained with the body until it was decomposed, some remained longer, while others departed for the spiritual realms. At certain times of the month or year, it was thought that the aspects of the soul would come together again at the grave site, providing the opportunity for the living to visit the grave and thus commune with the dead.[58] Beliefs such as this persisted despite previous efforts to eradicate them on the grounds of superstition. Basically, even conservative Jews, "grew to accept necromancy, asserting that the *Tanakh* forbade only the use of idolatrous-like rituals, marked by the use of special outfits and incense for conjuring up the dead. If the practitioner conjured up the dead through the use of holy names, as provided by Jewish mystical texts, then it was permitted."[59] So, the common belief that one can still communicate with the dead persisted despite the best efforts of the rabbis until it was finally accepted as a legitimate practice.

The notion of reincarnation in the Kabbalist philosophy requires special attention because it is unique in Jewish thought.

The Kabbalists describe three types of reincarnation: *gilgul*, *ibbur*, and *dybbuk*. *Gilgul* takes place during pregnancy. *Ibbur* (impregnation) occurs when an "old" soul enters the body of another individual at any time during its lifetime. The soul dwells in the new body for a limited period and performs certain acts or commandments. Finally, when an evil soul enters a person, causing mental illness and temporarily manifesting itself as a foreign personality, the invading soul is called *dybbuk*.[60]

The *dybbuk* have already been mentioned. *Ibbur* are benign souls who simply need to complete the tasks assigned to them in their own lifetime, but were prevented from completing these tasks due to a sudden death. This implies that every person has a certain purpose in life that must be completed before moving on. The notion of *gilgul*, unlike the notion that souls might occasionally possess people, is one not encountered in Judaism until the Kabbalists introduced it. In Kabbalist philosophy, the idea of reincarnation that had been drawn from Plato is adapted to fit the Jewish framework with the ultimate goal being eventual resurrection. It was first suggested by the earliest Kabbalists that reincarnation occurred only to the wicked as punishment for their sins. The righteous went to Paradise to await the resurrection and the "World to Come." Reincarnation, or the transmigration of souls, was a punishment meant to be both severe and just. This is an interesting reversal from the ancient notion that life itself was the reward and death the punishment. Later, the idea evolved to include everyone in the transmigration of souls with every soul reincarnated in order to purge itself from the sins of life. This idea echoes the Platonic conception of reincarnation in which souls continue to learn right living in successive lifetimes. It came to be viewed as, "an opportunity for the soul to fulfil its mission and make up for its failures in previous transmigrations."[61]

There is no evidence of the transmigration of souls appearing in any Jewish philosophy before the twelfth century. Still, some Kabbalists found references to their ideas in the writings of certain *Talmudic* rabbis, as well as in the *Tanakh* itself. The only passage consistently referred to in this context is extremely vague, however: "One generation passeth away, and another generation cometh; and the earth abideth for ever."[62] Certainly, this passage need not refer to anything other than the actual physical passage of time as the older generation dies off in the wake of a younger one. There is no explicit statement that these successive generations are made up of the same souls. Similarly, the following excerpt from Exodus 20:5 (*Shemot*) has been interpreted to refer to the punishment visited upon an individual in successive incarnations: "[F]or I the Lord thy God am a jealous God, visiting the iniquity of the fathers upon the children unto the third and fourth generation of them that hate Me."[63] Rabbi Phillip Berg argues that God could not be so vengeful as to punish the children of those that had sinned and so these subsequent generations must also be the same as those who had passed before them, thus implying reincarnation.[64] Within the wider context of the Bible, however, it is more likely that God is threatening subsequent generations only so far as they carry on the same iniquities of their forefathers, namely rejection of God. In any event, the Kabbalists took reincarnation for granted from their earliest writings. King David was said to be the reincarnation of Adam himself, who was then meant to later reincarnate in the form of the Messiah.[65] Successive incarnations between Adam and the eventual Messiah would fill specific roles all with the aim of preparing the way for the final incarnation.

Hasidic Judaism is one group among which the Kabbalist theory of reincarnation has been widely accepted, not to mention other mystical and supernatural aspects as well. Growing out of the public interest in magic and the supernatural during the eighteenth century in Eastern Europe, Rabbi Israel ben Eliezer, the *Ba'al Shem Tov*, or "Good Master of the Name," distinguished himself among other Kabbalist magicians and founded a distinct school of Jewish thought based on spiritual and allegorical interpretations. Hasidim are believed to have special God-given gifts, including the ability to heal, to speak with spirits of the dead and to read the past-lives of others, even recognizing those who have incarnated in inanimate forms or in those of plants and animals.[66]

Today, the many branches of Judaism embrace various forms and combinations of the beliefs described. As the *Tanakh*, being the ultimate authority in all schools of Judaism, makes so little mention of the afterlife, it is considered an open question to a large extent. Only the most orthodox Jews hold onto the notion of a literally physical resurrection, others preferring to view things more metaphorically instead. The resurrection that is to take place is more often considered to be one of a purely spiritual nature, having more in common with the dualism of Maimonides than with the older views of the rabbinic period and before. The concept of reincarnation is not widespread in Judaism in the least, but it remains for many a valid alternative all the same, the Kabbalah having been largely absorbed into the common Jewish mind. In any event, a life after death is expected at some point within Judaism despite the "this-life" orientation of many modern Jews. The resurrection will occur in one form or another once the Messiah finally arrives to usher in a world of paradise for the faithful, and either a world of suffering or simply complete annihilation for the unbelievers. The words of Aryeh Kaplan help maintain the proper perspective: "If man were immortal, it would be very easy for him to become totally immersed in the material world and forget life's spiritual values. Immortality and extreme longevity will therefore have to wait until the Messianic Age, when spiritual values will be firmly imbedded in man's nature."[67]

Notes

1. Simcha Paull Raphael, *Jewish Views of the Afterlife* (London: Jason Aronson, 1994), p. 13.

2. Joshua L. Liebman, *Peace of Mind* (New York: Simon and Schuster, 1946), p. 135.

3. Victor E. Frankl, *Man's Search for Meaning*(1959; rev. and updated, New York: Washington Square Press, 1984), p. 98.

4. It is suggested that the similarity may be due to a common Amorite origin of the cultures, though further discussion of this idea falls outside the bounds of this study. For further information,

see George E. Mendenhall, "From Witchcraft to Justice: Death and Afterlife in the Old Testament," in *Death and Afterlife: Perspectives of World Religions*, ed. Hiroshi Obayashi (New York: Greenwood, 1992).

5. Job 10:22 Jewish Publication Society.

6. Ps. 88:7.

7. Ps. 88:5.

8. Job 14:2.

9. Gen. 5:24.

10. C. H. Moore, *Ancient Beliefs in the Immortality of the Soul* (New York: Cooper Square, 1963), p. 61.

11. Deut. 18:10–12.

12. I Sam. 28.

13. W. Hirsch, *Rabbinic Psychology: Beliefs about the Soul in Rabbinic Literature of the Talmudic Period* (London: Edward Goldston, 1947), p. 75.

14. Raphael, *Jewish Views of the Afterlife*, pp. 46–50.

15. Robert Goldenberg, "Bound Up in the Bond of Life: Death and Afterlife in the Jewish Tradition," in *Death and Afterlife: Perspectives of World Religions*, ed. Hiroshi Obayashi (New York: Greenwood, 1992) p. 100.

16. Goldenberg, "Bound Up," p. 101.

17. For an introduction to Philo, see H. Chadwick, "Philo," in *The Cambridge History of Later Greek and Early Medieval Philosophy*, ed. A. H. Armstrong (London: Cambridge University Press, 1967), pp. 137–157.

18. Neil Gillman, *The Death of Death* (Woodstock, VT: Jewish Lights, 1997), p. 111.

19. Raphael, *Jewish Views of the Afterlife*, p. 50.

20. Deut. 32:39.

21. Is. 26:19.

22. Ez. 37:5–10.

23. Rifat Sonsino and Daniel B. Syme, *What Happens After I Die?: Jewish Views of Life After Death* (Northvale, NJ: Jason Aronson, 1994), p. 19.

24. Dan. 12:2.

25. Saul Lieberman, *Some Aspects of Afterlife in Early Rabbinic Literature* (Jerusalem: American Academy for Jewish Research, 1965), pp. 496–497.

26. Sonsino and Syme, *What Happens After*, p. 25.

27. Gillman, *The Death of Death*, p. 101.

28. Gillman, *The Death of Death*, p. 102.

29. Gillman, *The Death of Death*, pp. 104–105.

30. *Tos. San.* 13:2, cited in Sonsino and Syme, *What Happens After*, pp. 25–26.

31. Lieberman, *Some Aspects of Afterlife*, pp. 506–510.

32. Goldenberg, "Bound Up," pp. 101–102.

33. Sonsino and Syme, *What Happens After*, p. 29.

34. Joshua Trachtenberg, *Jewish Magic and Superstition* (New York: Meridian, 1961), p. 63.

35. *Moed Katan* 28b, cited in Raphael, *Jewish Views of the Afterlife*, p. 43.

36. *Midrash Tanhuma. Kallah*, ed. Coronel, 4b, and see quotations from *Tan.* in Aboab's *Menorat ha-Maor*, i. 1, 2, § 1, ed. Fürstenthal, p. 82, as cited in Louis Ginzberg, "Akiba ben Joseph," *Jewish Encyclopedia* (1901–1906), available online: <http://www.jewishencyclopedia.com/view.jsp?artid=1033&letter=A#2666>. January 25, 2008.

37. *Berakhot* 18b, cited in Hirsch, *Rabbinic Psychology*, pp. 261–262.

38. Numbers 12:6.

39. Trachtenberg, *Jewish Magic*, p. 234.

40. Angelo S. Rappoport, *The Folklore of the Jews* (London: Soncino, 1937), pp. 47–50.

41. *Berakhot* 22b, cited in Raphael, *Jewish Views of the Afterlife*, p. 43.

42. *Taanit* 11a, cited in Raphael, *Jewish Views of the Afterlife*, p. 132.

43. Martha Himmelfarb, *Tours of Hell* (Philadelphia: University of Pennsylvania Press, 1983).

44. Himmelfarb, *Tours of Hell*, pp. 106–126.

45. Himmelfarb, *Tours of Hell*, pp. 68–105.

46. Raphael, *Jewish Views of the Afterlife*, pp. 20–21.

47. Lee Naomi Goldfeld, *Moses Maimonides' Treatise on Resurrection* (New York: KTAV Publishing House, 1986), pp. 13–14.

48. Goldfeld, *Moses Maimonides*, pp. 31–51.

49. Maimonides, *The Guide of the Perplexed*, trans. M. Friedlander (New York: Hebrew Publishing Co., 1881), III, 235.

50. Trachtenberg, *Jewish Magic*, pp. 61–62.

51. Trachtenberg, *Jewish Magic*, p. 62.

52. Trachtenberg, *Jewish Magic*, pp. 63–64.

53. Raphael, *Jewish Views of the Afterlife*, p. 273.

54. Gershom Scholem, *Kabbalah* (New York: Quadrangle/The New York Times Book Co., 1974), p. 333.

55. Raphael, *Jewish Views of the Afterlife*, p. 287.

56. Eccl. 12:6–7.

57. Scholem, *Kabbalah*, pp. 158–159; p. 333.

58. Aryeh Kaplan, *Immortality, Resurrection, and the Age of the Universe: A Kabbalistic View* (New York: KTAV Publishing House, 1993), p. 101.

59. Raphael, *Jewish Views of the Afterlife*, p. 106.

60. Sonsino and Syme, *What Happens After*, pp. 48–49.

61. Scholem, *Kabbalah*, p. 161.

62. Eccl. 1:4.

63. Ex. 20:5.

64. Rabbi [Phillip] Berg, *Wheels of a Soul* (New York: The Kabbalah Learning Center, 1995), p. 25.

65. Scholem, *Kabbalah*, p. 334.

66. The following provides much detailed information on the development of Hasidism and specifically the types of miraculous wonders attributed to their leaders: Gedalyah Nigal, *Magic, Mysticism, and Hasidism: The Supernatural in Jewish Thought*, trans. Edward Levin (London: Jason Aronson, 1994).

67. Kaplan, *Immortality*, pp. 24–25.

CHAPTER THREE

~

Christianity

Near the beginning of the rabbinic period of Judaism, a charismatic figure emerged upon the Middle Eastern stage and attracted a loyal following who saw him as the promised Messiah that would usher in the Last Day and the Final Resurrection. This man was variously titled rabbi, prophet, and Son of God. To most in the modern world he is easily recognized by the name of Jesus Christ, from the Greek, *christos*, meaning "the anointed one," which is itself a translation of the Hebrew *messiah*. In the years following his death, and more importantly his resurrection three days later, a religion sprouted in his name that has since grown to become the most pervasive religion in the world today, molding the worldview of the Western world for centuries. Jesus was born into Judaism, his early followers were Jews, and his views reflect the Jewish ideology that he grew up with. Christianity and Judaism parted ways considerably as time went on, however, in no small part through the teachings of this new rabbi. Christians accepted the *Tanakh* of the Jews as scripture but added to it the so-called New Testament, referring to the Jewish Bible as the Old Testament. Together, the Holy Bible of Christianity records the deeds and sayings of God, his prophets, and Christ, mainly from the purported perspective of those who knew Christ or his disciples, culminating in the four Gospels and the writings of St. Paul.

The first significant divergence between Christ and the Jews came with his interpretations of the old scriptures. Whereas the Jews relied on their rabbis to interpret the *Tanakh* and to establish doctrine, Jesus preached from a very personal understanding of the word of God. The idea that one man could claim a specific understanding of scripture posed a real threat to the rabbinic authority that prevailed at the time. To properly describe the Christian understanding of death, one must realize that, "Christianity emerged as an interpretation of what Judaism should be—of how, in other words, the covenant promises and commands should be implemented in that day and at that time."[1] In some cases these interpretations agreed with the rabbis, in others they differed considerably. In the end, the only source of information as to what exactly Jesus said in terms of these interpretations has been filtered through the writing of others, as Jesus himself left no written texts. The Gospels provide the most detailed information on the life of Christ, having ostensibly been written by those who knew him or who were contemporaries, within several decades of his death. From what is told in these narratives, Jesus was born of a miraculous virgin birth. Miracles followed Jesus throughout his life as he healed the sick, transformed water into wine, caused limited food to spontaneously multiply, and even raised the dead back to life. While these miracles certainly where seen as proof of the divine provenance of Jesus as Messiah, the words that he spoke were always seen as much more important.

It was Christ's interpretation of the Old Testament that originally garnered his following, though it was his death and the subsequent miracle of his resurrection that proved, for Christians, his divine status for all time. He was persecuted by both the Jewish and Roman authorities and was eventually nailed to a cross and thus executed. Where Christianity could have died with Jesus on the cross, his resurrection three days later cemented the faithful into what would prove to be a formidable religious movement. In order to adequately understand the Christian understanding of life after death, it is essential not only to examine what Christ himself is reported to have said, but also to look more closely at the events surrounding his death and miraculous resurrection.

The Gospels refer to an afterlife much more often than the Hebrew Bible had, though there are only two instances of deliberate teaching on the subject, and only one of them by Jesus himself. Much of what is said in the New Testament assumes an understanding of the Jewish concepts of resurrection and judgment. The Gospels of both Matthew and Luke refer to the double-edged fate awaiting man after death, warning that the means to salvation are difficult and that many will fail to achieve it: "Enter ye in at the straight gate: for wide is the gate, and broad is the way, that leadeth to destruction, and many there be which go in thereat. Because straight is the gate, and narrow is the way, which leadeth unto life, and few there be that find it."[2] This division between two possible fates is further emphasized in the Gospel of Mark, where Jesus makes explicit mention of the fires of hell that await the unworthy, encouraging believers to do what must be done in order to remain true:

And if thy hand offend thee, cut it off: it is better for thee to enter into life maimed, than having two hands go into hell, into the fire that never shall be quenched: Where their worm dieth not, and the fire is not quenched. And if thy foot offend thee, cut it off: it is better for thee to enter halt into life, than having two feet to be cast into hell, into the fire that never shall be quenched: Where their worm dieth not, and the fire is not quenched. And if thine eye offend thee, pluck it out: it is better for thee to enter into the kingdom of God with one eye, than having two eyes to be cast into hell fire: Where their worm dieth not, and the fire is not quenched.[3]

The idea of a division of the world to come between the heavenly Kingdom of God and the torturous underworld of hell stems directly from intertestamental Judaism, the period within which Jesus was born and lived. As we have already seen, the traditional Jewish view of a shadowy *Sheol* was giving way to a varied state of torment or reward depending upon how one led one's individual life. The intertestamental Book of Enoch describes how the spirits of the dead are sent to *Sheol* to await judgment and following ascension or torment.[4] Jesus, then, echoes this evolution of Judaic thought, emphasizing the horrors of hell, what came to be called *Gehenna* among the Jews.

Jesus was particularly interested in the salvation of those who were among the more unfortunate members of society, preaching to the common people. While on the one hand there are those statements, as quoted previously, which denote an emphasis on good behavior symbolized through choosing the "straight path," Jesus also makes several references to the blessed future state of the poor and downtrodden. Luke recounts the parable of a pair of men who die, one rich and the other poor. Throughout life, the poor man, Lazarus, suffered, living a life of hardship. The rich man, named Dives, on the other hand, lived in the lap of luxury, ignoring the plight of his poor neighbor. Dives is forced to suffer the torments of hell while Lazarus is accepted into the bosom of Abraham after death. When the rich man begs for some respite, Abraham answers, "Son, remember that thou in thy lifetime receivedst thy good things, and likewise Lazarus evil things: but now he is comforted, and thou are tormented."[5] Here it becomes obvious that Jesus is preaching a philosophy of compassion for the less fortunate, both through encouraging those who can afford it to give to the poor, and also assuring the sufferers that they will be taken care of in the next life.

The most famous illustration of Christ's views on who is deemed worthy of rewards in the afterlife is that found in Matthew. Chapter 5 begins with Jesus's promise, "Blessed are the poor in spirit: for theirs is the kingdom of heaven," and includes the famous maxim, "Blessed are the meek: for they shall inherit the earth."[6] From such passages it is clear that Jesus preaches not only a doctrine of torment and punishment for the evil and salvation for the good, but additionally admonishes the rich for their excesses in this life and promises the poor comfort in the afterlife. Unfortunately, Jesus nowhere specifically outlines just what his views of this afterlife are, seemingly assuming some familiarity with such beliefs, likely closely related to those of Judaism.

There is, however, one instance where Jesus makes a clear statement about a specific aspect of the afterlife. The Sadducees, conservative Jews opposed to the notion of resurrection, posed what was meant to be a trick question to Jesus, confronting him on the issue of resurrection.[7] They proposed the hypothetical situation of a woman who was obliged by tradition to marry her husband's brother after his death. The husband had seven brothers, each of whom died one after the other, while the wife married each in his turn. The question, then, was after the resurrection, which brother would the woman be married to? Jesus answered simply: "Do ye not therefore err, because ye know not the scriptures, neither the power of God? For when they shall rise from the dead, they neither marry, nor are given in marriage; but are as the angels which are in heaven."[8] From this simple passage it is obvious, first, that Jesus supports the notion of an eventual resurrection of the dead, but more interestingly, that the state of man after resurrection is different from that before death. No more will such worldly matters as marriage have any meaning, but men will be "as the angels."

On this last part of the statement, and the meaning of what it might mean to be "as the angels" there is no small debate. For instance, in placing the emphasis on the reference to angels, Franz Mussner interprets as follows: "'Like angels' means that through the resurrection we shall be liberated from all those conditions to which we are subjected on earth; above all, we shall be liberated from death and from all conditions of the flesh, so that we shall no longer need to procreate."[9] This interpretation certainly bears the mark of Plato in the dichotomy of spirit and body. From another point of view, Alois Winklhofer, in seeming contradiction to Christ's words, states, "The soul is not 'like the angels'; it does not become a pure spirit, but always keeps its essential ordering to a body as its organs. As long as it is separated from the body it remains imperfect."[10] Winklhofer here implies that the angelic state of perfection requires the union of body and soul, which he would argue occurs at the day of resurrection, a contention not unfamiliar in particular Jewish circles. It will be helpful to examine the nature of angels to gain a better appreciation for exactly what it is that Jesus was talking about in this important passage before going further into the developing debate.

The Jewish Old Testament was already replete with images of angels, the messengers of God. In the New Testament, this function as messengers is carried over and angels play an active role. Tradition established that angels were created before man and were given the same freedom to choose good or evil.

Those that chose good were made ministers of God, while those that chose evil were condemned to hell.[11] This new conception of angels indicates an interesting evolution. For the pre-Christian Jews, there were no fallen angels. Satan was a title of office, not a personal name. The personification of Satan, associated with the name Lucifer in the New Testament,[12] reflects a growing partisanship for dualism over the older Jewish notions.[13]

On the actual nature of angels, there is agreement in large part, however. The Bible describes a distinct hierarchy of beings from Seraphim and Cherubim to the Archangels and Angels, all of which share certain common characteristics.[14] They are described as ethereal, nonmaterial beings. In his book on the subject, Father Pascal Parente states: "Being spiritual and completely immaterial [the angel] does not fill or occupy space, not even the smallest dimension, not even a single point. His presence in a place is determined, and occasionally made known, by his activity there and not by his substance which has nothing in common with matter."[15]

Angels became increasingly important in later theological discussions, forming the theme of lengthy discussions by the church fathers and later, writers. The notion of angels still captures the modern imagination as a recent poll states that 69% of Americans believe in their existence.[16] St. Augustine authoritatively summed up the nature of angels, in the fourth century CE, as follows:

> The Angels are spirits . . . but it is not because they are spirits that they are Angels. They become Angels when they are sent, for the name Angel refers to their office not to their nature. You ask the name of this nature, it is *spirit*; you ask its office, it is that of an Angel, (i.e., a messenger). In as far as he exists, an Angel is a spirit; in as far as he acts, he is an Angel.[17]

It seems obvious, then, that when Jesus refers to resurrected humans as being like angels, he is referring to a spiritual element, which allows them to simultaneously remain ethereal and occasionally appear as a seemingly physical manifestation in the pursuance of their duties. It later became a matter of Catholic doctrine that the angels are, "pure spirits, incorporeal substances, free and independent from any material body, ethereal or otherwise."[18] Certainly, this does not agree with the position held by Winklhofer and others who contend that the resurrected body must be the same physical body that died, or indeed any physical body at all. One must turn back to the biblical narratives of Jesus's life and death to see whether the New Testament supports the Judaic notion of a physical resurrection or this concept of a spiritual form for humans after the Last Day.

The key evidence in Christianity for a physical resurrection as imagined by the pre-Christian Jews lies in the four Gospel accounts of the crucifixion and resurrection of Jesus Christ himself. It is most certain historically that Jesus, the man, was crucified; the only question is over the veracity of his resurrection. All four Gospels tell a similar tale of the resurrection, though they each differ on certain specific details.[19] From these, a composite story can be constructed that runs as follows. Three days after the crucifixion of Jesus, and his subsequent burial in a tomb, Mary Magdalene, and perhaps some other women, went to the tomb bearing spices with which to anoint the dead savior. Upon arrival, the tomb was found to be open. The body of Jesus was missing from the tomb and in his place are one or two angelic men who explain that Christ has risen from the dead. Three of the four accounts have Jesus then appearing to Mary Magdalene to prove that what the angels have said was indeed true. In all cases, Mary and the women return to tell the apostles of what has become of their Messiah and they are not believed. The apostles assume that the women are seeing things. Following this, Jesus appears to the apostles in various scenarios. Though they doubt their sight at first, they invariably come to accept that Christ has been resurrected from the dead, at which time he then ascends into heaven.

From this account, it is often considered a given that the Gospels tell a story of the bodily resurrection of Christ and not a spiritual one. The references to physical phenomena are few but significant. Matthew claims that the women, when Jesus appeared before them, fell to their knees and held his feet.[20] Mark explains that Jesus appeared at dinner with the apostles, though it does not say here that he specifically ate with them, only that he was with them while they ate.[21] In Luke, however, Jesus is first described as breaking bread and later shown to actually eat fish and honeycomb in order to prove his existence.[22] Finally, John, in typical form, expands with the story of Thomas; the sole doubter among the apostles even after Christ shows them his wounds. He is invited to touch the wounds, which after doing so convinces him of the truth of Christ's return.[23] Of course, there is also the important fact that the body of Christ is missing from the tomb, begging the question as to where the body has gone. And so, there is ample grounds for the belief that Christ had risen in a physical body, but this is not an unambiguous conclusion.

Jesus appears, seemingly out of thin air, in all four Gospels. He is described as appearing to two of the apostles in "another" form,[24] and in Luke, further details are given as Christ appears in the form of an unrecognized man and travels with the unknowing apostles for a short time, after which time he vanishes before their eyes.[25] Jesus also appears in an unrecognized form during a fishing expedition, according to John's Gospel.[26] Finally, Jesus appears several times throughout the four accounts, and disappears at will, even being taken up to heaven before the eyes of the apostles. Certainly, feats such as this lend themselves more readily to a spiritual form, rather than a purely physical one.

Other books of the New Testament, particularly those attributed to St. Paul, seem to confirm the idea of a nonphysical resurrection. While the Acts of the Apostles describe much about Christ's resurrection and appearances to his apostles, it is in the Epistles that we find the clearest statements about life after death. I Corinthians, chapter 15, gives an account of Christ's death and resurrection similar to those found in the Gospels, but it then goes into a focused commentary upon the event and what it means to others. Paul goes into quite a bit of detail in discussing the state of man before and after the resurrection. The core argument can be summed up with verse 44: "It is sown a natural body; it is raised a spiritual body. There is a natural body, and there is a spiritual body."[27] Clearly, Paul indicates that the post-resurrection man is fundamentally changed from his present state. The corruptible, physical body is dead and gone and in its place is a fresh, incorruptible spiritual body. Alan Segal clearly links Paul's thought to Jewish mysticism and the notion that Paul, agreeing with the Hebrew prophet Enoch, believed that in his conversion he had been transformed into a higher state of being that would only be fully realized upon his death.[28]

Unfortunately, the specifics of what exactly a spiritual body consists are left out of Paul's writing, and this is perhaps the source of the continued debate over resurrection. What is much more important than the form of the resurrected, to the average Christian at least, is the fact of resurrection itself. The fact that Jesus died and then was resurrected, in Paul's belief, is proof enough that every person will share in that same fate on the Last Day.[29] The philosopher, C. D. Broad disagrees with the logic of this, however, and enters a debate that has lasted centuries, stating:

> if Christianity be true, though Jesus was human, He was *also* divine. No other human being resembles Him in this respect . . . the body of Jesus did not decay in the tomb, but was transformed; whilst the body of every ordinary man rots and disintegrates soon after his death. Therefore, if men do survive the death of their bodies, the process must be utterly unlike that which took place when Jesus survived His death on the cross. Thus the analogy breaks down in every relevant respect, and so an argument from the resurrection of Jesus to the survival of bodily death by ordinary men is utterly worthless.[30]

It seems difficult to justify, in light of the New Testament writings, a belief in the literal physical resurrection of one's body after its death. In addition to the apparent dearth of scriptural evidence, there are many logistical problems facing this view of resurrection as opposed to the spiritual-body form envisaged by St. Paul. Obviously, the earliest pressure to imagine a physical resurrection comes from the prevailing Hebrew view discussed in chapter 2. The Jews believed that the body and soul were inextricable from one another and that the resurrection of the chosen people would return the dead to their original bodies to live eternally. As John Hick argues, any reappearance of Jesus Christ after death would have to have been seen within this Hebrew context by the apostles and thus described in terms of a physical resurrection, leading to the accounts recorded in the Gospels.[31] Certainly, there was some tradition of spirits that might have accounted for apparitions of the dead; there are several instances in the Gospels when witnesses to a resurrected Jesus do not at first believe their eyes and doubt that they have even seen him. Luke goes so far as to say of the apostles, upon seeing Jesus: "But they were terrified and affrighted, and supposed that they had seen a spirit."[32] So, while the apostles would have been familiar with the notion that ghosts might sometimes appear, they preferred to interpret the appearances of Jesus in terms of the resurrection, especially when considering that the Gospels were written with the missionary intent of converting a largely Jewish population.

The visions of Jesus after his death were all the more important as it was no ordinary man who had died, but one who was believed to be the Messiah. This fact alone required a different framework from which to describe these visions. William Neil explains that the very concept of Jesus's divinity required: "A crucified Messiah was so complete a travesty of all that had ever been hoped for and promised that Jesus's claim to be what the prophets foretold would never have been countenanced for a week, let alone two thousand years, if the cross had been the end."[33] Since the Jews anticipated the coming "end times" and resurrection, the death of the Messiah required a resurrection to validate his significance. Krister Stendahl, in the introduction to *Immortality and Resurrection*, echoes these ideas in stating that the resurrection served both to pinpoint the dawning of a new age as well as vindicating Jesus as the true Messiah.[34] Thus, one can see that whatever form Christ took, be it physical or not, the visions of his return would be interpreted to fit the Procrustean bed of contemporary ideology, namely Jewish beliefs of an imminent resurrection.

The argument has haunted Christianity through the ages, and continues to do so even today. The church fathers, who laid down much of the church doctrine, encouraged the physicalist interpretation, despite what seems to be the exegetical conclusion drawn from a strict reading of scripture. They began to outline their theology throughout the second century. Growing slowly out of Judaism and still unable to conceive of a life without a body, they leaned more heavily upon the Hebrew tradition over the Hellenized intertestamental ideas that seem to have influenced Jesus and the biblical accounts of his resurrection. Distinctions were constantly drawn between pagan Platonism and fledgling Christianity. Many such distinctions were simply pedantic, such as the contrast between the immortal nature of the soul in the Greek concept and the Judeo-Christian idea that the soul was fundamentally mortal, relying upon the grace of God for eternal life.[35] In a paradoxical endeavor, they sought to defend their conviction in a physical resurrection using both the scripture of the Bible as well as the Greek philosophical works they were trying to distinguish themselves from. Justin Martyr, in his *Dialogue With Trypho*, uses the Socratic method in true Platonic style in order to reveal the obvious benefits of a belief in resurrection over the Greek transmigration of souls.[36]

Eminent among the early church fathers, we find the contentious genius of Origen (ca. 185–ca. 253).[37] A prolific writer, he is said to have written thousands of treatises, and to have developed the style of exposition known as the homily. Origen endeavored to defend theological ideas most effectively through philosophical means, for which many Christians have harshly criticized him. Well versed in Platonic doctrine, he was accused of allowing too much paganism into Christianity. Still, Origen's accepted tenets gave Christianity the core of the Platonic concept of the soul.[38] Such was the controversy surrounding some of his ideas, however, that Origen and his followers were made anathema at the Fifth Ecumenical Council, circa 553 CE. For the most part, however, his ideas were very influential, and he has certainly regained a position of esteem in modern times. In stark contrast to other church fathers, Origen argued that the resurrected body was not, in fact, the exact same body as that in life. He did not believe that the individuality of a being rested in its physical shape and thus did not require it be restored by the resurrection.[39] Another of his most contested views was that of a universal salvation. He disagreed with the body of church fathers, who held that only a chosen few would be permitted eternal life in the presence of God. The church fathers were split on whether the evil ones would be tormented eternally or would simply be annihilated, but Origen did not hold either opinion. For him, some sinners were tormented in hell, but only as a preliminary stage for eventual resurrection into eternal life. His main argument rested on what he believed was a mistranslation from the Greek, the idea of "a very long time" rather than eternity.[40] Finally, he also believed in the preexistence of souls, against the prevalent view of each soul being created upon the birth of the individual. This belief has since been manipulated into supporting a belief in the transmigration of souls and reincarnation, though there is little evidence to support such a leap, nor is there sufficient grounds for the contention that Origen himself espoused the doctrine of the transmigration of souls.[41] Though Origen's ideas were considered at one time highly controversial, he retains his place as one of the most influential of the church fathers and many of his ideas have again been accepted into the Christian canon.

The preeminent among church fathers was St. Augustine of Hippo (354–430). More than any other church father before or after him, Augustine set down a framework of belief that has been viewed as authoritative for centuries. He is held in the highest esteem of any church father. In terms of eschatology, Augustine is the most important source of doctrine from this early period through the Middle Ages. First, he stated clearly that those who are resurrected, "will be bodies and not spirits," and that "as far as regards substance, even then it shall be flesh."[42] And not just any flesh was indicated by Augustine, but the specific flesh that once made up the living individual. While most church fathers already agreed with Augustine before these official proclamations, there was some degree of debate, such as the ideas of Origen. Once Augustine had spoken, however, there was no further debate. To counter any possibility of argument against the plausibility of the doctrine, Augustine resorted to the omnipotence of God, arguing: "Far be it from us to fear that the omnipotence of the Creator cannot, for the resuscitation and reanimation of our bodies, recall all the portions which have been consumed by beasts or fire, or have been dissolved into dust or ashes, or have decomposed into water, or evaporated into the air."[43] And so, this became the official line of the church, being set down as doctrine a couple of centuries later by the Council of Toledo in 675.

In addition to the problem of the actual state of the resurrected, there was also the issue of the intermediary period between death and resurrection. The Jewish concept assumed that the dead "slept" in a kind of suspended animation until they were reawakened for the Last Judgment, and Jesus refers to the dead sleeping in the New Testament as well.[44] Even still, there remained a belief that the dead also had experiences and might sometimes contact the living in the form of apparitions, especially in dreams. On this, Augustine provided additional insight to placate growing concerns over the true fate of humans between death and resurrection. Accepting what might seem to be a compromise with the Platonic system, he proclaimed that at death the soul left the body for an intermediary state where it awaited the coming resurrection. The body itself was something that was no longer important, as it was the soul that increasingly held meaning. As the Jews became increasingly sophisticated in their understanding of *Sheol* and the waiting state of the dead before the coming resurrection, so too the church fathers adapted to the situation in their own way. Upon an individual's death, Augustine taught, the soul left the body and if not immediately taken up to heaven—a privilege reserved for the most pure of men, including Elijah in the Old Testament—it went to a *Sheol*-like transitional state. Here are the first inklings of what was to become known as purgatory; an interim place where souls would go to be purged of their sins before finally being judged on the Last Day and either resurrected to live eternal life with God, or sent back to hell to suffer the eternal damnation described by Jesus.[45] According to Hick, this marks the beginning of a trend moving away from a concentration on the resurrection and looking more purposefully to the immediate fate of one's soul upon death.[46]

The contemporaries of Jesus believed that Christ's own resurrection marked the beginning of the "endtimes" and expected that they would see the Judgment Day in their own lifetimes. Obviously, as years and then centuries went by, it became less and less tenable to believe in an imminent resurrection.

> But as the Last Day distanced itself into the remote future, the thought of a second judgement naturally also faded within the christian imagination. The sentence pronounced upon the individual as he passed out of this life became the real crisis upon which men's hopes and fears were fixed, and the popular christian view came to be that each man as he died went to heaven (directly or via purgatory) or to hell.[47]

And so, as the years ticked by, Christians looked increasingly to this interim state and began to ignore the now distant idea of an eventual resurrection. Passages such as Psalm 90:4, which says: "For a thousand years in thy sight are but as yesterday when it is past, and as a watch in the night," were invoked to reinterpret the chiliastic expectation of the Judgment Day and to account for the passing years with biblical authority.[48]

As the clouds of the Dark Ages parted, medieval Christians had all but relegated the final resurrection to some distant and unimaginable time. The official doctrine still held the same line as that delineated by Augustine, but the average believer now saw the resurrection as a far-off anticlimax. At death, each individual was judged in order to determine the level of purgation one was to undergo; some would go directly to heaven, some to hell, but most required some degree of purification to be meted out in purgatory. Once this initial judgment had been rendered, the idea of a Final Judgment lost its power and became no more than a reiteration of one's immediate death.[49] Purgatory became a formalized belief within the church during the twelfth century. Scriptural references to anything resembling purgatory are thin if they exist at all, yet the state of the faith required the notion in order to respond to the concerns of believers. People needed to know what their postmortem fate would be between death and the ever more distant resurrection, and so this notion of purgation was supposed as a stopgap between this life and the eventual next one. Thus, the tendency grew to place more emphasis on the immediate fate of humans upon death and less on the distant Last Day.

Centuries after St. Augustine, the most important Christian thinker to emerge is undoubtedly St. Thomas Aquinas (ca. 1225–1274). Aquinas was instrumental in formalizing the notion of purgatory, making some of his greatest contributions to Christian eschatology in the details of the intermediary state. He was among those who instructed the faithful not to concern themselves with timelines, instead being ready for Christ's appearance at any time, and ultimately being a good Christian in the event that it should happen sooner than later. He toed the line on resurrection, and reinforced the importance of the resurrection of the flesh, introducing the subtle accession of forms, echoing to some degree the ideas of Plato once again. For instance, he describes the soul as the "form" of the body and vice versa. With the growing interest in the immediate fate of the soul after death, however, Aquinas made numerous statements as regards the souls of the dead between death and resurrection.

He admits that the soul is immaterial in nature, while still retaining a "form" that is material. The importance of this seems to be in creating a kind of hierarchy in which God is the obvious head, and is completely immaterial. The angels, which we have discussed already, are one step away from God in that they are also immaterial. The angels, however, as messengers to men, are forced to call upon material forms in order to get the message across. According to Aquinas: "an intellectual substance which is not united to a body is more perfect than one which is united to a body."[50] Thus, the human soul is closer to perfection upon death than during life. This begs the question, however, of the state of one's soul after the resurrection of the flesh. In order for the argument to remain logical, Aquinas must assume that the resurrected body is somehow less material than the original one; however he seems to say the opposite when he affirms the materialistic view of resurrection of the flesh. Not only are the dead resurrected in the flesh, but paradise itself is a physical location.[51] On the other hand, the discarnate soul is something so immaterial that it can have no knowledge of the material world of the living,[52] and must speak to other souls through some form of what today would be called telepathy.[53] One can easily see that the problems of maintaining a belief in a physical resurrection in the face of a concurrent belief in a dualistic survival of the soul remained unresolved even after twelve hundred years of Christianity. These problems only contributed to a continuing ignorance of the resurrection among average Christians. Hick aptly suggests that Dante's *Divine Comedy* and Milton's *Paradise Lost*, accurately depict the medieval idea of the afterlife, and have shaped the way Christianity has been perceived by those outside the religion as well.[54] Both of these works deal almost exclusively with the immediate fate of the individual upon death and ignore any idea of resurrection.

As time went on, the emphasis on the immediate afterlife took an increasingly ominous turn. The fate of the soul became a matter of everyday concern for the general population. One could die at any moment and immediately face judgment. According to Aquinas, humanity was placed upon this earth with the intention of aspiring toward heaven. This quickly evolved from a striving for heaven to an overwhelming fear of facing hell, which had people scrambling to atone for sins before it was too late. Joseph Ratzinger (the future Pope Benedict XVI) points out that this move led to an increasing focus on the individual's own preservation, quite in opposition to the brotherhood envisioned by Christ and far removed from Origen's intimations of a universal salvation.[55] With a growing fear of hell, many worried for the fates of their departed friends and family and sought to ensure that they would not suffer either in purgation or eventually in hell. Prayers on behalf of the dead were thought to be helpful, and the church began to accept alms in exchange for such prayers as services on behalf of the dead. Alternately, the living could also see their sins absolved by similarly paying the local clergy in order to ensure safe passage to heaven after death. In some respects, then, the church seemed to some to be resorting to fear mongering and extortion as they practiced the selling of indulgences and forgiveness at a price. Purgatory thus became a profitable venture for the church as souls gathered there to wait for the Final Judgment.

It was this kind of policy that finally induced Martin Luther and other Reformers to break away from the Roman church.[56] The main force of opposition to the church came from a deep sense that it was not necessary as an intermediary between man and God. Anyone could pick up a Bible and read the Word of God for themselves. Protestant Reformers felt that the church had overstepped its bounds and corrupted the true meaning of the Bible and sought to return to an older, and truer, form of belief. In doing so, they rejected the notion of purgatory, which had long been concomitant to eventual resurrection. Luther believed it to be no more than a tool used by the church to fleece believers as they paid tribute in order to "save" deceased souls.[57] Instead, Luther readopted the Judaic concept of "sleeping" dead, as being more true to the scriptural sources. Accordingly, an individual would simply have no experience between death and resurrection, but would simply slip into suspended animation until being awakened at the Last Day. In such a state, resurrection was experienced as instantaneous upon death, with no personal experience of the dormant intermediary state. Among Reformers there was not agreement, however, as Calvin argued against Luther's torporific state.[58] Calvin instead posited that the souls of the dead were transported immediately to either heaven or hell, there experiencing their eventual fates in actuality rather than in the purgatorial sense. The reunion of body and soul at the resurrection was thought to simply serve to intensify either the joys or pains of the afterlife. In either case, the end result was a rejection of purgatory as a mediating experience between life and the "World to Come," and the elimination of perceived corruptions such as the selling of indulgences. Still, the general concepts of resurrection, heaven, and hell remained relatively unchanged throughout the Protestant schism.

In the Christian context, there exists one important group whose views did differ quite widely from the accepted doctrine, that of the poorly understood, and heretical, system known as Gnosticism. The origins of Gnosticism are shrouded in mystery, though their philosophy can be seen as far back as the intertestamental period. Kenneth Rexroth explains: "Most of the elements of all the Gnostic systems can be found somewhere in the vast mass of Jewish Apocrypha and Pseudepigrapha."[59] He goes so far as to draw a connection between Jewish Kabbalism and Gnosticism, but though they do share some similarities, Gnosticism is certainly a unique system. Indeed, it might be said that Gnosticism is only superficially Christian. The Gnostics refer to the Bible for support in their arguments and incorporate Christ fully into their religion. However, Gnosticism gives an entirely different interpretation to all of these things, actually integrating a vast array of ideas under the umbrella of Christianity. As Paul Tillich puts it, "gnosticism was an attempt to combine all the religious traditions which had lost their genuine roots, and to unite them in a system of a half-philosophical, half-religious character."[60] Benjamin Walker, in his history of Gnosticism, describes how much was salvaged from the crumbling paganism at the time and added to this hybrid form of Christianity.[61]

Going back to the oldest sources relating to Gnosticism, one may refer to the intertestamental Qumran texts. These texts suggest that humanity is already in an exalted state and that physical death has little meaning. The body, and the material world in general, are seen as illusions to be avoided lest they bring one to a base and impure level. The Nag Hammadi *Treatise on Resurrection* states that to place any significance on the material world will bring "spiritual death," and that things of matter, "are deceiving shadows and images of clay that will dissolve and pass away as if they had never been."[62]

The dichotomy between body and soul is even more clearly delineated. Some have drawn connections with Origen as the Gnostics also argued for the preexistence of souls. The similarity is only passing, however, as the Gnostics went a step further and allowed for successive lives, believing that preexistent souls may have lived lives previous to the present one. In addition, where Origen angered the church fathers with his insistence upon universal salvation, the Gnostics agreed that only some will be saved and the impure would remain forever in hell. The Gnostic model of successive lives resembles the one described by Er in Plato's *Republic*; individuals choose their successive lives based upon the purity they have attained, leading to an eventual union with God, or for those who have not the will or desire to be pure, eternal damnation.[63]

The Gospel of John reveals that some of Christ's apostles, if not Christ himself, held a belief in the possibility of reincarnation. Speaking of a blind man in the street, they asked Jesus, "Master, who did sin, this man, or his parents, that he was born blind?"[64] Obviously, the question implies the possibility that this man may have sinned before his birth and that through some system of karma-like justice, he has been made blind. That Jesus responds by denying anyone the blame for this man's misfortune does not alter the fact that the belief had been suggested, nor does it form an argument on Christ's behalf that reincarnation is false. It might also be noted that the other Gospels also make reference to reincarnation when Jesus discusses the prophecy of the prophet Elias's return in reference to John the Baptist.[65]

Not only did the Gnostics introduce the notion of reincarnation into the fringes of Christianity, they also denied any physical resurrection, even that of Christ himself. Christ's appearances were described as coming in the form of a "phantasmal body,"[66] a kind of quasi-material form permitting mortals to see him, similar to the notion of angels discussed previously. Essentially, the Gnostics posit that Christ appeared as a ghost to his apostles. While such a notion was anathema to the church fathers, it is a topic of debate that has been revived in modern times in light of recent research into apparitional experiences. Leslie Weatherhead theorizes that Jesus may have been transformed into a nonphysical state while in the tomb, thus enabling him to escape unnoticed and subsequently appear to his disciples and disappear into thin air.[67] That a belief in ghosts was prevalent in the time of Christ has been shown, but the relative dearth of actual apparitions in the Bible is certainly responsible for their lack of treatment in Christian theology. The Witch of En-dor is one example in which a spirit is said to have appeared, but it is clear from the passage that only the witch can perceive the spirit, while Saul, who sought communication with the dead, can only achieve it through her as a medium. The New Testament provides a second instance of apparitions in the appearance of both Elias and Moses at the transfiguration of Jesus in which his divine self is revealed to the apostolic inner circle.[68] The latter case must be seen as exceptional as both the figures represented are among the most revered of the Judeo-Christian tradition and their appearance can properly be called a miracle. The former instance, however, is more reflective of the desire of common people to communicate with the dead, a practice that is clearly condemned in the Old Testament, as seen in chapter 2. The church fathers agreed with the condemnation of mediumship and denied the existence of ghosts, though with some very rare exceptions. Augustine, for instance, admitted the possibility that people might encounter what they believed to be the spirit of a deceased loved one. He believed, however, that the vast majority, if not all, of these experiences were surely induced by demonic influences, especially afflicting people in their sleep.[69] Angels, prophets, and sometimes saints, were considered capable of appearing to the living for divine purposes, but the ordinary person was believed incapable of any contact with the spirit world.

Between the eleventh and fifteenth centuries, a number of autobiographical accounts of ghost sightings began to appear.[70] Up until this time, motives for apparitions had been fairly constant, focusing on divine messages of comfort and love. Angels appeared to comfort and lift a weary soul;[71] apparitions of Mary appeared to the young and innocent in order to share her eternal love;[72] and saints appeared to comfort the flock and urge the avoidance of sin.[73] Despite the official denial of contact with the dead, however, these new stories clearly indicated persistent encounters with the spirit world. Jean-Claude Schmitt reports the case of Thietmar of Merseberg, for instance:

> Thietmar was in his domain of Rottmersleben on December 18, 1012, a Friday, when at the first crowing of the rooster, a light filled the church and he heard a groaning. Questioning some old men, he learned that a similar phenomenon had already occurred several times and had announced a death. In fact, the death of his niece Liutgarde soon confirmed the prognostic, and afterward Thietmar and his companion several times heard at night, while everyone else was sleeping, a noise that sounded like a tree falling; he even heard "the dead who were speaking to each other," and this was always the sign of an imminent death in the domain.[74]

Throughout the hagiography of mystics and saints, we find apparitions, visions, and discarnate voices. In addition to these types of experiences, the mystics are subject to many other strange phenomena as well. Levitation; the temporary separating of soul and body; automatic writing; speaking in tongues; the stigmata; and the direct experience of either heaven or hell are all reported in the lives of mystics.[75] By way of example, Robert d'Uzes (1263–1296), experienced visions both while asleep and awake, heard voices from within his head, and from without. While the apparitions took various forms, he attributed the ultimate source always to have been Jesus Christ.[76] While some of these experiences relate directly to issues of life after death and the nature of the relationship between body and soul, they had no serious impact upon the orthodox teachings of the church.

In any event, with the changes of the medieval period and the Reformation, Christian beliefs in the afterlife went relatively unchanged to present times, with the general view of heaven and hell combined with a future resurrection held by all, if even only nominally. As church control has weakened, more debate and discussion has appeared on all matters of theology. In general, the Catholic Church still officially holds the same view as handed down through the church fathers and later theologians such as Aquinas. Protestants generally hold to a strictly scriptural law, relying solely on what is specifically laid down in scripture to guide them, though there are obviously alternate interpretations.

While there is still a strong voice preaching the horrors of eternal damnation, a more moderate tone seems to be prevalent in modern times. Some, like Pope Benedict XVI, have argued that, despite the difficulty in accepting the injustice of hell meted out by a loving God, "[d]ogma takes its stand on solid ground when it speaks of the existence of Hell and of the eternity of its punishments."[77] For them, dogma cannot be denied, regardless of sentiments to the contrary. Pope John Paul II described heaven, hell, and purgatory as being more state than actual places, and then specifically the states of being near or away from God.[78] The likes of Oscar Cullmann argue that the immortality of the soul that now provides the focus for Christian eschatology is no more than an "accommodation to the mythical expressions" of the early Christians, and is not as compatible with the notion of resurrection as is commonly assumed.[79] On the other hand, others, like Paul Badham argue that the two are not so much incompatible as they have evolved into new usage to reflect modern sensibilities:

> When twentieth-century Christians have pondered on these issues almost all have come to acknowledge the impossibility of returning to the original creeds. Thus, although the Biblical Theology movement has encouraged some theologians to prefer talk of "resurrection" to talk of "immortality" we find that when we clarify what they actually mean by 'resurrection' it is clear that there has been no real return to the older ways of thinking.[80]

And on a more personal level:

> Having taught both subjects [immortality vs. resurrection] over the last twenty-five years, I have to say that, whereas lectures relating to the soul always attract lively discussion, any attempt to interest people in bodily resurrection goes down like a stone.[81]

The resurrection for the most part has been completely relegated to some distant metaphor. It is still referred to as something that makes Christianity different from anything else, but there is general agreement that at death, the individual immediately goes to either heaven or hell, and that hell is not truly a place of eternal damnation but rather some state in which the soul is purified in order to share in eternal life with God after the resurrection, essentially taking the place of purgatory. "Graphic depictions of hell notwithstanding, the biblical references to hell still leave room for the understanding of hell simply as the opposite of God's blessing."[82] Rather than eternal torment, the punishment for sin is now seen as isolation from the grace of God and a temporary one at that, for an all-loving God must forgive even the most evil among us.

Unanimous among Christian theologians is the importance of the individual. Russell Aldwinckle encourages, "the Christian hope that we exist after death as real persons, that we have communion with God and with each other without losing our individuality."[83] Former Archdeacon of Durham, Michael Perry proffers: "Unless John Jones knows that he has survived and that he is still John Jones despite the traumatic experience [death] through which he has gone, no meaning can be given to the word 'survival.'"[84]

Still, the mystical notion of merging with the divine is not lost in Christianity, however the mystics are relegated to the fringes. Hans Küng speaks of a union with the absolute, while still maintaining one's individuality: "By losing himself into the reality of God, man gains himself. By *entering into the infinite, the finite person* loses his limits, so that the present contrast of personal and impersonal is transcended and transformed into the *transpersonal*."[85] Such a view takes into account the character of angels, and of God, and by extension human souls, as being nonlocal. That is to say, as nonmaterial they have no spatial dimension and thus are both nowhere and everywhere at once. If a human soul shares this feature in its similarity to the angels, then it makes sense that it should merge with the absolute in some way. Karl Rahner also seems to concur with this position when he speaks of man's relationship to the universe after death, "becoming a fully open, pancosmic relationship, no longer meditated by the individual body."[86] In this sophisticated system, the resurrected "spiritual body" of St. Paul would be a transpersonal body unlike anything known to humankind, with the exception of the rare few who glimpse the mystical union. Jesus would have died and been immediately merged into the absolute, a "resurrection" into another form. His appearance to the disciples would have been in a semiphysical form, such as that used by the angels when they appear on earth. Still, to many these ideas will be unacceptable, as they seem to severely reinterpret the resurrection as the Gnostics had done. In any case, it is obvious that the notion of the resurrection causes certain difficulties to the rational mind that have not been adequately dealt with in over two thousand years. Many who consider themselves Christians have instead adopted the more convenient concept of the immortality of the soul, while accepting that something called resurrection, whatever that may be, will occur in the distant future.

Notes

1. John Bowker, *The Meanings of Death* (Cambridge: Cambridge University Press, 1991), pp. 75–76.

2. Matt. 7:13–14, which is echoed in Luke 13:23–24 KJV.

3. Mark 9:43–48.

4. George W. E. Nickelsburg, *Resurrection, Immortality, and Eternal Life in Intertestamental Judaism* (Cambridge, MA: Harvard University Press, 1972), p. 123.

5. Luke 16:19–31.

6. Matt. 5:3, 5:5.

7. Mark 12:18–27, Luke 20:27–38.

8. Mark 12:24–25.

9. Franz Mussner, "The Synoptic Account of Jesus' Teaching on the Future Life," trans. Mark Hollebone, in *Immortality and Resurrection*, eds. Pierre Benoit and Roland Murphy (New York: Herder and Herder, 1970), p. 52.

10. Alois Winklhofer, *The Coming of His Kingdom* (London: Nelson, 1962), p. 27.

11. Fr. Pascal P. Parente, *Beyond Space* (Rockford, Ill: Tan, 1973), pp. 43–46.

12. The complexities of identifying Satan and Lucifer source in large part to biblical citations. See, for instance: Ez. 28; Rev. 12:9; Isa. 14:12.

13. An important aside must be taken here to say a brief word about demons and devils. Demonology is a vast field in both Judaism and Christianity. From one perspective, the gods of the non-Jewish neighbors to the Hebrews came to be recognized as demons. They do not qualify for god status when there is only one God. For instance, the well-known Jewish demon Lillith originates in Mesopotamian roots as a Sumerian storm goddess. From another (Christian) perspective, devils are angels who fell from God's graces along with Satan. Still another (popular) perspective sees demons as the departed spirits of particularly evil humans. This last belief has no official religious sanction, but is a common modern concept. Insofar as demons relate to conceptions of the afterlife, one might simply surmise that the popular conception reflects the terror of both personified evil and the power of devils generally, at the same time as it reflects a general fear of both the evildoers and the doing of evil. This is a vast area that would require its own book.

14. See, for example: Isa. 6:2; Gen. 3:24; Col. 1:6; Eph. 1:21; Rom. 8:38.

15. Parente, *Beyond Space*, p. 37.

16. Nancy Gibbs, "Angels Among Us," *Time Magazine*, December 27, 1993, p. 10.

17, St. Augustine, *Serm. in Ps.* 103, I, 15, quoted in Parente, *Beyond Space*, pp. 18–19.

18. Parente, *Beyond Space*, p. 20.

19. See Matt. 28; Mark 16; Luke 24; and John 20, 21 for the four accounts.

20. Matt. 28:9.

21. Mark 16:14.

22. Luke 24:30, 24:42–43.

23. John 20:27–28.

24. Mark 16:12.

25. Luke 24:13–31.

26. John 21:4–14.

27. I Corinthians 15:44.

28. Alan Segal, *Life After Death* (New York: Doubleday, 2004), pp. 399–440.

29. G. C. Berkouwer, *The Return of Christ* (Grand Rapids: Eerdmans, 1972), p. 183.

30. C. D. Broad, *Religion, Philosophy, and Psychical Research* (New York: Harcourt, 1953), pp. 236–237.

31. John Hick, *Death and Eternal Life* (London: Collins, 1976), pp. 171–172.

32. Luke 24:37.

33. William Neil, *Life and Teaching of Jesus* (London: Hodder and Stoughton, 1965), p. 153, quoted in Paul Badham, *Christian Beliefs About Life After Death* (London: MacMillan, 1976), p. 25.

34. Krister Stendahl, ed., *Immortality and Resurrection* (New York: MacMillan, 1965), p. 7.

35. Harry A. Wolfson, "Immortality and Resurrection in the Philosophy of the Church Fathers," in *Immortality and Resurrection*, ed. Krister Stendahl (New York: MacMillan, 1965), p. 57.

36. St. Justin Martyr, "Dialogue With Trypho," in *The Ante-Nicene Fathers*, Vol. 1, trans. And eds. Rev. Alexander Roberts and James Donaldson (1885), online (1997), http://www.newadvent.org/fathers/0128.htm.

37. For an excellent introduction to the works of Origen and his history, see Rowan A. Greer, trans. *Origen* (New York: Paulist Press, 1979).

38. Werner Jaeger, "The Greek Ideas of Immortality," in *Immortality and Resurrection*, ed. Krister Stendahl (New York: MacMillan, 1965), p. 112.

39. Wolfson, "Immortality and Resurrection," p. 69.

40. Origen, *In Exod., Hom.* 6, 13, quoted in Wolfson, "Immortality and Resurrection," p. 65.

41. For an example of how such arguments for reincarnation in Christianity have been made, see J. Head and S. L. Cranston, eds., *Reincarnation: The Phoenix Fire Mystery* (New York: Julian Press/Crown, 1977).

42. St. Augustine, *Enchiridion* 91; and *De Civ. Dei* XXII, 17, quoted in Wolfson, "Immortality and Resurrection," p. 70.

43. St. Augustine, "City of God," in *The Essential Augustine*, 2nd ed., comp. Vernon J. Bourke (Indianapolis: Hackett, 1978), XXII, 20–22, p. 190.

44. See, for example, John 11:11; Mark 5:39.

45. Hans Küng describes the logical and historical transitions from *Sheol* to purgatory in his, *Eternal Life?* trans. Edward Quinn (New York: Doubleday, 1984), pp. 124–125. For very specific details of the history of purgatory, see Jacques LeGoff, *The Birth of Purgatory,* trans. Arthur Goldhammer (London: Scolar, 1984).

46. Hick, *Death and Eternal Life*, p. 198.

47. Hick, *Death and Eternal Life*, p. 194.

48. Joseph Ratzinger, *Eschatology: Death and Eternal Life*, trans. Michael Waldstein (Washington, D.C.: The Catholic University of America Press, 1977), p. 36.

49. Hick, *Death and Eternal Life*, pp. 195–196.

50. St. Thomas Aquinas, "Summa Theologica, I, Questions 50–64," *Basic Writings of Saint Thomas Aquinas*, ed. Anton C. Pegis (New York: Random House, 1945), p. 493.

51. Aquinas, "Summa Theologica, I, Questions 75–89," pp. 944–946.

52. Aquinas, "Sum. Theo. I, Questions 75–89," p. 863.

53. Aquinas, "Sum. Theo. I, Questions 103–119," p. 990.

54. Hick, *Death and Eternal Life*, p. 198.

55. Ratzinger, *Eschatology*, p. 5.

56. For an excellent description of many Protestant groups, including Calvinism and Lutheranism, see the following collection by noted Protestant theologian, Paul Tillich: *A Complete History of Christian Thought*, ed. Carl E. Braaten (New York: Harper & Row, 1968).

57. See, among Luther's other works: Martin Luther, "Disputation of Doctor Martin Luther on the Power and Efficacy of Indulgences," Volume 1 of *Works of Martin Luther*, 6 volumes, trans. and eds. Adolph Spaeth, et al., (Philadelphia: A. J. Holman, 1915), pp. 29–38, online at: http://www.sacred-texts.com/chr/the9510.txt.

58. John Calvin, "Psychopannychia," in his, *Tracts & Treatises on the Reformation of the Church*, 3 volumes, ed. Thomas F. Torrance (Grand Rapids: Eerdmans, 1958).

59. Kenneth Rexroth, introduction to *Fragments of a Faith Forgotten*, by G. R. S. Mead (New York: University Books, 1960), p. xv.

60. Paul Tillich, *A Complete History of Christian Thought*, ed. Carl E. Braaten (New York: Harper & Row, 1968), pp. 33–34.

61. Benjamin Walker, *Gnosticism: Its History and Influence* (Wellingborough, Northamptonshire, UK: The Aquarian Press, 1983), p. 11.

62. Walker, *Gnosticism*, p. 59.

63. For a detailed account of this system, see Walker, *Gnosticism*, pp. 63–64.

64. John 9:2.

65. Matt. 17:10–13; Mark 9:11–13. It must be noted that John the Baptist is asked straight out in John 1:21 whether or not he is in fact Elias returned, and he denies that he is.

66. Mead, *Fragments of a Faith Forgotten* (1960), p. 141.

67. Leslie D. Weatherhead, *The Resurrection of Christ: In the Light of Modern and Psychical Research* (London: Hodder & Stoughton, 1959), pp. 47–49. Oliver Lodge is also cited as attesting to a similar belief in his "My Philosophy," (1930), quoted in Weatherhead, pp. 55–57.

68. Matt. 17:3–4; Mark 9:4–5.

69. Augustine, "Epistolae & De cura pro mortuis gerenda," quoted in Jean-Claude Schmitt, *Ghosts in the Middle Ages*, trans. Teresa Lavender Fagan (Chicago: University of Chicago Press, 1998), pp. 17–25.

70. Schmitt, *Ghosts in the Middle Ages*, pp. 35–36.

71. For example, see Parente, *Beyond Space*, p. 132.

72. For example, see Catherine M. Odell, *Those Who Saw Her: The Apparitions of Mary* (Huntington, Ind: Our Sunday Visitor, 1986), pp. ix, 15.

73. For example, see Schmitt, *Ghosts in the Middle Ages*, p. 30.

74. Schmitt, *Ghosts in the Middle Ages*, pp. 38–39, citing Thietmar of Merseberg, "Chronicon," in Nova Series 9, ed. R. Holtzmann (Berlin, 1955), vol. 1, pp. 112–113.

75. A very good source for an overview of mysticism remains Evelyn Underhill, *Mysticism*, 14th ed. (London: Bracken, 1995).

76. Paul Amergier, *La parole rêvée: essai sur la vie et l'oeuvre de Robert d'UZES O.P. (1263–1296)*. (Aix-en-Provence: Centre d'Études des Sociétées Méditerranéennes, 1982).

77. Ratzinger, *Eschatology*, p. 215.

78. Pope John Paul II, "General Audience," Wednesday, July 28th, 1999. Online: http://www.vatican.va/holy_father/john_paul_ii/audiences/1999/documents/hf_jp-ii_aud_28071999_en.html.

79. Oscar Cullmann, "Immortality of the Soul or Resurrection of the Dead: The Witness of the New Testament," in *Immortality and Resurrection*, ed. Krister Stendahl (New York: MacMillan, 1965), pp. 49–50.

80. Paul Badham, *The Contemporary Challenge of Modernist Theology* (Cardiff: University of Wales Press, 1998), p. 117.

81. Badham, *Contemporary Challenge*, p. 121.

82. Hiroshi Obayashi, "Death and Eternal Life in Christianity," in *Death and Afterlife: Perspectives of World Religions*, ed. Hiroshi Obayashi (New York: Geenwood, 1992), p. 116.

83. Russell Aldwinckle. *Death in the Secular City* (Grand Rapids: Erdmans, 1972), pp. 99–100.

84. Michael Perry, *The Resurrection of Man* (Oxford: Mowbrays London and Oxford, 1975), p. 9.

85. Küng, *Eternal Life?*, p. 112.

86. Karl Rahner, *On the Theology of Death*, trans. Charles H. Henkey (New York: Herder and Herder, 1961), pp. 23–24.

CHAPTER FOUR

~

Islam

Islam, the third of the world's great monotheisms, grew out of the harsh climes of the Arabian Desert in the sixth and seventh centuries. The emerging prophet Muhammad (570–632 CE) was an orphan living in the city of Mecca, raised among a clan charged with the care of a local temple. He gained employment as a trader and was otherwise inconspicuous but for his loyal and trustworthy nature. At the age of forty, his life—and the world with it—would change completely when he began to receive divine revelations. These revelations came to him throughout the latter part of his life and guided both him and those who would later follow him. He first spoke of his experiences only to his family and friends, but eventually expanded this circle as he preached the messages given to him by the Archangel Gabriel, setting the Muslim faith on the path to becoming what in modern times is the fastest growing religion in the world.

Before discussing the religion founded by the revelations of Muhammad, it is necessary first to understand the environment in which he lived.[1] Much has been made about the origins of Islam and what the spiritual influences upon Muhammad may have been. Some have linked Islam with strains of Christianity, Judaism, or Zoroastrianism that were present in Arabia during Muhammad's lifetime. Further, there appear to have also been purely Arabian monotheists, known as *hanifs*, as well. As the Judeo-Christian beliefs in death and the afterlife have already been discussed, I will turn now to uniquely Arabic influences and beliefs.

In the time before Islam took form, known as the time of ignorance (*jahiliyyah*) by Muslims, nomadic pastoral tribes wandered Arabia in an ongoing search for the scant resources of life. Some settled and formed communities based around oases that acted as rest stops for merchants moving along the trade routes linking the Middle East to Africa and India via the port cities at the southern tip of the Arabian Peninsula, in modern day Yemen. These people left little evidence of their beliefs, and what we can deduce must be extracted from archaeological evidence and what little poetry and folklore survived into the Islamic period. What can be pieced together forms an eclectic picture of belief. One can be sure that these people were of a polytheistic bent, worshipping a number of celestial and meteorological deities, as well as sharing the deities of other neighboring cultures, such as those of the Greeks and Mesopotamians. This polytheism does not lend itself to the construction of a pantheon, per se, as it appears more likely that nomadic clans preferred their individual gods and settled people worshipped local deities.[2] More common was an inclusive animism that perceived spirits of one sort or another, later to be called *jinn*, resident in all things. Related to this belief is the practice of ancestor worship, which appears to have been widespread and an integral aspect of pre-Islamic religious life.[3]

Archaeological evidence demonstrates that a great deal of care was taken with the burial of the dead, performance of which may be suggestive of a belief in some form of further existence.[4] Graves have been found to contain all manner of valuables, although what their intentions may have been can only be speculated upon. For the Bedouins, constantly moving from one place to another was an important part of normal life such that "the wandering aspect integral to nomadic existence is in sharp opposition to the state of the individual at the time of death, when he becomes a sedentary [*muqim*], a term used both for the grave and its occupant."[5] This combination of fear and reverence played itself out in the propitiation of the dead through sacrifice and libation.

Stone worship was well-known among the pre-Islamic Arabs, though this particular aspect of religious life has been often misunderstood. The Qur'an, the scriptural authority of Islam, denounces the use of stones as idols among the polytheistic tribes.[6] Blood sacrifices and libations of milk were poured before or upon stones erected as idols. Such sacrifices seem to have the aim of fortifying the dead whose spirits are incapable of taking care of themselves in the grave. While these idols eventually came to represent various deities, it is quite likely that they began as tokens of the dead, providing a lasting symbol of the grave for the living, and acting as intermediary for the transference of sacrificial material from the living to the dead. Powerful or heroic individuals were often exceptionally venerated, leaving open the possibility that some of the gods worshipped by the polytheistic Arabs may have begun as local mortal heroes. Joseph Henninger further points out that a similar ancestral cult exists among the Bedouins in modern times, strengthening the notion that such practices are traditional.[7] In some instances, these modern Bedouins are known to elevate certain ancestors to the level of a Muslim saint, or *wali*, much as their ancient predecessors might have deified their dead.

As a *muqim*, the dead person was thought to reside forever in the grave, thereby remaining eternally connected with the stones used in his or her burial. There was at least one major exception to this rule, however, as the pre-Islamic people did hold the notion that the spirit of one murdered might roam the world of the living. Only those who have been killed rather than those who died a natural death might be afflicted with such a fate, having had their lives cut short. "Cessation of breath was the means to a natural death; death as a result of the shedding of blood was unnatural and required retribution, without which the soul of the dead wandered restlessly in the desert until avenged."[8] This caveat to killing might be seen as an outgrowth of the uneasy state of tribal warring. This traditional belief is further colored by the notion that the spirit of the murder victim would fly out from the body and take on the form of a white owl, which would screech in the night demanding blood vengeance.[9] The demands for revenge for the murdered dead would normally be met by either a retaliatory killing or sometimes an animal sacrifice as a substitute.

Ibn Hisham's, *The Life of Muhammad*, tells the story of a similar problem in pre-Islamic times. In order to repay a debt, it was argued that Abdullah, the soon-to-be-father of Muhammad, should be sacrificed to make amends. Instead, he was brought before a "woman with a familiar spirit" who was then asked if he should indeed be allowed for sacrifice. The spirit medium went into seclusion to speak with her spirit and returned, explaining that camels should be offered in his stead, thus saving his life.[10]

Soothsayers were common among pre-Islamic Arabs, and continued to practice their feats well into the Islamic period. These individuals were renowned for their ability to communicate with all manner of spirits as well as to interpret dreams. *The Life of Muhammad* speaks of these Arab soothsayers alongside Jewish rabbis and Christian monks.[11] They had received prophecies of the coming of Muhammad from their familiar spirits and the *jinn*, though these messages had been widely ignored by the populace at large. When Muhammad finally began to proclaim his own prophetic revelations, he condemned the soothsayers and the *jinn* from whom they received their messages, saying:

> [Soothsayers] say that God has decreed so-and-so concerning His creation and the news descends from heaven to heaven to the lowest heaven where they discuss it, and the satans [evil *jinn*] steal it by listening, mingling it with conjecture and false intelligence. Then they convey it to the soothsayers and tell them of it, sometimes

being wrong and sometimes right, and so the soothsayers are sometimes right and sometimes wrong. Then God shut off the satans by these stars with which they were pelted, so soothsaying has been cut off today and no longer exists.[12]

The beliefs of these pre-Islamic people necessitates some discussion of the uniquely Middle Eastern beings called the *jinn*. They are seen as quasi-spiritual demons composed of fire, as opposed to the dust and clay that makes up humankind. They have the ability to remain invisible while engaging in all manner of earthly affairs, often being blamed for everything from sickness to accidents to sandstorms or other natural disasters. The origins of the *jinn* remain obscure, though their relationship to pre-Islamic animism seems certain. It seems highly likely that the *jinn* can be equated with the spirits of the dead, which had been deified by the Arabs, and then subsequently relegated back down to the level of demon. The Arab soothsayers would have therefore played a central role in the religious life of the pre-Islamic peoples through their connection with the spirit world, much like shamans and mediums in other cultures around the world. Further discussion of the *jinn* as they came to be conceived in Islamic thought will be reserved for later in this chapter.

Within this context, Muhammad emerged as a prophet. He was born in 570 CE. His father died shortly before his birth and his mother died when Muhammad was an infant. He was raised by his extended family in the Quraysh clan just outside the town of Mecca. His clan was charged with the care of a small temple called the *Kaaba*, or Cube, which was a center for pilgrimage from ancient times. Echoes of the pre-Islamic "stone worship" described previously can be found in the Black Stone mounted in the Kaaba even today, though it is no longer worshipped as an idol but venerated for its history and tradition. Muhammad gained a reputation as a loyal and trustworthy man and became a trader in the employ of a wealthy widow, who would eventually marry him. Suddenly, at the age of forty, he began to receive messages from Allah through the mediation of the Archangel Gabriel. Though the medium of communication was identical to that of the soothsayers and their spirits, Muhammad made clear, that whereas the *jinn* could be mischievous, deceitful, or just plain wrong, only Allah was all-powerful and all-knowing. These messages were revealed to Muhammad intermittently over the remaining twenty-three years of his life and were later recorded in the sacred text called the Qur'an, which provides the central doctrines of Islam. While Muhammad was himself more than likely illiterate, his teachings were memorized and later recorded by others.[13]

As Muhammad expanded the circle of those who listened to his teachings, there was a great deal of friction between the Prophet and those who refused his message, the adamant polytheists, not to mention Jews and Christians. Eventually, Muhammad was forced to flee Mecca and escape to the town of Yathrib, which later became known as Medina, to the north. This migration of Muhammad and his followers marks a turning point in the history of Islam of such significance that the Muslim calendar is dated around this event, with 622 CE marked as the year 1 AH (from the Latin *Anno Hegirae*, signifying Muhammad's momentous journey from Mecca to Medina). Here, he was accepted with open arms and attracted increasingly large numbers of followers. Due to the constant harassment of those who sought to destroy him and his message, Muhammad and his followers were forced to wage a number of battles before finally marching against Mecca itself and capturing it. The political nature of these conflicts led to a religious faith interwoven with politics, paving the way for future Islamic governments. As H. U. W. Stanton pointed out nearly a century ago, "Islam from the beginning was a theocracy, and it can still only be understood as ideally a religion and state in one."[14] Though there is some justification for such a perspective, it will be shown that the issue is not as straight-forward as this, especially when considering the main schism to come in Islam between Sunni and Shi'ites.

Despite these early conflicts, the perception of Islam as a religion spread "by the sword" is largely undeserved. Muhammad preached a missionary message open to any who would listen, but he explicitly denied that his message should be forced on the unwilling through violence. The Qur'an states: "There shall be no compulsion in religion."[15] Further, while warfare was a regular feature in the development of Islam, Muhammad's revelation specifically condemned fighting for any purpose other than self-defense: "Fight for the sake of Allah those that fight against you, but do not attack them first. Allah does not love the aggressors."[16] The polytheistic Arabs were aggressive in their attacks upon Muhammad and his followers, precipitating the need for war.

In addition to the polytheists, Christians and Jews were also fairly common in Muhammad's experience. Muhammad was believed to be the last in a string of prophets including Jesus, Moses, Abraham, and Adam. As Children of the Book, *ahl-i kitab*, their own religious texts, the Jewish *Tanakh*, and the New Testament of the Christians, were both granted a certain degree of credibility, though only as secondary sources in respect to the Qur'an itself. In Islam, Abraham, Moses, Noah, and Jesus are all recognized as prophets; a line in which Muhammad is the final and most revered, though this reverence certainly does not extend to any kind of actual worship as is the case with Jesus in Christianity. While the relationship between the three great monotheistic religions has been a strained one, especially in modern times, Muhammad maintained a link between the message of Allah and those prophets that had come before.

The holy book of Islam, the Qur'an, is a striking work in itself. It has often been confusing to the Western mind, as it seems to come from a number of different directions at once rather than following a linear narrative. Richard Bell typifies the ignorance of early scholarship with his opinion of the Muslim scripture as a veritable cornucopia of styles seemingly tossed together at random: "It is neither a treatise on theology, nor a code of laws, nor a collection of sermons, but rather a medley of all three, with some things thrown in."[17] Neal Robinson offers a much more studied description as he emphasizes the fact that the text is meant for oral presentation in the original Arabic, the sound of its recitation being enough to send one into reverie.[18]

Turning then to the special topic at hand in the present thesis, eschatology is central to Islam, as it is for the other great monotheistic faiths before it, though with Islam concepts of the afterlife are much more explicitly described in scripture. Life after death is discussed at length throughout the Qur'an, particularly in those chapters (suras) revealed during the Medinan era, corresponding to the latter part of Muhammad's life.[19] Eschatological details are outlined in the earlier suras, whereas the later revelations focused more upon the details of the world to come. Superficially, the Qur'an portrays a vision of the afterlife that would be familiar to followers of the Judeo-Christian traditions. There is a Last Day, resurrection of the dead, a judgment, followed by either reward or torment. The Qur'an describes:

> When the sun ceases to shine; when the stars fall down and the mountains are blown away; when camels big with young are left untended and the wild beasts are brought together; when the seas are set alight and men's souls are reunited; when the infant girl, buried alive, is asked for what crime she was slain; when the records of men's deeds are laid open and the heaven is stripped bare; when Hell burns fiercely and Paradise is brought near: then each soul shall know what it has done.[20]

All who have died will be raised up from their graves to experience the Last Day. The deeds of every person are made clear and revealed to all:

> Frail and tottering, the sky will be rent asunder on that day, and the angels will stand on all sides with eight of them carrying the throne of your Lord above their heads. On that day you shall be displayed before Him, and all your secrets shall be brought to light.[21]

The deeds, good and evil, of every person are recorded in books, which are then handed back to each individual as a sign of the judgment rendered. If the book is given into the right hand of a person, they are destined for paradise. A book placed in the left, however, is a condemnation to hell:

> Truly, the record of the sinners is in Sidjeen. Would that you knew what Sidjeen is! It is a sealed book . . . But the record of the righteous shall be in Illiyun. Would

that you knew what Illiyun is! It is a sealed book, seen only by those who are clos-est to Allah.[22]

He who is given his book in his right hand will say to his companions: "Take this, and read it! I knew that I should come to my account." His shall be a bliss-ful state in a lofty garden with clusters of fruit within reach . . .

But he who is given his book in his left hand will say: "Would that my book were not given me! Would that I knew nothing of my account! . . ." We shall say: "Lay hold of him and bind him. Burn him in the fire of Hell . . ."[23]

Those who have led their lives according to the will of Allah and have been good and just, will be granted access to paradise, which is described as lush gar-dens with flowing streams and cool breezes. The blessed can indulge in all man-ner of feasting and are wedded to lovely virgins. On the other hand, sinners are cast into hell, which is consistently described with allusions to fire and boiling water and where they have no joys and no pleasures at all.

This is the Paradise which the righteous have been promised. There shall flow in it rivers of unpolluted water, and rivers of milk for ever fresh; rivers of delectable wine and rivers of clearest honey. They shall eat therein of every fruit and receive forgiveness from their Lord. Is this like the lot of those who shall abide in Hell for ever and drink scalding water which will tear their bowels?[24]

Garments of fire have been prepared for the unbelievers. Scalding water shall be poured upon their heads, melting their skins and that which is in their bellies. They shall be lashed with rods of iron . . . And for those that have faith and do good works, Allah will admit them to gardens watered by running streams. They shall be decked with pearls and bracelets of gold, and arrayed in garments of silk.[25]

They shall recline on couches ranged in rows. To dark-eyed houris [maidens] We shall wed them . . . Fruits We shall give them, and such meats as they desire. They will pass from hand to hand a cup inspiring no idle talk, no sinful urge; and there shall wait on them young boys of their own as fair as virgin pearls.[26]

The wrongdoers shall be known by their looks; they shall be seized by their fore-locks and their feet . . . They shall wander between fire and water fiercely seething . . . But for those that fear the majesty of their Lord there are two gardens . . . planted with shady trees . . . Each is watered by a flowing spring . . . Each bears every kind of fruit in pairs . . . They shall recline on couches lined with thick bro-cade, and within their reach will hang the fruits of both gardens . . . They shall dwell with bashful virgins whom neither man nor jinnee will have touched before . . . Virgins as fair as corals and rubies . . . And beside these there shall be two other gardens . . . of darkest green . . . A gushing fountain shall flow in each . . . Each planted with fruit-trees, the palm and the pomegranate . . . Dark-eyed virgins shel-tered in their tents . . . whom neither man nor jinnee will have touched before . . . They shall recline on green cushions and rich carpets.[27]

While the overall image portrayed by these descriptions is plainly obvious, actual details are sparse. Discussions of paradise in the Qur'an provide more details, however, than those of hell. Lush gardens containing rivers of milk and honey flowing past bountiful trees, whose fruits hang within easy reach of the blessed inhabitant, all the while accompanied by beautiful virgins and handsome youths. Hell, on the contrary, is only described by its fire and the punishing use of boiling water to torture the sinners and unbelievers. While there may not be a great deal of detail in the Qur'anic revelation on the fate of humans beyond death, what is expressed therein sufficiently conveys the sense of reward and punishment at an emotional level.

Scholars and theologians have debated the words of the Qur'an and whether they should be taken literally in all cases, especially where the issue of life after death appears. In particular, descriptions of the sensuous pleasures of paradise, which seem clearly directed solely at male enjoyment with no mention of the fate of women in the afterlife, have stirred some degree of controversy. There has been some sense in modern times that these depictions are not to be taken literally. It is not surprising, then, that reinterpretation might be attempted. Hanna Kassis argues:

> Taken at face value, as regrettably has often been the case, the powerful and evocative symbolism can be readily distorted. What must be sought, instead, is the impact of the total picture of the mercy and compassion of God bestowed upon the faithful, a picture not unlike the *locus amoenus*, the location of pleasance, the garden motif borrowed by Christian poets to depict Paradise.[28]

Annemarie Schimmel makes a similar argument when she suggests that, "[o]ne could, however, interpret the houris and the fruits as symbolizing the greatest happiness, that of perfect union with the Beloved, and of the ancient belief that one can attain union with the Holy by eating it."[29] Sometimes, passages such as those cited that make reference to virgins are reinterpreted in a gender neutral sense in order to accommodate women in paradise as well. In this light, the chaste virgins are described rather as perfect spouses of either sex. One can also point to the presence of the youths, "fair as virgin pearls," as an indication that women will receive similar treatment to men in paradise.

Lest one assume from this discussion that the afterlife is reserved for men alone, two points should be borne in mind in addition to the aforementioned arguments. First, the Qur'an does not make any distinction between male and female believers when it mentions those who will be admitted to paradise, as can be seen in the quotes outlined previously. Second, a secondary scriptural source in Islam, known as the *hadith*, which details the deeds and sayings of Muhammad that were not part of the divine revelation, provides several examples of women in paradise. For instance, the following passage concerns Khadija, the first wife of Muhammad:

> "What did he (the Prophet) say about Khadija?" He (Abdullah bin Aufa) said, "(He [the Prophet] said) 'Give Khadija the good tidings that she will have a palace made of Qasab [precious stones] in Paradise and there will be neither noise nor any trouble in it.'"[30]

The preceding apologists notwithstanding, it is clear that the Qur'an deliberately depicts a sensual paradise, promising physical rewards in the hereafter. This is placed in juxtaposition with a spiritual reward that is even greater than the sensual ones. Not only do the good benefit from those bodily pleasures described, but they are also granted the vastly more important reward of spending eternity in the presence of God. "And what is more, they shall have grace in His sight. That is the supreme triumph."[31] The tenth century Muslim philosopher, al-Farabi, entered the debate on the literal interpretation of the Qur'an with a denial that any of the imagery of paradise or hell could be taken as anything more than poetry. He argued that such poetic visualization was the only means, however inadequate, to portray the true splendors of the afterlife.[32]

Still, there remains a strong connection in Islam to the physical body even beyond death and the notion that this body will be reincorporated at the Last Day when it is raised from the grave. The Qur'an affirms a physical resurrection: "Did He not give you life when you were dead, and will He not cause you to die and then restore you to life?"[33] Though the body was thought to lie dead in the grave, food for worms, it remained aware of the earthly realm above. After the first major battle between the Muslims and the Meccan polytheists, the Battle of Badr (623 CE), Muhammad speaks to the dead as they are buried in a mass grave, asking if they have seen that what he said of the afterlife was true. His companions are shocked by this and ask: "Are you speaking to dead people?" His reply indicates not only that they could hear his question but that they had in fact found that he had been right as they were surely suffering the fate of the nonbeliever in the grave.[34]

Thus, the obvious next question is what becomes of the individual in the grave between the time of death and the future day of resurrection? The Qur'an states that once a person has died, "[b]ehind them there shall stand a barrier till the Day of Resurrection,"[35] which keeps them from returning to the living world and separates the dead from their eventual fate in paradise or hell. This intermediary state is called barzakh. Unfortunately, the Qur'an itself gives little indication as to what is thought to happen on the other side of that barrier; for that one must turn to tradition and the hadith sources once again.

The *hadith* literature, in combination with a variety of commentary, philosophy, theology, and pre-Islamic traditional folklore, has created a vivid picture of the chain of events that befall one at the end of life, which can be described in the following composite narrative.[36] Upon death, or rather just before the actual time of death, the individual is visited by the Angel of Death, 'Izra'il, and attending angels. This Angel of Death is thought to be a fearsome being of immense power, symbolizing the fact that no one can escape his or her mortal fate.

> It is mentioned in the *Kitabu's-Suluk* by Muqatal ibn Sulayman that the Angel of Death has a seat in the seventh heaven. It is also said that it is in the fourth. Allah-ta'ala created it from light. He has 70, 000 feet and 4, 000 wings. All of his body is filled with eyes and tongues. Every creature among men and birds and that which is in possession of a ruh [soul] has a face, ear, eye, and hand on his body. The quantity is equal to the number of men. So the ruh is taken by that hand and he looks by the face which belongs to him. For that reason, the ruh of creatures is taken in every place.[37]

The individual is then separated from the dying body and brought briefly before God, only to be returned quickly to whence it came in order to witness the burial of his body. Again, two angels approach to question the dead, who is expected to know the correct answers to specific questions. A sinner would obviously not know the answers, while a true Muslim would have the answers at hand. The sinner is beaten and tormented by these angels, and then sealed into the grave with the body. These angels open a window within the grave to show the sinner the tortures of hell that await him or her after the Last Judgment. While the sinner feels the worms chewing upon his or her corpse, the sinner must also gaze into hell while waiting for this eventual fate to come. On the other hand, if the person has been good and followed the ways of Islam, the angels are kind and open a window looking out onto paradise. In either case, the dead remain in their grave until the time of resurrection, often thought to fall into an unconscious state not dissimilar to a dreamless sleep. Whilst in this state, tradition holds that the spirits of the dead can hear the laments and prayers of the living, though they have no power to answer them. The dead can certainly speak, but the living are unable to hear them and so only communicate amongst themselves and other spiritual beings, like the angels. In fact, as exemplified in the previous quote, this complete lack of communication between the living and the dead is strongly stated in the Qur'an.

There is one exception to this intermediary fate. Martyrs are exempted from the purgatorial *barzakh*, and are brought directly to paradise.

Al Tirmidhi and Ibn Maja report the following: the martyr has six privileges with God: his sins are pardoned when the first drop of blood falls; he is shown his seat in paradise; he is safe from the punishment of the grave and secure from the great terror (i.e., hell); a crown of dignity is placed on his head one jewel of which is worth more than the world and all that is therein; and he is married to seventy dark-eyed virgins; and he makes successful intercession for seventy of his relatives. "He who equips a warrior in the way of God has fought himself; and he who is left behind to take care of a warrior's family has fought himself."[38]

Ragnar Eklund outlines the evolution of cultural belief moving from the notion that all are condemned to the grave, as we have seen previously, through that of some chosen few being carried off to paradise immediately upon death, to the eventual acceptance of the idea that all souls will experience at least some degree of their fate to come while still in the *barzakh* state.[39] While in this intermediary state, the soul, while thought to reside with the body, might also be encountered by the living in the form of an apparition. In Islam, such phantom experiences are dealt with in two ways: either the apparition is assumed to be a dream or else it might be a *jinn* taking on the form of the deceased for its own reasons.

Dream interpretation, as practiced by the pre-Islamic Arabs, had developed into a respected science by the medieval period.[40] Like Daniel in the Judeo-Christian tradition, a skilled interpreter could divine the future from prophetic dreams. Joseph is described in the Qur'an as the key dream interpreter, having been given the gift of such divination by Allah.[41] Coming as messages from Allah, then, dreams can have only one meaning and are not open to multiple interpretations. There is also some evidence to suggest that incubation, such as that practiced in the temples of Asclepius, might have at one time taken place in mosques, with pilgrims sleeping so that they might dream in the presence of priests who could interpret their dreams.[42] Toufic Fahd, in his study of Arabic divination, *La Divination Arabe*, argues that this dream interpretation, combined with pre-Islamic attempts to summon the dead through necromantic techniques, signify a belief in the ability, however limited, of the living to communicate with the dead.[43] In the very least, if the dead can hear the living but not respond, they might communicate the answer by appearing in a dream. The Qur'an describes how during sleep, as in death, the soul of an individual is removed from the body, only to be replaced upon waking:

Allah takes away men's souls upon their death, and the souls of the living during their sleep. Those that are doomed He keeps with Him and restores the others for a time ordained. Surely there are signs in this for thinking men.[44]

In effect, the soul of the dreamer is thought to leave the body and thus encounter spiritual beings. Indeed, during sleep, a person's soul might encounter either angels or *jinn*; the angel's messages are to be believed while the *jinn's* are surely falsehoods.[45] Jane Smith and Yvonne Haddad relate an excellent example of the kind of dream one might have containing apparitions of the dead and the way in which these dreams may be prophetic:

> One delightful story describes a dream in which a man saw several (dead) women, but his own (dead) wife was not with them. He asked them where she was, and they replied that because he had been slipshod in wrapping her in the shroud, she was too shy to go out with them. So with the help of the Prophet the husband found a man of the *Ansar* who was dying, and he wrapped two saffron cloths in his shroud. When night came, the husband again saw the women, and this time his wife was with them, wearing yellow garments.[46]

The theme of the dead demanding proper burial attire is a common one across cultures. An interesting difference here, however, is the way in which the husband sends his wife the necessary accoutrements through the use of another person's body as intermediary. It is not necessary for him to place the saffron cloths in his wife's own grave but it is enough to send them along with another dying man, assuming that they will arrive on the "other side" regardless. Certainly, despite the common sense interpretation, which would have one believing the man had just seen the spirits of these women and later of his wife with them, Islam would insist instead that the images were sent by Allah in order to ensure that the husband showed the proper respect for his deceased wife.

On the other hand, there is also the possibility that apparitions of the dead may be *jinn* appearing in disguise. The line between spirits of the dead and the *jinn* is often blurred, just as with demons in Judaism and Christianity. An Egyptian tradition, for instance, holds that evil humans might become *ifrit*, a form of particularly malicious and powerful *jinn*, upon death. As described previously, *jinn* have the ability to appear in various forms and are sometimes mischievous and motivated toward their own ends. Just as they might provide false information to the polytheistic soothsayers, so too might they deceive people in false dreams. Where these demon-like beings were seen to have a close connection to spirits of the dead among the pre-Islamic Arabs, such is not the case in the thought of Muslim Arabs.

In his essay on the *jinn*, the thirteenth century Muslim thinker, Ibn Taymeeyah, describes several Christian visions, and argues that these are nothing more than *jinn* in disguise.[47] The case of the biblical Witch of En-dor is considered in Islam to be an example. The witch is thought not to have conjured up the actual spirit of Samuel, but a *jinn* who takes on his form to torment King

Saul for breaking the laws against consulting a witch. Edward Westermarck describes, among what he called "pagan survivals" in Islamic culture, how sacrifices to the dead continued, as had been done in pre-Islamic times, as some attempted to cajole the dead to aid the living, though such practices clearly run counter to Islamic law and the will of Allah.[48] Alongside such mediumistic communications, *jinn* are also believed capable of possessing the living in the same way that demons might possess humans in Christianity and Judaism. Exorcism can be employed by Muslims to rid the victim of such an affliction as well. This type of possession can be carried out by the *jinn* with goals as varied as boredom, loneliness, love, or simply malice.[49]

The *jinn* maintain an important place in Islam, appearing often in the Qur'an. They are generally condemned for leading humans astray: "Jinn, you have seduced mankind in great numbers . . . The Fire shall be your home, and there you shall remain for ever unless Allah ordains otherwise."[50] The Muslim equivalent of the Judeo-Christian Satan, Iblis, is variously described as a *jinn* or an angel, though Muslims have traditionally considered Iblis to be of the *jinn*, with angels being incapable of evil. It is said of Iblis: "And when We said to the angels: 'Prostrate yourselves before Adam,' they all prostrated themselves except Satan, who in his pride refused and became an unbeliever."[51] Another passage similarly states: "When We said to the angels: 'Prostrate yourselves before Adam,' all prostrated themselves except Satan, who was a jinnee disobedient to his Lord."[52] It thus appears that Iblis may have originally been an angel, such as Lucifer in the Christian tradition, who fell from grace for his pride in refusing to prostrate himself before a human. Thus, he becomes the leader of the evil *jinn*, as the *jinn* could be either good or evil, just as humans, depending upon their acceptance of the Qur'an. In the words of the *jinn*, "some of us are Muslims and some are wrongdoers. Those that embrace Islam pursue the right path; but those that do wrong shall become the fuel of Hell."[53] Traditionally, the *jinn*, as invisible demons who might be either good or evil, were credited with all manner of strange events, including mental illness, disease, accidents, or sometimes beneficial coincidences and the like. Additionally, most unexplained phenomena can also be attributed to the attempts of evil *jinn* to confuse and mislead humans. Basically, the *jinn* could be anywhere at any time, and could be responsible for just about anything that happened, most usually to the detriment of humankind.

Before leaving the *jinn*, it is interesting to note that they were also believed to be responsible for the same kinds of hauntings previously attributed to the spirits of the dead. "Haunted houses [in the Middle East] are there tenanted by Ghuls, Jinns and a host of supernatural creatures; but not by ghosts proper."[54] Again, in the Egyptian tradition, the *ifrit* or deceased spirits were thought to haunt a building to such an extent that dwellings in which a murder was committed would often simply be left completely abandoned for fear of the haunting spirit.[55]

The dominant opinion in Islam, then, is that the spirits of the dead leave the world of the living completely, travelling first to paradise and then to the grave in which to reside until the day of the resurrection, where each will be judged according to his or her deeds and sentenced either to eternal bliss or torture. Some modern scholars prefer to see the torment of hell as a temporary suffering, dependant upon the severity of the sin. Certainly, there is some precedent for such a belief, especially when looking at the more spiritual side of Islam.

The various schools of thought collectively known as Sufism mark the more mystical tradition within Islam. Some have argued that to categorize Sufism as a form of "mysticism" is inappropriate.[56] Still, in the broadest sense, the Sufi schools comprise, "anyone who believes that it is possible to have direct experience of God and who is prepared to go out of his way to put himself in a state whereby he may be enabled to do this."[57] Additionally, many Sufis, such as the famous whirling dervishes, are known to exhibit a number of miraculous powers, including such things as communicating with and controlling animals, healing the sick, and exorcising possessing *jinn*. In terms of an outlook on life, death, and what lies beyond, Sufi thinkers certainly use mystical language in their formulations. One popular Sufi saying encapsulates their view effectively: "Die before you die." Certainly, this idea is not wholly unfamiliar to the Muslim context in which the Sufis work. The Qur'an emphasizes the Judgment Day as the ultimate goal of life. Every person lives simply to die and the Sufis urge everyone to put their minds to it sooner rather than later, accepting it as not only inevitabile but also as a boon. The Sufi thinker, Al-Ghazali, tells the following story:

> When the angel of death came to take Abraham's soul, Abraham said, "Have you ever seen a friend take his friend's life?"
> God answered him, "Have you ever seen a friend unwilling to meet or go with his friend?"[58]

That is not to say that anyone should ever hurry toward death, or take his or her own life, but rather that one should not concern one's self with worldly things but should live instead always with the end firmly in mind.[59] Al-Ghazali goes on to cite a *hadith* that was recounted at a funeral. It is said that the Prophet spoke the following words, concerning the experience of a person upon death:

The dead man sits up and hears the footsteps of those that are present at his funeral, but none addresses him save his tomb, which says, "Woe betide you, O son of Adam! Did you not fear me and my narrowness, and my corruption, terror and worms? What have you prepared for me?"[60]

And so, every action taken in this life must always bear in mind the ultimate fate of death and the judgment that lies beyond. Even those flashes of divine meaning that come through in certain dreams and visionary experiences are not to be valued too highly, as they apply more to life in this world than in the next and are thus transitory.[61] Where Sufis diverge from the Muslim mainstream is in the state of being in the afterlife. Paradise is not for them a place of worldly pleasures, but a blissful union with God. The sensually described heaven and hell are thought to eventually fade. This inference derives from the Qur'an: "they shall abide [either in Heaven or in Hell] as long as the heavens and the earth endure, unless your Lord ordains otherwise."[62] Sufis argue that once the appointed time has come, the true fate of all humankind is a complete union with God transcendent of all description. Frithjof Schuon lays further emphasis on this point by mentioning the Sufi saying that paradise is the "prison of the gnostic" and that it is "inhabited by fools."[63] The reunion with God, from whom all of creation has emanated, is the goal of all life. As Parviz Morewedge states, "a salient aspect of Islamic mysticism is the normative prescription that we should follow a path of self-realization in which all entities become interrelated through their affinity with their origin, which is God or the One."[64] Certainly, this idea follows the same thinking as do the mystical traditions of the other world religions. The idea of a union with the divine is one that continues to recur, though it remains a belief held strongly only by the fringes of religion. Indeed, as in other religions, there are some Muslims who hold Sufis to be heretics for just such beliefs as this. Still, Sufism remains a vibrant piece of the Islamic fabric.

Sufism crosses the boundaries between the two major branches of Islam, Sunni and Shi'ite. This latter school deserves special consideration, having a number of beliefs that differ from those of the Sunni mainstream. It is estimated that the Shi'ite Muslim population makes up roughly 20 percent of the total Islamic population, with Sunnis comprising the majority 80 percent.[65] The main contention between the two areas of Islam stems from a conflict over the succession of authority after the death of Muhammad. Sunni Muslims adopted a series of leaders, known as Caliphs, who were first elected and then selected along hereditary lines. Shi'ite Muslims argued instead for an Imamate in which the successor was chosen by the preceding leader, as Muhammad apparently had done before his death. As the minority, the successive Imams were suppressed by the Sunni Caliphs until, in the most common Shi'ite schools of thought, the eleventh and twelfth Imams were virtually unknown.[66] Some Shi'ites believe that the twelfth Imam has not yet appeared, others hold that he entered into a state known as the Occultation in which he remains hidden from the material world; in either case, it is believed that his appearance will mark the sign of the coming of the Final Resurrection. At this time, it is thought that the twelfth Imam will lead a great apocalyptic battle against the forces of evil, and force the unbelievers to accept his authority under threat of prohibition from heaven, as has been revealed in numerous prophetic dreams in which the Imam himself has appeared to give warning. Alongside this belief in the authority of the Imams is an emphasis on the fate of martyrs in the world to come. While martyrs are considered to have a special place in the afterlife among all Muslims, Shi'ism is emphatic in its focus upon them as many Shi'ites were martyred during their early struggles to establish the authority of the Imamate over the Caliphate before being finally forced into a state of quiescence in anticipation of the coming of the twelfth Imam and thus vindication at the Last Day. Additionally, there is a much greater importance laid upon the tombs of martyrs, saints, and particularly those of the Imams, with pilgrimages being made to many of these. One branch of Shi'ite Islam has taken the aforementioned beliefs to a further extreme in adopting a belief in the reincarnation of the Imam in successive generations, thus reinforcing the authority vested in them by making them all incarnations of the same being. While the notion of reincarnation is focused primarily on the continued existence of the Imamate, it was extended to apply to regular people as well.

The Druze, dwelling mainly in Lebanon, represent a very small minority in Islam, and one that is viewed as heresy by orthodox Muslims generally, but their variation of Islam is of particular interest to the present discussion.[67] While they hold the Qur'an as the ultimate truth, as do all Muslims, they lean toward more esoteric interpretations where the soul is concerned. The strong connection believed to exist between the body and soul for the average Muslim has been shown. Sufism introduced the notion that this attachment is entirely superficial as Allah alone is eternal. "All things shall perish except Himself."[68] The Druze accept this radical separation of eternal soul and corporeal body, as well as the Sufi contention that life's goal is learning to die properly, that is, to die in good standing before Allah. The major difference, however, is that they do not feel that one lifetime is enough time in which to learn this. Instead, they assume a number of lifetimes, necessitating the notion of metempsychosis, or reincarnation. Every individual will be reincarnated in a new body after death, over and over again until the day of resurrection. It is hoped that by the Last Day the individual will have had the time to learn the necessary lessons and thus be deemed worthy to be united with God. While they accept the final resurrection, it is conceived of as something quite different from that of orthodox Islam. The resurrected body itself is of little importance, as it is the union with God that is sought after, with the resurrected body simply acting as the final incarnation, as it were. In support of these beliefs, many people have reported memories of past lives over the years. In recent years, the late psychiatrist Ian Stevenson carried out meticulous and detailed case studies of such memories and found striking correspondence between what, say, a child claims to remember of a particular life and the previously unknown facts of that same person's actual life. Stevenson's research will be examined in greater detail in a later chapter. Suffice it to say, for now, that there exists within Islam a small current of belief and experience of reincarnation in the Druze community.

In closing, a general picture of the Islamic view of the fate of humankind after death has been outlined. Little known practices involving an ancestral cult were followed by the pre-Islamic Arabs and were for the most part replaced by a sophisticated eschatology along similar lines to that of the Judeo-Christian tradition. Generally, Muslims look forward to a day of judgment when sinners are condemned to hell and the faithful are rewarded with heaven. The timing of the Last Day is unknown, though signs, such as the return of the twelfth Imam for some Shi'ite Muslims, might indicate that it is near. Immediately upon death, the individual soul is variously thought to remain in the grave either in a state of sleep-like torpor or experiencing a taste of the fate to come, to experience the intermediary *barzakh* state as a kind of purgatory preparing the soul for judgment, or they may travel immediately to paradise, especially in the case of martyrs. Actual descriptions of heaven and hell vary from purely sensual places to more symbolic representations of some form of union with Allah. On the fringes of Islam, the Druze consider the soul to reincarnate immediately upon death with no intermediary state until the final resurrection. While the pre-Islamic Arabs believed in substantial contact with spirits of the dead, Muslims relegate such experience, for the most part, to the work of *jinn*. Dreams are one instance in which the dead might still communicate with the living, but then only by the express will of God. All in all, Islam represents itself generally as a religion that holds eschatology in great importance and is well placed in the tradition of the great monotheistic religions.

Notes

1. Albert Hourani provides a great deal of detail in his historical overview of the Arabs, from pre-Islamic times into the present age: Albert Hourani, *A History of the Arab Peoples* (Cambridge, MA: Belknap Press of Harvard University Press, 1991).

2. Robert Hoyland outlines the vastness of the array of gods that have been identified in pre-Islamic Arabia: Robert G. Hoyland, *Arabia and the Arabs* (London: Routledge, 2001), pp. 139–145.

3. Joseph Henninger, "Pre-Islamic Bedouin Religion," in *Studies in Islam*, trans. and ed., Merlin L. Swartz (Oxford: Oxford University Press, 1981).

4. Jane Idleman Smith and Yvonne Yazbeck Haddad, *The Islamic Understanding of Death and Resurrection* (New York: SUNYP, 1981), pp. 148–150.

5. Smith and Haddad, *The Islamic Understanding*, p. 151.

6. Qur'an 5:3; 5:90. Two translations of the Qur'an have been consulted for the purposes of quotes throughout this chapter: *Qur'an*, 2nd revised ed., trans. N. J. Dawood (Harmondsworth, Middlesex, UK: Penguin, 1966); Mohammed Marmaduke Pickthall, *The Meaning of the Glorious Qur'an: An Explanatory Translation* (New York: New American Library, 1953). Quotations are derived mainly from the Dawood text.

7. Henninger, "Pre-Islamic Bedouin Religion," p. 10.

8. Hanna Kassis, "Islam," in *Life After Death in World Religions*, ed. Harold Coward (New York: Orbis, 1997), p. 49.

9. Smith and Haddad, *The Islamic Understanding*, pp. 151–153; Ragnar Eklund, *Life Between Death and Resurrection According to Islam* (Uppsala, Sweden: Almquist & Wiksells Boktryckeri, 1941), pp. 19–20.

10. 'Abdul-Malik Ibn Hisham, *The Life of Muhammad* (Lahore: Oxford University Press, 1968), pp. 67–68.

11. Ibn Hisham, *The Life of Muhammad*, p. 90.

12. Ibn Hisham, *The Life of Muhammad*, p. 91.

13. Neal Robinson, *Discovering the Qur'an* (London: SCM, 1996), p. 9.

14. H. U. Weitbrecht Stanton, *The Teaching of the Qur'an* (New York: Macmillan, 1919), p. 3.

15. Qur'an 2:256. This passage goes on to state that faith in Allah is the only true faith and those who do not accept it have only hell to look forward to. Basically, it is not the place of humans to compel faith, for Allah will judge all in the end.

16. Qur'an 2:190.

17. Richard Bell, *Introduction to the Qur'an*, (Edinburgh: Edinburgh University Press, 1953), p. 1.

18. Robinson, *Discovering the Qur'an*, pp. 9–14.

19. While the precise chronology of the *suras* has been debated, there is wide agreement as to the development of the ideas presented therein, whether they are believed to come directly from God, Muhammad, or a combination of the two. See the introduction to Thomas O'Shaughnessy, *Muhammad's Thoughts on Death* (Leiden: E. J. Brill, 1969). As for the debate over the chronology of the revelations, refer to Robinson, *Discovering the Qur'an*, pp. 60–96.

20. Qur'an 81:1–14. Dawood says of the reference to burying the child: "An allusion to the pre-Islamic custom of burying unwanted new-born girls." *Qur'an*, p. 17, note.

21. Qur'an 69:13–18.

22. Qur'an 83:6–7; 83:18–19.

23. Qur'an 69:18–28.

24. Qur'an 47:15.

25. Qur'an 22:19–23.

26. Qur'an 52:20–24.

27. Qur'an 55:37–76.

28. Kassis, "Islam," p. 61.

29. Annemarie Schimmel, *Deciphering the Signs of God* (New York: SUNYP, 1994), p. 238.

30. *Sahih Bukhari*, trans. M. Mushin Khan, Volume 3, Book 27, Number 19, online: http://www.usc.edu/dept/MSA/fundamentals/hadithsunnah/bukhari/027.sbt.html#003.027.019.

31. Qur'an 9:72.

32. Lenn E. Goodman, *Avicenna* (London: Routledge, 1992), p. 127.

33. Qur'an 2:28.

34. Ibn Hisham, *The Life of Muhammad*, p. 305.

35. Qur'an 23:100.

36. The information that follows has been culled from a variety of *hadith* and other sources in the following texts: Jan Knappert, *Islamic Legends*, 2 vols. (Leiden: E. J. Brill, 1985), vol. 2, pp. 461–463; Smith and Haddad, *The Islamic Understanding*, pp. 39–43, 48–49; Eklund, *Life Between*, pp. 9–10.

37. Imam 'Abd ar-Rahim ibn Ahmad al-Qadi, *Islamic Book of the Dead: A Collection of Hadiths on the Fire & the Garden* (Norwich, UK: Diwan, 1977), p. 32.

38. Alfred Guillaume, *The Traditions of Islam* (London: Oxford University Press, 1924), pp. 111–112.

39. Eklund, *Life Between*, pp. 47–48.

40. Toufic Fahd, *La Divination Arabe* (Leiden: E. J. Brill, 1966), pp. 247–367.

41. The story of Joseph is related in Sura 12 of the Qur'an.

42. Fahd, *La Divination Arabe*, pp. 363–365.

43. Fahd, *La Divination Arabe*, pp. 169, 174–176.

44. Qur'an 39:42.

45. Bess Allen Donaldson, *The Wild Rue* (1938; repr., New York: Arno, 1973), p. 174.

46. Jalal al-Din Suyuti, *Bushra al-ka'ib bi-liqa'I al-habib* (Cairo, 1969), p. 55, quoted in Smith and Haddad, *The Islamic Understanding*, p. 54.

47. Ibn Taymeeyah, *Essay on the Jinn (Demons)*, trans. Abu Ameenah Bilal Philips (Riyadh: Tahweed, 1989), p. 45, footnote on same page.

48. Edward Westermarck, *Pagan Survivals in Mohammedan Civilization* (1933; repr., Amsterdam: Philo, 1973), pp. 77–82.

49. Ibn Taymeeyah, *Essay on the Jinn (Demons)*. For some examples of such occurrences, see: I. M. Lewis, *Ecstatic Religion: A Study of Shamanism and Spirit Possession*, 2nd ed. (London and NY: Routledge, 1989).

50. Qur'an 6:128.

51. Qur'an 2:34.

52. Qur'an 18:50.

53. Qur'an 72:14–15.

54. Richard Burton, *Supplemental Nights to the Book of the Thousand Nights and a Night* (London: Stoke Newington, 1886–88), vol. 3, p. 252n, quoted in Robert Irwin, *The Arabian Nights: A Companion* (London: Allen Lane, Penguin Press, 1994), p. 183.

55. Irwin, *The Arabian Nights*, p. 183.

56. Sachiko Murata and William C. Chittick, *The Vision of Islam* (St. Paul, MN: Paragon House, 1994), p. 304.

57. J. S. Trimingham, *The Sufi Orders in Islam* (Oxford: Oxford University Press, 1998), p. 1.

58. James Fadiman and Robert Frager, eds., *Essential Sufism* (San Francisco, CA: HarperSanFrancisco, 1997), p. 253.

59. Hamid Algar, *Sufism: Principles and Practice* (New York: Islamic Publications International, 1999), pp. 22–23.

60. Al-Ghazali, *The Remembrance of Death and the Afterlife* (*Kitab dhikr al-mawt wa-ma ba'dahu*): Book XL of *The Revival of the Religious Sciences* (*Ihya 'ulum al-din*), trans. T. J. Winter (Cambridge, UK: Islamic Texts Society, 1989).

61. Algar, *Sufism: Principles and Practice*, p. 28.

62. Qur'an 11:106–108.

63. Frithjof Schuon, *Dimensions of Islam*, trans. P. N. Townsend (London: George Allen and Unwin, 1969), pp. 136–141.

64. Parviz Morewedge, "Sufism, Neoplatonism, and Zaehner's Theistic Theory of Mysticism," in *Islamic Philosophy and Mysticism*, ed. Parviz Morewedge (New York: Caravan, 1981), pp. 226–227.

65. Abdur-Rahman Ibrahim Doi, "Sunnism," in *Islamic Spirituality*, ed. Seyyed Hossein Nasr (New York: Crossroad, 1991).

66. Moojan Momen, *An Introduction to Shi'i Islam* (New Haven: Yale University Press, 1985), p. 147.

67. For a more general discussion, see Sami Nasib Makarem, *The Druze Faith* (New York: Caravan, 1974).

68. Qur'an 28:88.

CHAPTER FIVE

∼

Hinduism

Hinduism is undoubtedly the most venerable of the major world religions considered in this volume, dating as far back as the second millennium BCE, when the central scriptures of Hinduism, the *Vedas*, were first written down. Originally used by the Persians and Greeks, the term "Hindu" simply referred to those people who lived East of the Indus River. Muslims, and later British colonialists, further expanded the term to refer to those residents of India who were neither Muslim nor Christian. Modern scholarship has refined the term to refer to those "who follow the mainstream indigenous religious tradition of India and accept—at least nominally—the authority of the ancient scriptures known as the *Vedas*."[1] Far from monolithic, Hinduism should more accurately be seen as a kind of umbrella term for the wide variety of spiritualities that exist and have existed in India over centuries. In practice, Hinduism is a flexible and inclusive system allowing many different interpretations, called *margas* or "paths," for devotion, ritual, and religious practice, with the *Vedas* as the recognized sacred texts. In a uniquely inclusive way, Hinduism continues to build upon itself, adding new ideas to the older ones while the older beliefs remain options alongside the newer ones rather than being cast aside under the pressure of evolution.

The *Vedas* provide the first written records from the Indus valley area and give us the first inklings of Hindu beliefs. Earlier writings found in the area, from the mysterious Harappan civilization, linked with what has been called the Dravidian culture, have not yet been translated and so remain a mystery. A very common contention remains that a Northern race, known as the Aryans, descended into the Indus valley circa 1500 BCE and dominated the indigenous

Dravidians. The invaders ostensibly imported their religion and culture—that of the *Vedas*—and imposed it upon the existing culture. The *Vedas* are thus seen as an alien religious system superimposed upon an earlier native tradition. The theory, while widespread in its acceptance, rests on flimsy grounds based largely on linguistic evidence. A dearth of archaeological evidence makes the idea of an external source for the *Vedic* tradition unlikely, however, and archaeologists have not yet succeeded in locating the alleged source of the Aryan people. As Gavin Flood has said, "The predominance of Aryan culture over Dravidian culture is not disputed, but the origin of the Aryans as coming from outside the subcontinent has recently been questioned."[2]

Because of the lack of archaeological and other supporting evidence for an Aryan invasion, it is perhaps most prudent to accept the theory referred to by Flood as the "cultural transformation thesis." Basically, this theory states that the Aryan culture developed from the preexisting culture of the Indus valley. In this scheme, the *Vedas* were gradually composed from a combination of new and old ideas formed by the people of one geographical area.[3] Whether the Aryans represent a wholly external influence on the native Dravidians or simply an indigenous evolution cannot be known for certain. Whatever the case, the terms Aryan and Dravidian can be used to distinguish between two different aspects of Indian thought, the latter being more ancient than the former.

The texts of the *Vedas* themselves are a collection of hymns, tales, and rituals that had been transmitted through the ages by an oral tradition until the time of their being written down. They incorporate material that certainly spans a long period of history, incorporating ideas that surely belonged to the older Dravidians with the newer ideas developing with the growing Aryan culture. They were finally codified around the middle of the second millennium BCE, corresponding to the alleged date of the Aryan invasion. Conservative estimates date the oldest of the four *Vedas*, the *Rig Veda*, between 1500 and 800 BCE.[4] The influence of the *Rig Veda* is clear in the other three. The *Sama Veda* and *Yaju Veda* repeat much of what is contained within the *Rig Veda*, in the form of chants. The *Atharva Veda*, however, is interesting for its differences, containing ritualistic information that harks back to a more ancient past. The ultimate source for all of these sacred texts is, of course, believed to be the gods. "No *Vedic* bard designedly wrote poetry. He only gave effortless vent to the crowding emotions and ideas aroused in his heart during spiritual exaltation."[5] Thus, these texts are considered to have been divinely inspired and are therefore the ultimate scriptural authority.

Similarities exist between the *Vedic* ideology and that of Homeric Greece. Aside from the pantheon of gods and goddesses, the early conceptions of life after death described in Homer's epics are echoed in the *Vedas*. Hermann Oldenberg draws a comparison between the dark regions of Homeric Hades and the *Vedic pitrloka*, or World of the Fathers.[6] It is a place where individuality is almost nonexistent, though descriptions of it are quite a bit more hospitable than its Greek counterpart, as will be seen. Of the various ideas concerning death and the afterlife to be found within the *Vedas*, that of the World of the Fathers is likely the one of the greatest antiquity. These earliest ideas about the World of the Fathers are vague and impersonal but we do know that the Fathers themselves form a collective, invocations being directed more toward the group as a whole rather than to any individual among them. Obvious similarities exist between these ancient Indian ideas and the ancestral worship found in China, which are discussed in a later chapter. The Fathers might be propitiated into the service of the living with special offerings. On the other hand, regular offerings were mandatory to ensure that the Fathers would not cause ill to the living. In order for a person to travel to the World of the Fathers, the correct rituals were required. The dead person must have followed prescribed ritual actions (*karma*), as outlined in the *Vedas*, throughout his or her life, but even more importantly, those people left behind in the world of the living were left the duty of continuing the rituals to ensure their loved one a place in the afterlife. Specifically, the eldest son was expected to perform the requisite functions. In turn, while alive, every man was expected to beget a son in order to both ensure his own entry into the World of the Fathers and to ensure that all of his previous ancestors might retain their places in the afterlife as well. Family lines provided the ritual sacrifices necessary for the continued existence of their ancestors. In this patriarchal society, a woman's afterlife seems to have been contingent upon that of her husband.

Ritual offerings suggest a view of the afterlife as a kind of continuation of the earthly existence. Like the ancient cultures of Egypt and the Middle East, the earliest Hindus, though they had not yet been categorized thus, believed in a material afterlife in which dead ancestors could physically take advantage of those things being offered to them from the world of the living.

> During the earlier period gifts to the dead were buried or burnt with the corpse. These gifts consisted of food, weapons, clothes and domestic animals. Sometimes slaves and even wife were also burnt or buried with the dead. The *Atharvaveda* calls it "the ancient custom." This inhuman [sic] custom, however, was discontinued in the *Rgvedic* [sic] time, though the formality of lying on the funeral pyre by the widow was retained . . .[7]

A note, first, about widow-burning. That such a ritual should be called "inhuman" out of hand is inappropriate and ignorant of cultural factors. For one thing, we are dealing here with a belief that dictates that this life is not our only

life and that death in this world leads to birth in another. Catherine Weinberger-Thomas, in her thoughtful book on the topic,[8] points out that the tradition came to have strict limits. Those disqualified from sacrificing one's self included girls who had not yet reached puberty, pregnant women, or mothers of
young children, those who are coerced to sacrifice themselves, who are tied
down, drugged, or beaten into the fire, or those who change their minds at the
last minute.[9] What this leaves us with is the sincere Hindu who wishes to join
the one she loved in the journey to the next world. One can admire such
devotion. On the other hand, moral questions arise when coercion can be
observed. Ultimately, widow-burnings have become illegal in modern India,
though the tradition carries on regardless, though with greater difficulty. A
woman who is prevented from sacrificing herself for any reason can still be recognized as a living-sacrifice. Taking this another step further, some may symbolically sacrifice themselves at the funerals of their spouses, lying with the
body only to stand up once the fire is lit. In any event, the practice of widow-
burning is a controversial one, but one that has at its roots the same motivations
as any other forms of sacrifice—the continuing bonds of love and support for
the dead.

The offerings of food and such were intended as sustenance for the dead on
their journey to the afterlife and the means by which they might continue to
"live" in the World of the Fathers. "The grain and sesame, offered to the dead,
were believed to become respectively a cow and its calf in the heaven to provide milk for the dead."[10] These beliefs continue into modern Hindu thought,
and at death, the soul of the individual is believed to remain in the vicinity for
many days. Daily offerings must be made to appease the spirit and ensure it a
safe journey to the land of the dead. For thirteen days, offerings must be made
to both the ghost as well as various priests who in turn perform the requisite rituals necessary to aid the spirit to successfully transfer from life to death. During
this time, the soul is considered a malevolent and hungry ghost, called a *pret*.[11]
This spirit is a being to be feared for it demands offerings in order to sustain it
under threat of inflicting such repercussions as disease or natural disaster. Once
the rituals have been properly performed, the soul then transforms from a
malevolent *pret* into a benevolent ancestor, or *pitri*, and travels to the land of
the dead. *Vedic* priests are required to perform these rituals, as most Hindus simply have had no access to the sacred scriptures. Offerings of food and money are
given to these priests as well as to the dead. While acting as a form of payment
for the priests, the act also transfers merit to the dead, which can aid them in
the afterlife as well. Some Hindus offer milk and a special rice-ball mixture
called *pinda*. The purpose of these is to fortify the ghost so that it will not go
hungry during the yearlong journey to join the ancestors in the World of the Fa-

thers. Additionally, boiled rice is also cast to the ground to feed crows, echoing the belief that the souls of the dead take the form of birds.[12]

The descriptions of the World of the Fathers itself reveal a place of idyllic beauty. According to the *Atharva Veda*, those who perform the requisite rituals are promised the sensuous rewards of women, food, and drink in the comfort of a lush, breezy landscape.[13] The dead are also described in the *Rig Veda* as sharing rich banquets with the gods in a realm of light.[14] Such an afterlife is certainly one to look forward to, especially when contrasted to the bleakness envisioned by other ancient peoples, though one might remember the Mesopotamian caveat that allows for rewards for those who have many sons but nothing to those who have none.

Among the myriad gods of the *Vedic* pantheon, three are commonly associated with death or the realm of the dead: Yama, Lord of the Dead; Agni, God of Fire; and the enigmatic god Soma, who is associated with ecstatic experiences. One version of the story paints Yama as the first mortal, the primordial human being. He attained a state of immortality through overcoming selfishness and the fear of death itself through his loyalty to the gods.[15] Thus, all those who make the otherworldly journey to the World of the Fathers are said to revel in the company of Yama.[16] As a mortal hero who overcame death in some primordial time, Yama became the God of the Dead in Indian thought. Combined with the familial propitiation of ancestors, Yama, in this view, can be seen to represent an example of the trend in ancestral cults to deify certain particularly powerful or heroic individuals. While the residents of the World of the Fathers are offered sacrifices as semidivine beings in the other world, Yama and other gods are worshipped as full divinities, having exceeded the common ancestor in both life and death. The existence of such gods may illustrate the evolution from ancestral worship to the more focused worship of specific divinities, though the differentiation between spiritual beings is a subtle one in Hinduism.

Soma, to whom the entire ninth book of the *Rig Veda* is devoted, is closely associated with a drink of the same name. The true concoction of this magical beverage is unknown, but poetic passages in the sacred texts describe its ecstatic effects, indicating it may have been some form of psychoactive drug. The drink is often called "nondeath" as it triggered journeys outside of the body and encounters with the gods and other spiritual beings. For reasons unknown, the shamanic recipes for *soma* disappeared and later attempts to conjure similar experiences included such practices as asceticism, yoga, and meditation.[17]

Agni, for his part, is associated with the purification of the cremation rituals, as well as the fires of damnation. The *Rig Veda* describes how Agni, through cremation, carries the individual from the world of the living to that of the dead, thus safeguarding a continued existence in the hereafter.[18] Fire is seen as a facilitator in the individual's travels from life to the World of the Fathers, reducing the matter of life into a more ephemeral substance in the form of smoke that rises and disappears into the air. Items to be used by the dead in the next world are also burned on the funeral pyre. Importantly, however, it should be pointed out that the *Rig Veda* places no particular emphasis on the ritual of cremation as a necessary factor in bringing one safely to the hereafter. Whether the dead are burnt or buried, if the necessary rituals and offerings are made, they will still be admitted into the next world. It is possible that cremation was a later addition to ritual funerary practice. As ritual action became increasingly important throughout the later *Vedas*, however, the use of cremation came into the fore as the chosen method for the disposal of remains, implying the evolution of the practices concerning the disposal of the dead. The purifying nature of fire gained an increased emphasis in opposition to a growing concern over various kinds of spiritual pollution, including contact with the dead themselves.

The concept of hell, however, is not clearly delineated in the *Vedas*, though there are intimations of it in the later texts. R. C. Zaehner points out that while the *Atharva Veda* contains descriptions of an "abyss" into which evil doers are hurled, or a place of "lowest darkness" or "black darkness," the concept of judgment does not appear until the *Brahmanas*, commentaries on the *Vedas* dated from the seventh century.[19] Although even in these texts, the emphasis remains on rewards for the dead versus the punishments of the evil. Such passages as the following are often cited as references to a hell similar to that in Western traditions: "Guard us, O Agni, from above and under, protect us from behind us and before us; And may thy flames, most fierce and never wasting, glowing with fervent heat, consume the sinner."[20]

The fact that "sinners" are to be consumed in flames calls to mind images of hell as found in Western traditions, although the notion of sin as such does not appear in early Hinduism. When one considers, however, that Agni's role within the early pantheon is that of a god of fire, it only makes sense that his followers would ask that their enemies be destroyed by the weapon of choice of their favored deity. Those who worshipped Agni would certainly ask him to use his flames in their service to destroy their enemies, the "sinners." With this in mind, it makes more sense to view these references as simple supplications to a god rather than references to any form of hell in a Western sense.

Some of the later passages of the *Vedas* do seem to imply some form of divine retribution, particularly for transgressions against the priestly classes or for failure to adhere to sacred norms. The *Atharva Veda*, for instance, provides the following rather gruesome example: "They who spat upon a brahmin [a priest], or who sent [their] mucus at him—they sat in the midst of a stream of blood, devouring hair."[21] Another late *Vedic* text states that one who spills the blood of a brahmin shall, "not get to see the world of fathers."[22] Still, examples of such hellish retribution are very rare, with the overwhelming emphasis always being simply on the performance of the rituals and respect for those who know the details of them.

It is apparent that the earliest Hindu views of life after death involved a great deal of ritual observance. Paradise in the form of the World of the Fathers was available to any who carried out their duties while alive, including bearing offspring, and in particular male offspring, to continue lineage, caste, and ritual obligations. Emphasis lies squarely in ritual actions taken in this world with little detailed thought of the next, except for the notion that individuals will enjoy continued material happiness so long as the necessary actions are taken in the world of the living. This is the earliest of the three main Hindu paths, or *margas*, to the afterlife, the *karma marga*, the path of dutiful action.

The second path to salvation after death, the *jnana marga* or the path of knowledge and wisdom, is described in the next set of sacred texts, the *Upanishads*, which appeared around 800 BCE. Though the *Vedas* offer a rudimentary picture of life after death, the *Upanishads* demonstrate an acquired sophistication in philosophical thinking. We have seen that the *Vedas'* vision of postmortem judgment is based upon dutiful action in sacrificing to the deceased ancestors rather than on any concept of right or moral action. With the *Upanishads*, there is an attempt to deal with the problem of evil through the introduction of an alteration in the usage of the word *karma*. The *Vedas* mention *karma* almost forty times, always in the sense of ritual works and sacred actions, whereas the *Upanishads* introduce the notion in connection with that of rebirth.[23]

In fact, while orthodox Hinduism has always held the *Vedas* as the authoritative religious text, the *Upanishads* differ significantly from the earlier texts on a number of crucial points. As N. Ross Reat puts it in *The Origins of Indian Psychology*:

> . . . the two beliefs most obviously expressed in the *Rg Veda* [sic], 1) the existence of many gods, and 2) the efficacy of ritual, are denied or seriously subverted in the *Upanisads* [sic], which are nevertheless traditionally considered to be derived from the *Vedas*. On the other hand, three of the major *Upanisadic* concepts, 1) the soul as the innermost essence of the human being, 2) repeated rebirth, and 3) the possibility of spiritual release . . . are all lacking in the *Rg Veda*, though the pious often claim to find them there.[24]

It is not entirely accurate to say that the *Upanishads* completely overrule the rituals of the older *Vedas*, but a spiritual hierarchy of belief is clearly set out. The *karma marga* is open to those who perform the requisite rituals of the older faith, but the truly faithful and pure follow the *jnana marga* instead. The new path offers radically different ideas on the state of humans after death, as mentioned in the previous quote. While the *Vedas* had offered the loosely described material pleasures of the World of the Fathers, their focus always remained in a this-world orientation to ritual performance. The *Upanishads*, on the other hand, place the emphasis not on actions and deeds, but on the inner soul, the *atman*, and its eventual fate. The *atman* is thought to move from one life to the next after death, in a succession of reincarnations aimed at a spiritual perfection that will result in liberation from life on this world, called *moksha*. This liberation involves the realization that all things are interconnected and that the individual soul will merge into the underlying reality of all things, called *Brahman*.[25]

In this view, the World of the Fathers is but a temporary abode, and one of far lesser value than the ultimate goal of *moksha*, release. The dead who rest in that former paradise rely on the continued ritual action of their progeny. The earliest belief system indicated that should the rituals stop, and those who have passed on no longer receive offerings, they would lose their spiritual body and either be relegated to utter annihilation or else to return to the earth as a haunting spirit seeking only to once again receive offerings. The new concept of rebirth, however, incorporates the World of the Fathers into an ongoing cycle of life, death, and eventual rebirth on earth. Should any beings cease to receive the ritual sacrifices due them, they would not suffer any worse fate than a return to earthly existence in a new body and a new life.

> Now as a caterpillar, when it has come to the end of a blade of grass, in taking the next step draws itself together towards it, just so this soul in taking the next step strikes down this body, dispels its ignorance, and draws itself together [for making the transition].
>
> As a goldsmith, taking a piece of gold, reduces it to another newer and more beautiful form, just so this soul, striking down this body and dispelling its ignorance, makes for itself another newer and more beautiful form like that either of the fathers, or of the Gandharvas, or of the gods, or of the Prajapati, or of Brahma, or of other beings.[26]

The *Brihad-aranyaka Upanishad* describes how those who know the divine truths will travel to the World of the Gods after being consumed in the funeral fire. This heavenly realm is another form of paradise, not completely unlike the World of the Fathers, but more opulent and befitting a god rather than a human. After a brief stay, they might then, if truly pure enough, merge with the absolute reality. The brahmin priests of the *Upanishads* renounced their ritual Vedic roles, and the path of knowledge became central to their career and caste, making divine truths available only to an elite few, though theoretically anyone who could harness the wisdom of the *Upanishads* could achieve *moksha*. Those who simply perform the ritual actions will go on to the World of the Fathers for an indeterminate length of time before returning to the world of the living for a new life. Those who take neither of these two paths are said to return to life as insects.[27]

And so, a cycle of birth, death, and rebirth is envisaged, called *samsara*. The soul (*atman*) moves from one body to another in consecutive life cycles, a process which might continue ad infinitum unless appropriate action is taken. Eventually, one might break the cycle of births and deaths by coming to a specific understanding of the nature of reality. Brahman is seen as the only reality, out of which all other things come and go. Brahman is the overarching absolute of the universe. Life, death, and even the gods are all transient while Brahman alone is absolute. In order to break the cycle of reincarnation, the individual must understand that *atman*, at the heart of every being, is but an aspect of Brahman and thus is not truly a part of the transient day-to-day reality we know through our senses. Thus, upon death, rather than a rebirth of any kind, the individual *atman* becomes one with the essence of reality, Brahman, and achieves *moksha*, the cessation of birth and death. Much like a drop of water falling into the ocean, what was once thought to be an individual disappears into the greater whole of the true reality. "What the *Upanishads* teach finally is that this Ultimate Reality is nothing but pure Consciousness."[28] Composed of every *atman*, Brahman can be envisioned as a kind of universal mind in which all souls lose their individuality and merge with the collective.

R. D. Ranade has called the *Upanishads*, "merely a propaedeutic to their [the *Upanishadic* priests] mystical doctrine."[29] Certainly, in order to come to a full appreciation for the concept that the self is in fact only a small part of a greater whole, something more than words is required. Mystical experience must have formed a central component in the formalizing of these beliefs. The mystical experience of union with the absolute is a common one from one culture to the next, though it is rarely formalized as clearly as it is in the *Upanishads*, and it is certainly nowhere accepted as part of mainstream religion in the Western traditions.

En route to eventual salvation, every person must suffer a series of incarnations, each determined by one's *karma* as further determined by one's actions from one life to the next. The question of divine justice is addressed in the *Upanishads* by a reinterpretation of *karma*, from ritual action to *right* action. On the importance of *karma*, the *Upanishads* are clear, as described in this dialogue between a brahmin teacher and his pupil:

"Yajnavalkya," said he, "when the voice of a dead man goes into the fire, his breath into the wind . . . his body into the earth, his soul (*atman*) into space . . . what then becomes of this person?"

"Artabhaga, my dear, take my hand. We two only will know of this. This is not
for us two [to speak of] in public."

The two went away and deliberated. What they said was *karma* (action). What
they praised was *karma*. Verily, one becomes good by good action, bad by bad
action.[30]

One's actions in one's life will affect the form they take upon reincarnation,
with each new life reflecting the actions they had taken in past lives. As mentioned previously, those who reject the philosophies of either the *Vedas* or the
Upanishads are reincarnated in the form of some insect. Other evildoers are similarly punished for their actions, while those who do good see their lots improved from one life to the next.

. . . either as a worm, or as a moth, or as a fish, or as a bird, or as a lion, or as a
wild boar, or as a snake, or as a tiger, or as a person, or as some other in this or that
condition, he is born again here according to his deeds (*karman*), according to his
knowledge.[31]

In such a way, if one were to lead a good and honest life, following the duties
of one's station in life, one's *dharma*, one could be guaranteed a future life better than the present one. An individual living one life in a low caste might be
reborn into a higher station in life, for example. Every successive life should ideally bring the individual closer to the final release from rebirth that comes with
the true realization that life in this world had been nothing more than an illusion. The Indian caste system was organized with the brahmin at the pinnacle
of a strict hierarchy, being the closest to spiritual salvation, and so, the goal of
lower castes was to eventually accrue enough positive *karma* to be reborn into
the priestly brahmin caste. Beyond this lay the World of the Gods and then
Brahman and *moksha*.

Though the first two paths discussed show no similarities with one another,
it has become a characteristic of Hinduism to accept that there are multiple
paths available for the individual to choose from. As Gavin Flood has pointed
out, "[w]hile many non-[brahmin] do not claim to believe in reincarnation,
there is no cognitive dissonance experienced by Hindus who do, yet who nev-
ertheless perform the correct funerary procedures."[32] The beliefs are not mutu-
ally exclusive. The *Upanishads* became the official doctrine of the more educated higher castes, while common people tended to continue to participate in
the rituals of the traditional ancestral cult, relying on *Vedic* experts to oversee
their performance. In theory, the path of wisdom was open to people of any station. All that was necessary was the renunciation of this world and the acceptance that everything was an illusion hiding the true reality of Brahman and the

interconnectedness of all things. In practice, however, most people had little or no exposure to the details of these ideas and many who did simply rejected them, or could not understand them, as too esoteric in the face of the more immediate rewards of an afterlife in the World of the Fathers.

Alongside the growing influence of the mystical philosophy of the *Upanishads*, there continued to flow a variety of common beliefs. Myths, legends, and stories continued to be told and passed down through oral history. In the centuries after Christ, the great Indian epic, the *Mahabharata*, of which the popular *Bhagavad Gita* forms but a small part, appeared in written form, along with the series of tales known as the *Puranas*. Together, these works describe detailed folk traditions dating back as far as the original *Vedas*, having been similarly passed down orally for generations. These traditional legends formed a core for the common beliefs of the people of India, the vast majority of whom had never had access to the scriptural teachings of the *Vedas* and *Upanishads*, and these ideas intermingled with some of those presented by religious scholars through the ages. Having been written down at such a late stage in the historical development of Hinduism, the main texts of the *Mahabharata*, *Gita*, and *Puranas* might be seen as the manner in which common people understood the *Vedic* and brahminic philosophies combined with a fair dose of superstition and folk belief. It has been said that through these varied legends, a narrow and restricted brahminism was extended to become the all-inclusive Hinduism that accepts that there are many different paths through life.[33] Basically, the priestly caste had to incorporate the widespread beliefs of the common people.

The *Puranas* give us rich detailed descriptions of all manner of demon and spirit, as well as the otherworldly abodes of all of these creatures. There are said to be seven heavens, seven nether regions, and twenty-one hells.[34] The denizens of these realms range from demons, ghosts, and ghouls to angelic *devas* and the spirits of the dead. The World of the Fathers described in the *Vedas* appears among the seven heavens, as do the World of the Gods and the Ultimate Reality of *Brahmaloka*, the World of Brahman, found in the *Upanishads*. The layers of hell are described as places as equally radiant as those of heaven, but provide abodes to the myriad demons believed to share space with human beings. The Nether World, on the other hand, is that place where tortured souls reside. Any of these multiple worlds might be the future birthplace of any given person after death. They formed an obvious hierarchy, with Brahman at the top. To be born into the World of the Gods would doubtless be more pleasant than a birth into one of the demon worlds, but only the truly evil would be born into the torturous Nether World. The concept of punishment or reward in the afterlife for deeds done while alive will be more fully described.

The greatest sins are reported to be those of neglecting family responsibility, performing rituals poorly or wrongly, and disrespecting brahmin priests. Obviously, the *Vedic* influence is clear in this list. Murder, theft, and slander are all dealt with, though the focus is still primarily on the conduct of proper worship. Brutal punishments are described for those who are born into the tortures of the Nether World. Methods of punishment for such beings who had failed in their duties or committed other evils predominantly involve either physical mutilation or the forced ingestion of all manner of gruesome matter. Having one's intestines plucked out by birds; being forced to hold hot metal balls in the mouth; being torn in half; ingesting blood, pus, and urine; having one's eyes blown out—all of these represent the kinds of tortures one might endure if one does not follow any of the ways of right living.[35]

The *Puranas* also introduce the notion that one's fate after death might depend upon which god or goddess one chooses to venerate. For instance, to become a *Gana*, which are ghosts believed to make up the personal entourage of Shiva, god of creation and destruction, is considered one of the highest boons attainable by the followers of this god.[36] Those who worshipped Lord Shiva specifically might strive to be reincarnated into the particular level of heaven or hell that spawned these beings. Alternately, other Hindus might devote their prayers and sacrifices to any specific deity, entreating them to look over them after death and see that they be reincarnated into a beneficial life. Typically, Shiva and Vishnu are the prime beneficiaries of *bhakti*,[37] but ultimately any deity may receive personal devotion, especially if one considers that those gods might manifest in any number of forms. Devotional theism, or *bhakti marga*, the third of the Hindu paths to salvation, sprang from a need for personal salvation in a way that was not offered by the other two paths. The World of the Fathers provided a sensual heaven, but one in which people lost their individuality and required constant help from the living to survive, while the World of the Gods was nothing but a stepping stone to *moksha*, in which it was realized that the individual was only a part of a greater whole to begin with. Ramakrishna summed up the sentiment when he said, "I want to taste sugar, not become sugar."[38] And so, the notion took form that every individual could choose his or her own path, and his or her own deities. This new idea does not deny the cycle of rebirth cited in the *Upanishads*, nor does it deny that one might eventually escape that cycle to achieve *moksha*. Instead, it proposes a new path to *moksha*, a way of devotion that is simpler to follow and that provides a more personally rewarding relationship with one's god. Simply put, not every person is born into the same position in life, whether by caste, station, or other factors. The *bhakti marga*, the third path, that of simple devotion, provides every person with the possibility of some kind of afterlife.[39] Often the three paths are seen as leading to progressively more socially inclusive means of attaining salvation. In particular, the *Gita* eventually gained a place of great popularity as, "a text appropriate to all persons of all castes or no caste; its message transcends the limits of classical Hinduism."[40] Krishna, in the *Bhagavad Gita*, promises Arjuna, who is the protagonist of the poem and stands in for the reader, that through devotion and faith in him, Krishna will guarantee him salvation:

> Listen! I tell thee for thy comfort this. Give me thy heart! Adore Me! Serve Me! Cling in faith and love and reverence to Me! So shalt thou come to Me! I promise true, for thou art sweet to Me! And let go those—rites and write duties! Fly to Me alone! Make Me thy single refuge! I will free thy soul from all its sins! Be of good cheer![41]

Having described three paths to achieving salvation from mortality, it is also extremely important to recognize the importance of death rituals in the Hindu praxis. The *Vedic* sacrificial rituals have already been mentioned, involving offerings made to placate and aid the dead on their journey to the next world. Axel Michaels includes an interesting analysis of death rituals in his discussion of Hinduism.[42] Michaels describes the dead body as a form of sacrifice in itself, and as such can transcend death just as other sacrifices might be transmitted to the gods and so escape this mortal realm. In this light, the dead might actually become the sacrifices themselves.

Various priests and functionaries are required for these efforts, to ensure that the rituals are properly carried out for the safety of both the dead and the living. The issue of spiritual pollution, which is very important in many aspects of Hindu religion, combines with these basic fears, perhaps representing a reflection of them, to create a complicated system of people involved. One specialist is required to deal with the remains, another to deal specifically with the malevolent ghost upon death, and a third to handle the rituals related to the deceased once he or she has been transformed into a benevolent ancestor. These priests are often looked upon with trepidation despite their brahmin caste, simply because of the pollution they are steeped in by virtue of their proximity to the dead. At times, this proximity can go to extremes. For example, Jonathan Parry describes a case from Banaras, sometimes referred to as the religious capital of India, where a brahmin becomes "consubstantial" with the deceased.[43] That is to say, through ritual, the brahmin actually *becomes* the deceased, though only temporarily. In such a case, the priest wears the clothing of the deceased and allows the spirit to enter his body, sometimes even speaking its words. While certainly not always employed, such rituals are among those aimed at facilitating the passage of an individual from life to death and to help the families in dealing with such a loss.

Possession, in fact, is not an uncommon phenomenon, even in modern India. For instance, the Tamils of Southern India and Sri Lanka, also known as Ceylon, hold the belief in possession by both malignant spirits as well as gods.[44] Cults of the dead can be found throughout these areas. For centuries, spirits of the dead have been thought to possess the living, and gods have done likewise for almost as long. Just as ancient Indians worshipped the dead in ancestral cults before they worshipped distinct gods themselves, so too with beliefs in possession.[45] There is mention of possession and those who perform exorcisms as early as the *Atharva Veda*.[46] These priests provide the same function as exorcists in other religious traditions, dealing with all manner of possession by malignant ghosts, evil demons, or occasionally minor gods. In Hinduism, however, "possession" refers most commonly to domination by spirits of the dead or by goddesses (more so than gods), rather than by demonic forces, as is often the case in Western religions.

Three main reasons are most often cited to explain why a person might become a ghost, whether intent on actual possession or merely to appear as, say, an instance of haunting: (1) dying before one's allotted time, (2) dying a tortured death, or (3) behavior contrary to village custom or religious custom, including failure on the part of the living to properly perform the necessary rituals.[47] Typically, if the spirit has not been successfully conveyed to whatever land of the dead awaits it, the spirit will wander the world in anger, seeking some means to live again. Possession provides a means through which a ghost might thus live, if even vicariously through some other person. Unfulfilled obligations or desires may cause a ghost to seek some means of remaining in the world of the living. Often, if the exorcist, or someone else for that matter, can coax the possessing entity to reveal its purpose, the living might then make efforts to resolve the problem faced by the spirit. Should such action be taken, the possessing entity will usually leave in peace, and the exorcist will have proven successful. The *Brhadaranyaka Upanishad* provides an example of the identification of a deceased spirit in possession of a living person:

> . . . the sage Bhujyu, the son of Lahyayana, in his student days, went to the Madra country and came to the house of Patanchala, the son of Kapi. This Patanchala had a daughter who was possessed by a Gandharva, an aerial spirit, and who thus served as a medium. Bhujyu asked the spirit who he (the spirit) was, and received the answer that he was Sudhanvan, the son of Angirasa.[48]

As an aside, an interesting connection can be drawn between personal stress on the part of the *victim* and their subsequent possession. Waves of spirit possession have been known to occur in communities facing crises such as droughts, floods, and epidemics.[49] It might be posited in the face of this that severely stressful situations might invoke symptoms similar to actual possession by a dead person, and that the exorcisms accompanying these possessions somehow help to alleviate the stress of the community. On the other hand, such natural disasters might also be caused by the malignant spirits moving into the area and wreaking havoc before actually possessing certain individuals.

Sinister ghosts might also haunt an area rather than take possession of an individual. Common areas for hauntings include funerary grounds, ruined buildings, mines, caves, desert areas, or dark, lonely roads.[50] Often, spirits roam for a particular reason, aiming to rectify some wrong on Earth. The epic poem, the *Ramayana*, provides the following example:

> After Dasaratha has been dead for years, he appears in the sight of man, raised by Mahesvara [an epithet of Shiva], and stands dressed in bright garments, devoid of dust, and says he will never forgive Kaikeyi. Then [he] changes his mind, forgives her, and blesses Rama, whom he embraces, and finally goes back to Indra's heaven.[51]

William Crooke provides yet another example:

> Mr. Campbell tells a Marhata [sic] legend of a master who became a Brahma-parusha [a kind of ghost] in order to teach grammar to a pupil. He haunted a house at Benares, and the pupil went to take lessons from him. He promised to teach him the whole science in a year on condition that he never leave the house. One day the boy went out and learned that the house was haunted, and that he was being taught by a ghost. The boy returned and was ordered by the preceptor to take his bones to Gaya, and perform the necessary ceremonies for the emancipation of his soul. This he did and the uneasy spirit of the learned man was laid.[52]

In addition to those apparitions described, there are also cases where the ghosts involved remain invisible yet let themselves be known through their actions. Of course, common ailments and natural disasters are often blamed on malignant ghosts. In these instances, the presence of the ghost is only presumed. However, in certain hauntings, the ghosts' actions can be witnessed firsthand. An example of one such poltergeist, or noisy ghost, is given here, in the description of a house that had been infested by spirits for a hundred years:

> The *bhut* [ghost] began its activities by hurling down bricks from the wall. It is said that a Patidar neighbour, who was called in to witness this, observed, characteristically, that there would be a good deal more sense in the situation if the spirit were to throw down gold, whereupon, on that one occasion, a shower of gold descended. This spirit is still said to be active occasionally.[53]

While these examples all describe ghosts appearing in waking visions, it is also common for spirits to appear in dreams making demands for proper burials or for the righting of wrongs committed while they were alive. The dream state is conducive to such encounters with the dead. Indeed, during normal life, the soul of an individual is thought to depart from the body during sleep. It is such nocturnal journeys that dreams are made of, and also that encounters with the souls of the dead might occur. The *Catapatha Brahmana* warns of the dangers of waking a sleeper too hurriedly lest the soul not have time to return to the body. A Punjabi tale tells how a sleeping Hindu's soul became thirsty during one of its normal nocturnal travels. To quench its thirst, the soul entered a pitcher of water. At that moment, someone placed the cover back onto the pitcher trapping the soul inside. Friends thought the man dead and, making the necessary arrangements, carried what they considered his corpse to the funeral grounds. Luckily, someone happened to open the pitcher once again before the fire was lit and the soul returned quickly to its body, which awoke startled while lying upon the bier.[54]

In addition to those encounters with spirits of the dead, there are also cases in which living people remember details of a past-life. This phenomenon will be examined in a separate chapter, but it is important to touch upon it here in the context of Hindu beliefs, as reincarnation is such a central feature and many cases of past-life memories come from India. Recent case studies have found a growing number of instances in which individuals, typically children, claim memories of a past-life that are later verified to correspond to facts unknown to the child but known to the person the child claims to have been. It will suffice for the moment to provide one brief example of the kinds of memories exhibited in these cases:

Sukla, daughter of Sri K. N. Sen Gupta of the village of Kampa, West Bengal, was born in March, 1954. When she was about a year and a half old and barely able to talk, she was often observed cradling a block of wood or a pillow and addressing it as "Minu." When asked who "Minu" was, Sukla said "My daughter." Over the next three years she gradually revealed additional information about Minu and "he," meaning her husband of the previous life. She said "he," Minu, Khetu, and Karuna (the latter being brother and sister of her "husband") were all at Rathtala in Bhatpara. The village of Bhatpara is eleven miles from Kampa on the road to Calcutta. The Gupta family knew Bhatpara slightly; however, they had never heard of a district called Rathtala in Bhatpara nor of people with the names given by Sukla.[55]

When the child began to complain of wanting to travel to Bhatpara, her father began to talk about the case to friends and neighbors until he discovered that one of the people mentioned by his daughter did in fact live in the city mentioned. When she was five years old, the family made the trip. Once in Bhatpara, Sukla was able to guide the family to her former home and identified several people once they got there, and she swelled with deep emotion when she recognized her daughter and husband. Gradually, as in the vast majority of these cases, the child began to lose the memories as she grew older. Still, the fact is that cases such as these remain highly suggestive of reincarnation, especially for those predisposed to such a belief.

From these accounts, and innumerable others, it becomes clear that most Hindus perceive death as more than merely a brief transitory stage prior to rebirth. The souls of the dead must be treated with the utmost respect lest they become angered and cause trouble for the living. Correct ritual observances are expected in order to appease the dead whether they are destined for an afterlife in one of the seven heavens or whether they are due for rebirth shortly after death. Hindu society thus displays a layered system of belief, creating a kind of hierarchy from the most basic levels of ancestor worship and strict ritual observance to more complex philosophical systems dealing with beliefs about the afterlife and salvation. There is a story of a brahmin priest who sought personal release through solitude. He was once confronted by the Fathers who chastised him for neglecting them and his family duties. They threatened him with degradation and downfall unless he were to sire some children. Upon meditation, he realized that he had only one option. In order to keep the Fathers happy, he was obliged to find a wife with whom to have children, who might in turn continue the family line of ritual. Only once these familial duties had been performed could he return to the quest for personal release.[56] This is a reminder for us, as it was for the brahmin, that affairs of this life are as important as those of the next. Some modern Hindus do not even concern themselves with ideas of the next life in the slightest. According to Sri Aurobindo for instance, "rebirth is no longer taken for granted . . . but is merely a theory."[57] Still, reincarnation is accepted by most Hindus as a fact more so than an article of faith. In Hinduism, many alternatives are accepted as means to liberation after death. Ritual propitiation of the dead continues to be practiced overwhelmingly among Hindus, thus relying on the efforts of *Vedic* priests well versed in such rituals. Typically, the soul is thought to be reborn in some alternate realm depending upon the merit of the individual's deeds during life on earth. Some are born into a torturous existence, suffering for evils committed, while others are born into the paradisiacal Worlds of the Fathers or Gods. Eventually, the average person is bound to be reincarnated here on earth once again, continuing the ongoing cycle of life, death, and rebirth called *samsara*. Encounters with spirits of the dead, both while awake and asleep, as well as possession of the living by the dead encourage a belief in the continued existence of the individual beyond death. Memories of past-lives support the notion that people will eventually be reborn in this world. The long-term goal of this seemingly endless cycle is the ultimate realization that all things are part of a continuous whole and that the individual *atman* is really a part of a great world soul, Brahman. Every person is expected to simply do what they can and follow their *dharmic* path in life, living well and doing good. Through this, everyone can expect to eventually achieve liberation and ultimately *moksha*, release from the troubles of life.

Notes

1. Thomas J. Hopkins, "Hindu Views of Death and Afterlife," in *Death and Afterlife: Perspectives of World Religions*, ed. Hiroshi Obayashi (New York: Greenwood, 1992), p. 145.

2. Gavin Flood, *An Introduction to Hinduism* (Cambrdige, UK: Cambridge University Press, 1998), p. 31.

3. For an overview of this topic see Flood, *An Introduction to Hinduism*, pp. 31–35. See also David Frawley, *The Myth of the Aryan Invasion of India* (New Delhi: Voice of India, 1994).

4. N. Ross Reat, *The Origins of Indian Psychology* (Berkeley, CA: Asian Humanities Press, 1990), p. 6.

5. Mahuli R. Gopalacharya, *The Heart of the Rigveda* (New Delhi: Somaiya, 1971), p. 2.

6. Hermann Oldenberg, *The Religion of the Veda*, trans. Shridhar B. Shrotri (Delhi: Motilal Banarsidass, 1988), pp. 315–316.

7. Raj Bali Pandey, *Hindu Samskaras* (Delhi: Motilal Banarsidass, 1969), p. 252.

8. Catherine Weinberger-Thomas, *Ashes of Immortality: Widow-Burning in India*, trans. Jeffrey Mehlman and David Gordon White (Chicago, Ill: University of Chicago Press, 1999).

9. Weinberger-Thomas, *Ashes of Immortality*, p. 199.

10. Chanda Chakraborty, *Common Life in the Rgveda and Atharvaveda* (Calcutta: Punthi Pustak, 1977), p. 174.

11. For detailed example see Jonathan P. Parry, *Death in Banaras* (Cambridge, UK: Cambridge University Press, 1994), pp. 75–76.

12. Pandey, *Hindu Samskaras*, p. 255. William Crooke's investigation of Indian folklore also revealed a number of beliefs associating the spirits of the dead with owls and bats. See: William Crooke, *Popular Religion and Folklore of Northern India*, 2 vols. (1896; repr., Delhi: Munshiram Manoharlal, 1968), vol. 1, p. 279.

13. *Atharva Veda* (AV) 4.34 *Atharva-Veda-Samhita*, trans. William Dwight Whitney (Delhi: Motilal Banarsidass, 1971 [1962]).

14. *Rig Veda* (RV) 7.76.4 *The Hymns of the Rgveda*, trans. Ralph T. H. Griffith, ed. J. L., Shastri (Delhi: Motilal Banarsidass, 1973), p. 372.

15. Raimundo Panikkar, trans. and ed. *The Vedic Experience: Mantramanjari* (Berkeley, CA: University of California Press, 1977), p. 544.

16. AV 10.14.8–10.

17. Mircea Eliade, *A History of Religious Ideas*. vol. 1. trans. W. R. Trask (Chicago: University of Chicago Press, 1978), pp. 210–212.

18. RV 10.16.1–4.

19. R. C. Zaehner, *Hinduism* (London: Oxford University Press, 1962), p. 76.

20. RV 10.87.20.

21. AV 5.19.4.

22. *Taiit. samhita* II, 6, 10, 2, cited in Oldenberg, *The Religion of the Veda*, p. 320.

23. Panikkar, *The Vedic Experience*, p. 539.

24. Reat, *The Origins of Indian Psychology*, pp. 7–8.

25. One must here be aware of a potential confusion that can result from the similarity of the terms Brahma and Brahman. The former refers to the personified creator god, while the latter refers to the primordial stuff from which everything has come. Further complicating matters, the priestly caste is also designated as the Brahman caste, which I refer to in this book by the anglicized form, brahmin, for clarity. Readers must be aware of which is being discussed at any one time.

26. Brihad-aranyaka Upanishad (BA) 4.4.3–4 *The Thirteen Principle Upanishads*, trans. Robert Ernest Hume (Delhi: Oxford University Press, 1921), p. 140.

27. BA 6.2.15–16.

28. Swami Muni Narayana Prasad, *Karma and Reincarnation* (New Delhi: D. K. Printworld, 1994), p. 22.

29. R. D. Ranade, *A Constructive Survey of Upanishadic Philosophy* (Bombay: Bharatiya Vidya Bhavan, 1968), p. 45.

30. BA 3.2.13.

31. Kaushitaki Upanishad (KU) 1.2, in *The Thirteen Principle Upanishads*, trans. Robert Ernest Hume (Delhi: Oxford University Press, 1921).

32. Flood, *An Introduction to Hinduism*, p. 208.

33. Cornelia Dimmitt and J. A. B. van Buitenen, trans. and eds. *Classical Hindu Mythology: A Reader in the Sanskrit Puranas* (Philadelphia: Temple University Press, 1978), p. 13.

34. Dimmitt and van Buitenen, *Classical Hindu Mythology*, pp. 24–26.

35. Dimmitt and van Buitenen, *Classical Hindu Mythology*, pp. 50–51.

36. Dimmitt and van Buitenen, *Classical Hindu Mythology*, p. 248.

37. Though Brahma, the creator god, makes up the third of the trinity of major gods, he has not had a cult in his honor for many centuries.

38. Hopkins, "Hindu Views of Death and Afterlife," p. 152.

39. Hopkins, "Hindu Views of Death and Afterlife," p. 154.

40. Christopher Chapple, foreword to *The Bhagavad Gita*, trans. Winthrop Sargeant (Albany: SUNYP, 1984), p. xix.

41. Sir Edwin Arnold, trans. *The Song Celestial or Bhagavad-Gita* (London: Routledge & Kegan Paul, 1961), Book 18, p. 109.

42. Axel Michaels, *Hinduism: Past and Present*, trans. Barbara Harshav (Princeton, NJ: Princeton University Press, 2004 [1998]), pp. 131–158.

43. Parry, *Death in Banaras*, p. 76.

44. George L. Hart III, "The Theory of Reincarnation Among the Tamils," in *Karma and Rebirth in Classical India*, ed. Wendy Doniger O'Flaherty (Berkeley, CA: University of California Press, 1980), pp. 117–118.

45. Deleury, *The Cult of Vithoba* (Poona, 1960), cited in Hart, "The Theory of Reincarnation," p. 118.

46. Ruth S. Freed and Stanley A. Freed, *Ghosts: Life and Death in North India* (Seattle: University of Washington Press, 1993), p. 46.

47. Freed and Freed, *Ghosts*, p. 84.

48. Ranade, *A Constructive Survey*, p. 92. Unfortunately, we are not told how this possession case was resolved, but one might presume that Bhujyu assumed the role of exorcist; the first question as to the identity of the individual being asked and answered, his role is thus established.

49. Freed and Freed, *Ghosts*, pp. 313–314.

50. Crooke, *Popular Religion and Folklore*, vol. 1, pp. 277–278; 280–283; 290–294.

51. *Ramayana* 6.120.10f, quoted in E. Washburn Hopkins, *Epic Mythology* (1915; repr., Delhi: Motilal Banarsidass, 1974), pp. 29–30.

52. J. S. Campbell, "Notes on the Spirit Basis of Belief and Custom" (Bombay, 1885), p. 146, quoted by Crooke, *Popular Religion and Folklore*, vol. 2, pp. 78–79.

53. D. F. Pocock, *Mind, Body and Wealth* (Oxford: Basil Blackwell, 1973), pp. 34–35.

54. Anon., "Panjab Notes and Queries," 4 vols, Allahabad, 1883–87, vol iii, p. 166, quoted in Crooke, *Popular Religion and Folklore*, vol. 1, p. 231.

55. Ian Stevenson, *Twenty Cases Suggestive of Reincarnation* (New York: American Society for Psychical Research, 1966), p. 51.

56. Dimmitt and van Buitenen, *Classical Hindu Mythology*, pp. 340–342.

57. Robert N. Minor, "In Defense of Karma and Rebirth: Evolutionary Karma," in *Karma and Rebirth: Post Classical Developments*, ed. Ronald W. Neufeldt (Delhi: Sri Satguru, 1986), p. 25.

CHAPTER SIX

~

Buddhism

From within the atmosphere of the myriad gods, rituals, and ideas that made up religion in India, what today are known collectively as Hinduism, a child who would change religious thought was born. Named Siddhartha Gautama, of the Shakya clan, he would eventually be known simply by the title of Buddha, founder of what was to become the most pervasive religion in Asia. Buddhism may be traced back to a single semi-historical/semi-legendary man, but centuries have brought it a life of its own as the religion and philosophy have evolved and adapted to an ever-expanding environment, its adherents bringing Buddhism across Asia and the world.

Though history is vague, scholars have made some conclusions about the man who would be the Buddha.[1] Most importantly, it is likely that Gautama was a real person and that he was born circa 563 BCE and lived for eighty years.[2] Much else is a mixture of history and legend. He was a prince, heir to become chief of his clan, whose father made every effort to raise his son in a sheltered atmosphere far from the troubles of the outside world. Astrologers had warned that the young prince would forsake his royal heritage after encountering four men, so his father did all he could to prevent it. Gautama's curiosity brought him to explore beyond the walls of his home, however, and the shock of what he experienced put him on a journey toward enlightenment. Specifically, he encountered the four men prophesied; each of who brought home the hitherto unknown reality of suffering through life and death. After seeing a terribly sick and crippled man, followed by an old and withered man, and finally the rotting body of a dead man, Gautama was struck by the fact that sickness, old age, and death were the natural process of every person and that all the wealth and comfort of his father's home was useless in avoiding this. In his despair, he then encountered a fourth man, a wandering mendicant who inspired Gautama to follow certain ascetic methods of the Indian tradition in order to find escape.

This he did, leaving his wife and family behind. Depictions of the Buddha invariably include the long, pierced earlobes, which symbolize, among other things, the extravagances of wealth and his subsequent rejection thereof. His ascetic efforts led only to more suffering, however, and after years of wandering Gautama decided there must be a better means of discovering the truth and meaning of life. To this end, he adopted the concept of the Middle Way, between self-denial and self-indulgence. He sat under a type of fig tree, since called the Bodhi tree, and waited in deep meditation. After a great deal of time, enlightenment suddenly came to him and he realized the doctrines, *dharma*, that would become the foundation of Buddhism.

As his faculties for awareness grew ever broader, he was struck with three visions. First, memories of his past incarnations came to him, revealing that he had lived through the cycle of birth and death for eons. Second, he became acutely aware of the procession of humankind through the suffering of birth, old age, and eventually death. Finally, he achieved knowledge of the workings of the universe and understood that "all things, except for *nirvana* and space, arise and pass away, and that the existence of all things is dependent upon a number of causal conditions."[3] Once realized, Gautama went forth as the Buddha, preaching his insights to all that would listen.

India had long been open to new religious ideas, new gods and goddesses, but Gautama, as the Buddha, was proposing something very different. He attained enlightenment not through some exterior forces, nor through devotion to some god or another, but through and within himself. For Gautama, the power of enlightenment was, as Walpola Rahula puts it, a wholly mortal affair.[4] The realization of truth was not a divine revelation but came to the Buddha through his own efforts as he sat and thought.

Merv Fowler delineates three important distinctions between the Hinduism from which Gautama sprung and the early Buddhism that he espoused.[5] First, ritual was rejected as an impairment to personal enlightenment, and with it was rejected the hierarchical caste system of karmic advancement. The Buddha completely rejected the notion that enlightenment should only be available to those who practiced rituals and read the *Vedas*, which were only available to the brahmin caste. Second, asceticism and excess were to be avoided in favor of the Middle Way, a path anyone could follow given the will to do so. Finally, while the Hindu pantheon was recognized, the existence of these gods had no bearing upon enlightenment and truth. Peter Harvey calls Buddhism "trans-polytheistic," as it accepts many gods but always looks beyond them for what is of real importance.[6] The Buddha did accept the common Indian concept of successive lifetimes, however, and adapted that of *karma* to avoid the need for rituals.

As for the teachings of the Buddha himself, we must rely on the words of later writers. Gautama spread his message orally, and his followers did likewise after his death. The first Buddhist Council met soon after the Buddha's death, around 483 BCE, with the purpose of preserving the central doctrines of Buddhism, and organized them into three sections, known as the *Tipitaka*, or three baskets. This collection of rules, parables, anecdotes, and quotations from Gautama Buddha were handed down from one generation to the next for centuries. They were finally committed to writing in the Pali language during the first century BCE, by which time a certain amount of schism had created numerous different schools of Buddhist thought.

Of the eighteen early schools of Buddhism, only the Theravada tradition, the "Doctrine of the Elders," remains to this day. The Pali canon contains the fundamental texts of the Theravadins and, translated into English, runs thousands of pages long. It is impossible to know exactly what was said by the Buddha himself, and certainly, the vast majority of debate among the various early schools of thought is lost. Still, the Pali canon provides the earliest written source to the historical Buddha, thus providing the closest insight into the original ideas of the Buddha that is possible.

In order to understand the Buddhist conception of death, one must look first at how the Buddha conceived life. Gautama's philosophy of life is encapsulated in the concept of the Four Noble Truths, as described (ostensibly) in his own words:

> Bhikkhus [monks], it is through not realizing, through not penetrating the Four Noble Truths that this long course of birth and death has been passed through and undergone by me as well as by you. What are these four? They are the noble truth of Dukkha [suffering]; the noble truth of the origin of Dukkha; the noble truth of the cessation of Dukkha; and the noble truth of the way to the cessation of Dukkha. But now, bhikkhus, that these have been realized and penetrated, cut off is the craving for existence, destroyed is that which leads to renewed becoming, and there is no fresh becoming.[7]

The long course of birth and death is the cycle of rebirth from one life to the next (*samsara*), which is based upon the Indian notion of reincarnation, and will be discussed later. *Dukkha* is suffering stemming from the impermanence of all things in this world. Rahula argues that simply translating *dukkha* as suffering is misleading, as it may tend to portray Buddhism as a pessimistic religion.[8]

On the contrary, Buddhism should be seen as a *realistic* faith, and a proper understanding of *dukkha* will help to make this clear. It is not that *dukkha* is simply suffering, though pure suffering plays a role in its meaning, but it is also the kind of suffering that comes with the passing of happiness, as when a good friend leaves for a long trip, and also includes the general suffering that is contingent on a failure to understand the true nature of reality as preached by the Buddha. Accordingly, material reality is transitory and reliance upon it and craving after it can only lead to suffering. The ultimate fate of every person is to grow old, become ill, and die. The process of birth, life, and death is thus fleeting and cause for suffering. The origin of *dukkha* can be found in the craving for and longing after the impermanent. By continuing to chase after the temporary pleasures of life, suffering will always exist. Attachment to this world will result in rebirth after death, remaining stuck in the cycle of *samsara* and suffering. Cessation of *dukkha* and escape from this torturous cycle can only come through enlightenment and the elimination of ignorance and desire. Finally, the way to enlightenment is outlined in the so-called Eightfold Path, which instructs followers to be vigilant in their conception of the world, and everything in it, as merely temporary and thus to behave accordingly. That is, by bearing in mind the impermanence of all things, including most importantly the individual self, the three evils of desire, anger, and ignorance will be eliminated.

Whereas Hinduism stressed the underlying unity between the self, *atman*, and the surrounding reality, Buddhism denied any such reality for either the self or its surroundings as these things remained wholly impermanent and ephemeral. In the words of P. T. Raju, "the I-am has no ontological status."[9] What each individual experiences as a continuing and consistent self is in reality an illusion obscuring the fact that there are only fleeting moments coming together in aggregates and passing away as quickly. The self that is now is already different from the self that was a moment ago. The continuity of selfhood is a fallacy perpetuated by ignorance. Raju further states that, "[r]ealizing this renders one immune to the fear of death since there is really nothing which death can attack."[10] In fact, death and birth are unimportant. The goal is *nirvana* and release from the continuum of rebirth.

Unlike the Hindu concept of *moksha*, in which the self escapes *samsara*, often uniting with the underlying order of the universe, *nirvana* takes on a wholly different meaning for Buddhists. A Sanskrit word meaning "to extinguish," or "to blow out," *nirvana* has commonly been misinterpreted to mean the extinction of the individual self, but this is inherently false, "a Buddhist heresy."[11] Since the Buddha claimed that there was no real, permanent self in the first place, there is no "self" to be extinguished. *Nirvana* instead represents the extinguishing of desire, anger, and ignorance. It is the state in which all attachments to the illusions of self and this world are utterly eliminated. The Buddha says of *nirvana*: "Calming of all conditioned things, giving up of all defilements, extinction of 'thirst,' detachment, cessation, Nibbana [Nirvana]."[12] *Nirvana* is a state of mind in which no attachments whatsoever impinge upon the peacefulness of simply being without striving to become or to cease.

Buddhism is often considered a mystical tradition because of the emphasis on *nirvana*, and Gautama doubtless felt the expansion of awareness of the mystical experience as he sat meditating under the famous fig tree. Mystical experiences, as a distinct class of human experience, appear cross-culturally, and have been mentioned briefly in the context of other religious traditions in preceding chapters. The psychologist William James famously delineated four main features of such experiences: a noetic quality, subsequent ineffability, transiency, and the feeling of passivity throughout.[13] The noetic quality is essentially the core of the experience in that the mystic gains an expanding awareness of his or her place in the universe. These experiences have variously been interpreted as a union with God, Brahma, the absolute, or *nirvana*, as in the present context. Most importantly, these experiences demonstrate to those who have them that the boundaries we perceive between self and other in daily life are arbitrary distinctions and that the ultimate reality does away with separateness. With this in mind, it is likely that there is some empirical connection between the Hindu *moksha* and Buddhist *nirvana*, though the theoretical frameworks used to explain the experiences are diametrically opposed. That is to say, the core experience of some union with an absolute is common to all mystical traditions, though a variety of religious frameworks have been elaborated to account for these experiences.[14]

The attainment of *nirvana* is no simple task, having come to the Buddha after many years of intellectual seeking and meditation. According to Theravada Buddhists, the Eightfold Path describes the prescription for living appropriately so that eventual enlightenment will take place, but it is a process that could take eons. As Gautama's awareness expanded, he remembered countless past lives leading to his final incarnation as Shakyamuni. Indeed, Buddhaghosa's "Path to Purity" describes how every person has the capacity to recall previous incarnations through meditative practice, as well as a number of other psychic abilities like clairvoyance.[15] Through each lifetime, the thoughts and actions of each individual cause the accretion of either good or bad *karma*. Again, there is a major difference between Hindus and Buddhists in their ideas of how *karma* works.

Whereas in *Vedic* Hinduism ritual sacrifice and prayer was enough to increase good *karma*, Buddhism emphasizes the role of intention over simple action. Part and parcel with the Buddha's rejection of *Vedic* authority, this move allows any person the ability to improve his or her *karma* simply through earnest devotion to doing good, rather than relying upon the brahmin priest for salvation. Thus, by following the Eightfold Path and avoiding such unwholesome acts as killing, stealing, lying, or slander, good karma, or merit, may be amassed. Karma is important as it has a direct cause-and-effect relationship to each individual's life-state. Happiness is brought by good karma, while suffering stems from bad karma. Not only can suffering and misery in this life be attributed to bad deeds done within this lifetime, but the evils of past lives certainly have their impact as well. Just as Hindus believe accumulated karma will determine one's subsequent incarnation, so Buddhists acknowledge the role in determining the fate one is to be reborn into, however different their definitions of karma itself and the mechanisms behind it.

For many, there seems to be an inherent contradiction in the ideas discussed thus far. Since there is no self, how can it be said that one will be reborn after death? Raju expresses the problem thus:

> The Buddhists, unlike the Vedantists, do not seem to have elaborated the idea of a subtle body, apparently because the idea of a durable subtle body conflicts with their doctrine of momentariness. But for logical reasons, the idea of a subtle body must be posited. Otherwise, we cannot understand what transmigrates. If it is only some *karmic* ("ethical") potencies which transmigrate, then the being from which they are transmitted will have to be different from that to which they are transmitted. Thus, the former being need not worry about transmigration at all because it perishes absolutely after only a moment. Its perishing must be as good as emancipation, and salvation, consequently, ought to be spontaneous and instantaneous. But such could not have been the view of the Buddhist teachers. There is, therefore, a lacuna in their argument.[16]

In fact, no such lacuna appears, and one could hardly expect a philosophical system to remain effective with such a gaping hole. The problem seems to stem more from semantics than from a problem of logic. Just as the illusory self exists throughout one lifetime, so it carries over when reborn. Raju argues that a person would need not worry about bad karma for there is no soul connecting this life with the next, but this misses the point that there is no soul in this life to begin with. *Vijnana*, consciousness, is made up of ever-changing aggregates that manifest a semblance of continuity through the effect of memory. Just as I might have vague memories of being three years old, so I might also have memories of living a previous life. In either case, that which is being remembered and that which is doing the remembering are connected only through a series of cause-and-effect relationships, called karma. Certainly, *vijnana*, as the locus of thought-moments, shares some affinity with the Hindu *atman* or Christian soul, but Buddhists reject the reality of both. "The exact nature of this distinction has been differently stated, but in essence the Vijnana is not an Atman or soul because it is neither eternal nor substantial."[17] Much of the confusion surrounding these notions is the outgrowth of a pernicious desire to think of one's self as a distinct, separate, and real individual. "The Buddha knew this quite well. In fact, he said that his teaching was 'against the current' (*patisotagami*), against man's selfish desires."[18]

With this in mind, it is possible to speak of rebirth as related to karma and the individual. One's actions lead to karmic consequences along a linear chain of cause-and-effect linked with a series of ever-changing aggregates and thought-moments. These aggregates make up the illusory self. As long as there is karma that requires resolution, there will continue to be aggregates. Once detachment from the material world is achieved, the aggregates cease to come together and the state of *nirvana* is achieved.

Rebirth itself can take many forms, depending upon the karma involved. Good or bad karma is reflected in the birth-state of each individual. There are basically six modes of existence, divided into three good and three bad modes, at least in the present realm of reality. These modes are further divided into more and more detailed states, but for the sake of simplicity and ease of understanding, it is sufficient to discuss primarily these six. The higher modes of being consist of humans, lower gods (*asuras*), and higher gods (*devas*). The lower modes are animals, hungry ghosts (*pretas*), and hell-beings (*naraka*). On this, the Buddha said:

> Because of their wicked conduct, their unjust conduct . . . some beings with the break up of the body, after death . . . go the bad way, come to places of pain, to hell . . . Owing to their conduct in agreement with the teaching, their considerate conduct, some beings with the break up of the body, after death, go the good way, come to the heavenly world.[19]

None of these states is permanent, however. Every life comes to an end and results in either rebirth or *nirvana*. The chances of avoiding rebirth are very slim, though, as the human mode of being is the only one that may lead to *nirvana*. Both the higher and lower beings remain attached to material things. The higher gods are either distracted by the excessive lavishness of heaven, or overly wrapped up in philosophical thoughts. The lower beings are stuck in the sensual world, remaining either too dull to achieve enlightenment or forced to purge themselves of tremendous evils. While Gautama urged his followers to focus upon following the right path in this world, there are a great many descriptions of the heavenly and hellish realms in the early Buddhist literature.

Ashvaghosha's poem, "Nanda the Fair," provides great detail into one of the higher heavens, that of the god Indra. The poem tells the story of the monk Nanda and how he was carried to the higher realm to witness its splendors and learn a special lesson. Here, lush trees, beautiful flowers, and wondrous fragrances fill the landscape. Musical instruments grow like flowers, and the flowers and trees are themselves made of precious jewels. All manner of beautiful birds flit about happily singing. But the real prizes are the celestial nymphs: "They are always in the prime of their youth, and libidinous enjoyment is their only concern."[20] The warning is given, however, that even these are impermanent lives and how much worse suffering would be to lose paradise than it is to lose life now.[21] Thus, a sensual heaven exists but it is to be rejected just as the material reality of here and now should be rejected.

Another tale describes the otherworldly journeys of King Nimi.[22] In addition to visions of the *devaloka*, King Nimi actually met with Indra and sat with the gods. He also visited a great number of other heavenly realms, and was taken on a tour of the hells as well. In the lower regions, he witnessed countless tortures of the most horrible kind. He watched as sinners were tossed onto heaps of burning ash. Others had their throats cut before being hurled into boiling water. Starving sinners were forced to sate themselves on urine and feces while the thirsty drank pus and blood. Gossips and liars were dragged about by hooks in their tongues. The *Anguttara Nikaya* describes how the evil person after death is seized by hellish beings and brought before the Hindu god, Yama, who then reviews his or her evil deeds and directs them to the appropriate hell for purgation.[23] Accumulated karma determines the actual fate, and Yama's presence here seems more as an intermediary and a carry-over from Hinduism, than anything else. In fact, Bimala Charan Law notes that the descriptions of hell-states found in Buddhism and Hinduism are essentially the same. Where they differ is in the mechanism behind the process.[24]

Ray Billington argues that the lowest modes of being should be considered as merely states of mind rather than actual modes of existence. He further suggests that the notion of animals being reborn as humans is preposterous as no creature lacking the freedom to choose could build up good karma.[25] Though Billington draws support from later thinkers, both assertions are poorly founded, based upon highly biased suppositions. For one thing, there is no reason to consider negative modes of existence as mental states while still considering the higher heavenly states and *nirvana* as somehow real. Certainly, the Pali Buddhist texts follow the Hindu tradition of regarding them as real, inasmuch as Buddhists can regard anything as real. To assume that animals cannot accrue karma can only be based upon Western notions of human superiority. Additionally, some states of being simply act as means to purge bad karma and do not engender the building up of any more, whether good or bad.

In any case, the individual's rebirth will somehow be justified by past actions. In fact, the new state is actually directly caused by these actions, whether good or evil. Performing good deeds leads to a better life, while evil ones lead invariably to a hellish existence in a subsequent life. The Pali texts are full of examples of such just rewards or punishments. People who give gifts of food will live long and healthy lives; those who offer houses gain palaces full of wealth; those who dig wells for the public will never need water; those who offer medicine are forever free from disease. And so the list goes. And the same is true of sinners and their punishments. Those who oppress others by confining them suffer madness; those who assault and batter, become lepers; those who steal cannot earn money even with great effort.[26] The tale of King Nimi describes a number of similar fates. The closer one stays to the Eightfold Path and the doctrines of the Buddha, the better life one is to be born into. To oppose these doctrines, however, and to have no faith in what the Buddha is alleged to have said, leads to hell.

Another common form of punishment comes from being reborn as a hungry ghost. Individuals whose sins may not have been grave enough to warrant hell, but who continue to harbor base attachments to the material world may be reborn as ghostly beings continually starved but never able to satiate themselves. The *Petavatthu* details a number of tales involving these tortured spirits. A variety of forms are available in which the hungry ghosts might appear, some withered and emaciated, others bleeding and full of pus. As a whole, these spirits take on a form that is sufficiently horrible to reflect their hell-like state, and like other forms of purgation, such existence often teaches the individual the error of his or her ways and leads to a better life when that one ends.

The situation of hungry ghosts is problematic, however, in that the stories of the *Petavatthu* introduce the possibility of transferring merit from a person living in the human world to one in the *petaloka*, the world of these hungry spirits.[27] There is the story, for instance, of a woman of Benares who was known for her luxurious hair. Out of jealousy, some local women had some special drugs mixed into her shampoo that caused her hair to fall out from the roots. This woman from Benares was often generous and kind, but once fell victim to the temptation to steal some particularly fine raiment. After she died, she was then reborn in a huge palace with her flowing locks restored. The problem was, she had no clothing and therefore could not leave the ghostly palace. When a passing ship found her castle, the sailors offered to help. She told them that she could not accept clothing from them, being a ghost, but that if they were to donate the clothing to a monk, the merit might be transferred to herself. They carried out her instructions and she soon emerged "with a sweet smile on her face, draped in the finest garments."[28]

That every person is uniquely responsible for his or her own karma and fate is seen as a cornerstone of Buddhist philosophy. The transfer of merit seems originally to have been rejected as a reflection of the brahminic control of karma in the traditional Indian system. As ritual experts, the brahmin regularly received offerings that would in turn bring favor upon those who gave them, in effect making the brahmin the distributors of good karma. The Theravadin monks apparently fell into the same situation and eventually filled this role, despite the philosophical rejection of it. This apparent contradiction was one of many that emerged within Buddhist thought in the centuries after the Buddha's death. As stated earlier, the Theravada school was one of eighteen early Buddhist schools of thought. As the centuries ticked by, the differences between these schools widened until a second Buddhist Council was convened in 383 BCE to deal with the conflicts. The teachings of Gautama were again discussed, with divergent utterances harmonized. The early view taught that since the Buddha's enlightenment had been the instantaneous source of his wisdom, nothing new could be added and there could thus be no development in thought. This traditional way of thinking came into conflict with a new view that conceived the Buddha as a semidivine being capable of updating his ideas through the inspiration of others. Somewhere between god and man, the Buddha was believed to have the power to transmit enlightenment to humans, of which Gautama was but one of many. It became clear at this council that the orthodox traditions of the Theravadin were in a minority as a new form of Buddhism had risen in popularity. Mahayana, or Greater Vehicle, remains the more popular form of Buddhism today, encompassing a great number of further subdivided schools. Theravada was pejoratively labeled Hinayana, or Lesser Vehicle, by this new faction.

The third Buddhist Council of 250 BCE saw the Pali canon finally written down. Until this point, oral history had been passed from one generation to another, and it is easy to imagine how more than two hundred years of oral history might have led to variance of understanding. In addition, an infusion of Hindu ideas had crept back into Buddhism in forms such as the transfer of merit. By this point, Mahayana had begun to solidify as an alternative within the larger spectrum of Buddhism.

H. Wolfgang Schumann effectively delineates eight key differences between the orthodox Theravadin and the Mahayana traditions.[29] (1) Mahayana holds a more idealized view of the human condition, emphasizing that not only is the self an illusion but all suffering is also an illusion. (2) Mahayana posits an idea similar to the Hindu notion of an underlying unity in all things, the underlying connectedness of all things. (3) Whereas Theravada sees the Buddha as a man like any other, who achieved enlightenment through his own efforts, Mahayana believes the Buddha to have been a projection of enlightenment. (4) Theravada urges followers to take the example shown by Gautama and seek enlightenment individually, whereas Mahayana holds that one might achieve enlightenment simply through devotion. (5) Mahayana teaches that the transference of merit and karma is possible, though it was shown that this concept had begun to creep into later Theravadin thought as well. (6) While Theravada teaches that the goal is individual enlightenment, the Mahayanists argue that the goal is the state of bodhisattva, where the enlightened wait to help others achieve the same state before going on to *nirvana*. (7) The concepts of *nirvana* differ in that the Theravada school believes it to be a release from *samsara* and complete liberation, while the Mahayana tradition believes it to be the realization of the underlying interconnectedness of all things and that the self and absolute are inseparable within this life. (8) Finally, Mahayana aims to transcend illusion and help the world, whereas Theravada aims to live practically in the effort to defeat and escape the world.

These differences mark the Mahayana tradition as a more populist form of Buddhism appealing directly to the average Indian rather than the devoted monk, though it probably arose originally from the practices of progressive monks. Also, it incorporates several elements of traditional Indian culture, folklore, and religion, which no doubt made this brand of Buddhism more appealing to a broader audience as well. Despite some distinct differences, however, Mahayana still remains within the context of Buddhism by virtue of its reliance upon the teachings of the Buddha and many of the fundamental doctrines.

> The analogy of the wheel is often used to describe the relationship between the two, the hub of the wheel being Theravada and the spokes Mahayana. Core beliefs are inevitably derived from orthodox doctrines, but Mahayana has given these beliefs different and extended interpretations.[30]

Mahayana had an early advantage over the Theravada tradition in its greater appeal to the masses. The Doctrine of the Elders was considered too constricting for lay people to follow. The average person is incapable of strictly following the Eightfold Path, and thus incapable of entering into *nirvana*, except in the most extraordinary cases. Indeed, only Theravadin monks could normally succeed in this goal with a lifetime devoted to practicing the Eightfold Path, once again placing liberation in the hands of the clergy in a way similar to that aspect of brahminism originally rejected by the Buddha. Impatient with the eons it might take a Theravadin to achieve a birth favorable to achieving *nirvana*, Mahayana provides the means by which anyone can achieve awakening in this lifetime. Carl Becker argues that the apparent self-centered nature of Theravadin meditation can be "ironically" contrasted with Gautama's *anatta* theory of no-self.[31] This interpretation of Theravada simplistically states a perceived inner contradiction in that Theravada denies the existence of a self yet urges its adherents to meditate without a care for any other person. In reaction to this, the Mahayana tradition posited that the Buddha, and subsequent bodhisattvas, had achieved enlightenment but refrained from entering completely into *nirvana*. Instead, these individuals existed in some other form of existence in order to wait for every other being to achieve enlightenment, and in fact help them to achieve that end.

The beginnings of such ideas can be traced to the Buddha's death and his subsequent veneration. There is a link between the growing devotion to the bodhisattvas and the *bhakti* cults that were emerging in India in the second century BCE. Certainly, both of these phenomena grew out of the increasing tendency for people to turn to individual worship of chosen deities, rather than rely heavily on the brahmin, or Theravadin monk as the case may be, as intermediary between humans and the ultimate goal of personal liberation from *samsara*. After the Buddha's death, his remains were burned according to Hindu custom and his bones were then passed on amongst monks as sacred relics. Many of these relics were buried in mounds called *stupas*, which became sites of veneration. Buddhist temples were often later erected at these locations. Alongside the monks, many lay people came to visit these sites to make offerings to the memory of the Buddha. With a genuine reverence was combined the hope that such veneration would lead to the acquisition of good *karma*. Already at this early stage, many assumed that the Buddha was able to bear witness to their entreaties from some other realm.

By the first century CE, Mahayana scriptures, which emphasized universal salvation, were being added to the Buddhist canon. Buddhism had entered China at this point and was influenced by the indigenous ideas it encountered. One of the best known of these new texts is the *Saddharmapundarikasutra*, or the Lotus Sutra. This is the first written source that describes the Buddha as a universal savior. These texts, as a whole, outline the methods by which every person might achieve transcendent *nirvana*—no longer a higher quest for enlightenment in terms of endeavoring to the means to correct living, but simply the escape from the general suffering of daily life. Schumann describes three means of salvation for the common person as the Bodhisattva Way, the Way of Faith, and the Cultic Way.[32]

The Bodhisattva Way relies heavily upon the compassion of the bodhisattvas, those who have attained enlightenment but have delayed *nirvana* in order to help save the masses. By their very nature, the bodhisattvas define compassion. It is thought that because of their desire to see every person released from suffering, they are incapable of refusing any request for help. To attain help from a bodhisattva, all that one must do is ask. In exchange for this help, however, the supplicant agrees to commit to the strict morals of compassion espoused by the bodhisattvas themselves. In doing so, an individual comes into a moral pact with the bodhisattvas. On the one hand, they will ensure the safety of the supplicant, but on the other, this individual must also show equal compassion to all he or she may come across in life. So, while the Bodhisattva Way seems at first to be quite a simple path, the commitment required of it remains too lofty for many of the weaker willed. "The Bodhisattva Way being easy to follow in its passive aspect, is in its active portion the most difficult way to deliverance which Buddhism offers."[33]

The Way of Faith offers a more comfortable route to bliss. It is thought that maintaining a devout faith in Gautama, and others who have attained Buddhahood, will lead to salvation. Of the many schools of Mahayana thought that have arisen, Pure Land Buddhism is that most readily associated with the Way of Faith. This particular school predominates the Buddhism of the Far East, and will be discussed in more detail in the next chapter. For now, it is sufficient to explain that through devotion to a particular Buddha, the most common of which is a figure variously named Amitabha, Amitayus, or Amida, a person might be reborn in a heavenly Pure Land. These Pure Lands are similar in many respects to the *devaloka* described previously in that they represent sensual realms of beauteous paradise, but they are conceived of as much more fortuitous and closer to *nirvana*. This is a reversal of the notion that humankind is closest to achieving *nirvana*, placing increasing emphasis on the supernatural. However these paradises might be imagined, the ultimate goal remains, at least nominally, that of transcending even that and achieving *nirvana*. Still, it is not difficult to see how the masses might be satisfied with reaching such a paradise, especially given the density of the philosophical notion of *nirvana*, not to mention the common-sense connection to one's self that every individual experiences in conscious life. Certainly, to the common person, existence in some form of concrete paradise holds a far greater appeal than does the relatively esoteric idea of *nirvana*.

Straying further afield from the intentions of older forms of Buddhism, the Cultic Way provides a means to *nirvana* for even the most superficial Buddhist. The Lotus Sutra describes how the worship of relics, *stupas*, and images of the Buddha, as well as offerings of flowers and incense, combined with music making at the temples are a ritualized path to *nirvana*.[34] Such rituals are easily practiced by even the most noncommittal Buddhist, many placing the emphasis on the actions much more so than on the intention.

In the Mahayana tradition, two Buddhist scholars stand out as being of primary importance to the evolution and establishment of key ideas. They are Nagarjuna and Vasubhandu, and the ideas of each are important to Buddhist notions of life and death.

Nagarjuna is the earlier of the two, though there is, as is so often the case, debate over when he actually lived. Recent scholarship conventionally dates Nagarjuna to between 150 and 250 CE, placing him firmly during the revolutionary period when the Mahayana texts came into existence and Buddhism most radically changed upon entering China.[35] While at the forefront of Mahayana thought, Nagarjuna made efforts to harmonize the new scriptures with the traditional ones to keep the new doctrines closely aligned to the original teachings of Gautama. He is most famous for blurring the line between *samsara* and *nirvana*, arguing that there was in fact no distinction between the two at all. This school of Mahayana Buddhism became known as Madhyamika, or the School of the Middle Way, where the Middle Way eliminates the need for binary opposites. The following passages from the Madhyamika Karika are attributed to Nagarjuna:

> 17. It is not maintained that "the Venerable One exists after death" nor is it maintained "he does not exist" or "both or neither."
>
> 18. It is not maintained that "the Venerable One exists while remaining in the world" nor is it maintained that "he does not exist or both or neither." [sic][36]

While both the Theravadin and Mahayana traditions accept the doctrine of no-self, this idea becomes increasingly obscured in the Mahayana popular tradition, and Nagarjuna's goal was to maintain a conservative stance and keep any notion of dualism out of the picture. There is no belief in a self that is extinguished in *nirvana*, although Western scholars have often mistakenly picked that up as the core teaching of Buddhism. Similarly, there is not an underlying unity hidden by other states of existence. Though paradoxical, according to Nagarjuna, both life and death, *samsara* and *nirvana*, are the same and different at once. Further expressing this paradoxical reality, Nagarjuna states:

> 30. It is not established that I existed in the past, because this one is not the very same one who existed in previous lives.
>
> 31. It is not established that I did not exist in the past, because this one is not different from the one who existed in previous lives.[37]

By attacking the dichotomy of opposites, Nagarjuna wished to reveal the relativity of reality. Three levels of truth are distinguished. The first two levels form the bivalence of untruth and relative truth. Within the context of ignorance, certain things seem to be either true or false. The third category of truth, however, is that of ultimate truth, which defies description, being beyond the pale of rational discourse. *Nirvana* and enlightenment are the only means of experiencing the ultimate truth. It is as if those who are unenlightened are living in a fantasy, not recognizing reality for what it is. "Defilements, karmans, bodily entities, doers and effects are all similar to the nature of an imaginary city in the sky, a mirage and a dream."[38] Simply put, all that one perceives as normal reality is in fact a misperception, and the only way to lift the veil is through *nirvana*, which obviously has considerable influence on related concepts of life and death. Certainly, this line of argument is much more esoteric than rationally logical, requiring direct experience or faith to accept, but Nagarjuna seems not to have been as concerned with the effectiveness of the argument as much as simply breaking down common modes of thought, for it is these modes of thought that keep one locked in the cycle of life, death, and rebirth. In this relativity of truth and the negation of opposing concepts, the door is open for further speculation and thus begins the wide history of Mahayanist thought.

The second great father of Mahayana Buddhism is Vasubhandu, who, with the help of his brother Asanga, converted to Mahayana philosophy after being sufficiently impressed with the new ideas put forward in the texts. Again, his dates are debated, but a fair estimate would place him around 316 and 396 CE.[39] His philosophy took Nagarjuna's train of thought one step further. Accepting first that absolute truth was wholly ineffable, and second that our concepts of truth and falsity in this realm were subjective and relative, Vasubhandu surmised that the essential element in reality was consciousness, *vijnana*. Consciousness, that which thinks, is necessary in order to make the distinctions between relative truth and untruth. Yogacara, as the school of Vasubhandu and his brother is known, is sometimes also known as the "Consciousness-Only School," or Vijnanavada. Consciousness is that which conceives thoughts. Most of these thoughts are illusory, based upon ignorance, especially when the consciousness turns upon itself and conceives of a self, as in Descartes's famous axiom, cogito ergo sum. The perceived self is, of course, an illusion, but the consciousness itself is real. It must be pointed out that consciousness here does not indicate a self in any sense, but simply that a thought processor of some kind exists. The mystical experience of enlightenment provides the empirical evidence that there is both consciousness and no-self at once.

The notion of *alaya-vijnana*, or store-house consciousness, was introduced to explain the transmigration of a person from one life to the next. R. C. Amore describes the *alaya-vijnana* underlying regular consciousness in the same way as the ocean underlies a wave.[40] In this analogy, each lifetime is but one wave that rises and falls, always drawing from the same store-house. This represents an attempt by Vasubhandu to resolve the problem of a transmigrating consciousness. Once the string of lifetimes related to a particular store-house consciousness achieved enlightenment, then the underlying store-house consciousness itself would simply come to an end.

With consciousness at the core of experience, Vasubhandu argues against the traditional notions of hell in Buddhism, which describes them as actual realms into which individuals might be reborn in order to purge themselves of certain sins and bad karma. Vasubhandu says that these infernal places must be internal states of consciousness, as, "assuming 'an approved place for the infliction of suffering' is to him abhorrent."[41] As with the arguments of Billington, compassion for humankind and the inability to believe that torture could ever be inflicted upon a being led to the philosophy of subjective hells. Logic dictates that if these states are purely internal, then so are heavenly states, as well as present existence. To single out hell-states as somehow more internal than any other seems to cater more to the fear of increased suffering than to anything else.

Further developments occurred as Buddhism spread North into Tibet by the eighth century CE. In fact, Tibetan Buddhism evolved to the extent that it is so different from either Mahayana or Theravada that it is often considered a distinct type of its own. Called Tantrayana after its scriptures, the Tantra, the third of the "Three Wheels of Buddhism" is also known as Mantrayana, the Vehicle of Mantras (sometimes referred to as spells, other times as forms of prayer), and also Vajrayana, the Diamond or Thunderbolt Vehicle. J. R. Haldar laments that Mahayana Buddhism had lost its idealistic motivation for universal salvation and, in the magic of Tantrayana, "yielded to gross superstitions and esoteric and immoral principles."[42] Tibetan Buddhism certainly is esoteric, particularly in its tantric and mantric forms, but it is an over generalization to apply such judgment across the board. Tibetan Buddhism remains under the umbrella of Buddhism as a whole, and its moral grounding rests well within the Buddhist tradition.

The indigenous religion of Tibet, called *Bon*, held a number of beliefs that seem at face value to be incongruous with Buddhist tenets. Basically, each person was believed to have twin spirits, the *pho-lha* and *dGralha*, which separated and left the body at death. A number of rituals, including exorcism, were required to ensure that these departed spirits would not haunt the site of the individual's death or grave. Shamans routinely made contact with the dead to determine the causes of all manner of ills, as have ancient cultures worldwide. The general idea was that the souls of the deceased would travel either to a heavenly realm or a hellish one depending upon their deeds in life. Buddhism therefore adapted to these beliefs, incorporating otherwise non-Buddhist ideas with traditional Buddhism.

The shamans of Tibet became incorporated into the Buddhist framework as mediumistic mouthpieces of both the gods and the dead. Mediums were incorporated into monasteries and would become possessed with either some minor god or goddess or the spirit of a dead person. Depending upon the nature of the entity, the words might be considered prophetic or not.[43] The mediums in these cases are often not in control of the communications and are considered possessed by the entities involved. This is an important counterpoint to the Theravada belief that possession of any kind, despite its appearance in Theravadic cultures, is to be avoided as it disrupts the inner calm regularly sought. Alongside the passive mediums, there are also shamanic sorcerers who wield magical powers over the dead, as well as possessing a number of other powers such as the ability to summon hail and rain. While the mediums can convey messages from beings in other realms, it is these necromancers who must actually deal with them on their own planes. These shamans have the ability to leave their bodies at will and travel to the worlds of spirits or demons and, when the entities are malignant, negotiate amicable terms or battle them psychophysically. Alexandra David-Neel, during her ten years with the hermit monks, or lamas, of Tibet, encountered numerous reports of such voyages, as well as a great variety of other magical and paranormal phenomena.[44] In addition to psychic battles, she found these shamans also conducted exorcisms, had the power to kill with a word, and routinely facilitated the journeys of the spirits of the deceased to the next world.

This "next-world" in Tibetan Buddhism is an in-between state after death but before rebirth. This state is called *bardo*, and it is the unique contribution of Tibetan Buddhism found in the famous *Tibetan Book of the Dead*. The title of this text (*Bardo Thos-Grol*) is actually better translated as *The Great Book of Natural Liberation Through Understanding in the Between*, but the former title has stuck in the Western mind.[45] The purpose of this great text, written by the "great adept's adept,"[46] Padma Sambhava around the eighth century CE, is to help guide the dying and the dead through the period of being in-between. A combination of maintaining the right frame of mind and knowing how to entreat various deities and saints is essential. The readings in the text are aimed not only at providing instructions for the subsequent journey, but also at maintaining a clear and positive mental state upon entering death. The text is to be read to the dead person's body in the belief that the consciousness will gain from such reading while it remains near the body, preparing to depart for the *bardo* state. The fourteenth Dalai Lama points out that, "the attitude just before death is very important; for, if even a moderately developed practitioner is disturbed at that time, manifest desire or hatred will be generated."[47] Obviously, desire and hatred are to be avoided at all costs as two of the three karmic roots of all suffering.

The opportunities to purge such evils from one's consciousness extend past the moment of death, however, and for those who have the benefit of the *Book of the Dead*, the in-between state might be used to consciously influence the rebirth state. Where the Bon shamans saw multiple spirits departing from the body, Tibetan Buddhism describes the consciousness (*vijnana*, or *rnam-shes* in Tibetan) as that which leaves the body at death. Just as the Bon shamans would also guard against the haunting presence of these spirits, so too the Tibetan Buddhists must guard against evil spirits invading the dead body and causing it to rise from the dead as a kind of zombie or revenant.[48] While karma is still seen as the final arbiter of rebirth, the "evolutionary momentum"[49] is seen as fluid in the *bardo*, thereby creating an atmosphere lax enough to leave room for last minute change. Thus, a continuing consciousness from one life to the next exists in Tibetan Buddhism, perhaps reflecting the influences of both the native Bon religion and Hindu ideas.

During the *bardo* state, the individual adopts a spiritual body, in effect an ethereal double similar to that described in ancient Egypt. Without guidance, the individual might not realize that he or she is dead and will wander in a ghostly form until the next birth. The intermediary state may last for as long as forty-nine days after which time rebirth is thought to be certain.[50] Still, rebirth could take any number of forms as described in the Pali canon.

An interesting feature of the *bardo* state is the perception of *nirvana* as a kind of light. The natural tendency is to shy away from the awesome power of it and only those who have mastered the appropriate methods will be able to overcome this fear. Becker sees similarities between this description and that of modern near-death experiences involving a tunnel and a being of light.[51]

Because Tibetan Buddhism suggests the continuation of consciousness between life and rebirth, their notion of rebirth is considerably more like the reincarnation of Hinduism than any other major form of Buddhism, though it still retained the quintessential Buddhist denial of the self. This fact is exemplified in the spiritual head of Tibetan Buddhism, the Dalai Lama.[52] Dalai Lama, or Oceanic Master, is a title given to the reputed incarnation of Chenrezi, the Bodhisattva of Compassion and patron of Tibet. The first Dalai Lama was discovered in the sixteenth century CE when a boy began to make claims that he was the reincarnation of the great Tibetan renaissance leader, Gendun Drubpa. From the moment he could speak, the child claimed memories of the recently dead icon, who had himself been considered by many to be the embodiment of the Bodhisattva of Compassion. The claims were thoroughly tested until it was determined that the uncanny memories that the boy had of this other life could be verified and that this child possessed knowledge that he could not have unless he were in fact who he claimed to be. After the death of this newly incarnated Drubpa, yet another boy was found who exhibited similar capabilities and claimed to be a subsequent incarnation. While Gautama had claimed that it was possible to recall all of one's previous births, there is no clearer example of a continued being living from one life to the next than the Dalai Lama.

And so, a clear evolution of thought can be drawn out in the history of Buddhism in India and neighboring countries. Further developments will be examined in the next chapter as Buddhism encounters the religious ideas of China. While there has been some tendency toward laicization, especially in many forms of Mahayana Buddhism, in the transformation from Theravada through Mahayana to Tibetan Buddhism, the core teachings attributed to Gautama Buddha have remained unchanged. The ability of individuals, and not necessarily those well-versed in the sacred texts of Buddhism, to achieve personal awakening has replaced the strict codes of conduct espoused by the early Theravadin monks. Today, Theravada Buddhism is predominant in southern India and Sri Lanka, as well as in southern Asia, namely Thailand, Burma, Laos, and Cambodia. Mahayana is more popular in Nepal, China, Vietnam, Korea, and Japan. And Tibetan Buddhism, in addition to being the religion of Tibet, also attracts a great deal of interest in the West from those interested in more esoteric ideas.

Notes

1. For a good, basic introduction to the life of the Buddha, see Michael Pye, The Buddha (London: Gerald Duckworth, 1979).

2. Though these dates have been widely accepted, there remains dispute, leaving any conclusion far from certain. See R. F. Gombrich, "Dating the Buddha: A Red Herring Revealed," in The Dating of the Historical Buddha Part 2, ed. H. Bechert (Gottingen: Vandenhaeck & Ruprecht, 1992), pp. 237–259.

3. R. C. Amore, "The Heterodox Philosophical Systems," in Death and Eastern Thought, by Frederick H. Holck (Nashville, TN: Abingdon, 1974), pp. 118–119.

4. Walpola Rahula, What the Buddha Taught (New York: Grove, 1974), p. 1.

5. Merv Fowler, Buddhism: Beliefs and Practices (Brighton: Sussex Academic Press, 1999), pp. 36–37.

6. Peter Harvey, "Buddhism," in Human Nature and Destiny, ed. Jean Holm, with John Bowker, (London: Pinter, 1994), p. 18.

7. The Last Days of the Buddha: The Maha-parinibbana Sutta (Digha Nikaya 16), trans. Sister Vajira and Francis Story, revised ed. (Kandy: Buddhist Publication Society, 1998), online (2002), http://www.accesstoinsight.org/ptf/sacca.html.

8. Rahula, What the Buddha Taught, pp. 16–20.

9. P. T. Raju, foreword to Holck, Death and Eastern Thought, p. 10.

10. Raju, in Holck, Death and Eastern Thought, p. 10.

11. Richard Gombrich, Theravada Buddhism (London: Routledge & Kegan Paul, 1988), p. 63.

12. *Samyutta-nikaya* I, quoted in Rahula, *What the Buddha Taught*, p. 36.

13. William James, *The Varieties of Religious Experience* (London: Collier-MacMillan, 1961).

14. To enter the debate over the universality of mystical experience in any depth would take this book on a lengthy tangent. Suffice it to say that a great number of scholars of renown have reached the same conclusion upon close scrutiny of the reports of mystics from traditions world-wide; namely that there is a common unitive core to all mystical experience. The interested reader is directed to the following: Martin Buber, *Between Man and Man*, trans. R. G. Smith (London: Kegan Paul, 1947); Abraham H. Maslow, *Religions, Values, and Peak-Experiences* (Harmondsworth, UK: Penguin, 1964); Walter T. Stace, *Mysticism and Philosophy* (London: MacMillan, 1961); Rudolph Otto, *Mysticism East and West*, trans. B. L. Bracey and R. C. Payne (New York: Meridian, 1957); Margaret Smith, *An Introduction to the History of Mysticism* (London: Sheldon, 1977); R. C. Zaehner, *Mysticism Sacred and Profane* (London: Oxford University Press, 1967); ____, *Concordant Discord* (London: Oxford University Press, 1970). On the other hand, there are those who oppose the notion of a common core, led by the much respected scholar, Stephen Katz. For a variety of arguments from this side of the coin, see Stephen T. Katz, ed. *Mysticism and Philosophical Analysis* (New York: Oxford University Press, 1978).

15. Edward Conze, trans. *Buddhist Scriptures* (Harmondsworth, UK: Penguin, 1959), pp. 131–132.

16. Raju, in Holck, *Death and Eastern Thought*, pp. 15–16.

17. Amore, "The Heterodox Philosophical Systems," p. 121.

18. Rahula, *What the Buddha Taught*, p. 52.

19. *Anguttaranikaya* 2, 2, 6, I, quoted in H. Wolfgang Schumann, *Buddhism: An Outline of its Teachings and Schools*, trans. Georg Fenerstein (London: Rider, 1973), p. 55f.

20. Conze, *Buddhist Scriptures*, p. 223.

21. Conze, *Buddhist Scriptures*, pp. 222–224.

22. *Nimi Jataka*, quoted in Bimala Charan Law, *Heaven and Hell in Buddhist Perspective* (Sonarpura, Varanasi, India: Bhartiya, 1973), pp. 16, 101–102.

23. *Anguttara Nikaya*, Vol I., pp. 138–141, cited in Law, *Heaven and Hell*, pp. 97–98.

24. Law, *Heaven and Hell*, pp. 115–116.

25. Ray Billington, *Understanding Eastern Philosophy* (London: Routledge, 1997), p. 67.

26. Law, *Heaven and Hell*, pp. 19–21.

27. James Paul McDermott, *Development in the Early Buddhist Concept of Kamma/Karma* (New Delhi: Munshiram Manoharlal, 1984), pp. 97–98, 110–111.

28. Law, *Heaven and Hell*, pp. 53–55.

29. Schumann, *Buddhism: An Outline*, pp. 91–93.

30. Fowler, *Buddhism: Beliefs and Practices*, p. 35.

31. Carl B. Becker, *Breaking the Circle: Death and the Afterlife in Buddhism* (Carbondale and Edwardsville, IL: Southern Illinois University Press, 1993), pp. 44–45.

32. Schumann, *Buddhism: An Outline*, p. 127.

33. Schumann, *Buddhism: An Outline*, p. 129.

34. *Saddharmapundarikasutra* 2, 78–94, cited in Schumann, *Buddhism: An Outline*, p. 138.

35. Nancy McCagney, *Nagarjuna and the Philosophy of Openness* (Oxford: Rowman & Littlefield, 1997), p. 1.

36. McCagney, *Nagarjuna*, p. 209.

37. K. Satchidananda Murty, *Nagarjuna* (New Delhi: National Book Trust, 1971), pp. 108–109.

38. Kenneth K. Inada, *Nagarjuna: A Translation of his Mulamadhyamakakarika with an Introductory Essay* (Tokyo: Hokuseido, 1970), Chap. 17, verse 33, p. 112.

39. Stefan Anacker, *Seven Works of Vasubandhu: the Buddhist Psychological Doctor* (Delhi: Motilal Banarsidass, 1998), p. 10. Anacker provides the details for much of the debating dates and attempts to synthesize them in the most logical way possible in an effort to arrive as closely to the actual dates as can be done.

40. Amore, "The Heterodox Philosophical Systems," p. 121.

41. Anacker, *Seven Works*, p. 160.

42. J. R. Haldar, *Links Between Early and Later Buddhist Mythology* (Calcutta: Grantha Parikrama, 1972), p. 2.

43. Réne de Nebesky-Wojkowitz, *Oracles and Demons of Tibet* (London: Oxford University Press, 1956), pp. 409–443.

44. Alexandra David-Neel, *Magic and Mystery in Tibet* (New York: Dover, 1971), pp. 131–166.

45. Robert A. F. Thurman, trans. *The Tibetan Book of the Dead* (New York: Bantam, 1994).

46. Thurman, *The Tibetan Book of the Dead*, p. 83.

47. The fourteenth Dalai Lama, foreword to *Death, Intermediate State and Rebirth in Tibetan Buddhism*, by Lati Rinbochay and Jeffrey Hopkins (London: Rider, 1979), p. 8.

48. Turrell Wylie, "Ro-langs: The Tibetan Zombie," in *History of Religions* 4 (1), (1964), pp. 69–80.

49. Thurman, *The Tibetan Book of the Dead*, p. 28.

50. Rinbochay and Hopkins, *Death*, p. 19.

51. Carl B. Becker, "The Centrality of Near-Death Experiences in Chinese Pure Land Buddhism," *Anabiosis—The Journal for Near-Death Studies* 1 (1981): 154–171; Idem, "Views from Tibet: NDEs and the *Book of the Dead*," *Anabiosis—The Journal for Near-Death Studies* 5 (1985): 3–20.

52. For an historical overview, see Ram Rahul, *The Dalai Lama: The Institution* (New Delhi: Vikas Publishing House PVT, 1995).

CHAPTER SEVEN

~

Chinese Religions

China is home to what may be the most poorly understood, especially to Western scholars, of the world's major religious traditions. Much of this lack of understanding stems from a difficulty in differentiating between philosophy, theology, folk belief, and religion, or perhaps more accurately, from the difficulty in recognizing that these are all fundamentally interrelated. Traditionally, scholarly convention divides Chinese religion into the triumvirate of Confucianism, Taoism, and Buddhism. Jordan Paper argues that this tripartite distinction is wholly a Western construction, reflecting more the Western associations with religion, established canons, and faiths often named after historical founders, rather than the complex realities of Eastern thought.[1] Certainly, Chinese religion has become a composite of beliefs ranging the spectrum of the three religions mentioned as well as an important element of folk belief. Still, through an examination of the historical developments of these ideas, particularly where they involve belief in life after death, it will become apparent that the tripartite distinction traditionally outlined not only facilitates discussion of Chinese ideas but is also well founded in history with each of these three schools of thought contributing to one another in its own individual way.

The earliest information on Chinese belief in a life after death comes from the Shang period, circa 1500 to circa 1050 BCE. Early funerary practices reveal the attempts of the ancient Chinese to prevent the departure of the life-giving spirit through the stopping up of all bodily orifices. J. J. M. De Groot, in his massive study of Chinese beliefs, provides examples of this belief's continuance in modern times as, for example, a candle or other light source will be placed near the dead body in order to coax the spirit to return to the corpse.[2] This ghost, or *kuei*, was conceived of as a shade-like spirit that left the body to inhabit a subterranean realm called the Yellow Springs. This realm was not unlike the Greek Hades or Jewish *Sheol*, being a dark world where the dead wandered as ghosts without individuality or purpose. The Yellow Springs existed just below the surface of the earth, and so the *kuei* was thought to either inhabit the underworld or to actually reside in the grave itself. As in other ancient systems of thought, this was the fate of the dead regardless of class or merit.

Political upheaval in the form of a change of dynasties from the Shang to Chou dynasty led to the adoption of important new ideas. Most importantly, the usurpers instituted the notion of *t'ien ming*, the Mandate of Heaven, to justify their new rule. This effectively gave the ruling class divine authority over the common people. Under such an authority, the powerful and influential individuals of society—kings, princes, aristocrats—were thought to avoid the bleak fate of the dead in the underworld, as they would travel instead to heaven. The Shang rulers had already envisioned a heavenly hierarchy of spiritual beings,[3] but the Chou expanded that notion to include the human realm as well. The Mandate of Heaven grew with time not only to apply to the relation of rulers over their subjects but became a symbol for family units as well.

The worship of ancestors represents the cornerstone of popular religion in China to this day. In this mode of thought, the shades of the dead wandered aimlessly only when ignored by the living, otherwise their lot was to merge with former family members in an amalgamated ancestral unit. Offerings to the dead would provide them the means of becoming ancestors and escaping the dreariness of the Yellow Springs. The dead eventually lost their individuality, but the ancestral unit formed a continuum so long as the descents maintained their duty to remember and propitiate their dead. The living members of the family formed, in effect, a physical component to this group soul. New family members were often conceived of as new incarnations of the familial substance. This connection between the living and the dead within a family structure became all encompassing. On the one hand, the living are required to make offerings to their ancestors as a sign of respect and to provide the means by which an individual can remain a part of the group soul. On the other hand, the ancestors have the responsibility to provide comfort and fortune to their living progeny from beyond the grave. Such was the reverence for the dead among the living that the ancestors were ritually consulted before any major undertaking, such as war, hunting expeditions, or major agricultural projects, with oracular records being made of the ancestors' answers to these important questions.[4] Should the living fail to uphold their end of the arrangement, the vengeful spirits would visit calamity upon them. For the ancestors, the need for propitiation was essential for the maintenance of their very existence.

The following modern example of the interaction between the living and the dead is typical, revealing both the familial connection and the fear associated with such an offering. This brief story was recorded by anthropologist Charles Emmons, and comes from a thirteen-year-old girl relating the events transpiring after an offering had been left out to her grandfather: "My grandpa came back on the seventh night after his death. His room window made a lot of strange noise. It was very horrible. The next day, all the food, water, and candy had been eaten or moved around."[5]

Normally, ancestors would be remembered for a number of generations on an individual basis. Special tablets bearing the names of these recently deceased family members are made. As generations pass, eventually the older ancestors are thought to merge into the ancestral unit proper. As the living members of the family grow increasingly distant from the earlier generations, memories of them fade and the dead are no longer individually worshipped. So, generally any family will worship and make offerings to the last three or four generations individually. For those having died earlier than this, any offerings made are simply directed to the ancestors as a group.[6] Where this complex system was likely first a means for the ruling class to honor and remember their historical heroes and also to instill the requisite reverence in their own rule, as it expanded to apply to every family unit it became a means of establishing family bonds and a sense of community. This facet of ancestor worship was propounded by Confucius, whose ideas had a profound effect on Chinese cultural development.

The ideas of Confucius have influenced the development of Chinese culture perhaps more fundamentally than any other single thinker. Confucius (the Latinized form of K'ung Fu Tzu), who lived from 551–479 BCE, formalized the preexisting religious thought of the elite with a heavy emphasis on practical results in the here-and-now. During the lifetime of Confucius a number of competing schools of thought emerged as attempts to rescue the country and its people from political strife. During the latter part of the Chou dynasty, China had become divided into factious warring states in what came to be known as the Spring and Autumn Period (771–401 BCE) of Chinese history. At the end of this, the proliferation of philosophical ideas came to be known as the Period of The One Hundred Schools (551–233 BCE). Of the ostensible "hundred schools," Confucianism became a bedrock of Chinese thought forever more. In the words of Xinzhong Yao: "Confucius and his faithful followers made the first efforts to formulate a new philosophy based on the old tradition and propagated it as the path to peace and harmony."[7]

Confucian thought has often been described as an atheistic ethical philosophy. Confucius was certainly a humanist who preferred to deal with the issues of this life over those of the next, but he in no way denied the existence of gods or an afterlife. He simply preferred not to discuss the supernatural as such consideration would distract from the earthly pursuit of virtue. The following dialogue is representative of the pragmatic Confucian outlook:

> Chi Lu asked about serving the spirits of the dead. The Master said, "While you are not able to serve men, how can you serve their spirits?" Chi Lu added, "I venture to ask about death?" He was answered, "While you do not know life, how can you know about death?"[8]

This practical view of life and death rested prime importance upon action in this world with a view to improving the lot of humans in this life. Still, the worship of the ancestors was encouraged for its ritual significance. While Confucius emphasized life here-and-now, he accepted the traditional view of life after death. Coming from an aristocratic background, Confucius upheld the traditional notions of a privileged afterlife for the elite, with the commoners relegated to the anonymity of the Yellow Springs, though, as stated previously, the rituals eventually included the family units of all people and not only the aristocrats. In the words of Kristofer Schipper: "The aristocratic religion, that of the feudal class, considered the human being only in terms of his social role, codified in rituals which themselves expressed the entire feudal order."[9] Very much a traditionalist, Confucius taught that the most virtuous of humans would reflect the divine order through the ritualized and stylized behavior of utmost benevolence and duty. The rituals of ancestral worship were important symbols of the continued respect of the hierarchy within not only the family but within the entire feudal system.

One of the classic texts promoted by Confucius, the *Li Chi*, or Classic of Rites, describes the spiritual nature of humans and outlines the methods for proper ancestral worship. At some point in this period of Chinese history, the conception of the human spirit became one of a dual sort, aligning with the burgeoning theory of *yin* and *yang*, which described the world in terms of cooperating opposites. Varying interpretations of the human spiritual condition, notably those of the more esoteric Taoism, had evolved a complex set of spirits within each person, and these were focused into a dichotomy through the doctrine of *yin* and *yang*. According to the evolving ancestral cult, the lower, animalistic or *yin* souls would go down into the ground upon death, to reside either in the grave or the Yellow Springs (and, as stated previously, these may be seen as identical). There were thought to be as many as seven such lower souls, called *p'o*, which would become *kwei*, or ghosts, upon death. The higher, or *yang*, souls, would leave the body and drift upwards toward heaven to unite with the ancestors or, for the exceptional few, to become deified. These higher souls were thought to number as many as three, called *hun*, and would become synonymous with spirits known as *shen* after death.[10] The following dialogue from the *Li Chi* represents, according to De Groot, the "fundamental theory about the human soul in a nut-shell:"[11]

> [Tsai Wo] said, "I have heard the names *Kwei* and [*Shen*], but I do not know what they mean." The Master [i.e., Confucius] said, "The (intelligent) spirit is of the [*shen*] nature, and shows that in fullest measure; the animal soul is of the *kwei* nature, and shows that in fullest measure. It is the union of *kwei* and [*shen*] that forms the highest exhibition of doctrine.
> "All the living must die, and dying, return to the ground; this is what is called *kwei*. The bones and flesh, moulder below, and, hidden away, become the earth of the fields. But the spirit [*shen*] issues forth, and is displayed on high in a condition of glorious brightness."[12]

The veneration of the ancestors was upheld as morally right in Confucian culture. Evolution of Confucianism through Mencius (Meng Tzu), the great student of Confucius, incorporated an egalitarian philosophy derived from the likes of Mo Tzu and his Moist philosophy and eventually extended the ritual observation to all levels of Chinese society. The position of Confucianism on life and death developed into a basic idea that built upon ancient beliefs, clearly summarized in the words of Yao:

> In Confucianism eternity exists in self-cultivation as well as in the collective and practical life of the family. Confucians believe that a sense of eternity can be obtained through the continuity of the family in which each generation is treated as a necessary link in the family chain and every life is considered a contribution to the huge enterprise that was initiated by the ancestors and continued by their descendants. Confucians taught that through the performance of their duties in the family, the young would obtain a sense of moral responsibility, the elderly gain respect, the dead live in the hearts of their descendants and the new-born be given a mission. In these ways an individual would last as long as his family lasted, and would acquire a sense of eternity in the midst of temporal life.[13]

The second quintessentially Chinese school of thought to emerge during The Period of The One Hundred Schools is Taoism. While Confucianism, and other schools of lesser importance, all aimed at improving the lot of humans in the turbulence of warring states, Taoism approached the problem from a completely different angle. The early Taoist texts are clearly written from the perspective of a mystic as opposed to that of a philosopher, promoting an extreme laissez-faire style of government and of living in general.

Philosophical Taoism, as this early form of it might be called for its impenetrable nature, and to distinguish it from the institutionalized religious Taoism to be discussed later, first appeared with the self-titled work of Chuang Tzu. Chuang Tzu lived and wrote the core Inner Chapters[14] during the fourth century BCE, making him a contemporary of Meng Tzu. Later chapters were added and attributed to him after his death until reaching its present form in the third century CE.[15] The text itself is a mixture of parable, metaphor, satire, and dialectic.

Unlike the pragmatism of Confucianism, Chuang Tzu presents a more esoteric path. The concept of the Tao, present in all schools of Chinese thought, is given a strictly metaphysical meaning, thereby defining philosophical Taoism itself. Here, the Tao represents an anonymous Divine Will, linked to heaven or simply nature, permeating all things. Holmes Welch illustrates the confusion in translating this term: "English translations of Tao are many: Nature (Watters), Reason (Carus), Logos (Legge), Truth (Cheng Lin), Undifferentiated Aesthetic Continuum (Northrop) and, most often, the Way."[16] It is the order of the universe and the nature of all things, including humans. In order to live well, according to Chuang Tzu, one must not strive after success, but should passively obey the Way of Tao. The concept of *wu-wei* represents this "active inaction," a doing-without-trying in ultimate harmony with the world and one's self. One is simply to do as the Way dictates without personal will or thought interfering with the natural order of things. Death is seen as but another inevitable and natural aspect of life to be accepted calmly and without fear. The following words from one of the Inner Chapters are typical of the mystical attitude found throughout the *Chuang Tzu*:

> After he had managed to see his own aloneness, he could do away with past and present, and after he had done away with past and present, he was able to enter where there is no life and no death. That which kills life does not die; that which gives life to life does not live.[17]

In the Tao, there is neither life nor death, and yet both together. Upon stating this mystical position, Chuang Tzu goes on to illustrate how such a viewpoint can be practically applied, spoken through the voice of a misshapen cripple:

> I received life because the time had come; I will lose it because the order of things passes on. Be content with this time and dwell in this order and then neither sorrow nor joy can touch you. In ancient times this was called the "freeing of the

bound." There are those who cannot free themselves, because they are bound by things. But nothing can ever win against Heaven—that's the way it's always been. What would I have to resent?[18]

In the same chapter, Chuang Tzu reports the dialogue between two wise men. One of the men, Master Lai, is nearing death and the other approaches to ask him about the impending change that will take place and what death might have in store for the living. Master Lai responds by pledging his passive acceptance of whatever may come. "A child, obeying his father and mother, goes wherever he is told, east or west, south or north."[19] He goes on to invoke the analogy of the Creator being like a skilled smithy melting down one metal object to form another.

> Now, having had the audacity to take on human form once, if I should say, "I don't want to be anything but a man! Nothing but a man!", the Creator would surely regard me as a most inauspicious sort of person. So now I think heaven and earth as a great furnace, and the Creator as a skilled smith. Where could he send me that would not be all right? I will go off to sleep peacefully, and then with a start I will wake up.[20]

Chuang Tzu encourages the reader to accept death with the same passive contentment that he encourages one to accept all things in life. Chuang Tzu differs from the general agnosticism of Confucius toward an afterlife only in placing a trusting faith in the workings of the Tao. There is no detailed speculation upon what is to come after death, only a calm obeisance to the natural order.

The Outer Chapters of the *Chuang Tzu* repeat much of what is said in the first chapters, however there is some insight provided, albeit limited, into the fate of the dead. Chapter 18 describes Chuang Tzu himself finding a skull on the ground outside as he is lying down to sleep. In his dreams, the same skull speaks to him and offers to reveal the state of being after death, and Chuang Tzu consents to listen. The skull explains:

> Among the dead there are no rulers above, no subjects below, and no chores of the four seasons. With nothing to do, our spring and autumns are as endless as heaven and earth. A king facing south on his throne could have no more happiness than this![21]

This brief description gives the immediate impression of a bleak afterlife "with nothing to do." Chuang Tzu responds in disbelief by stating that surely the skull must pine for its body and life on earth. The skull answers adamantly, "Why would I throw away more happiness than that of a king on a throne and take on the troubles of a human being again?"[22] Evidently, the postmortem existence is one of blissful stasis and total harmony with nature and the universe, far removed from the worries of day-to-day life shared by all humans whether king or pauper.

The second eminent text of Taoism is the *Tao Te Ching*, attributed to the pen of Lao Tzu. It is now highly doubted that Lao Tzu was in fact an historical figure, but seems instead to be a mythical one. He is mentioned as a character in the *Chuang Tzu*, and was thus thought to predate the writer of that work. The man, whether he ever existed or not, is considered to have lived between 600 and 500 BCE, while the book attributed to him was not penned until the third or fourth century BCE. Whoever the author of the *Tao Te Ching* was, the text has become central to Taoism in all its forms just as Lao Tzu has become a central figure in its mythology.

The *Tao Te Ching* echoes the sentiments of Chuang Tzu in the following succinct statement on death:

> Tao endures.
> Your body dies.
> There is no danger.[23]

Simply, the death of the body is unavoidable, but so long as one bears in mind the overbearing unity of all things in the Tao, there is no fear. Death is but another change in an infinite evolution of forms. And so, the philosophical Taoist point of view urges a passive acceptance of death as simply another aspect of nature.

It should be pointed out that just as Confucius accepted the worship of ancestors, albeit with a pragmatic caveat, these early Taoists accepted the existence of spirits and ghosts, though with reservations as well. Certainly, especially when taking into account the often satirical style of the *Chuang Tzu*, tales such as that of the skull appearing in a dream cannot be taken as anything more than parables. There are other appearances of ghosts in the work of Chuang Tzu, as well. For instance, there is the story of Duke Huan who, while out in the marshes with his carriage driver Kuan Chung, thought he saw a ghost. The result of this trauma was that the Duke immediately became very ill, and feared he would soon die as a result of the ghostly curse. A wise man appears and declares to the Duke that he is causing his own problems for a ghost cannot harm a man. The Duke then asks whether ghosts actually exist at all, and the answer he receives is that they certainly do. The wise man then goes on to list a number of different types of spirits and ghosts. One in particular catches the attention of Duke Huan, who asks for a more detailed description of it. The wise man describes the spirit, adding that any who should see it would one day become a ruler. The Duke's mood improves instantly as he exclaims, "*That* must have been what I saw!" Though he barely noticed any more, his illness was coincidentally cured upon his acceptance of this explanation.[24] Obviously, there is a not-so-subtly-implied skepticism toward the apparition, and an outright rejection of any ghostly influence on humankind even if they did truly exist. It appears that here, as in Confucianism, there is the recognition of the traditional beliefs in ancestors, though it is obvious that such beliefs are viewed with amusement as superstition.

A range of practices coalesced under the banner of Taoism toward the end of Chuang Tzu's time with the common goal of discovering the secret of physical immortality. Henri Maspero argues that these various branches of Taoism were always a consistent group integrating a number of ideas that sometimes seem contradictory.[25] Whether these disparate ideas formed an evolving movement or the coming together of various schools under the same banner will not be argued here, however, but the important ideas emerging under the title of Taoism will be discussed separately for the sake of clarity. This eclectic group drew inspiration from philosophical Taoism, but doubtlessly misunderstood the central message of the works as discussed previously. Where the message Chuang Tzu and Lao Tzu sought to inculcate was that life and death are natural processes both to be embraced, these other all-too-human Taoists focused upon the fact that death would mark the end of life and therefore should be staved off indefinitely. Certainly, some passages in Chuang Tzu's work can be seen as encouragement to search for eternal life, such as the following line that equates happiness with life: "Perfect happiness, keeping alive—only inaction gets you close to this!"[26] To interpret this literally, however, is to miss the ultimate point of philosophical Taoism.

Of the practices aimed at lengthening humankind's allotted time on earth, a complex system of meditative breathing exercises and yoga-like body postures is mentioned in the *Chuang Tzu*.

> To pant, to puff, to hail, to sip, to spit out the old breath and draw in the new, practising bear-hangings and bird-stretchings, longevity is his only concern—such is the life favored by the scholar who practices Induction, the man who nourishes his body, who hopes to live to be as old as P'eng-tsu.[27]

These breathing exercises were aimed at inhaling enough good air to nourish the tiny gods or spirits that dwelt within each person. Holding one's breath for extended periods of time would keep the good air available to these inner gods for a longer period of time. If the adherent could hold his breath long enough—reported to be up to several hours at a time—the inner gods would eventually project themselves outside the body in order to communicate with the practitioner. It was the well-being of these gods that would enable the individual to live longer on this earth.

James Legge represents a different school of thinking from that of Maspero, arguing that passages such as that just quoted refer to an older Taoist tradition extending back thousands of years.[28] While Maspero argues for the contiguity of these various Taoist forms, it is clear that they did not all come together under one banner until much later in Chinese history. Certainly, the quotation from Chuang Tzu mentions the breathing exercises and yogic posturing of this so-called Hygiene School, but the context is one of mockery and not support for its methods.

Other passages seem to reinforce the notion that accepting the Tao would bring exceptionally long life. One of the Inner Chapters recites a long list of mythical individuals who are said to have gained insight into the workings of the Tao and subsequently to have had long or even eternal lives. Among those who have become immortal are the anthropomorphized Sun, Moon, and stars, as well as the mythic Yellow Emperor. Others have attained extraordinarily long life spans, including the Chinese Methuselah, P'eng-tsu, whose life spanned nineteen centuries. When one ignores the concept of transcendence in which life and death are both overcome in total harmony with the Tao, such passages can be taken literally as placing an emphasis on attaining immortality.

Alongside the Hygiene School, there appeared also a school of alchemy aimed at discovering the elixir of life. Not very much is known of Tsou Yen, the man to whom the founding of Taoist alchemy is normally attributed. He was active around the year 325 BCE, and propounded a philosophy that stressed the importance of the Five Elements: wood, fire, earth, metal, and water. By the second century BCE, his followers, the *fang-shih*, were well-known as magicians with powers over the spirit world who sought to uncover the recipe for an elixir of eternal life. They integrated the spiritual beliefs of traditional shamanism and the ancestor cults with both the theories of the Five Elements and the texts of philosophical Taoism, however misunderstood. When they gained entry to the courts of the early Han Emperors, they persuaded the rulers to accept their ideas and fund alchemical experiments and great journeys to locate P'eng-Lai, and other Isles of the Blest, whereupon those who knew the secrets of immortality lived.

Chuang Tzu mentions P'eng-Lai as well as special beings known as Immortals, the *hsien*, though seemingly only as allegorical devices. Chapter 12 contains a brief description of the eventual fate of a "true sage": "And after a thousand years, should he weary of the world, he will leave it and ascend to the immortals, riding on those white clouds all the way up to the village of God."[29] Elsewhere, the typical *hsien* is described as living the life of a hermit in the mountains, living off of nothing but dew and air, while climbing into the clouds and riding a flying dragon.[30] Though these passages demand critical interpretation, they have been taken quite literally and incorporated with existing folk tales of spiritual beings and legendary dwelling places to form a philosophy of possible immortality quite unlike what appears to have been the intention in the philosophical branch of Taoism.

Alchemy took on an established role in 133 BCE when the wizard Li Shao-chun convinced the Han Emperor, Wu Ti, of the need to transform cinnabar into gold.[31] Li Shao-chun described himself as an immortal, claiming to have lived for centuries, thus lending his claims the authority necessary. Rather than react with utter shock when the wizard actually died himself, Wu Ti explained that Li Shao-chun had simply transformed himself into another form and departed, much like the "true sage." This outward appearance of death was enacted so as not to disturb the everyday world of ordinary people who had yet to attain immortality. If the grave of such an immortal were to be examined after burial, all that would be found would be a robe and a cane or sword, the body having lived on.[32]

One can plainly see where these variant schools of Taoism diverge from the teachings of Lao Tzu and Chuang Tzu. The censure of any discussion of an afterlife in order to focus upon this life led to a quest for physical immortality. The mystical transcendence of everyday reality becomes a spiritual ascendance from eventual death to eternal life. This is not to say that the search for immortality grows directly out of a misunderstanding of philosophical Taoism. As stated previously, it is likely that many of these ideas existed before either of the key texts discussed had been written. Still, later Taoists of all colors turned to the *Tao Te Ching* and *Chuang Tzu* for inspiration and authority, if only nominally. Kenneth Ch'en argues that adherents of these practices chose for themselves the name of Taoism in order to garner a certain degree of respectability.[33]

Confucianism was also forced to adapt under the pressure of popular ideas and practices. Toward the end of the third century BCE, China was unified under the ill-fated Ch'in dynasty, which managed, during its short reign, to transform Chinese government from the feudal system supported by Confucius into a highly bureaucratic hierarchy under the rigid school of Legalist thought. Though the Ch'in were in power for only fifteen years, the bureaucracy they introduced came to define the government of China into the twenty-first century. The early Han dynasty, coming into force in 207 BCE, installed Confucianism as the state religion, though in so doing they altered the face of it and its central tenets.

Just as Taoism had grown to incorporate a number of varying elements, the Han Synthesis forced Confucianism to become a more eclectic philosophy. Perhaps as a means of placating as many people as possible, or perhaps for purely benevolent governmental purposes, this neo-Confucianism added such esoterica as *yin* and *yang*, the Five Elements, and astrology to its core beliefs. This likely provided the kind of intellectual setting of tolerance that fostered the alchemical search for immortality and the nautical quests for the magical island upon which those who already attained it dwelt.

Around the time that these developments in Chinese thought were taking place, Buddhism was carried onto the scene via the silk trade routes. While it is most likely that Buddhist ideas would have circulated for some time shortly before the turn of the millennium, the first Chinese Buddhist texts do not appear until 67 CE. Buddhist missionaries imported the popular Mahayana tradition and translated their texts into Chinese. The translators availed themselves of Taoist terminology, which lent itself more readily to the mystical message of Buddhism, leading to an early perception of Mahayana Buddhism as yet another form of Taoism. In reality, both Buddhism and Taoism intermingled and incorporated certain elements from each other.

The idea that the individual consciousness was but an illusion created by an aggregate of elements in constant transition was central to Buddhism in India. The Chinese could either not understand or not accept the notion of non-self, so Buddhism in China taught the indestructibility of personal identity as it passed through numerous rebirths depending upon one's karma instead. In turn, one's karma was defined by how harmonious one's relationship was with the Tao. In this way, death still represented the kind of change from one state to another depicted in the *Chuang Tzu*, and the prospect of rebirth was looked upon as a continuation of the physical life so cherished. So enveloping was the identification of Buddhism with Taoism that an early tradition even claimed that Lao Tzu had traveled West to India and was identified there as the original Buddha. This ability of Buddhists to adapt to the Chinese climate enabled the faith to gain a foothold in the country and to grow into one of the three religions of China. By the second century CE, due to a continuous translation of Indian texts, Buddhism was strong enough to proclaim its independence as a legitimate train of thought distinct from Taoism, though altered by years of co-opting the latter's terminology.

Just as Buddhism was coming into its own as a recognized mode of religious thought, Taoism went through yet another major transition. In 142 CE a man named Chang Tao-ling, of whom very little is known, claimed to have received a divine message directly from the deified Lao Tzu. Through this revelation, Chang Tao-ling was granted the title *T'ien Shih*, or Heavenly Master, and thus became the founder of the first institutionalized religious form of Taoism. He is said to have been able to perform faith healings and exorcisms, and to have been given the elixir of immortality. The Way of the Heavenly Master, as the Taoist Church is also known, found enormous popular support alongside Buddhism as the two continued to borrow heavily from one another.

Since Chang Tao-ling, the title of Heavenly Master has been handed down to selected initiates into the present day. Throughout the history of religious Taoism, further revelations have been received and a lengthy Taoist Canon, the *Tao Tsang*, which spans over a thousand volumes, has been written. Often, the texts of religious Taoism were written in a trance state using automatic writing, the divinity using the adept's hand to write the Canon personally. Spirit mediumship has been, and continues to be, a part of Chinese religious life since time immemorial. More will be said of the common use of such mediums.

The main appeal of the Taoist Church for the common person was the element of individual salvation. Before Buddhism entered China, the prevailing belief in the state beyond death was an anonymous one in which individuals were simply absorbed into the ancestral family collective. Spirits might interfere in the world of the living, but only if the requisite rituals of remembrance and sacrifice were ignored, and then only out of some base instinct for ancestral survival. For many, such a prospect seemed increasingly bleak, encouraging an educated few to seek physical immortality. The revelation to Chang Tao-ling revealed that immortality was achievable by every person, and that it was not, in fact, a continued physical existence but a spiritual immortality to which one would depart upon the death of the body. Centuries later, the eleventh century Heavenly Master, Chang Po-tuan, argued that alchemical terms were not to be taken literally, but that an inner transformation was to be inferred. In this way, the elements of lead and mercury were defined as the symbols of yang and yin respectively, and the search for immortality was placed in a wholly spiritual context of self-transformation.[34] The Chinese interpretation of Buddhism had introduced the concept of postmortem immortality, and religious Taoism incorporated this idea enthusiastically into the Chinese culture.

The Mahayana concept of the bodhisattva, an individual who had attained enlightenment but withheld personal salvation in order to aid the rest of humanity in achieving the same, appealed to the masses in China as it had in India. These beings were looked upon as minor divinities, like the immortal *hsien*, who would attentively listen to entreating prayers by the faithful. Taoism countered with the addition of *T'ien Tsun*, Heavenly Elders who form a divine hierarchy and listen to the prayers of devotees and who mercifully sought the salvation of all humankind.[35] The *T'ien Tsun*, like the bodhisattvas, were for the most part former mortals who attained immortality (*hsien*) and vowed to ensure that others could do the same. Again following Buddhism, the attainment of immortality was often considered to require multiple lifetimes. Lao Tzu, who himself was said to have incarnated a multitude of times since well before the construction of heaven and Earth, is but one of these beings atop an ever-growing hierarchy of divinities.

Buddhism in China experienced a major development in 402 CE, when Hui-yuan, a former Taoist and Confucian who had wholly converted to Buddhism, gathered one hundred and twenty-three of his followers together to make a vow before the bodhisattva Amitabha, also known as Amida especially in Japan,[36] to be reborn in the Western Paradise, or Pure Land. And so, with this legendary pledge, the Pure Land school of Buddhism was born.[37] While the Mahayana notion of bodhisattvas had already elaborated upon the existence of so-called Buddha-lands, multiple heavens, as well as hells for that matter, the determined devotion to one specific figure, and his realm, endemic to the Pure Land sect has been described as the "paradigmatic example of a well developed Mahayana view of the afterlife."[38]

Of the three main texts of Pure Land Buddhism, the *Larger* and *Smaller sutras* (*Wu-liang-shou ching* and *A-mi-t'o ching* respectively) originated in India, while the third shows the distinct Chinese influences of the fifth century CE, and is called the *Meditation sutra*, or *Kuan Wu-liang-shou ching*. The older sutras describe how the bodhisattva Dharmakara vowed to forgo his own entrance into *nirvana* until every person who called him to mind had first entered before him, and in so doing became the Amitabha Buddha. According to his vow, the mere act of invoking the name of Amitabha, or Amida, at the moment of death would enable one to be reborn in the Pure Land of his Western paradise. The *Larger sutra* describes the Pure Land in similar terms to those of other Mahayana heavens. It is a realm of eternal light, filled with lakes and rivers. Flowers bloom in abundance while jewels grow upon trees and music whistles through their branches. Evil is nonexistent and there is no need for food to survive.[39] Being born into the Pure Land was seen as a stepping stone before the inevitable entrance into *nirvana*, but the sensual images of paradise appeal much more readily to the more immediate concerns of the average person.

The *Meditation sutra* points out that these heavenly realms are not mere fantasies, but places that can be seen through the practice of sincere meditation. Through practicing various visualization techniques, anyone can receive visions of the world to come. Similarly, it is crucial to continue the meditative process on one's deathbed and focus the mind on the image of Amitabha, while reciting his name. Much as it is in Tibetan Buddhism, the thoughts of the dying are paramount to determining the fate of the individual after death. The *Meditation sutra* describes how different types of meditation, and varying levels of faith, will result in different deathbed experiences. To the most accomplished meditators, Amitabha appears in his full brilliance. Others see only flowers and splendid colors, while the lowest of the worthy must first get a brief taste of hell before being reborn in the Pure Land.[40] Additionally, Carl Becker explains that due to the importance placed upon the state of mind at the moment of death, detailed descriptions of deathbed visions were recorded. The *Ching-t'u-lun* lists twenty accounts of deathbed visions in which monks as well as laypeople report seeing various spiritual beings approach from the other world. Included is one report in which even those present saw the Buddha appear to the dying Master.[41] Alternate visions involve the appearance of Kuan-yin, the popular companion of Amitabha, who then plays the role of *psychopomp*, leading the dead into the Pure Land.[42] In any event, all of these reports are meant to impress upon the populace the fact that rebirth in the Western paradise is an empirical fact experienced by many believers. Though the Pure Land sect became widely popular in its own right in both China and, later, Japan, Buddhist ideas entered the popular imagination through its interaction with Taoism and traditional beliefs.

As both Taoism and Buddhism grew alongside each other, borrowing ideas, terminology, and even deities from one another, the beliefs increasingly overlapped to the point where the average Chinese person now feels free to follow both systems interchangeably. Confucianism was also integrated with Taoism to form a union of ideas known as Dark or Mysterious Learning. The tale of sixth century CE scholar, Fu Hsi, who was renowned for his flamboyant manner, provides an excellent allegory for the intermingling of philosophical schools. He was said to go about wearing a Taoist cap, Buddhist scarf, and Confucian shoes. When the Emperor of the time saw him, he was brought to ask the scholar if he were a Buddhist. In response, Fu Hsi simply pointed at his cap. The Emperor then asked if he were a Taoist, to which the scholar pointed at his shoes. When the Emperor then asked if he were a Confucian, Fu Hsi pointed to his scarf, thus signifying that he was none of the three individually but all three together.[43] With this in mind, it is necessary to therefore speak more generally of Chinese beliefs as a whole with only passing reference to the possible roots of individual beliefs.

As David Jordan states the problem: "All three of these strains, Taoism, Buddhism, and folk religion, have contributed heavily to Chinese religious life, and their interpenetration is so extensive as to prevent a thoroughgoing sorting of the elements one might associate with each in its 'primal' state."[44] The typical Chinese person will draw upon all of the sources discussed in formulating their conception of their fate after death. Traditional sacrifices to the ancestors are maintained as families feel a strict filial duty to continue the rituals propounded by Confucius. The details of these rituals are outlined in the Confucian classics for all to read.[45] Food is seen as a particularly good form of sacrifice, and it is normally laid out as a meal for the deceased. Upon death, the individual is thought to have at least two spirits. There are varying accounts of exactly how many spirits reside in one person's body, however, which may stem from attempts to accommodate the variety of traditions. In any event, one of these souls is considered to reside in a special tablet reserved for that purpose and which is used as a representative in the sacrifices. The belief remains that in sacrificing to the ancestors, these spirits will in turn bring blessings to the living family. On the other hand, failure to carry out the appropriate rituals will result in the spirits becoming angry and malicious. In addition, those who have died violent or lonely deaths, or who have no family to carry out the requisite rites, become particularly nasty and vengeful. Calamities such as a collapsed or burnt house, or worse still, illness and death, such as was feared by Duke Huan in the previous example, would all be attributed to troubled spirits.[46] Many other examples of such spectral encounters exist throughout Chinese history and literature.

David Jordan provides a modern tale of a haunted building near Tainan. Five men decided to stay in the building to test their mettle. The ghost of an old beggar woman appeared and in their fright they attacked her with clubs, at which she vanished. Subsequently, the men all became ill. Four of the men returned to the house to beg forgiveness and offer sacrifices to her. They got better forthwith, while the fifth man is said to remain ill "to this day" for his stubbornness.[47] There are also many other tales of benevolent spirits that help friends in exams, reveal hidden money, or simply appear to console the living.[48]

There is a long-standing tradition of communicating with the spirits, often as a means of determining the cause of certain afflictions or the reasons for a certain spirit's rage. Indeed, it has been said that spiritualism of this kind forms the core of Chinese religious practice in many parts of the country today.[49] Under the guidance of a special priest, known as a *tang-ki*, a group of people can be "transported" to the spirit world.[50] Typically, the priest effectively hypnotizes those who wish to contact the dead and guides them through what they perceive as the realm of spirits. Other methods of entering an altered state are also found, such as the inebriation of the spirit medium.[51] In other cases, the priest might go into a trance himself—these priestly mediums are most often males—and channel a spirit or even a god, as is the case with the divinely inspired Taoist Canon. Various types of ouija board-type implements, like using a stylus or a miniature spirit-throne to spell out characters, are employed in efforts to communicate with the dead as well.[52] While the communications with gods may often be aimed at receiving some kind of divine revelation or guidance, messages from the dead for the most part revolve around the consolation of the living. One example of such a spiritual message comes from the spirit of a 70-year-old woman who had been summoned to speak to her son:

It is a happy thing that I died a natural death; It is a result of good accumulated in my last life; Happily my case has been noticed, and I have asked for immediate reincarnation.

Already I have the document and am only waiting for my turn to say farewell to the Tenth Judge.[53]

And so, messages such as this illustrate a seeming paradox in belief, for on the one hand the dead are thought to reside in the funeral tablet until they eventually merge into the ancestral community, while on the other hand the Buddhist notion of rebirth insists upon the reincarnation of each individual, and not necessarily in the form of a human. One possible explanation might be an equation between *nirvana* and the ancestral unity, though this is not a typical formulation of the ideas. Instead, the common Chinese person is inclined today to simply accept both possibilities as existing somehow side by side.

One of the spiritual elements of every person is thought to enter the underworld at death to receive judgment before their eventual rebirth in this world or some heavenly paradise, such as the Pure Land. This underworld is constructed in the rigid bureaucracy that has become characteristic of Chinese government.[54] A being known as Ch'eng-huang is the first to be seen. His job is to evaluate the extent to which the deceased has lived a balanced life. Depending upon one's sins, each person would be directed to one of ten, or sometimes eighteen, levels of hell. These levels of hell are variously described, with such gruesome tortures as being hung upside down, being shredded, ground to dust, burnt, boiled, frozen, or being forced to eat filth, blood, or excrement.[55] Prayers, often incorporating other ancestral sacrifices, from the living can be used to ease the sufferings of the dead and speed them to rebirth. In any event, a certain amount of purgation is necessary for the average person between each new birth.[56]

Normally, nothing is remembered from one life to another, either of the previous lifetime or of the tortures in between as people are instructed to imbibe a concoction inducing forgetfulness. Still, some accounts appear of past-life memories. For instance, an eighth century story tells of one Ku Huang, whose son died at the young age of seventeen. Witnessing the intense sorrow of his father, the son appeared to him and promised to be reborn as another son in his family. Upon being reborn, the son remembered nothing until, at the age of seven, a slap from his older brother prompted him to exclaim, "I am *your* elder brother, why do you beat me?" After this, he remembered all of the details of his past life, and amazed his family with the accuracy of what he knew.[57]

In addition to the spirit's continued survival after death, there is also a consistent belief in the ability of the spirit to leave the body while still alive. One of the legendary Taoist deities collectively known as the Eight Immortals, Li T'ieh Kuai, also called Iron-Crutch Li, was originally a sage who asked a disciple to mind his body while he traveled into the spirit world for several days. Due to the negligence of his charge, when Li returned he found his body destroyed and was forced to occupy that of a crippled beggar who had recently died himself.[58] De Groot discusses the possibility of regular people having the ability to depart the body in order to glean information from distant locations as well.[59] An example of this appears in the story of Ch'ien-pu, the son of a military official called Fan Wen-cheng, who was said to be capable of traveling to the distant headquarters of the enemy in order to spy.[60]

In conclusion, the development of Chinese thought on life after death has led to an intricate system in which the various spirits that make up every person disperse at death. One aspect remains in a funerary tablet where it receives ritual sacrifices from the living family members. These rituals are necessary to the well being of the spirits, and can help them to be reborn into paradise more quickly. Spirits enter a bureaucratic system of purgation designed to punish transgressions against a balanced and harmonious existence. Being in perfect harmony with the Tao will allow a person to bypass the cycle of rebirth and achieve spiritual immortality in a Heavenly Paradise, while some aspect of the individual also merges into an ancestral community. The Pure Land sect of Buddhism provides a special means of attaining the heavenly state. And so, the three religions of China come together so as to form a very intricate system of belief in the fate of humans after bodily death.

Notes

1. Jordan Paper, *The Spirits are Drunk* (New York: SUNYP, 1995), pp. 7–8.

2. J. J. M. De Groot, *The Religious System of China*, 6 vols. (Leiden: E. J. Brill, 1892–1910), vol. 1, pp. 21–22.

3. See David Keightly, "The Religious Commitment: Shang Theology and the Genesis of Chinese Political Culture," *History of Religions* 17 (1978), pp. 211–225, cited in Meir Shahar and Robert P. Weller, *Unruly Gods: Divinity and Society in China* (Honolulu: University of Hawaii Press, 1996), p. 4.

4. For example, see Jessica Rawson, ed., *Mysteries of Ancient China* (New York: George Braziller, 1996), p. 87.

5. Charles F. Emmons, *Chinese Ghosts and ESP* (Metuchen, NJ: Scarecrow, 1982), p. 72.

6. For much detailed information on the specifics of ancestor worship in China, see Emily M. Ahern, *The Cult of the Dead in a Chinese Village* (Stanford, CA: Stanford University Press, 1973).

7. Xinzhong Yao, *An Introduction to Confucianism* (Cambridge, UK: Cambridge University Press, 2000), p. 7.

8. Confucius, *Analects*, trans. James Legge (1893; New York: Globusz Publishing, n.d.) http://www.globusz.com/ebooks/ConfucianAnalects/. (accessed February 11, 2008).

9. Kristofer Schipper, *The Taoist Body*, trans. Karen C. Duval (Berkeley, CA: University of California Press, 1993), p. 6.

10. Henri Maspero discusses these various souls, and mentions the *Pao-p'u-tzu*, an early alchemical text, as an early source for such beliefs. Henri Maspero, *Taoism and Chinese Religion*, trans. Frank A. Kierman, Jr. (Amherst: University of Massachusetts Press, 1981), pp. 266–267.

11. De Groot, *The Religious System of China*, vol. 4, p. 4.

12. *The Book of Rites*, James Legge, trans. Sacred Books of the East, vol. 28 (Oxford: Oxford University Press, 1885), Part 2, Book 21, Section 2, p. 220.

13. Yao, *An Introduction to Confucianism*, p. 204.

14. These are the first seven chapters of the *Chuang Tzu* as we see it now.

15. Chuang Tzu, *The Complete Works of Chuang Tzu*, trans. Burton Watson (New York: Columbia University Press, 1968), p. 13.

16. Holmes Welch, *Taoism: The Parting of the Way* (Boston: Beacon Press, 1965), p. 86.

17. Chuang Tzu, *Complete Works*, Chapter 6, p. 83.

18. Chuang Tzu, *Complete Works*, Chapter 6, pp. 84–85.

19. Chuang Tzu, *Complete Works*, Chapter 6, p. 85.

20. Chuang Tzu, *Complete Works*, Chapter 6, p. 85.

21. Chuang Tzu, *Complete Works*, Chapter 18, p. 193.

22. Chuang Tzu, *Complete Works*, Chapter 18, pp. 193–194.

23. Lao Tzu, *Tao Te Ching*, trans. Stephen Addiss and Stanley Lombardo (Indianapolis: Hackett, 1993), p. 16.

24. Chuang Tzu, *Complete Works*, Chapter 19, pp. 203–204.

25. Maspero, *Taoism and Chinese Religion*.

26. Chuang Tzu, *Complete Works*, Chapter 18, p. 191.

27. Chuang Tzu, *Complete Works*, Chapter 15, pp. 167–168.

28. James Legge, trans., *The Texts of Taoism*, Sacred Books of the East, Vol. 39 (1891; repr., New York: Dover, 1962), pp. 1–5.

29. Chuang Tzu, *Complete Works*, Chapter 12, p. 130.

30. Chuang Tzu, *Complete Works*, Chapter 1, p. 33.

31. Welch, *Taoism*, p. 99.

32. Welch, *Taoism*, p. 102.

33. Kenneth K. S. Ch'en, *Buddhism in China* (Princeton, NJ: Princeton University Press, 1964), p. 25.

34. Carl Jung later seized upon the notion of inner alchemy, seeing the whole process as analogous of his theory of archetypes and the individuation of the self. See C. G. Jung, *Jung on Alchemy*, ed. Nathan Schwart-Salant (Princeton, NJ: Princeton University Press, 1995).

35. Welch, *Taoism*, pp. 135–136.

36. Japanese beliefs are not being considered in the present study, though many of the particulars bear a striking similarity to Chinese beliefs, those in Japan having been influenced by their larger neighbors. Ancestor worship appears in Japanese culture in a similar form to that in China: Robert J. Smith, *Ancestor Worship in Contemporary Japan* (Stanford, CA: Stanford University Press, 1974). A good introduction to Shintoism, the indigenous religion of Japan, can be found in John Breen and Mark Teeuwen, eds. *Shinto in History* (Richmond, UK: Curzon, 2000). An overall study of the mixture of religious beliefs in Japan can be found in Ichiro Hori, et al., eds. *Japanese Religion* (Tokyo: Kodansha International, 1972); also Ian Reader, *Religion in Contemporary Japan* (Honolulu: University of Hawaii Press, 1991). An excellent study of beliefs and experiences relating to death and the afterlife can be found in Carmen Blacker, *The Catalpa Bow* (London: George Allen & Unwin, 1975).

37. The facts of the founding of the Pure Land sect by Hui-yuan are more legendary than fact, but the story is the traditional one. For historical details, see: Ch'en, *Buddhism in China*, pp. 106–108. For a more recent account of the Japanese stream of Pure Land, see Mark Laurence Blum, *The Origins and Development of Pure Land Buddhism: A Study and Translation of Gyonen's Jodo Homon Genrusho* (New York: Oxford University Press, 2002).

38. Carl B. Becker, *Breaking the Circle: Death and the Afterlife in Buddhism* (Carbondale and Edwardsville, IL: Southern Illinois University Press, 1993), p. 52.

39. Fujita Kotatsu, "Pure Land Buddhism in India," trans. Taitetsu Unno, in *The Pure Land Tradition: History and Development*, eds. James Foard, Michael Solomon, and Richard K. Payne (Berkeley, CA: Regents of the University of California, 1996), p. 22.

40. Carl B. Becker, "The Pure Land Revisited: Sino-Japanese Meditations and Near-Death Experiences of the Next World," *Anabiosis–The Journal for Near-Death Studies* 4 (1984), p. 58.

41. Becker, *Breaking the Circle*, p. 74.

42. For instance, see Reginald Fleming Johnston, *Buddhist China* (1913; repr., San Francisco, CA: Chinese Materials Center, 1976), pp. 100–109.

43. Johnston, *Buddhist China*, p. 3.

44. David K. Jordan, *Gods, Ghosts, and Ancestors* (Berkeley, CA: University of California Press, 1972), p. 27.

45. The minutiae to which these rituals are carried out is detailed in the following paper: Patricia Ebrey, "The Liturgies for Sacrifices to Ancestors in Successive Versions of the Family Rituals," in *Ritual and Scripture in Chinese Popular Religion*, ed. David Johnson (Berkeley, CA: Chinese Popular Culture Project: Distributed by IEAS Publications, 1995), pp. 104–136.

46. Francis L. K. Hsu, *Under the Ancestors' Shadow* (New York: Doubleday, 1967), p. 38.

47. Jordan, *Gods, Ghosts, and Ancestors*, pp. 33–34.

48. For some excellent compendiums of Chinese ghost stories, see the following: Herbert A. Giles, trans. *Strange Stories from a Chinese Studio* (London: T. Werner Laurie, 1916), which has been described as the Arabian Nights of the Asian world; Yuan Mei, *Censored by Confucius*, trans. and eds. Kam Louie and Louise Edwards (Armonk, NY: M. E. Sharpe, 1996), which contains 100 stories from the eighteenth century.

49. Hock Tong Cheu, *The Nine Emperor Gods: A Study of Chinese Spirit-Medium Cults* (Singapore: Times Books International, 1988), p. xi.

50. Ahern, *The Cult of the Dead*, pp. 229–235.

51. Paper, *The Spirits are Drunk*, pp. 111–120.

52. Jordan, *Gods, Ghosts, and Ancestors*, pp. 64–84, describes the use of a small spirit-throne as a means of contacting the dead. A similar device is described in Wei-pang Chao, "The Origin and Growth of the Fu Chi," *Folklore Studies* 1, pp. 9–27, cited in Graeme Lang and Lars Ragvald, *The Rise of a Refugee God* (Hong Kong: Oxford University Press, 1993), pp. 186–187.

53. Hsu, *Under the Ancestors' Shadow*, p. 174.

54. Francis L. K. Hsu, *Under the Ancestors' Shadow* (New York: Doubleday, 1967), p. 174.

55. Anne Swann Goodrich, *Chinese Hells* (St. Augustine, FL: Monumenta Serica, 1981).

56. Stephen Teiser details the development of this purgatory in Chinese belief in the following text: Stephen F. Teiser, *The Scripture of the Ten Kings* (Honolulu: University of Hawaii Press, 1994).

57. G. Willoughby-Meade, *Chinese Ghouls and Goblins* (London: Constable, 1928), p. 77.

58. T. C. Lai, *The Eight Immortals* (Hong Kong: Swindown, 1972), pp. 22–23.

59. De Groot, *The Religious System of China*, vol. 4, p. 103.

60. Willoughby-Meade, *Chinese Ghouls and Goblins*, p. 10.

PART TWO

AN OVERVIEW OF THE RESEARCH INTO EXPERIENCES OF AN AFTERLIFE

CHAPTER EIGHT

~

Mediumship

During the early months of 1848, strange knocking sounds began to be heard in the New York home of Mr. J. D. Fox and his family.[1] These sounds continued unabated for quite some time, disturbing the sleep of everyone in the household and generally putting the entire family on edge. Finally, a frustrated Mrs. Fox, with her daughters, began to attempt communication with the invisible mischief-maker, whom they believed to be a ghost. With the desperate hopes of putting an end to the whole affair and regaining peace of mind, not to mention a good night's sleep, firmly in mind, they were shocked and amazed when they actually received intelligent replies to their queries. A system was worked out whereby the "spirit" would answer questions with yes or no answers; for instance, knocking once for "yes" and twice for "no." It seemed that the two youngest girls, Katie and Maggie, were the focus of the communications, and they were the ones who assumed the role of asking the questions. The spirit claimed to be one Charles Rosa, murdered and buried in the basement of the Fox's home by a former owner, named John Bell. Later digging in the cellar uncovered what were reportedly human teeth, hair, and bones.[2] The local press had a field day with this story. Word of the Fox sisters' amazing ability spread like wildfire through the area, then the whole of America, and finally on to England and Europe. As word spread, others discovered that they too had the ability to communicate with discarnate entities in the same way that the young girls could. A great number of so-called mediums (named for the fact that the individual becomes the medium through which a discarnate spirit might communicate) began to appear all over. These mediums performed for audiences and in private, impressing the masses with dramatic displays and convincing many that the dead were in fact the true source of each medium's fantastic powers. This soon led to an entire religious movement based about these mediums, called Spiritualism. Still active today, its main tenet is that the immortality of the human soul can actually be proven through these ostensible communications with the dead.

Spiritualist mediums, as the conduits through which spirits proved their existence, first performed using similar techniques to those employed by the Fox sisters. The simple rappings and knockings were later supplemented by increasingly sophisticated methods. To prove the existence of spirits, mediums typically utilized such techniques as table-tipping, *ouija* boards (or the similar *planchette*), levitation, apports, discarnate voices speaking, and even the appearance of ghostly hands, faces, or entire beings. These so-called "physical mediums," named for their use of physical manifestations, often operated in the dark, supposedly to maintain the delicate integrity of "ectoplasm," the ethereal material of which the spirits and their apports were formed. While conducting séances in darkened rooms enhanced the mediums' performances by creating an ambiance akin to watching a scary movie with the lights out, this feature also incited many skeptics to allege fraud. As shall be shown, this claim was justified more often than not.

Alongside the physical mediums was another kind of medium, known as "mental mediums." These mediums stemmed in large part from the absorption by the Spiritualist movement of its precursor, the practice of Mesmerism. Modern hypnotism traces its roots to Franz Anton Mesmer and what he termed "animal magnetism." Subjects were induced into trance by the mesmerist, in a similar fashion to that of hypnotists today. It was thought that the mesmerist could then influence the subject through a transfer of mystical, and invisible, fluids, or energies, from the mesmerist to the subject. The trance state thus induced was also found to be conducive to spirit communication. While in a state of trance, varying from a slight change of perception to complete unconsciousness, the mental medium thus claims to actually see, hear, or be completely possessed by the spirit of some deceased entity. While, on the one hand, physical mediums provided displays supposedly demonstrating the presence and powers of discarnate agents, mental mediums offered direct communication with the dead. Some mediums might have employed a combination of these two techniques. As a source for proof of an afterlife, the methods of mental mediumship have proved themselves much more fruitful than those of physical mediumship.

Mediumistic phenomena have appeared throughout time, as has been shown throughout the preceding chapters. On the topic of the historical occurrence of such phenomena, William James points out:

We suppose that "mediumship" originated in Rochester, New York, and animal magnetism with Mesmer; but one look behind the pages of official history, in personal memoirs, legal documents, and popular narratives and books of anecdote, and you will find that there never was a time when these things were not reported just as abundantly as now.[3]

What is important to bear in mind is that the events at the Fox residence, combined with the work of Mesmer and his ilk, brought these phenomena to the attention of the general populace in a way that had not been seen for some time in a society increasingly reliant on materialistic modes of thought.

As the appearance of such phenomena spread and captured the attention of an increasingly large portion of the popular imagination, a group of Cambridge scholars decided to band together with the express interest of finding out, through honest empirical investigation, what was actually going on. The Society for Psychical Research (SPR) came into being in 1882 with the purpose of scientifically examining those phenomena commonly referred to as "spiritualistic." Mediums provided an immediate source for research, and physical mediums, extremely common by this time, were among the first to be examined.

Very quickly after its inception, the SPR unearthed the fraudulent practices of a surprisingly—or perhaps not surprisingly, depending upon one's point of view—high number of mediums. As Tom Harpur put it, "The sad truth is that it would take almost a library of books to contain the full accounts of all the past deceptions and frauds perpetrated by would-be spiritualists and psychics. Their number is legion."[4] Any interested student need not delve far into the annals of psychic research to find the myriad cases studied in the earliest days of this fledgling field.[5] SPR investigators quickly found that many mediums were indeed, as the skeptics had alleged, operating under cover of darkness in order to perpetrate shams. They used a number of tricks facilitated by darkness: sleight of hand was used to manipulate objects and touch people eager to make contact with deceased loved ones; flour or white linens would give the illusion of spectral white hands or faces; accomplices were even stashed under tables or in secret rooms to lend support in the plot. Accomplices, or the mediums themselves, might even go so far as to appear before onlookers as a wispy, white ghost—an effect created by the simple draping of a gauze sheet. As the investigations of the SPR, and other skeptics, were made public, many fraudulent mediums saw their careers ruined and many unsuspecting clients were enraged at the deception perpetrated. The result of these findings was to effectively make the physical medium extinct except as a kind of illusionist or magician; no longer were their physical manifestations taken as any true sign of contact with the dead. Even the Fox sisters eventually admitted that they had faked the original phenomena that had awakened the populace to the means of possible communications beyond the grave. Committed Spiritualists ignored these claims in any case, preferring to believe that the Foxes were lying in their confession rather than in their original claims. Some years later, it should be noted, one of the sisters tried to recant her confession but it was of no use as the final nails had already been driven into the coffin of physical mediumship. In any event, mediumship had outstripped the Fox sisters, leaving the girls irrelevant but for their role in its modern inception.

While such physically manifesting phenomena have largely been cast into disrepute, it is important to note that it has not ceased altogether, and there are some in modern times who maintain that there might remain some evidential material to be gleaned from them. The most important and well-known example of such recent research can be found in the controversial "Scole Report," published in the *Proceedings of the Society for Psychical Research*.[6] Over a three-year period, members of the SPR investigated a group of mediums purporting to produce a variety of spiritualistic phenomena, physical manifestations in particular, including the appearance of images on film, floating glowing lights, and various discarnate sounds. In general, the phenomena produced and the methods employed by the mediums have not changed in over a hundred years, most importantly the fact that they remained cloaked in darkness throughout the séance. While the investigating group in this instance was convinced of the genuine character of their experiences at these séances, their investigation suffers from many criticisms. Not least among these criticisms is the fact that the mediums themselves dictated the kinds of controls that could be placed upon them, including that the séances be held only under cover of darkness. Alan Gauld, who had been present at some sittings with the Scole Group, is most diplomatic in his criticism, stating:

> The central problem with Scole is that though there is no direct evidence for hoaxing, there is quite a lot of indirect evidence for it, while on the other hand, though there is a fair amount of possible direct or indirect evidence for genuineness, very little of it seems good enough to defeat the methodological hypothesis of production by normal means.[7]

The one physical medium who, historically, has been most often cited as having impressed and confounded investigators is Daniel Dunglas Home, who has been called, "the most acclaimed physical medium of the nineteenth century."[8] Home found patronage amongst the upper elite and royalty of Europe and the United Kingdom. He was never proved to be fraudulent despite surrendering himself to the careful scrutiny of eminent British scientist Sir William Crookes. Home even published a book of his own detailing the practices of fraudulent mediums, whom he claimed to despise.[9] Despite all this, many magicians have often claimed that they could perform identical feats to those of Home, though none ever proved their claims through action. Harry Houdini, a rabid debunker of physical mediums, is quoted as saying, "every one of them [his feats] can be duplicated by modern conjurers under the same conditions."[10] Houdini went so far as to declare that he could recreate Home's most famous stunt, in which the medium went into trance and floated out a third floor window and then floated back into another window leading into an adjacent room. Houdini was forced to call off his demonstration, however, ostensibly due to illness, and never rescheduled.[11] Modern magicians have made similar claims to the replicability of physical mediumship through normal means as well,[12] but Home still remains famous as the most remarkable of the physical mediums. While Home is indubitably the most renowned physical medium ever, the jury must remain out on his actual veracity. As was pointed out many years ago:

> Opinions as to the genuineness or the reverse of Daniel Home's mediumship are sharply divided. [. . .] Still, it must be admitted that he had the support of men of scientific distinction in Crookes, Barrett, de Morgan, and Wallace, etc. Against this, experts of more pronounced calibre, in Darwin, Faraday, Huxley, and Tyndall, regarded his "phenomena" with something very near contempt. Which of them was right? Which of them was wrong? [. . .] The solution can only be found with [Home] himself.[13]

A. R. Wallace, co-founder of the modern theory of evolution, and mentioned as a supporter of Home in this quote, studiously catalogued the phenomena associated with mediumship.[14] He delineated six key characteristics of physical mediumship, which can be summarized as follows:

(1) So-called simple physical phenomena, which form the core of physical mediumship, include such things as the production of all manner of sounds, the ability to make objects move or levitate without human agency, sometimes even moving them through sealed containers, doors, or other similar barriers.

(2) The ability to touch heat and flame without harm was also a common feat.

(3) Often drawings or writing would be elicited from the spirits, and such would be done again without human agency.

(4) Adding to the spectacle of these performances were musical numbers played by the spirits themselves, with instruments that would be provided to them by the medium.

(5) The climactic finale of many such shows was the actual appearance of the spirit in a quasi-physical, *ectoplasmic* form. This form might appear simply as a face in a gauzy bit of material emanating from the medium through some orifice, or might actually be a materialized hand, head, or entire spirit. Such materialized forms would walk about the room touching attendees to prove their existence.

(6) Several of these spirits have been photographed over the years as well, and these photographs surprisingly convinced many, including the creator of the ultimate logician, Sherlock Holmes, Sir Arthur Conan Doyle.

In looking at this list, some observations must be discussed. First, the first four features do not seem to have any a priori relation to a proof of life after death as they do not directly involve anything that necessarily indicates the presence of a spirit versus some other paranormal or supernatural manifestation. If one supposes a supernatural or paranormal explanation, that an instrument should play music seemingly of its own accord does not necessarily indicate the presence of a deceased spirit any more than it might suggest the presence of some other type of spiritual entity (demons or *jinn*, perhaps?). The possible evidential exceptions might be where the sounds described in the first point are actually a recognizable voice speaking out of thin air, though normally such voices simply whisper indistinctly. Another exception might be found in the written words or drawings, depending on what has been drawn, though in actuality these have also usually been very vague and limited in what they said or described, allowing a subject to interpret as they see fit. Where one prefers a nonsupernatural, perfectly normal explanation, then it would seem that a good illusionist could easily perform any of these feats. Basically, the key point here is that none of these first features of physical mediumship can be seen as strong independent evidence for the ongoing existence of a deceased spirit.

The last two features described by Wallace, those of the materialization and photography of spirits, require further comment. It is important to observe what exactly Wallace states about the figures seen. He says they are generally draped in flowing garb. This is usually described by mediums and Spiritualists as some kind of ectoplasmic form. As Wallace admits, only a portion of the face and hands are shown. Given that such figures manifest only in darkness, it is easy see how one might perceive features that are not present, or misperceive those that are. Any child can describe the experience of seeing in a darkened room many things that are not physically there. Shapes easily appear to take on different forms in the murky depths of darkness. The other thing that strikes one as strange is the fact that the figures are described as being not only visible but tangible to all present. Dr. J. M. Gully, an experienced physician, sat in on séances with the medium Florence Cook, who was reputedly capable of producing full body manifestations of a spirit named Katie King. Upon examining just such a manifestation, Gully proclaimed:

> I have not the smallest doubt, and have the strongest conviction, that such materialization takes place and that it is not the slightest attempt at trick or deception. . . The feel of the skin was quite natural, soft and warm; her movements were natural and graceful . . . When that photograph was taken, I held her hand for at least two minutes . . . but I was constrained to close my eyes by reason of the intense magnesium light which shone directly upon me [from the camera's flash]; moreover she desired that none of us would gaze at her whilst the lens was directed upon her [the spirit].[15]

This flies in the face of all other research that has been done on apparitions to date. As we will see in a later chapter, apparitions are very rarely seen by more than one person at a time and it is unheard of that they should be even remotely tangible. In fact, the very concept of a *spiritual* form, as it is commonly understood, would seem to deny the possibility of any substantial tangibility. That the claims of spirit manifestation during mediumistic séances are much grander than other spontaneous cases is enough to raise red flags.

Wallace seems to feel that his last feature of physical mediumship justifies all the others—that of spirit photography. Even today, many continue to pursue photographic evidence of spirits as evidence for an afterlife. Sir William Crookes conducted numerous studies of the medium Florence Cook and produced some of the most famous pictures of materializations in the history of psychical research.[16] It is difficult to look at such photographs, however, and not have the impression that one is looking at a living woman dressed in white simply posing for what must have been a credulous audience. One might forgive those living in a less technologically sophisticated age for failing to recognize what seems obvious to us, but there is no reason today to take such photographs as anything other than hoaxes.[17] It should be seen as no coincidence that as photographic techniques have become more sophisticated, the appearance of full-bodied materializations have all but ceased.

So, when considering the research on mediumship, it is difficult to refer to physical mediumship as anything other than showmanship, if only because of the high number of revealed frauds. While there may be some who were impressive, as was Daniel D. Home, their feats still do not provide any solid support for an afterlife. Even if these phenomena were found to be paranormal in nature, they do not necessarily support a belief in any form of life after death. One may witness a table rise off the ground and circle the room while at a séance, but that the spirit of some deceased loved one is responsible is far from certain. The medium can claim that it is the ghost of one's great-grandfather who is picking up the table, but how does anyone know that this is so? One might be convinced that the force levitating the table around the room were one's great-grandfather only if there were something more to prove it were so, unless said great-grandfather had some particular fetish for carrying tables about or some distinctive way of doing just that. More likely, one will need to have some kind of information to prove the spirit's identity, information he might have known in life and which would prove to those who knew him that it were truly him. The rapping and knocking of physical mediumship might be able to answer certain questions, but this process is long and tedious, and in cases where the spirit answers simply with yes or no, the chances of correctly guessing are much higher. Techniques such as the *ouija* and *planchette* might provide even more detailed information, though both suffer from being somewhat slow and awkward to use. Still, if a medium could relay *specific and detailed information* through such a device, then one might be inclined to believe that the spirit of one's great-grandfather were actually present.

It is here where "mental mediumship" can be seen as providing more fertile grounds in the search for proof of the existence of a discarnate entity. Physical mediumship can produce incredible feats and the manifestation of wonders, but mental mediumship offers the kind of information necessary to identify a spirit as such. While physical mediumship has all but disappeared, mental mediumship by contrast is still very much alive and well. Spiritualist churches continue to hold weekly meetings at which the existence of spirits is believed to be demonstrated through the giving of personal messages from the dead to the living. New Age channelers borrow heavily from the spiritualistic practices of shamans while still carrying on the tradition of Western mediumship established over one hundred years ago. Messages from the dead are even accessible by phone via certain pay-by-the-minute phone services, claiming to be for entertainment purposes only. Certainly, among this branch of mediumship there has been found to be much fraud, but investigators have found some interesting mediums who seem to be capable of something more interesting. Whether the mediums can be shown to be legitimate or not, those who receive messages via a medium often feel a genuine sense of relief at the ongoing existence of their loved ones. That mediums might serve some social function in grief and bereavement is a separate issue, however, from that of whether they provide genuine evidence for an afterlife.

We may once again refer to Wallace's categorizations as he provides a similarly detailed list for mental mediumship as that given for the physical phenomena, this time finding five distinct features:[18]

(1) The first feature described by Wallace is what is known as automatic writing. The medium involved in this practice writes involuntarily, sometimes in a state of trance, and often on subjects of which she is not thinking about, does not expect, and does not like. Occasionally definite and correct information is given of facts of which the medium has not, nor ever had, any knowledge, sometimes even including predictions of future events. Often the handwriting appears to be similar to that of the deceased, and sometimes it comes through in languages unknown to the medium. Much of the mental mediumship done at the turn of the twentieth century was of the automatic writing type, though today it has become substantially more rare.

(2) Some mediums see the forms of deceased persons unknown to them, and describe their peculiarities so minutely that friends at once recognize them. They often hear voices, through which they obtain names, dates, and places, connected with the individual so described. Others read sealed letters in any language, and write appropriate answers, through a psychic faculty known as clairvoyance.

(3) Many mediums go into a more or less unconscious trance state, and then speak, often on matters and in a style far beyond his or her own capacities. Automatic writing also normally involves such trances.

(4) Also during a trance, impersonation of the deceased often occurs. The medium seems taken possession of by another being; speaks, looks, and acts the character in a most marvelous manner; in some cases speaks foreign languages never even heard in the normal state.

(5) Finally, Wallace adds healing to his list of feats performed by mental mediums. Sometimes this is accomplished by the laying on of hands, an exalted form of simple mesmeric healing. Sometimes, in a trance state, the medium at once discovers the hidden malady, and prescribes for it, sometimes describing in exact detail the morbid appearance of internal organs. In either case, it is not entirely clear where the spirits are involved in the process, but since many mediums were capable of such feats, they are included in Wallace's list.

To begin discussing these features, it must be said that healing has very little to do with the subject of life after death. While certain mediums are famed for their diagnostic abilities, as for example Edgar Cayce,[19] the ability to identify illness is not strictly speaking healing and thus should not be covered under this heading. Certain mystics and faith healers have exhibited the ability to heal the sick by the laying on of hands, but such abilities are more accurately categorized under the physical phenomena as healing is certainly an effect upon the physical world.

Those instances of clairvoyant diagnoses and prescriptions would also best be categorized under clairvoyance. In any event, it is difficult to imagine why the ability to heal people might somehow be related to the spirits of the dead unless the spirit in question was a medical doctor in life. The other four characteristics, however, do relate to the pursuit of evidence for an afterlife. Further, such features have been demonstrated in outstanding mediums that were investigated by scientific researchers. A handful of these mediums have been dealt with extensively in the literature, with the following examples representative of the best among them.

One such medium is Leonora Piper, the first medium found to yield truly impressive results suggesting paranormal faculties. She was discovered by the eminent psychologist, William James who himself subjected her to careful scrutiny. James was impressed by Mrs. Piper and became convinced that she was not perpetuating a fraud. He concluded:

> I am persuaded of the medium's honesty, and of the genuineness of her trance; and although at first disposed to think that the "hits" [correct statements] she made were either lucky coincidence, or the result of knowledge on her part of who the sitter was, and of his or her family affairs, I now believe her to be in possession of a power as yet unexplained.[20]

While James accepted her powers as extraordinary, he was not convinced that they originated from actual spirits of the dead. The possibility of telepathy on the part of the medium was always considered a likely explanation by James, and so he imagined that the medium might simply be gaining her information through mind reading, albeit of an unconscious type. The sittings at which James conducted his investigations revealed much information that was personal to him and his wife and of which there was no way, as far as James could conceive, that the medium could have known. Subsequent investigations involved several other investigators. James sent twenty-five people to see Mrs. Piper for sittings under pseudonyms so that she would have no way of knowing anything of these people. Ultimately, James stated, "I am prepared to stake as much money on Mrs. Piper's honesty as on that of anyone I know, and am quite satisfied to leave my reputation for wisdom or folly, so far as human nature is concerned, to stand or fall by this declaration."[21]

As Mrs. Piper produced such remarkable results in the eyes of a man of such repute as William James, Richard Hodgson, a leading member of the Society for Psychical Research in London, made the trip to the United States in order to investigate her himself. Hodgson was renowned for his debunking of a great many mediums in England and he applied the same stringent methods to Mrs. Piper. Careful notes were taken at all sittings, with special attention paid to first sittings, which might provide useful background information on an unscrupulous medium. Private investigators were hired to shadow Mrs. Piper and verify that she was not meeting with any contacts or seeking other sources of information. Finally, Mrs. Piper was even brought back to England where she was both out of her own environment, and thus cut off from any sources of clandestine information she may have had, and placed under the scrutiny of an entire group of Society members. By the end of his investigations, Hodgson, originally a staunch skeptic, had accepted the validity of Mrs. Piper's abilities and came to conclude that they did indeed derive from the afterlife.[22] One feature of Mrs. Piper's mediumship which seemed to particularly influence Hodgson's conclusion was the fact that shortly after he took over the investigation, a "control," sometimes known as a familiar spirit, appeared during sittings. This control claimed to be an old friend of his named George Pellew. Mrs. Piper relayed very personal information through this control spirit that ended in convincing Hodgson of her authenticity.

Controls were a very important part of modern mental mediumship in its earliest days. Controls, or familiar spirits, are no longer central to mental mediumship today, though many mediums still employ them. For some, the control is unnecessary as the personality of the medium can commune directly with the spirit world. Normally, when a medium went into a trance one specific entity came to the fore. This entity is known as the control. This secondary personality acts as a kind of Master of Ceremonies, speaking through the medium on behalf of the spirits "on the other side." The control acts as a buffer between the mind of the spirit and the mind of the medium. It is thought that this buffer serves to somehow protect the intellect of the medium. In any event, this secondary control-personality can be seen as the medium's trance-personality. Trance mediums who do have a control communicate mentally with the spirit. They may claim a kind of telepathy or even that the spirits actually enter their body and use them to speak through. In such cases, the control is essential to explain the communication and at the same time retain the medium's sanity. It is as if the main personality of the medium, his or her true personality, retreats in place of an unconscious one in order to maintain the former's integrity. The secondary, unconscious personality can then be broken up and allow various other entities to "come through" while the medium, per se, is safely tucked away somewhere else.

It is possible to discuss the typical control by using Mrs. Piper's controls as an example, as there is a great similarity between the controls of mediums. Mrs. Piper had a slew of strange, and sometimes famous, controls in her first year of practice but finally settled on one regular control, though this was not a decision made of her conscious will. Her main control claimed to be a Frenchman named Dr. Phinuit. He had a personality distinct from Mrs. Piper's waking state and would relate to the sitters what it was that certain spirits wanted to say. He was a very flamboyant personality and would often prattle on when at a loss for answers to questions the sitters might have asked. It was found, however, that there existed no record of a French physician named Phinuit having ever lived anywhere in France. In addition, Phinuit (through Piper) could speak only a smattering of French—not more than could Mrs. Piper herself. In addition to Dr. Phinuit, Mrs. Piper's controls included such famous personalities as Bach, Longfellow, as well as an Indian girl with the unlikely name of Chlorine. These odd facts suggest that the control is not exactly what it claims to be; in fact, the conclusion has been reached that these controls are likely aspects of the medium's own mind. Some controls have had more or less developed personalities, but when analyzed critically, they all seem to stem directly from the imagination of the medium, albeit unconsciously. On this, William James commented:

> One curious thing about trance utterances is their generic similarity in different individuals. The "control" here in America is either a grotesque, slangy, and flippant personage ("Indian" controls, calling the ladies "squaws," the men "braves," the house a "wigwam," etc., are excessively common); or, if he ventures on higher intellectual flights, he abounds in a curiously vague optimistic philosophy-and-water, in which phrases about spirit, harmony, beauty, law, progression, development, etc., keep recurring. It seems exactly as if one author composed more than half of the trance messages, no matter by whom they are uttered. Whether all subconscious selves are peculiarly susceptible to a certain stratum of the *Zeitgeist* and get their inspiration from it, I know not; but this is obviously the case with secondary selves which become "developed" in spiritualist circles.[23]

It would seem, then, that the alleged spirit control is actually no more than an imaginary character portrayed by the medium during the sitting. That more recent mediums often have no need for a control might be seen as a result of the indication that the controls are nothing more than aspects of the medium. Today, many mediums simply communicate with the spirits directly, without the need for this fictive intermediary. Those mediums who have clairvoyant visions and the like, without entering a trance, generally do not have this unconscious personality. The difference between these mediums and the ones who use a control is the fact that clairvoyant mediums see the spirits as external from themselves and communicate face-to-face, so to speak, thus preserving the integrity of the medium's identity. Whether the control is present or not, much of what mediums relay from the spirit world continues to be constituted of the same kind of "philosophy-and-water," popular in New Age circles today, as William James observed.

Since it is obviously not from the mediums' controls that one will derive proof of an afterlife, one might instead turn to the actual information purporting to come from deceased individuals. Certainly, more recent mediums have recognized the importance of information over the showmanship of the control and have generally dropped the latter. The most important things one looks for in determining the veracity of a medium is whether the information they provide can be verified as true and whether the medium could have had any possibility of gaining this information through normal means. Mrs. Piper once again provides the template for the kind of information that might be communicated.

In one instance, Mr. J. Rogers Rich gave a dog's collar to Mrs. Piper while she was in a trance. Her control, Dr. Phinuit, then stated that he could see a dog bounding toward him. He said, "Here he comes! Oh, how he jumps! There he is now, jumping upon and around you. So glad to see you! Rover! Rover! No— G-rover, Grover! That's his name!" In fact, the dog's name had once been Rover, but had had its name changed in honor of the U.S. president, Grover Cleveland.[24]

In a series of other instances, Piper's George Pellew control correctly recognized twenty-nine of thirty anonymous sitters who had known Mr. Pellew in life. Mrs. Piper had no previous contact with any of these people and only recognized them once Pellew was the control. The last of the thirty was also accounted for when Pellew's failure to recognize the individual was attributed to the fact that he had not seen this person since he were a child.[25]

A final example is one in which the spirit of a man came through Mrs. Piper and related some private stories of his youth. The young sitter, who was his son, knew nothing of these stories and could not attest to their accuracy. When investigators sought confirmation of the stories, they had to go to two of the deceased man's brothers before they could piece together the whole story. Neither of the two men remembered all of what the spirit told, but together, their stories corroborated the spirits, thus confirming that the information received was in fact veridical.[26]

The literature is rife with just such examples. As Alan Gauld points out, "The material on this topic published in the *Proceedings* of the S. P. R. alone would, if added together, yield a dozen or two bulky volumes."[27] Most of the information being revealed involves trivialities of no great importance—the name of a dog, or a childhood memory. The purpose of these tidbits seems less directed to giving helpful, practical information and more focused on proving that the spirit is indeed who it says it is. Though Mrs. Piper was the early star of

psychical research, other mediums were similarly successful, and many were subjected to increasingly sophisticated experimentation.

Some have argued that the kinds of information provided by Mrs. Piper and
others could have been gathered by the medium herself. The normal explanation that the medium was gathering information from informants or spying had
been ruled out by the employment of private investigators and strict surveil-
lance of the medium. The possibility remained for some, however, that the
medium might be using alternate paranormal means to gather information,
namely telepathy. The fact that information like childhood memories or the
name of a dog or an old friend was held in the mind of another living person
left open the possibility of mental communication between the living. William
James was among those who remained unconvinced that successful mediums
proved the continuing existence of deceased spirits, while still accepting that
they did indicate some poorly understood faculty for gathering information. Efforts were made early on to determine the source of the information that was
being conveyed.

Mrs. Leonard was another medium eager to be investigated by psychical researchers. She was subjected to similar methods to those used in the investigations of Mrs. Piper (i.e., private investigators and the like). Mrs. Leonard was
involved in a series of experiments that have been called the "book tests." These
tests required that the spirit seeking to communicate would give directions to a
specific book on a shelf in the sitter's home. The spirit would say something like,
"The third book from the left on the second shelf from the top." It would then
also give a page number upon which would be found a significant message confirming that the spirit was who it said it was. The sitter would more often than
not be unaware of the book until it was discovered. In some cases, the book
might not even have been known to the spirit in life, but the message on the
page described would still be significant to that person. The idea of these experiments was to somehow prove that the spirit was actually a spirit; that the
communicator could retrieve information from a specific book on a shelf far removed from the medium was thought to indicate agency beyond the medium
herself.

Mediums sometimes relate information that does not seem to come from any
spirit at all. Yet another medium, Eileen Garrett, who often clairvoyantly saw
the spirits she communicated with, provides some interesting examples. She
once claimed to see the spirit of a woman's son. The son passed on the simple
message: "Don't worry." The interesting thing in this case is that the boy was
in an accident *one hour later*, and did not actually die until the following day.[28]
Obviously, unless spirits can spontaneously leave bodies well before death, the
medium in a case such as this is gaining information from some other source and

simply imagining the spirit. Believers in the ongoing existence of the spirit often have little trouble attributing all manner of powers to the spirit—they can
foretell the future, have practically limitless abilities of clairvoyance, and they
can travel effortlessly over great distances.

To give another example of Mrs. Garrett's mediumship, she reported seeing a
dirigible crash one afternoon while out walking. The vision was so real that she
expected to hear about the crash on the news that night. When she did not hear
of the news she became concerned. Again, a year later, she saw the same crash
once more. This time, she noticed that nobody else seemed to witness the crash.
It was not for some time that she finally heard about a dirigible that was sched-
uled to take off soon. The dirigible matched the description of the one she had
twice seen crash. Her efforts to stop the flight were ignored by the authorities
and indeed the dirigible crashed, killing the crew. She was later contacted by
the spirit of a crew member whom she had personally tried to dissuade from flying. He explained to her what the cause of the crash had been. When officials
heard her detailed account, as related by the spirit, of how the dirigible had
gone down, they were convinced that she could not possibly have known the
technical information necessary to offer such a description.[29] Here we have
the account of a medium who both predicted a crash and learned of the cause
through ostensible communication with a crew member *postmortem*.

There have been shown to be some mediums of quality and character amongst
the legions of charlatans. These few have shown that they can gain information
by means that cannot readily be explained. The explanation preferred by mediums is that they gain this information from the spirits of the dead themselves.
Certainly, many who have sat with mediums and have heard, or read, the information coming through have been convinced that it is in all actuality the spirit
of a dead friend or relative communicating. However, in certain instances, some
of the information received cannot be explained by the presence of spirits. Why
should a son's spirit appear to Mrs. Garrett before his life was even in danger—
and a full day before he actually died? Can this be considered as a communication with his spirit? If his spirit knew in advance that he was going to die and
wanted to tell his mother, "Don't worry," could not his spirit have prevented the
accident from occurring? Then there is the problem of the dirigible. Without an
investigation, the details of the crash could not have been known to anyone
other than a crew member, and certainly not to a woman who had no knowledge
of dirigibles whatsoever. This appears to be a clear case of spirit communication
as the deceased crew member is the claimed source of information. However,
Mrs. Garrett predicted the crash years before when she "saw" the dirigible crash.
Surely, dirigibles cannot be thought to possess spirits. What did Mrs. Garrett
see? Many other examples exist in the literature of mediums seeing nonhuman

visions. That a dog, as seen by Mrs. Piper, might have a spirit might not challenge the beliefs of everyone, that a blimp should have a spirit would surely have
few proponents. If Mrs. Garrett gained this knowledge through some form of
clairvoyance, could she not have also gained the information about the crash details via clairvoyance? Indeed, if the actual spirits who do the talking through the
medium—the controls—are imaginary representatives of the medium's own
subconscious, could not also the spirits themselves be deeper hallucinations? The
argument over the actual source for mediumistic communications is not easily
resolved.

The so-called cross-correspondences are often seen as the best source of evidence for the survival of spirits as the source for mediumistic communications.
These communications began to occur after the deaths of a number of the most
prominent members of the Society for Psychical Research. Frederic W. H. Myers, one of the Society's founders, was a staunch supporter of the belief in an afterlife and it was his spirit that supposedly initiated the cross-correspondences.
The early correspondences mainly involved five mediums and others to a lesser
degree, who lived in India, England, and the United States. These mediums began to receive messages, first claiming to be from Frederic Myers, then from
other deceased members of the Society. Each of the mediums received messages
that held little meaning individually, but once the messages were examined by
the Society in London it was found that the messages formed puzzles. Separate,
the messages were meaningless, but once two or three were put together, they
were seen to be meaningfully connected. Each of the individual pieces matched
up with other individual pieces from mediums around the globe. H. F. Saltmarsh
described three types of correspondence: (1) simple correspondences involving
two or more mediums who produce the same words or phrases; (2) complex correspondences involving topics rather than specific words; and (3) ideal correspondences, in which the messages form intricate linguistic puzzles.[30] Not only
did the mediums receive messages which corresponded to one another, often
while at different ends of the Earth, but some messages even came through in
Latin or Greek, often involving complex allusions from classical scholarship.
Myers himself was a classical scholar, as was one of the mediums, however most
of the mediums had little education, including the famous Leonora Piper. Investigators have recognized that it is possible for mediums to receive information not normally available to them. The problem presented by these cross-
correspondences comes from their complexity. The number of mediums involved and the distances between them would seem to preclude collusion and
fraud. Further, the fact that no single communication contained the totality of
the actual message and that multiple mediums would be involved in order to
complete the message would seem to rule out the telepathic abilities of a single

medium. For many, the most parsimonious explanation is that a single discarnate spirit is moving from one medium to another in order to deliver pieces of a larger puzzle, in an effort to prove its own existence. One would not be surprised to find that such an elaborate demonstration would claim to arise from the postmortem minds of the founders of the SPR. Taken at face value, it seems as though Myers, and others, continued to conduct their experiments from the other side, as if they were trying to create a source of evidence which could not be denied. On the complexity of the messages, and sheer number of them that appeared over a span of over thirty years, many have accepted the cross-correspondences as just such experiments. If one tries to imply fraud, one must blame a great number of people, including several respected members of the Society for Psychical Research as well as mediums like Mrs. Piper, whose honesty has already been attested to.

Aside from fraud, there is, however, the very real possibility that the cross-correspondences are more a result of the ingenuity of the investigators and less the result of a complicatedly coordinated puzzle from beyond. In a recent study, I demonstrated that randomly selected passages from works of literature might be substituted for mediumistic scripts and still reveal similar patterns to those found in the original cross-correspondences.[31] Basically, given enough material and enough time, investigators with the right motivation and level of ingenuity can discover patterns without the need for any agent having left them there to be found. Arguments against my findings have been of an interpretive kind, arguing that the patterns I found are not as complex as those of the cross-correspondences themselves.[32] The large numbers of cross-correspondences that are remarked upon as adding to their value must be seen instead as a detriment as one would expect increasingly complex patterns to emerge from a larger data set. In any case, the evaluation of the complexity of one pattern over another is subjective. That patterns appear in a random set of writings indicates that the complexity of the cross-correspondences need not be seen as anything more than a reflection of investigator ingenuity and should not be seen as anything near the strongest evidence for a spiritual survival of bodily death.

Aside from the largely anecdotal and case study evidence provided, recent work has been done to test mediumship in a laboratory setting. Gary Schwartz, et al., have been particularly involved recently in conducting controlled laboratory experiments in which he has shown that selected mediums can achieve levels of success exceeding what might be expected by chance, in terms of the number of pieces of correct information they can receive about a given sitter.[33] Schwartz and his colleagues have adapted mediumistic study to a laboratory setting with some success. Employing professional mediums, including John Edward (who appeared on the television show *Crossing Over with John Edward*),

Schwartz's experiments aim to control for fraud on the parts of both mediums and experimenters. These experiments establish protocols that keep the mediums separate from sitters, thus reducing the likelihood of information being subtly transferred from sitter to medium. Such study allows for statistical analysis and has repeatedly demonstrated that these professional mediums can convey information relating to the dead at a rate higher than would be predicted by chance.[34] To provide some sense of the kind of information being received, I offer one excerpt from the transcript of a sitting:

Medium: Now, I don't know if they mean this by age or by generation, but they talk about the younger male that passed. Does that make sense to you?

Sitter: Yes.

Medium: Okay, 'cause wherever he is is [sic] claiming he was the first one in the room. So I guess he wants the credit of coming first. He states he's family, that's correct?

Sitter: Correct.

Medium: This I don't understand. If you do, say yes, you understand, but don't explain. He speaks about his dad, does this make sense?

Sitter: Yes.

Medium: I don't know why yet. I don't know if he's trying to tell me his dad is there or if he's calling to his dad. So don't say anything, I want them to say it.

Also, another male presence comes forward to you and says, "Dad is here." Is it correct your dad passed?

Sitter: Correct.

Medium: Okay, 'cause he's there. But this younger male, these are two different people, correct?

Sitter: Correct.

Medium: Yeah,'cause I don't, he's already explained "Don't get me mixed up." You know, they know each other but don't forget about him. Yeah, so your dad comes forward. Now your dad, okay, again, don't explain, just say you understand. Your dad speaks about the loss of a child. That makes sense?

Sitter: Yes.

Medium: Twice?

Medium: 'Cause your father says twice.

Sitter: Yes.

Medium: Wait a minute, now he says thrice. He's saying three times. Does that make sense?

Sitter: That's correct.

Medium: 'Cause your father said, "Once, twice, thrice."

Sitter: That's correct.

Medium: It . . . there's talk of the son that passed on. That is correct?

Sitter: Yes.

Medium: Okay, he's claiming to be the first male who came in the room. That would make sense?

Sitter: Yes.

Medium: Okay. So him and his grandfather are together. Now your son's dad is still on the earth, I take it, yes?

Sitter: Yes.

Medium: 'Cause he's . . . that's why I was hearing him talk about dad. Now that's why I didn't want you to explain. Let him explain where his father is. His father is on the earth. Please tell dad you've heard from me, whether he believes in this or not. Who cares? It's the message that's important, not the belief system. And as your son says, besides, he'll find that I'm right as usual someday anyway.

Wait a minute now. There's talk of loss of another son, is that correct? Wait a minute now. Wait a minute, don't answer yet. Your father speaks about a miscarriage. Is it correct, you did have one?

Sitter: Yes.[35]

This exchange shows the kind of information that is typically conveyed by mediums—namely of little importance but to prove the existence of the continuing personality beyond death and to console the living. Further, it demonstrates how the style of communication used by mediums has changed little since the earliest days of psychical research—mediums appear to struggle for each piece of information, trying desperately to understand just what the message is. Critics have responded to Schwartz's work revealing serious methodological flaws in his experiments that severely limit their impact as solid evidence.[36] That Schwartz and his colleagues have been able to adapt studies to a laboratory situation remains a remarkable advance, however, and one can remain hopeful that further studies in other labs can improve and correct methodological flaws. Such improvements might either confirm or refute the claims that select mediums can succeed in gaining information otherwise unavailable normally.

In closing, what has been provided is a brief review of the modern phenomena of mediumship. Empirically minded scientists have spent much time researching these phenomena and have found, in large part, fraud and deceit. Researchers have also found, however, that there are some mediums who do exhibit extraordinary abilities. While these mediums are the metaphorical needles in the haystack, they have been found and appear to possess some kind of ability to gain information through extraordinary means. Certain phenomena exhibited by mediums are more suggestive of an afterlife than others. While these phenomena are highly suggestive, there remain lingering doubts. While mediumship has provided no incontrovertible proof one way or the other, the experience of it remains consistent and appears cross-culturally. Tom Cross says of mediumship that "as a method of enquiry—though requiring time and effort—it is repeatable though not by its nature in the precise terms of presently accepted scientific enquiry."[37] Mediums continue to ply their trade, often with a sincerity that belies fraud. Those who receive messages from deceased loved ones remain moved by relief at the hope for eternal life. Still, we must continue to seek for answers. Is there some other way the mediums might gain their information? Do the souls of the dead truly speak to these few special people? In 1871, before the founding of the Society for Psychical Research, a committee was set up in the name of the London Dialectical Society to investigate the growing number of mediums. Their conclusion reads:

> In presenting their report, your Committee, taking into consideration the high character and great intelligence of many of the witnesses to the more extraordinary facts, the extent to which their testimony is supported by the reports of the sub-committees, and the absence of any proof of imposture or delusion as regards a large portion of the phenomena; and further, having regard to the exceptional character of the phenomena, the large number of persons in every grade of society and over the whole civilized world who are more or less influenced by a belief in their supernatural origin, and to the fact that no philosophical explanation of them has yet been arrived at, deem it incumbent upon them to state their conviction that the subject is worthy of more serious attention and careful investigation than it has hitherto received.[38]

Over one hundred years later, their conclusion remains appropriate, however modest it may be.

Notes

1. For a very good historical account of the Fox sisters and the beginnings of modern Spiritualism, see Barbara Weisberg's *Talking to the Dead: Kate and Maggie Fox and the Rise of Spiritualism* (San Francisco, CA: HarperSanFrancisco, 2004). For discussion of some of the (relatively minor) problems with this account, see my review: Christopher M. Moreman, "Review of *Talking to the Dead: Kate and Maggie Fox and the Rise of Spiritualism* by Barbara Weisberg," *Journal of Parapsychology* 68:2 (2004): 436–438.

2. It must be noted that the research done at the time was far from thorough. It has been suggested that the remains were not, in fact, human, as reported, (if indeed bones were found at all) but were the remains of some animal. While this may very well be true, the reports at the time still had the effect of fueling a widespread interest in spirit communication.

3. William James, "What Psychical Research Has Accomplished," in *William James on Psychical Research*, eds. Gardner Murphy and Robert O. Ballou (London: Chatto and Windus, 1961), p. 27.

4. Tom Harpur, *Life After Death* (Toronto: McClelland & Stewart, 1991), p. 82.

5. One might refer to the *Journal of the Society for Psychical Research*, and also that of its American counterpart, the *Journal of the American Society for Psychical Research*, as well as the *Proceedings* of both of these organizations.

6. Montague Keen, Arthur Ellison, and David Fontana, "The Scole Report," *Proceedings of the Society for Psychical Research* 58 (1999).

7. Alan Gauld, "Comments on the Scole Report," *Proceedings of the Society for Psychical Research* 58 (1999), p. 420.

8. Milbourne Christopher, *ESP, Seers & Psychics* (New York: Thomas Y. Crowell, 1970), p. 174.

9. Daniel Dunglas Home, *Lights and Shadows of Spiritualism* (London: Virtue, 1877).

10. Horace Wyndham, *Mr. Sludge, the Medium: Being the Life and Adventures of Daniel Dunglas Home* (London: Geoffrey Bles, 1937), p. 289.

11. Rosemary Ellen Guiley, "Home, Daniel Dunglas," *Encyclopedia of Mystical and Paranormal Experience* (San Francisco, CA: HarperCollins, 1991), pp. 266–267.

12. For instance, see Christopher, *ESP*, pp. 176–187. Also, such modern magicians as The Amazing Randi and the duo of Penn & Teller remain skeptical based on the notion that if it is possible to recreate similar feats through magic, then the medium must be assumed to be using the same technique. See various issues of both *The Skeptical Inquirer* and *Skeptic Magazine*.

13. Wyndham, *Mr. Sludge*, pp. 294–298.

14. A. R. Wallace, *Miracles and Modern Spiritualism* (1896; repr., New York: Arno, 1975), pp. 205–209.

15. Quoted by Epes Sargent, *The Proof Palpable of Immortality: An Account of the Materialization Phenomena of Modern Spiritualism* (Boston, MA: Colby and Rich, 1876), pp. 54–55.

16. William Crookes, *Researches into the Phenomena of Spiritualism*, 7th ed. (London: Two Worlds, 1904).

17. A comprehensive collection of ghostly images can be found at the website of the International Survivalist Society: http://www.survivalafterdeath.org/photographs.htm. The following text contains what have been called the best photographs taken of the mysterious spiritual substance known as ectoplasm: Margaret Hamilton, *Is Survival a Fact?* (London: Psychic Press, 1969). Additionally, the following text includes more photographs taken by the photgrapher and father of the previously mentioned author, T. Glen Hamilton: Hamilton, *Intention and Survival* (Toronto: MacMillan, 1942).

18. Wallace, *Miracles*, pp. 205–209.

19. Edgar Cayce is often cited as a modern medium, though his most remarkable ability was a type of clairvoyance in which he entered a trance and claimed to consult a great library in the tradition of the Akashic Records. For more information on Edgar Cayce, consult the Association of Research and Enlightenment (ARE), founded by Cayce himself: http://www.are-cayce.com/index .htm.

20. F. W. H. Myers, O. J. Lodge, W. Leaf, and W. James, "A Record of Observations of Certain Phenomena of Trance," *Proceedings of the Society for Psychical Research* 6 (1889–1890), p. 653.

21. Myers, "A Record of Observations of Certain Phenomena of Trance," p. 654.

22. See Richard Hodgson, "A Record of Observations of Certain Phenomena of Trance," *Proceedings of the Society for Psychical Research* 8 (1892), pp. 1–167; Hodgson, "A Further Record of Observations of Certain Phenomena of Trance," *Proceedings of the Society for Psychical Research* 13 (1897–1898), pp. 284–582; see also Alan Gauld, *Mediumship and Survival* (London: Paladin, 1983), pp. 32–44.

23. James, *On Psychical Research*, pp. 48–49.

24. Gauld, "Comments on the Scole Report," p. 35.

25. Guiley, "Piper, Leonora E.," p. 446.

26. Gauld, "Comments on the Scole Report," pp. 42–43.

27. Alan Gauld, "Discarnate Survival," in *Handbook of Parapsychology*, ed. Benjamin B. Wolman (New York: Van Nostrand Reinhold, 1977), pp. 584–585.

28. Allan Angoff, *Eileen Garrett and the World Beyond the Senses* (New York: William Morrow, 1974), pp. 105–106.

29. Angoff, *Eileen Garrett*, pp. 28–30.

30. H. F. Saltmarsh, *Evidence for Personal Survival From Cross Correspondences* (London: G. Bell & Sons, 1938).

31. Christopher M. Moreman, "A Re-examination of The Possibility of Chance Coincidence as an Alternative Explanation for Mediumistic Communication in the Cross-Correspondences," *Journal of the Society for Psychical Research* 67 (2003): 225–242.

32. See Montague Keen and Archie E. Roy, "Chance Coincidence in the Cross-Correspondences," *Journal of the Society for Psychical Research* 68:1 (2004): 57–60, and Christopher M. Moreman, "Response to Keen and Roy re: Chance Coincidence in the Cross-Correspondences," *Journal of the Society for Psychical Research* 68:1 (2004): 60–62. See also David Fontana, *Is There an Afterlife?* (Deershot Lodge, UK: O Books, 2005), pp. 184–185.

33. See Gary E. R. Schwartz, Linda G. S. Russek, Lonnie A. Nelson, and Christopher Barentsen, "Accuracy and Replicability of Anomalous After-Death Communication Across Highly Skilled Mediums," *Journal of the Society for Psychical Research* 65:1 (2001): 1–25; Gary E. R. Schwartz and Linda G. S. Russek, "Evidence of Anomalous Information Retrieval between Two Mediums: Telepathy, Network Memory Resonance, and Continuance of Consciousness," *Journal of the Society for Psychical Research* 65:4 (2001): 257–275; Gary E. R. Schwartz, Linda G. Russek, and Christopher Barentsen, "Accuracy and Replicability of Anomalous Information Retrieval: Replication and Extension," *Journal of the Society for Psychical Research* 66:3 (2002): 144–156; Gary Schwartz, with William L. Simon, *The Afterlife Experiments: Breakthrough Evidence of Life After Death* (New York: Pocket Books, 2002).

34. For the reader interested in the methodology, please consult Schwartz, et al., mentioned in the above note.

35. Schwartz, "Accuracy and Replicability," pp. 14–15.

36. Richard Wiseman and Ciaran O'Keefe, "Accuracy and Replicability of Anomalous After-Death Communication Across Highly Skilled Mediums: A Critique," *The Paranormal Review* 19 (2001): 3–6; Ray Hyman, "How Not to Test Mediums: Critiquing *The Afterlife Experiments*," *Skeptical Inquirer* 27:1 (2003): 20–30.

37. Tom Cross, "The Himalayas Case; Strong Survival Evidence Through Three Mediums," *Journal of the Society for Psychical Research* 62 (1998): 352.

38. *Report on Spiritualism of the Committee of the London Dialectical Society* (London: Longmans, Green, Reader and Dyer, 1871), pp. 5–6.

CHAPTER NINE

~

Apparitions and Hauntings

Phantoms, specters, ghasts, wraiths, shades, and ghosts. Since time immemorial, humankind has been beset by denizens no longer of this world. The typical fireside ghost stories have been told time and again. Spectral voices calling out to loved ones; ghostly hands lighting upon the unsuspecting; phantom heads floating mournfully above one's bed; or the disembodied moans of a tortured soul—these are all familiar motifs in such ghastly tales. Many still feel a chill run up their spines as they hear these strange tales from beyond the grave. Surely, they can be no more than mere fancy—myths and legends told in the wee hours to entertain and pass the time—but when pondering the question of whether or not humans survive death, ghostly apparitions present the careful investigator with many issues that deserve more serious examination. The simple fact is that people *do* see ghosts, people *do* hear disembodied moans, and people *do* sometimes feel as if they have been in close, personal contact with the dead. Given this reality of human experience, one must wonder at the source.

One of the first endeavors of the Society for Psychical Research was the so-called Census of Hallucinations.[1] The purpose of the survey was to determine the prevalence of apparitional experiences, what were deemed a form of hallucinatory experience by the psychical researchers carrying out the census. The census found that 10% of respondents reported having had actually seen, heard, felt, or otherwise sensed the presence of a person who was not actually there in the flesh, so to speak. This striking finding was the first scientifically verifiable indication that at least some ghost stories might stem from actual human experience. When one considers that one out of every ten people has experienced an apparition and realizes the vast numbers of people this represents, one has no choice but to stand up and take note. Even those of us who have not actually experienced ghostly phenomena first hand may know someone who has. It thus became obvious that these claims could not be sloughed off as trifling nonsense, but instead begged the question of what it was that people have been experiencing, be it spirit, hallucination, or something else.

During the past one hundred years or so, many have sought the answer to that very question. While the answers themselves are divergent to say the least, many facts have been learned concerning these evanescent experiences. What follows is a summary of the knowledge gathered on the subject to date, beginning with some examples of just what sorts of experiences will be considered herein. The following are both typical and contain many characteristics common to most apparitional experiences.

Laurence Orchard, of London, England, reported in an early case:

On Christmas Day at 12.50 p.m. I was in the bathroom, when I heard footsteps and doors being opened and closed quite distinctly, and as I was the only one in the house it surprised me, so [I] opened the door and looked out, and to my astonishment I saw Mother [who was alive and well in Canada at the time] (or thought I did) in a black dress at her bedroom door and her arms full of parcels. I made an exclamation—"Mother," I think—and I think there was some sort of response, but I forget now, and then all disappeared suddenly. I then left the house, and told Gerty [his sister] what a vision I had.[2]

In another early case, Prince Victor Duleep Singh reported:

On Saturday, October, 1893 I was in Berlin with Lord Carnarvon. We went to a theatre together and returned before midnight. I went to bed, leaving, as I always do, a bright light in the room (electric light). As I lay in bed I found myself looking at an oleograph which hung on the wall opposite my bed. I saw distinctly the face of my father, the Maharajah Duleep Singh, looking at me, as it were out of the picture; not like a portrait of him, but his real head. The head about filled the picture-frame. I continued looking and still saw my father looking at me with an intent expression. Though not in the least alarmed, I was so puzzled that I got out of bed to see what the picture really was. It was an oleograph common-place picture of a girl holding a rose and leaning out of a balcony, an arch forming the background. The girl's face was quite small, whereas my father's head was the size of life and filled the frame.

I was in no special anxiety at the time, and had for some years known him to be seriously out of health; but there had been no news to alarm me about him.

Next morning (Sunday) I told the incident to Lord Carnarvon.

That evening (Sunday) late on returning home, Lord Carnarvon brought two telegrams into my room and handed them to me. I said at once, "My father is dead." That was the fact. He had had an apoplectic seizure on the Saturday evening at about nine o'clock, from which he never recovered, but continued unconscious and died on the Sunday, early in the afternoon. My father had often said to me that if I was not with him when he died he would try and come to me.[3]

Celia Green and Charles McCreery cite the following more recent example in their excellent book, *Apparitions*:

When living in Oxford . . . I had an odd experience when walking from New College to Broad St. There is a curve in the road with the back gates of Queen's College on the left and before reaching Hertford bridge. As I came down the road I saw two undergraduates in short gowns, one was sitting on a chestnut colored horse with white socks, the other was holding the bridle rein with one hand and had the other hand on the horse's neck. I was surprised to see a horse there and took a good look at it. Just as I came near the group another undergraduate on a cycle, with a tennis racket, came round the curve very quickly. I shrank back as I thought there would be a nasty accident, but to my surprise the cyclist came through the hindquarters of the horse. Very startled I realised the horse and the young men were no longer there.

It is the only time I have ever seen anything unusual and the group looked quite ordinary. The undergraduates were, however, wearing riding breeches. They both had short hair, and short black gowns. They were talking to each other quite naturally.

It was not until later, when I made some enquiries, that I learnt that these large doors had led to the Queen's College stables in the past.

I was going to a meeting of the Oxford Writer's Circle at the time and I was sufficiently pale when I arrived to make members ask if I was all right. They were very intrigued when I told them the story—although I think very few believed me![4]

While these examples are typical of the types of experiences reported, they are far from exhaustive in describing the characteristics of apparitions. It is important to note that while we generally refer to one's "seeing" a ghost, and even the more technical term "apparition" connotes the visual aspects of the phenomena, any and all senses might be involved in the perception of such spiritual forms. Again, the authors of the census found that it was, "legitimate to infer that *impressive* hallucinations of the visual class are considerably more frequent than those of the auditory, and that auditory hallucinations in general are considerably more frequent than tactile."[5] That is to say, the vast majority of apparitions are in fact of a visual kind. The next highest group of experiences being of a purely auditory nature, while sensations such as touch, smell, and taste are very rare indeed. This said, it also seems that most apparitions consist of only one sensory aspect. Green and McCreery confirmed the earlier findings in their study of apparitions. They note: "It will be seen that the number of experiences falls off rapidly as the number of senses increases. It seems that the more complicated types of hallucinatory experience may occur less frequently than the simple ones."[6] These two findings together indicate that by far the most common type of apparition is one that is both silent and visual. For this reason, it is simpler to continue to speak of an individual seeing an apparition, while keeping in mind that in the minority are cases in which it might also be heard, felt, or perhaps a combination of any of these sensations.

Former SPR president, G. N. M. Tyrrell, with his knack for cataloguing, expertly presents an analysis of apparitional experiences in his monumental work, *Apparitions*.[7] This text has been recognized in the field of psychical research as a modern classic and a seminal work on the study of apparitions. Tyrrell outlines common features found throughout accounts of ghostly encounters. In the next few pages, I will summarize Tyrrell's findings, supplementing them with confirmation from the work of Green and McCreery.

Tyrrell found that spatial presentation of the spirit is at odds with normal reality. That is to say, the apparition does not appear in ordinary space. The apparition will typically appear to be perfectly normal except for certain strange spatial characteristics. Prince Duleep Singh's report is a good example; his father's head seemed to be life-sized and with "an intent expression," though it was squarely placed within the frame of a picture. As Tyrrell puts it: "There is an unbroken transition from appearances in space, through appearances in detached and private spaces, to appearances in crystals, in dreams, or in inward types of vision."[8] Other oddities include certain attributes being greatly enhanced. Examples include such things as the label of a hat being clearly visible at over one hundred yards; objects being perceived which would normally be blocked from view by the apparition; or even the perception of the apparition while it is out of the range of normal perception. By way of example, Green and McCreery cite the case of a man who, while seated, reading, by a fire, clearly *saw* the figure of his friend standing behind him, completely out of normal, or even peripheral, visual range. The man was able to describe an injury to the apparition's jaw, which was later corroborated by his friend who had fallen on a curb and injured himself in just such a way. The apparition only vanished when the man turned around to actually look at it.[9] Green and McCreery also found that certain percipients with poor eyesight or hearing were able to perceive the apparition with clarity far exceeding their normal senses.[10]

Further, apparitions display a distinctly nonphysical character, as defined, according to Tyrrell, by the following characteristics: (1) they appear and disappear in locked rooms; (2) they vanish while being watched; (3) they sometimes become transparent and fade away; (4) they are often seen and heard by some of those present but not by all; (5) they disappear into walls and closed doors and pass through physical objects; (6) people might put their hands through them or walk through them without encountering any resistance; (7) they leave no physical traces behind. Green and McCreery further point out:

> subjects frequently do not comment spontaneously on whether things moved by the apparition were or were not found in a new position at the end of the experience. However, when asked they almost always say that the apparition left no permanent physical effects behind.
>
> Those few subjects who do perform some action at the time of the experience which has the effect of testing whether the physical effect really happened, usually find that it did not.[11]

Despite the nonphysical character of apparitions, the fact that they are perceptible at all suggests an objective reality. This presents a paradox in terms of the reality of the experience. A. R. Wallace, for instance, argues for the objectivity of apparitions, and ultimately their *physical* existence.[12] He cites that in certain cases, phantasms *can* have physical effects upon their environment, counter to Tyrrell's point that they leave no physical traces. It is clear that Wallace is referring to cases of what are now termed *poltergeist* phenomena, which are commonly thought of as spirits who smash or move objects while remaining invisible. Strictly speaking, these are not true apparitions for reasons that will be dealt with in their own turn further on in this chapter, though it might be noted briefly here that such phenomena often do not involve any experience of an apparition per se, whether seen or heard, though there may rarely be some apparitional experiences reported.

Wallace further argues for the objectivity of spirits on the basis of spirit photography, an idea briefly mentioned in the preceding chapter. Wallace states overconfidently that it is a "fact that phantasms, whether visible or invisible to persons present, can and have been photographed."[13] He goes on:

> The first person through whom spirit photographs were obtained was a New York photographer named Mumler . . . evidence of extraordinary tests having been applied was given. A professional photographer, Mr. W. H. Slee, of Poughkeepsie, watched the whole process of taking the pictures, and though there was nothing unusual in Mumler's procedure, shadowy forms appeared on the plates . . . Yet a third photographer, Mr. W. W. Silver, of Brooklyn, gave evidence to the same effect. He frequently went through the whole process himself, using his own camera and materials, yet when *Mumler was present,* and *simply placed his hand on the camera during the exposure,* additional forms besides that of the sitter appeared upon the plates.[14] [Italics mine]

There are a couple of problems with Wallace's assertion. The first is that he is dealing with turn-of-the-century equipment, which required a long time to actually take pictures. The long exposure times lent themselves easily to forgery and there are numerous examples of these fakes available.[15] These forgery techniques were also used in conjunction with physical mediumship, as mentioned in the preceding chapter. Modern technology has all but done away with the notion of spirit photography. Those who now claim to have pictures of spirits actually show quite different images from those of a hundred years ago. Modern images are no longer of ghostly human figures, but of wisps of smoke or tiny orbs of light. They certainly have no semblance to anything that should be assumed to be a priori human. This dramatic shift in results hardly seems like a reasonable occurrence given the stability of eyewitness accounts of apparitions over the centuries. Rather, they seem more likely to be the fraudulent, or to give the benefit of doubt, the merely credulous attempts of spirit photographers to salvage their beliefs that apparitions can indeed be captured on film.

Another problem with Wallace's argument lies within his own example. He states that "when Mumler was present and touched the camera" the effect would be noticed. If it were indeed possible to photograph an apparition, whether invisible or visible, it hardly seems likely that the photographer would have anything to do with it. If a camera were somehow able to register this information, one would believe that it is the camera itself that is capable of the feat. Since this does not appear to be the case, lest every camera in the world has developed spirit photographs already, one can only assume that the feat lies with the photographer, in this case with Mumler himself. At this point it does not matter whether this was the result of fraud, incompetence, or some latent psychic faculty possessed by the photographer. The point of the matter is that over a hundred years of effort have not provided any convincing pieces of photographic evidence for ghosts. Having said all of this, it would seem that, based upon the evidence, Tyrrell's second characteristic of apparitions, namely that they are distinctly nonphysical forms, can be accepted as accurate.

Returning to Tyrrell's finding, he notes that apparitions generally behave as though aware of their surroundings. Despite having a nonphysical nature, apparitions will behave as if physically occupying space. Typically, the apparition will move about an area paying attention to the topography of the environment, perhaps, for instance, moving to one side to avoid bumping into a chair. Also, most apparitions seem to take note of the presence of the percipient(s). In the case of Laurence Orchard's mother, the apparition apparently made some response when called after, and once again in Prince Duleep Singh's account, his father's face was looking intently at him. Apparitions also usually take special note of percipients that try and touch them. Apparitions are notoriously shy and tend to avoid all contact, even disappearing to avoid physical contact with a person, similar to the fashion in which the two undergraduates and their horse vanished when the cyclist drove into them.

Tyrrell adds a number of miscellaneous features to his list, including such things as the appearance of clothing, accessories, and animal companions. Generally, apparitions appear wearing some form of clothing, and it is often the clothing itself that makes identification of the apparition possible. As far as animal companions go, a great majority of human apparitions appear alone, though there are a few, like the example of the undergraduates, who appear with another human form or with animal companions (or indeed, as in said example, both). Occasionally animals might appear on their own, without human companions. An interesting aside on animal apparitions finds that cats appear far more frequently than any other animal, followed by dogs, horses, and then other domestic animals. Wild animals appear far less frequently still. As statistics also show that cats are the most common pets, one can easily deduce the human element even in animals that appear alone. The greater the expanse in the relationship between man and animal, the less common the apparition of said animal.[16] There are also rare cases where an entire scene, including background and environment, appears to the percipient.[17] This last feature can be compared to the example of Eileen Garrett's perception of the phantom dirigible crash describe in the previous chapter. A couple of questions are raised by these nonhuman elements of apparitional experience. That animals appear would seem to force one to accept that they also have spirits. More problematically, if apparitions are to be the spirits of the dead, then how does one account for their wearing clothes unless clothing is also thought to possess a soul? And as far as phantom scenery and other accessories go, if the apparitions are truly spirits of the dead, must all the rest of these additional features also be somehow composed of the same "spirit stuff?"

Tyrrell makes special mention of apparitions perceived by more than one person collectively. This is perhaps the single most troubling piece of evidence surrounding apparitions in terms of the question of whether they are objectively real or simply subjective hallucination. The fact that more than one person may see a given apparition certainly weighs heavily toward asserting that it is objectively real. Tyrrell suggests that the evidence is overwhelmingly in favor of the fact that multiple observers of an apparition are in fact seeing the exact same thing. However, there are reasons to believe that the situation may not be as straightforward as this. Green and McCreery observed that, "we do not know how precise the correspondence is between the images perceived by the various subjects. There are cases on record where, although the reports of the different subjects show some resemblance to one another, there are distinct indications of discrepancies.[18] Given the discrepancies between individual witness accounts, it is difficult to determine with certainty that any two people have in fact perceived the same objective reality. And there is always the possibility that one person's perception of events might affect another's by means of suggestion alone. If one thinks of watching clouds take shape, the fact that one's perception of patterns might be easily influenced by the observations of others should be easy to understand.

Green and McCreery provide the case of a group of three people who, after leaving the home of an ailing man, all saw a figure drift across a lake. The figure was identified as the man they had just left. One of the three clearly saw the man standing in a boat, another saw that there was no boat and that the man was simply floating along the surface. Interestingly, the witnesses discussed the apparition, and the differences they saw, as they watched the figure drift across the lake.[19] One might consider the conflicting reports as illustrating the common fallibility of eyewitness testimony, but the fact that they all reported discussing the apparition as they watched it argues against this. Instead, differences in perception remained despite the suggestions from one another. Such discrepancies, while minor in their detail, have great implications. It is often assumed that in eyewitness cases where there is a discrepancy that one report must be the "true" report and the others are misperceptions of that truth. The problem with this assumption is that it is impossible to tell which of the reports might be the true one as all witnesses may have the same certainty in what they perceive. As in the case just mentioned, the differences can hardly result from misperception when the witness' attention is drawn to the difference as it is happening and still sees the apparition as originally perceived. Green and McCreery come to the conclusion that what is instead occurring here is that each percipient is having an individual subjective experience of an overall scene. However, this still leaves open the question of the original source.

There remain other interesting findings relating to the collective perception of apparitions that may shed more light upon them. Analyses of case studies show that by far most apparitions are seen while the percipient is alone, thus accounting for the relative scarcity of collective cases. In those rare cases where an apparition appears to an individual while another is present, it is not always the case that everyone present will witness the event at all. Many cases illustrate that only one or some of a group will perceive the apparition with others remaining completely oblivious to the phenomenon. Also, as the group of people becomes larger, the cases of apparitions becomes smaller and smaller. To quote from Green and McCreery once again: "There are reports of groups numbering from two up to about eight people seeing the same apparition at the same time, but there are no well authenticated cases of groups much larger than this doing so. For example, audiences in theatres or other public places do not seem to witness collective apparitions."[20] It would seem that the more eyes added to a given situation, the less likely an apparition is to manifest. An exception to this rule against large numbers witnessing the same apparition would be cases of haunting, or what might be termed recurrent apparitional phenomena. Haunting cases have other differences from the typical apparition as well and so will be dealt with separately later.

Now, it must be stressed that while the number of cases in which more than one person sees an apparition are quite small in comparison to those in which there is only one witness, this does not necessarily weaken the fact that there *are* those cases in which the apparition is seen by multiple observers. Such collectively perceived cases would present the strongest evidence that apparitions are real, to some extent, and not simply subjective fantasy. As W. H. Salter points out, "Given poor light and a fit of nerves, 'how easy does a bush become a bear,' and there is little doubt that percipients sometimes take for apparitions what are nothing else than quite ordinary persons or things."[21] However, when several witnesses all describe the same bear, chances increase that they have actually seen more than just a bush. The question, then, is not whether they have experienced something but what it is exactly that they have experienced.

Tyrrell ends his list of apparitional features with a number of experiences he collects under the vague title of "other subjective feelings." By such "other" feelings, Tyrrell refers to those experiences where a person "feels" the presence of a person who remains undetected by the normal senses, or any other sensations which are difficult to put into words. People may occasionally have reason to believe they have been in the presence of a ghost but be unable to describe why they feel this way. William James also refers to a "sense of presence" when discussing religious experiences. This sense of presence is a well-established feature of apparitions. James provides the following example, related to him by a close personal friend:

> After I had got into bed and blown out the candle, I lay awake awhile thinking on the previous night's experience, when suddenly I *felt* something come into the room and stay close to my bed. It remained only a minute or two. I did not recognize it by any ordinary sense, and yet there was a horribly unpleasant "sensation" connected with it. It stirred something more at the roots of my being than any ordinary perception.[22]

Sometimes this sense of presence can be quite vivid. The case of the man who could "see" his friend standing directly behind him though not using his actual eyes, might be seen as an extreme example of this sense. A similar example can be found in the story of a girl who simply knew that a strange man was seated in her room, but was too afraid to turn and actually look. The feeling was so intense that she was sure of what he looked like and what he was doing without even physically looking at him. In her words: "I suddenly awoke . . . with a sort of certainty that a tall, thin, old man, in a long flowered dressing gown, was seated and writing at the table in the middle of the room. I cannot say what gave me this certainty, or this distinct picture, for I did not once turn my eyes to the place where I felt that the intruder was seated."[23]

Having discussed the general characteristics of the apparitions themselves, the situations in which an apparition is likely to be experienced require consideration. It has already been shown that apparitions typically reveal themselves to a person when not in the company of others. One of the correlates to this is the fact that the percipient is usually in a relaxed state. Generally the witness to an apparition is neither anxious nor terribly troubled with worry before the experience occurs. Typically, an apparition will appear when the percipient is in bed, largely accounting for the dearth of corroborative observers. Those periods between sleep and wakefulness, called hypnopompic and hypnagogic states, seem particularly conducive to these experiences. "Edmund Gurney [one of the founders of the SPR] observed that the transition states between sleeping and waking—or, more generally, the time when a person is in bed but not asleep—seem to be specially favorable to *subjective* hallucinations of the senses."[24] In one quarter of the cases gathered by Green and McCreery, the subject states that the experience occurred just after waking up, usually at night.[25] They also go on to point out that most subjects were lying down at the time, followed by being in a sitting position, with the least accounts occurring to those either standing or walking.[26] That is to say, apparitions tend to appear while one is in a relaxed state, not when one is partaking in vigorous activity. To further point out the necessity of relaxation for the appearance of apparitions, Green and McCreery further discovered that in 61% of their cases, the apparition appeared in the subject's home. Only 12% occurred in places the subject had never visited before.[27] Generally, reports of apparitions occur overwhelmingly in situations where the witness would normally be quite comfortable. Andrew MacKenzie points out that, "It is now generally accepted that apparitions are experienced in what are termed altered states of consciousness (ASC)."[28] Certainly, ASCs are regularly induced by relaxation. Meditation and daydreaming are normal parts of life, and the altered state of consciousness that comes with such calming activity is conducive to liminal experience. ASCs like trances, hypnosis, and the hypnopompic and hypnagogic states are simply deeper types of ASC. It is important to note that altered states of consciousness are also central to the work of mediums. In both mediumistic and spontaneous apparitional cases we find the importance of the altered state in the perception of the paranormal event, be it actual contact with the dead or not.

With the common characteristics of apparitions thus outlined, it becomes obvious that there are a great many paradoxes surrounding these phenomena. The question is how to best account for all of the characteristics adequately. As has been shown, there are striking reasons that suggest that the spiritualistic explanation may not be the best, unless one is to assume that ghosts possess a great number of powers not possessed by the living. That people witness apparitions, and especially that they sometimes witness them in groups, suggests an objective reality. That apparitions appear to be nonphysical, defy rules of normal perception and limits of space, and that multiple witnesses might perceive the ghost differently from another combine to suggest hallucination. Further, that nonhuman aspects might also appear as apparitions argues against a straightforward acceptance of them as spirits of the dead. Aside from the commonsense response that they are all created by the strange and little understood powers of spirits, a common theory since the earliest days of the SPR has involved telepathy among the living. Tyrrell subscribes to the telepathic theory, constructing an elaborate system to account for the possibility of multiple witnesses to a given apparition somehow sharing the basic structure of the apparition but then independently experiencing their own subjective versions of it.[29] Basically, this theory posits that the apparitions are hallucinations caused by the unconscious mind in order to reveal a telepathic message to the conscious mind. In the instant when a person dies, he or she may send out a subconscious cry to loved ones. This telepathic cry is received subconsciously and may be revealed to the conscious mind through the most vivid means available, as in a dream, potentially accounting for the preponderance of nocturnal visitations as well as the dreamlike qualities of the apparitions.

The only reason one might need to invoke a telepathic theory at all rather than simply rejecting all apparitions as hallucinations stems from a potential transfer of information. A great many apparitional experiences transfer information to the living—information that was otherwise unknown to any but the dead themselves. Most often, the information transferred is simply that the person appearing as a spirit has actually died. Many apparitions are simply loved ones already known to be deceased, their appearance serving to console the living but offering no real evidence of their reality. Those who experience such apparitions often feel a sense of relief from their grief and will trust in their experience itself as evidence for the reality of the spirit. In terms of verifiable evidence of the objective reality of the spirit, however, such experiences offer nothing. On the other hand, many apparitions bear important information that once corroborated can serve to suggest more than mere hallucination. Most scholars today follow Tyrrell in referring to four categories of apparition. Experimental cases are those in which an agent deliberately attempts to cause his apparition to appear to a particular percipient. "Crisis-apparitions" are those that appear at the time of, or in close proximity, to a trauma to the appearing individual; such cases often involve the death of the person in question. A third category (what Tyrrell calls "postmortem cases") accounts for those cases in which a recognized apparition appears long after the death of the person, such as I mentioned in connection with apparitions of bereavement. Tyrrell finishes with a fourth category of haunting apparitions, which we have yet to deal with in detail.[30] A fifth category can also be added, which includes those cases where one experiences the apparition of one who is living and has gone through no coincidental trauma; the implications of these latter apparitions will be dealt with in more detail later in this chapter.

Crisis-apparitions are a common type of spontaneous experience that also serves as proof that the apparition is a spirit of the dead. The proof stems primarily from the transference of information that occurs when the percipient becomes aware of the death or trauma of the individual represented by the apparition only through the experience of the apparition itself. Essentially, the experience of the apparition can be seen to transmit the information regarding the crisis in question itself—death, accident, and so forth. Other pieces of information might also be transmitted, ranging from such matters of import as the location of a lost will to trivialities that seem to have no other purpose than simply to prove that they are "still there." Carl Jung describes a situation in which a friend whose funeral he had recently attended appeared to him and showed Jung his library. Jung had never been to this friend's library but saw it in great detail while in this dreamlike state. The friend then pointed to a specific book on a certain shelf. When he later had the opportunity to visit the library in the flesh, Jung found the library to be just as seen in his vision and sought the book to which his friend had pointed. Sure enough, he found the exact book, one of a distinctive red color in the exact spot pointed to. The book was a translation of Emile Zola's appropriately titled *The Legacy of the Dead*.[31] Jung's entire experience can be considered veridical as the information was confirmed after the experience and was unknown to him before it. Of course, the information transmitted served no practical purpose other than to suggest that there was a life after death and that Jung's friend was not gone forever. In the other examples previously described, we find similar kinds of information transfer; the apparition of Prince Duleep Singh's father informed the prince of his father's death, while the apparition of the undergraduates did no more than indicate that the gates had once led to the Queen's stables. In each case, some information that was otherwise unknown to the living witnesses was somehow relayed. The source for such information, just as it was with mediums, is again the ultimate question.

It must also be stated that there are cases of apparitions of the dead that simply convey no information at all. Many of these remain unrecognized apparitions. Why they should appear to any given subject is a mystery. Those that are recognized but convey no veridical information often simply bear messages of reassurance. Other cases refer to loved ones simply smiling or saying hello and the like. This quote from U.S. General George S. Patton makes the point: "Father used to come to me in the evenings to my tent and sit down to talk and assure me that I would do all right and act bravely in the battle coming the next day. He was just as real as in his study at home at Lake Vineyard."[32] The emotional tone of such experiences leads Raymond Moody to believe, "that the subjects [of apparitions] see the person they *need* to see."[33] Dennis Klass describes in some detail the experiences of bereaved parents who maintain continuing bonds with their deceased children, often experiencing their actual presence in a variety of ways.[34] There is also a direct relationship between the appearance of ghosts and the time after which the person has died. As the time gets further away from the time of death, the number of apparitions decreases sharply. Thus, apparitions can be considered quite common at the time of death or shortly thereafter, but quickly become increasingly less common as the length of time increases.

Complicating the issue of the nature of apparitions is the fact that apparitions of the living, bearing the obvious distinction from those apparitions already mentioned, can be found in a surprisingly high number of accounts. Living apparitions might appear either spontaneously or may actually be willed by a living agent. The latter, referred to by Tyrrell as "experimental cases," are caused by the express will of the agent. Basically, one person wills him or herself to be seen by a subject at some distant location. Actual laboratory experiments have been conducted in this area, though in-depth discussion of the results will be related in the next chapter on out-of-body experiences (OBE). Since the agent is attempting to project some image of him or herself at a distance, such cases are closely related to other forms of OBE, also known as astral projection. An example from Tyrrell's study can again be used to illustrate just how such living apparitions might appear.

Mrs. Wilmot was at home in North America when she learned of bad weather on the oceans. As her husband was travelling by sea overnight, she was worried. She wished to herself that she might visit him and be sure that all was well. As she wished this, she had the impression of leaving her body and flying over the ocean to the boat on which her husband slept. She imagined walking into his cabin but being momentarily taken aback by the man in the top bunk above her husband staring at her in disbelief. She chose to ignore him and moved to her sleeping husband to bestow a kiss upon his head. Meanwhile, the husband had the most pleasant dream, as he referred to the experience, which exactly dovetailed with his wife's account. Upon receiving his wife's kiss, he awoke to find a much chagrined bunkmate. The bunkmate, a Mr. Tait, chastised Mr. Wilmot for having a woman in his room in the middle of the night. Mr. Wilmot was understandably awed that Mr. Tait should have seen what he had only just been dreaming. When he returned home, he excitedly told his wife about his strange experience and that of Mr. Tait. It was only then that he learned of his wife's nocturnal out-of-body journey.[35]

Here, then, it appears that not only one, but two witnesses saw Mrs. Wilmot's double as she willed herself to appear to her loved one.

Living apparitions may also appear spontaneously. Rare cases exist where a person has seen the double, or *doppelganger*, of someone only to find later that they had not even been near where they were seen. In these spontaneous cases the object of the apparition has no knowledge that he has been seen until they are told after the fact. An interesting feature in these types of cases is the fact that the object of the apparition not only is completely oblivious to the event, but is probably even asleep or otherwise unconscious, in an altered state of consciousness, one might say. In these spontaneous versions of living apparitions no information is relayed. The apparition generally behaves in a very robotic manner, expressing no agency whatsoever. I myself can recount a personal experience of this kind. While working a summer job at a factory, I saw one of my foremen approaching out of my peripheral vision. Because I was in the process of making a weld, I could not turn to acknowledge the foreman's approach but instead concentrated on my work. As I completed the weld, I perceived the foreman walk right up next to me and stand waiting for my attention. When I turned to speak with him, the vision disappeared. The foreman had not approached me or been in the immediate vicinity at the time of my experience. Given that such apparitions convey no information at all, there is no purpose for them. It is thus simple to explain these away as hallucinations. I am certain that the fatigue of shift-work had a part to play in my own particular experience.

Recurrent apparitions, commonly referred to as either hauntings or poltergeists, form another group of apparitional phenomena. Hauntings are a special kind of apparition in that while other apparitions appear only once, these are perceived over and over again in the same locale, as with the typical haunted house. The Cheltenham ghost, or so-called "Morton case," is one of the best-verified and documented cases on record, and so provides an appropriate example.[36] Starting around 1882 when the Despard family moved into the house, the figure of a black-clad woman, apparently weeping into a handkerchief, was seen during a two-year span by about seventeen different people, and heard by about twenty. Since that time, many other people have reported seeing the apparition in and around the house, and the surrounding neighborhood, through to the 1980s. Andrew MacKenzie points out that the location of the apparition has changed as the original house, and later neighboring houses, were renovated and modernized. In fact, it is a common belief in folklore that a ghost will stop haunting a place if it is rebuilt or renovated, perhaps even with something as simple as the application of new wallpaper. Ultimately, haunting experiences are interesting for the fact that they have several witnesses, who often do not know one another. They do not convey information, but are more difficult to attribute to subjective hallucination given the amount of witnesses involved. Normally, the apparitions in a haunting situation remain unidentified, not even transmitting enough information to declare their own identity. Those interested in doing the research can often find some indications of who the spirit might be, but this amounts to no more than conjecture. For instance, the Cheltenham ghost is believed to be the widowed wife of a drunk who originally owned the house based simply on records of occupancy and rumors about the husband's drinking and supposed treatment of his wife.

Hauntings are generally harmless, characterized by a sense of sadness or moroseness. The apparition will appear from time to time, perhaps performing some domestic chore or other completely benign activity. Perhaps some strange noises may accompany these apparitions, such as the sounds of footsteps or furniture being moved about. The more dramatic descriptions of moans, or even shrieks, occur in only very rare cases, blurring the line between haunting and poltergeist phenomena.

Poltergeists are quite different from any of the phenomena that have been discussed thus far. The word itself is of German origin, and means "noisy spirit." Normally, with such a poltergeist there is no apparition, but a spiritual presence is inferred from its apparent effects. Objects are aggressively moved across tables or hurled across rooms, doors are slammed, thuds and bumps of all kinds can be heard, and other violent phenomena are characteristic. The fact that these phenomena are normally not related to any apparitional experiences has led many investigators to conclude that they should not be considered in the same class as apparitions. As William Roll points out in his groundbreaking study of the poltergeist: "I do not know of any evidence for the existence of the poltergeist as an incorporeal entity other than the disturbances themselves," and these, he thinks, can be explained without resorting to the use of a spiritual theory.[37] However, the connection between poltergeist phenomena and hauntings necessitates some discussion.

First, unlike hauntings, which center on a particular location, poltergeists seem to center upon one person. Whereas a haunting will continue to plague a house

regardless of how many people move in and out, the poltergeist may follow a particular person, or family, from one location to the next. Investigations have shown
that the center of attention is most often a prepubescent or pubescent child,
though in some cases, the focus might be an emotionally unstable adult. The rule
seems to hold that the person on whom the poltergeist focuses is someone in a state
of emotional turmoil or frustration of some kind, which is then related to the often violent phenomena of the poltergeist.

The kinds of phenomena that characterize a poltergeist seem to imitate this
emotional turmoil. Objects are typically thrown about violently, and noises are
frighteningly loud. Shrieks and moans would be much more common in these
types of situations. In the midst of all this chaos, however, no one ever seems to
get hurt. Though there are cases of people receiving phantom bites and
scratches, leaving marks and all, none of the wounds are very serious, and certainly not life threatening. Herbert Thurston, after extensive research into poltergeists, made the following comments:

> I cannot at the moment recall a single instance . . . in which the human subject
> in such a case has sustained any serious or permanent injury. The damage to prop-
> erty is often considerable. Windows are broken by flying stones until not a sound
> pane of glass is left in the house. Chairs and tables are rendered unserviceable;
> plates, dishes and china ornaments are shattered wholesale; wearing apparel is
> torn to shreds or disappears mysteriously just when the owner wants to use it; but,
> however unpleasant this form of horseplay may be to the parties concerned, life
> and limb are apparently always respected.[38]

Another important difference between these and haunting cases is that where
a haunting might last for years, even decades, a poltergeist case usually does not last
much more than a few months. The haunting is a much more sedate and drawn
out experience, while, on the other hand, the poltergeist burns fast and fierce.

A parallel can be drawn between poltergeist cases and what has already been
learned about mediums from the previous chapter. The "medium" in these instances of poltergeist activity would be the individual at the center of all the activity, though unknowing they may well be. In fact, if not for their violent nature, the phenomena attributed to these disturbances would not be unfamiliar
to the old séance rooms of the physical mediums. The connection between the
poltergeist and mediumship was noticed early in psychical research. Salter argues that "it has been shown that the childish mentality, which gives rise to poltergeist disturbances, has a close kinship with some phases of advanced dissoci-
ation. Kinship with some kinds of mediumistic 'controls' is equally obvious."[39]
To draw this connection even more clearly, we may resort to the case of a poltergeist that attacked the small town of Shawville, Québec in 1889.[40]

What is special in this case is that, in addition to physical disturbances, the Shawville poltergeist was actually heard to speak in a deep, gravelly voice. This gruff voice would answer questions put to it, but would only speak in the presence of the family's eleven-year-old daughter. The voice would alternate between cordiality and crudity, reflecting the turbulent emotional state characteristic of poltergeist cases. The spirit variously claimed itself to be a devil, an angel, and the departed spirit of an 80-year-old man. The similarity to the ambiguity of mediums' controls is apparent. Further, similarities between the Shawville case and that of the Fox sisters are remarkable, though here the alleged spirit reportedly spoke rather than simply communicating through physical manifestations. No identity could be traced to the Shawville entity and it eventually disappeared after attracting the attention of the entire town. A telling aspect of the voice's origins lay in the fact that a main concern of the entity was to ensure that the young girl didn't get blamed for anything "he" had done or said. While it is impossible to ascertain that this girl faked the phenomena, she was certainly central to their appearance and was conveniently protected by the otherwise hostile poltergeist.

On another note, this case also demonstrates the roots of the confusion between poltergeists and hauntings as the girl and her two younger siblings all claimed to actually see the apparition of the spirit, though again in various forms. From surveys of case studies, it would appear that poltergeist cases and standard apparitional experiences are very different. The apparition never has any influence on physical objects, as noted by Tyrrell. However, in cases of poltergeist activity, an apparition may sometimes appear. For a number of reasons, which will be discussed momentarily, there are good reasons for assuming that apparitions in these cases are not evidence for any form of a life after death. The apparitions which so rarely appear in a poltergeist case never bear veridical information and generally remain unrecognized. Also, in a haunting the apparition itself is the whole of the event, while in a poltergeist case, the apparition appears only after the disturbance is well under way. Once people are victimized by a poltergeist, they become tremendously anxious to the point where, to use Salter's saying again, any bush *does* become a bear. Indeed, who would expect a bush to be capable of such destruction? Given the lack of information transferred by the poltergeist, it is easy to chock up any related apparitions to hallucination, especially given the emotional trauma that might lead to a kind of hysterical expectation.

From looking at the evidence from poltergeist cases, one can see why many investigators choose to place them in a completely separate category from apparitions, some going so far as to completely remove them from the discussion of life after death. They are an enigmatic type of phenomenon, encompassing aspects of both mediumship and hauntings. It is interesting to note that the modern form of mediumship described began with what might have been deemed a poltergeist in the vein of the Shawville case. The young Fox sisters simply harnessed the sporadic rapping sounds to become full-fledged mediums. Much like physical mediumship, which fell by the wayside in terms of evidential value to any effort to prove the ongoing existence of spirits, so too does the poltergeist suffer the same fate.

Now, it is an obvious hindrance to scientific inquiry that, with the exceptions of hauntings and experimental cases which will be discussed in the next chapter, apparitions are a spontaneous creature. Even hauntings, which do provide the advantage of staying in one place over a length of time, are notoriously coy. The analogy of the watched pot can equally be applied to apparitions; they seem only to appear when least expected and refuse to accommodate the waiting observer. There have, however, been a few attempts by scholars to bring these phenomena into the laboratory.

Michael Persinger, a neuroscientist at Laurentian University in Sudbury, Ontario, is one such individual. He has found that through the stimulation of certain parts of the brain, namely the temporal lobes, by electromagnetic fields, he is able to produce sensations similar to those found in some forms of haunting.[41] Among those sensations simulated are visual and auditory hallucinations, the sense of presence, and feelings of cold and horror. The hallucinations produced are very vague, however, and do not seem to resemble the lifelike apparitions described. Though haunting apparitions are generally unidentifiable, and perhaps even stereotypical in their appearance as, for instance, a grey nun, or a woman in black, they are still more clearly human than those created in Persinger's lab. Instead, Persinger's induced hallucinations are described as flashing lights, formless clouds, and strange, barely identifiable sounds. These types of visions and noises, it can be noted, are commonly found in those cases of hauntings that are borderline poltergeist cases. One might surmise that the difference between expectations in a laboratory setting compared to those of a familial home might account for differences in the interpretation of experience. Persinger theorizes that naturally occurring electromagnetic fields in certain areas might be the cause of haunting experiences, explaining why they occur over long periods of time in the same locations. William Roll agrees in large part with Persinger's theory, and extends it from the area of hauntings to that of the poltergeist as well.[42] Field studies have confirmed the possibility of magnetic fields playing a role in anomalous experiences at specific locations.[43] However one might explain both of these kinds of phenomena, it is clear that neither carries any weight in terms of direct evidence for the continuing existence of spirits of the dead. They may be strange experiences, perhaps even challenging a materialistic paradigm, but they do not force one to the conclusion of post-mortem human agency.

Other experimental studies of apparitions have taken a different approach to creating ghosts in the lab. Raymond Moody, who gained notoriety for first bringing the near-death experience to public attention in 1975 with his book, *Life After Life*, later turned his attention to apparitions. In more recent explorations, he was driven by the ancient notion that ghosts could be seen in reflective surfaces.[44] Reflective surfaces have featured prominently in the necromantic practices of a wide range of cultures from ancient Greek oracles to the modern child's game of looking into a mirror while saying "Bloody Mary" three times. Andrew Lang sums up the situation:

> Among the superstitions of almost all ages and countries is the belief that "spirits" will show themselves, usually after magical ceremonies, to certain persons, commonly children, who stare into a crystal ball, a cup, a mirror, a blob of ink (in Egypt and India), a drop of blood (among the Maoris of New Zealand), a bowl of water (Red Indian), a pond (Roman and African), water in a glass bowl (in Fez), or almost any polished surface.[45]

Moody's method involved constructing a so-called *psychomanteum* modeled after the Greek Oracle of the Dead at Ephyra. Basically, the psychomanteum is a small, enclosed area containing only a comfortable chair, dim lighting, and a mirror placed at such an angle that nothing but darkness could be seen in the reflection.[46] Moody's method has a subject prepare to see a certain departed individual by thinking about that person, and describing them in detail to another person before entering the enclosed psychomanteum. Once inside, the subject is to sit alone and relax, gazing into the mirror. In his book, Moody claims that approximately 50% of the subjects who entered his chamber succeeded in seeing an apparition. These apparitions appear as the actual deceased person themselves, unlike Persinger's vague sensations. Moody was himself a subject of his psychomanteum and was convinced of the genuineness of his own experience.

> I realize how people can assume that these apparitional facilitations are hallucinations. As a veteran of altered states of consciousness, I can say that my visionary reunion with my grandmother was completely coherent with the ordinary waking reality that I have experienced all my life. If I were to discount this encounter as hallucinatory, I would be almost obliged to discount the rest of life as hallucinatory too.[47]

Certainly, the experiences have the ring of truth about them, what William James referred to as a noetic quality. Such a feeling does not rule out the possibility of hallucination, however, and does not provide any evidence for there being an objective spirit present in these studies. Moody's work has since been replicated by a number of other studies, deriving results that correspond, for the most part, with the claim that the psychomanteum can actually induce the experience of apparitions.[48] That such apparitions can be induced does seem to provide some solace to the grieving, but they do not provide any evidence of a genuine spiritual presence. None of the apparitions generated in Moody's studies provided any evidential information that might suggest anything more than hallucination, and all of those that appeared were individuals known to be already deceased, and in fact, missed by the subject. While all subjects were instructed to seek a specific deceased person, there were cases where a different, but no less familiar, apparition appeared. This lead Moody to conclude, as mentioned earlier, that witnesses often perceive the apparition that they personally need to in order to resolve their grief. These observations notwithstanding, Dianne Arcangel reports a strange instance in which unrecognized apparitions sent messages intended for third parties, thus suggesting a certain level of information transfer in that the apparitions were later identified by the intended recipients of the messages. She reports that "2 participants saw images previously unknown to them and were given verbal messages to deliver to someone else. Interestingly, when the 2 people delivered their respective messages, the third parties identified the visions as *their* departed loved ones."[49] Arcangel's finding here is an anomaly among such studies. Interestingly, where Green and McCreery found that spontaneous apparitions rarely spoke a word, but rather looked as if they were unable to communicate, Moody reports that in fully 50 percent of the facilitated apparitions there was actual dialogue. Perhaps even more remarkably, in only 15 percent of these dialogues was the communication verbal instead of through some apparent mental communication, or telepathy.[50]

That the subjects in the psychomanteum cases are seeing an apparition, and a most convincing one at that, need not be denied. However, the facts as they stand are more suggestive of subjective wish fulfillment than the presence of some surviving agent. The subject has come seeking to reunite with a specific deceased individual, and then receives just that message which they most need in order to resolve their grief. There is nothing in that to add to the evidence for survival. Moody reports one case of an ostensibly collective apparition, however it is not clear what other causes may have led to this as the apparition appeared to several students in a demonstration, not under any scientific protocol.[51] As for veridical information, the Arcangel case cited is one of extremely few examples. That apparitional hallucinations can be induced experimentally suggests that other apparitions may well be hallucinations. The transfer of information in other spontaneous cases remains to be resolved, however.

As Andrew Lang points out: "It is said that, as sights may be seen in a glass ball, so articulate voices, by a similar illusion, can be heard in a sea shell."[52] And so a corollary to the psychomanteum studies can be found in what is today referred to as EVP, electronic voice phenomena, or more generally as Instrumental Transcommunication, or ITC. Apparent voices recorded accidentally in the background of other audiocassette recordings were first reported as evidence for the existence of spirits by Konstantin Raudive,[53] and Friedrich Jürgenson.[54] Such recordings begin to cross over into the territory of mediumship where the mechanical instrument becomes, naturally, the medium in place of a human being (or perhaps in concert with one). That these represent another attempt at physically recording the existence of a spirit allows us to consider them briefly here. Hans Bender suggested that such recordings might be caused by psychic faculties of the living and so should not constitute evidence for the spirits of the dead.[55] David J. Ellis later determined that the voices were in fact nothing more than auditory hallucinations.[56] If one listens hard enough to the static of a regular television set or radio, one will eventually hear voices whispering in the noise, especially if one is specifically looking for such voices to appear. Expectation can influence one's experience, and the ingenuity of a motivated listener can certainly hear signs of voice in the hiss. Of course, there remain those who in their commitment to proving the reality of an afterlife by any means necessary continue to mine this particular area for evidence of ghostly voices. Anabela Cardoso, for one, founded a journal dedicated to the study of recorded voice phenomena, the *ITC Journal*. She and David Fontana also recently waged a renewed debate with the author of the original rejection of EVP, David Ellis, in the pages of the *Journal of the Society for Psychical Research*.[57]

Finally, another means of creating apparitions can be found in hypnosis. Certainly, the preparation for the psychomanteum can be seen as a kind of planted suggestion in that the subject sets one's self up to perceive a specific vision. Sitting comfortably in the dark, gazing into a mirror is likely to induce a relaxed state akin to the hypnotic trance. Hypnotically induced hallucinations can appear completely lifelike and indistinguishable from reality, even when the hallucination is the double of another individual present, even a friend of the subject. Thomson Jay Hudson describes an example, which will suffice to elucidate the relevance for our present discussion. A subject was hypnotized and the apparitional form of Socrates was suggested to be seated in front of him. As he much admired the great sophist, "he catechised the Greek philosopher for over two hours, interpreting the answers to the professor as he received them."[58] The dialogue was filled with such lofty ideas about life and the universe that many witnesses became convinced that Socrates must truly be sitting invisibly where he was suggested to be. Following this, the subject was given an array of other equally great thinkers with whom he could discuss further ideas. The experiment concluded with the subject being instructed to converse with the reincarnation of a Hindu priest, *in the form of a pig*. Once completed, it was clear that the entire series of dialogues were so coherent as to suggest a single mind's work rather than several. Nobody is expected to believe that the long-dead spirit of Socrates was actually summoned up by the hypnotist. One might recognize some similarities to mediumship as the hypnotized subject, having entered into an altered state of consciousness, sees visions of the dead and converses with them. One will here recognize once again James's "philosophy and water."

Having reviewed the varieties of apparitions and those characteristics common to them all, we can reach some final comments. Basically, everything that has been learned about apparitions to date can be boiled down to two paradoxical points. On the one hand, apparitions appear very solid and lifelike. They move about in physical space and behave as though they exist within the confines of their environment. The fact that several people may see the apparition, either all at once as in spontaneous cases, or over a span of time as in a haunting, suggests that they are objectively real in space. Those who have the experience of an apparition often feel as if their experience could be nothing but real. On the other hand, the apparitions perform feats that would be impossible for a physical being to perform, such as passing through doors, vanishing into thin air, walking without leaving footprints, or making any noise whatsoever. In some cases, only one or two people in a group will perceive the apparition while others present do not. And what is one to make of such things as ghostly animals? What about ghostly plants? Carriages, clothing, or dirigibles? Scientific experimentation, while attempting to create ghosts within a laboratory setting, has succeeded only in imitating some of the features of apparitions, and these are typically only the most vague of characteristics. In relating apparitional research to that on mediumship one can see similarities and overlap. It seems that any person, under the right conditions and in the right state of mind, might be able to experience these "spirits" just as some mediums are wont to do. The difference is that the medium can do so at will, while the general population is merely at the mercy of unpredictable spontaneous intrusions. While collective apparitions, however rare, are suggestive of objectivity, the most troubling aspect of apparitional experiences remains the same as that emerging from mediums: the transfer of information and its source. Possible answers to these questions require further speculation, and some ideas will be put forth following the discussion of further evidence in the following chapters.

Notes

1. Henry Sidgwick, A. Johnson, F. W. H. Myers, F. Podmore, and E. M. Sidgwick, "Report on Census of Hallucinations." *Proceedings of the Society for Psychical Research* 10 (1894): 25–422.

2. William Henry Salter, *Ghosts and Apparitions* (London: G. Bell & Sons, 1938), Case XII, pp. 37–38.

3. Salter, *Ghosts and Apparitions*, Case XV, pp. 43–44.

4. Celia Green and Charles McCreery, *Apparitions* (London: Hamish Hamilton, 1975), p. 1.

5. Sidgwick et al., "Report on Census of Hallucinations," p. 130.

6. Green and McCreery, *Apparitions*, p. 81.

7. G. N. M. Tyrrell, *Apparitions*, revised ed. (New York: Collier, 1970), pp. 53–84.

8. Tyrrell, *Apparitions*, p. 58.

9. Green and McCreery, *Apparitions*, pp. 18–19.

10. Green and McCreery, *Apparitions*, p. 169.

11. Green and McCreery, *Apparitions*, pp. 205–206.

12. A. R. Wallace, *Miracles and Modern Spiritualism* (1896; repr., New York: Arno, 1975), p. 234.

13. Wallace, *Miracles*, p. 234.

14. Wallace, *Miracles*, p. 248.

15. For a description of how fraudulent ghostly photographs were taken in the dawn of photography, as well as a great amount of detail on photographic fakery in general, see: Dino A. Brugioni, *Photo Fakery: The History and Techniques of Photographic Deception and Manipulation* (Dulles, VA: Brassey's, 1999), especially pp. 157–161.

16. Green and McCreery, *Apparitions*, p. 63, pp. 192–196.

17. Green and McCreery, *Apparitions*, pp. 275–277.

18. Green and McCreery, *Apparitions*, p. 41.

19. Green and McCreery, *Apparitions*, pp. 42–48.

20. Green and McCreery, *Apparitions*, p. 41.

21. Salter, *Ghosts and Apparitions*, pp. 31–32.

22. William James, "What Psychical Research Has Accomplished," in *William James on Psychical Research*, eds. Gardner Murphy and Robert O. Ballou (London: Chatto and Windus, 1961), p. 63.

23. Green and McCreery, *Apparitions*, p. 121.

24. Andrew MacKenzie, *Apparitions and Ghosts* (London: Arthur Barker, 1971), pp. 46–47.

25. Green and McCreery, *Apparitions*, p. 70.

26. Green and McCreery, *Apparitions*, p. 124.

27. Green and McCreery, *Apparitions*, p. 123.

28. Andrew MacKenzie, *Hauntings and Apparitions* (London: Granada, 1983), p. 16.

29. Tyrrell, *Apparitions*, pp. 124–125.

30. Tyrrell, *Apparitions*, pp. 35–36.

31. C. G. Jung, *Memories, Dreams, Reflections*, ed. Aniela Jaffé (London: Collins and Routledge & Kegan Paul, 1963), p. 289.

32. F. Ayer, *Before the Colors Fade*, cited in Raymond Moody, *Reunions: Visionary Encounters With Departed Loved Ones* (New York: Ivy, 1993), p. 11.

33. Moody, *Reunions*, p. 22.

34. Dennis Klass, *The Spiritual Lives of Bereaved Parents* (Philadelphia, PA: Brunner/Mazel, 1999).

35. Tyrrell, *Apparitions*, pp. 128–131.

36. MacKenzie, *Hauntings and Apparitions*, pp. 47–74.

37. William G. Roll, *The Poltergeist* (Garden City, NY: Nelson Doubleday, 1972), p. 159.

38. Herbert Thurston, *Ghosts and Poltergeists* (London: Burns Oates, 1953), p. 27. For cases of phantom bites, see pp. 14–26.

39. Salter, *Ghosts and Apparitions*, p. 135.

40. Thurston, *Ghosts and Poltergeists*, pp. 162–171.

41. Michael A. Persinger, S. G. Tiller, and S. A. Koren, "Experimental Simulation of a Haunt Experience and Elicitation of Paroxysmal Electroencephalographic Activity by Transcerebral Complex Magnetic Fields: Induction of a Synthetic 'Ghost,'" *Journal of Perception and Motor Skills*, 90:2 (2000): 659–674.

42. Roll, *The Poltergeist*, pp. 158–178.

43. Jason J. Braithwaite, Katty Perez-Aquino, and Maurice Townsend, "In Search of Magnetic Anomalies Associated with Haunt-Type Experiences: Pulses and Patterns in Dual-Time Synchronized Measurements," *Journal of Parapsychology* 68:2 (2004): 255–288 and Jason J. Braithwaite, "Magnetic Variances Associated with 'Haunt-Type' Experiences: A Comparison Using Time-Synchronized Baseline Measurements," *European Journal of Parapsychology* 19 (2004): 3–28.

44. Moody, *Reunions*. A preliminary report was also made in 1992: Raymond Moody, "Family Reunions: Visionary Encounters with the Departed in a Modern-Day Psychomanteum," *Journal of Near-Death Studies* 11:2 (1992), 83–121.

45. Andrew Lang, *The Book of Dreams and Ghosts* (London: Longmans Green, 1899), p. 57.

46. For the description of Moody's psychomanteum and the methods of its use, see Moody, *Reunions*, pp. 65–82.

47. Moody, *Reunions*, p. 22.

48. Dianne Arcangel, "Investigating the Relationship Between the Myers-Briggs Type Indicator and Facilitated Reunion Experiences," *Journal of the American Society for Psychical Research* 91 (1997): 80–95; Dean Radin and J. Rebman, "Are Phantasms Fact or Fancy? A Preliminary Investigation of Apparitions Evoked in the Laboratory," *Proceedings of Presented Papers*, Parapsychological Association 38th Annual Convention, Durham, NC (Charlottesville, VA: Parapsychological Association, 1995), pp. 342–365; William G. Roll and B. A. Braun, "Psychomanteum Research: A Pilot Study," *Proceedings of Presented Papers*, Parapsychological Association 38th Annual Convention, Durham, NC (Charlottesville, VA: Parapsychological Association, 1995), pp. 438–443.

49. Arcangel, "Investigating," p. 92.

50. Moody, *Reunions*.

51. Moody, *Reunions*, pp. 131–132.

52. Lang, *The Book of Dreams and Ghosts*, p. 66.

53. Konstantin Raudive, *Breakthrough: An Amazing Experiment in Electronic Communication with the Dead* (New York: Taplinger, 1971).

54. Friedrich Jürgenson, *Sprechfunk mit Verstorbenen* (Freiburg: Verlag Hermann, 1967).

55. Hans Bender, *Verborgene Wirklichkeit: Parapsychologie und Grenzengebiete der Psychologie* (Olten, Freiburg: Walter Verlag, 1973).

56. David J. Ellis, "Listening to the 'Raudive Voices,'" *Journal of the Society for Psychical Research* 48 (1975), pp. 31–42 and David J. Ellis, *The Mediumship of the Tape Recorder: A Detailed Examination of the Raudive Voice Phenomenon of Voice Extras on Tape Recordings* (Pullborough, UK: D. J. Ellis, 1978).

57. See the *Journal of the Society for Psychical Research* 69:1–4 (2005), 70:3 (2006), and 71:2–3 (2007).

58. Thomson Jay Hudson, *The Law of Psychic Phenomena* (Chicago: A. C. McClurg, 1902), pp. 34–38.

CHAPTER TEN

~

Near-Death
and Out-of-Body Experiences

Raymond Moody provides the following fictional idealized version of a near-death experience (NDE), combining the common features that he identified in actual reports from those who had come close to death:

A man is dying and, as he reaches the point of greatest physical distress, he hears himself pronounced dead by his doctor. He begins to hear an uncomfortable noise, a loud ringing or buzzing, and at the same time feels himself moving very rapidly through a long tunnel. After this, he suddenly finds himself outside his own physical body, but still in the same immediate physical environment, and sees his own body from a distance, as though he is a spectator. He watches the resuscitation attempt from this vantage point and is in a state of emotional upheaval.

After a while, he collects himself and becomes more accustomed to his odd condition. He notices that he still has a "body," but one of a very different nature and with very different powers from the physical body he has left behind. Soon other things begin to happen. Others come to meet him and help him. He glimpses the spirits of relatives and friends who have already died, and a loving, warm spirit of a different kind he has never encountered before—a being of light—appears before him. This being asks him a question, nonverbally, to make him evaluate his life and helps him along by showing him a panoramic, instantaneous playback of the major events of his life. At some point, he finds himself approaching some sort of a barrier or border, apparently representing the limit between earthly life and the next life. Yet, he finds that he must go back to the earth, that the time for his death has not yet come. At this point he resists, for by now he is taken up with his experiences in the afterlife and does not want to return.

He is overwhelmed by intense feelings of joy, love, and peace. Despite his attitude, though, he somehow reunites with his physical body and lives.

Later he tries to tell others, but he has trouble doing so. In the first place, he can find no human words to describe these unearthly episodes. He also finds that others scoff, so he stops telling other people. Still, the experience affects his life profoundly, especially his views about death and its relationship to life.[1]

Studies have reported that as many as 35–40 percent of all people who have reached the brink of death, but were subsequently resuscitated report an experience similar to that described,[2] with even more conservative estimates citing the pervasiveness of these experiences around 20 percent.[3] A recent long-term study involving 344 patients who had been resuscitated found that 18 percent reported some kind of near-death experience.[4]

Near-death experiences, such as the one Moody recounted, will be familiar to most readers due to the fact that the subject has received a great deal of publicity in recent years. Raymond Moody coined the term "near-death experience," and brought it to popular attention in the mid-seventies with his book, *Life After Life*. While admittedly not a thoroughly scientific study of this new type of experience, the book did succeed in setting the framework from which other research could be initiated, and it has, for this reason, become a classic in the field.

The account described is not a true report of an NDE, but is a prototypical construct created by Moody himself to illustrate what the "perfect" near-death experience would look like. Many of the features are particularly recognizable, such as the tunnel and the light. These archetypal features seem to have garnered the better share of the popular spotlight, appealing particularly to the public imagination. Moody, however, is quick to point out that the prototypical NDE does not exist; instead, several of the features described, but never all, will appear in any given individual experience. All of the features in this experience have been described in numerous accounts, though no one case has contained them all. In order to get a flavor of the near-death experience, it is necessary to see an example of a real NDE as reported by a person who actually experienced it. The case used as an example here is that of a woman in her mid-thirties, who, before having the NDE, was undergoing surgery for a chronic intestinal disorder. She reports her experience as follows:

[She remembers hearing someone say that they were going to do a "cut down" on her and then] I remember being *above* the bed—I was not *in* the bed anymore—looking down on *me* lying in the bed and I remember saying to myself, "I don't want you to do a cut down on me." . . . I know [from what she was told afterward] that the doctors worked on me for many hours. And I remember being first above my body and then I remember being in, like a valley. And this valley reminded me of what I think of as the valley of the shadow of death. I also remember it being a very *pretty* valley. Very pleasant. And I felt very *calm* at that point. I met a person in this valley. And this person—I realized it later on—was my [deceased] grandfather, who I had never met. [She then describes how she was able to identify him after talking to her grandmother about it.] I remember my grandfather saying to me, "Helen, don't give up. You're still needed. I'm not ready for you yet." It was that kind of a thing. And then I remember *music* . . . It was kind of like church music, in a sense. Spiritual music . . . it had . . . somehow a *sad* quality about it. A very awesome quality to it.[5]

Now, it is important to place reports such as this within the proper context before continuing any further. What Moody coined as near-death experiences are just that; experiences had by persons who actually come very near to being dead. In many cases, the people who have these experiences have been declared clinically dead; that is to say, their heart has ceased to beat. It is only once the person has been resuscitated and brought back from the brink of physical extinction that the patient reveals the seeming otherworldly journey just undertaken.

Since Moody's groundbreaking book, and his subsequent further studies, the near-death experience has been the subject of much scientific scrutiny. Of the phenomena dealt with here, NDEs are by far the most well established in scientific circles, if for no other reason than that they have elicited a great deal of curiosity among scientists at large, primarily those in the medical profession. That some people do report this strange set of experiences is beyond a doubt; what is under debate now is what to make of them and how to explain them.

To begin with, having already seen the "perfect" NDE, it will now be helpful to review the standard features delineated by Moody in individual detail.[6] These characteristics have been debated since Moody's pioneering efforts, and though there have been changes made to this preliminary list, it will be important to discuss them for their historical importance to this field of research. It must be borne in mind that not all features need appear in any given experience, and that in some cases, certain aspects may appear in differing order from one experience to the next. Let us now turn to the characteristics.

Ineffability is often cited as a key feature in such deeply moving experiences, encouraging some to liken the NDE to a mystical experience. People who have experienced an NDE have a truly difficult time expressing in words what they have experienced. The experience is one of such emotion and intensity as to be beyond words, much like the awesome sense of mystical union with the absolute described by mystics the world over. William James cited ineffability as one of his defining characteristics of mystical experiences as well.[7] The woman in the previous example exhibits this common element as she obviously struggles with the words, at points speaking in metaphors, as she says, "like a valley," reminding her of the biblical valley of the shadow of death.

The person often hears someone, a doctor or nurse most likely, report that the patient has been lost and that he or she is now dead. There may also be the subjective sense of, "ah, now I am dead." In the previous example, there is no mention of the subject's death, but only the imminent incision, the "cut down."

Feelings of peace and quiet overwhelm them. Nothing seems to matter any more, least of all the fact that they have died. Reports one near-death survivor, "I knew I was going to be perfectly safe, whether my body died or not."[8] Feelings of calm combined with a pleasant atmosphere are common, and are illustrated in the previous example. Pim van Lommel, et al., found that positive emotions were the most commonly agreed upon characteristic of the experience among those who report them, citing the appearance of positive emotions in 56 percent of cases.[9]

The patient often hears a loud noise, which seems to mark the beginning of the transition from the body to the spiritual realm. Buzzing, ringing, clicking, roaring, banging, or whistling like the wind, even music, are all typically reported. Music is heard in the case of the woman provided.

The image of a dark tunnel has become synonymous with the NDE for many people, being the most readily accessible symbol of any experienced. This "tunnel" may take various forms, from a tube or funnel to a valley. In many cases there is not an actual tunnel so much as simply a dark void. Kenneth Ring has pointed out that an actual tunnel is but one interpretation of what appears more accurately to be a dark space in which a light gradually appears.[10] A more recent study concluded that the tunnel appears to be influenced by societal expectation deriving from the publication of Moody's list more than any other component.[11] The valley reported in the previous example is in keeping with the common tunnel phenomenon, as is the religious interpretation.

The out-of-body experience (OBE) is central to the near-death experience for logical and obvious reasons. The person feels themselves exit from their body and can observe it from a vantage point elsewhere in the room, usually floating up into the air. He or she may find that their own body is different from their physical one in that it may have a ghostly, transparent quality. Alternatively, he or she may perhaps not even have any body as such, but merely exists as a point of consciousness in space. Moody's collection of cases drove him to claim that there was always a "spiritual body" in the OBE. The work of others, notably Celia Green, has shown, however, that there are rare cases in which there is no body to speak of, or at least the percipient did not perceive their own spiritual body.[12] Descriptions of people in the room with the unconscious, or "dead" person, as well as details of their actions are generally correct, as if seen from this new vantage point. In some cases, the person leaves the room where their body is and wanders freely, sometimes for quite some distance. Further descriptions of events outside the environment of the physical body, such as overheard conversations in other parts of the building, are accurately reported upon waking. Because of the possibility for veridical information in this state, and thus scientific testing, the out-of-body experience has received a lot of attention on its own and will therefore be dealt with in detail in the second part of this chapter. The previous example includes an out-of-body experience, as the patient reports being *above* her body.

Meeting with others is commonly cited as a component of such experiences. Deceased friends and relatives typically appear to meet the percipient and to assist in the process of dying. These other spirits play the role of *psychopomp*, leading the newly dead person away from the body and into the next world. They are, "beings who apparently were there to ease them through their transition into death."[13] On these ghostly visions, Karlis Osis made two interesting observations. First, he points out that close to 40 percent of near-death patients perceive these types of visions compared to only about 4 percent in the general healthy population. Even if one considers the 10 percent figure cited by the Census of Hallucinations mentioned in the previous chapter, there is still a wide range between the experiences of those living and those nearing death. Second, dying patients most commonly see apparitions of the dead, compared to those witnessed by the general population that often include apparitions of the living, or *doppelgangers*, again described in the preceding chapter.[14] The woman in our example encounters such a being in the form of her grandfather who appears during her experience.

The so-called "Being of Light" appears in many reports, though like all features mentioned, not in all. Moody's description of this feature is best provided in full:

> The love and warmth which emanate from this being to the dying person are utterly beyond words, and he feels completely surrounded by it and taken up in it, completely at ease and accepted in the presence of this being. He senses an irresistible magnetic attraction to this light . . . Interestingly, while the above description of the being of light is utterly invariable, the identification of the being varies from individual to individual and seems to be largely a function of the religious background, training, or beliefs of the person involved. Thus, most of those who are Christians in training or belief identify the light as Christ . . . A Jewish man and woman identified the light as an "angel." It was clear, though, in both cases, that the subjects did not mean to imply that the being had wings, played a harp, or even had a human shape or appearance. There was only the light.[15]

It is important to note that while in Moody's sample, the Being of Light was always perceived as such, other surveys have shown differences. Notably, the Being may not even appear as a light at all, but may only make itself known through a voice, or even what seems to be thought transference, or telepathy. A better term might be simply to refer to a presence, rather than Moody's Being of Light.[16] The example includes no other beings than the grandfather, though this figure does assume certain aspects of the Being of Light.

In some instances, one literally has one's life flash before one's eyes. Typically, at least in Moody's sample, it is the presence referred to as the Being of Light who brings the person to the life review. One is asked a question along the lines of, "What have you done with your life and is that enough so that you might die now?" Then, one experiences the life review. This process is both very quick and detailed at the same time. Percipients often report seeing all of life's experiences bound up together so that suddenly everything that had ever happened, both good and bad seemed to fit and to make sense. Life seems to come together perfectly and the point and purpose of everything is revealed. Two points always seem to be emphasized during these reviews—namely learning to love other people and the importance of gaining knowledge are of paramount importance. Again, our example does not include a life review.

The percipient often comes to some border or point beyond which there is no return. Upon reaching this area, the percipient is sent back to life. This border can be described in a vast array of ways, from a river to a white picket fence to an area of dense fog. Sometimes, the percipient is even vouchsafed a brief glimpse of some heavenly city of sorts. This stage of the NDE is, along with the "tunnel," among the most easily recognizable forms of Jungian symbolism provided by such experiences. It is just such archetypal images that suggest a psychological explanation for the phenomena versus a purely survivalist interpretation. Van Lommel, et al., found that while the tunnel, the most popularly imagined aspect of the NDE, appeared in 31 percent of cases, the notion of some other border appeared in only 8 percent. It would be interesting to know whether these two characteristics often appear in the same account as both would appear to symbolically indicate the same thing—a liminal state of transition from one state of being (life) to another (death). The example above makes no mention of a border or barrier of any kind, instead referring only to a valley in the place of a tunnel.

While many experience some degree of fear and trepidation at the outset of their experience, these initial feelings often change to such blissful joy that the percipient is often upset to actually return to his or her body and carry on living, preferring instead to have remained dead. This reaction is temporary, however, as will shortly be discussed. The actual return itself is generally not experienced, but the percipient simply wakes up back in his or her body. Again, the return is not described in detail in the example used here, although the words of the percipient's grandfather urge her back to life with the contention that she is still needed and it is not her time, signaling her return to the world of the living. Our example ends with the completion of the actual experience, and so the next few points are not mentioned therein, though one can assume that the remaining characteristics might well apply to this woman as they apply to others who have experienced an NDE.

Telling others is always a difficult thing for the percipient to do. Their own certainty in what they have experienced is balanced by the fear that they will be thought insane. As with all paranormal experiences, the fear of ridicule is both normal and justified, given the present climate of social rejection and contempt for such phenomena. However, Moody's books, and the scientific attention now given the NDE, have enabled many people to realize that they are not alone in their experiences and have helped these people to talk more freely about them. While a hefty degree of ignorance still fosters some rejection and ridicule, as more research is conducted and disseminated to the population at large this will gradually change for the better.

For many researchers, especially those of a more religious bent, the effect that these experiences have on those who experience them is of immense importance. People's lives are broadened by the near-death experience. They are made more reflective and more concerned with ultimate philosophical issues. Life itself becomes more precious in every detail. For some, intuition becomes more pronounced, or perhaps psychic abilities may manifest themselves. "Almost everyone has stressed the importance in this life of trying to cultivate love for others, a love of a unique and profound kind."[17] The two main lessons learnt from the life review become realities in the lives of survivors. David Lorimer has discussed the extent to which the NDE is a transformative experience akin to a truly mystical experience, stressing the unitive consciousness, loss of selfishness, and desire to obey the "Golden Rule" that all become important issues for survivors of an NDE.[18]

Furthermore, Moody states, "Almost every person has expressed to me the thought that he is no longer afraid of death . . . They all feel that they have tasks to do as long as they are physically alive."[19] Life is seen as something precious and to be fully lived every moment, as death is no longer to be feared. There is no doubt to the percipient that there must be an afterlife as they have died and seen what was there. In addition, "the reward-punishment model of the afterlife is abandoned and disavowed, even by many who had been accustomed to thinking in those terms."[20] Now, while it is certainly important to take the interpretation of percipients into consideration, one cannot accept the conclusion that there truly is an afterlife on subjective testimony alone. The fact that people who have NDEs almost universally feel that they have died and seen a world beyond does not prove that this is necessarily so. That there is such a wide agreement on such aspects of the experience as has been seen certainly requires some form of explanation, however.

From a scientific perspective, the corroboration of some or all of the above-mentioned phenomena is essential. Certain features of the percipients' descriptions of their experiences can be verified, which is especially impressive where some form of information that would otherwise lie outside of the patient's range of knowledge is revealed through the experience. Moody explains, "Several doctors have told me, for example, that they are utterly baffled about how patients with no medical knowledge could describe in such detail and so correctly the procedure used in resuscitation attempts, even though these events took place while the doctors knew the patient involved to be 'dead.'"[21] It is this type of corroboration that might enable us to determine empirically whether the near-death experience is truly an experience of an afterlife. Our example includes some degree of such corroboratory evidence, namely stemming from the encounter with her grandfather whom she was unable to identify, having not met him in life, until her description was seen to conform to her grandmother's memory of him.

Having seen the various stages of the near-death experience, what is one to make of it all? Does this experience actually provide any proof for an afterlife, as the typical percipient's own interpretation contends? As the philosopher Christopher Cherry states it, whether people do or do not actually experience an afterlife during an NDE, "is an *empirical* matter, albeit a hugely complicated one."[22] Such being the case, one can look to see if there are any veridical and/or testable aspects to the NDE. Michael Grosso points out that there are three key components of NDEs that require explanation: (1) the consistency and universality which they generally display, (2) their power to modify attitudes and behavior, and (3) their paranormal aspects—that is, the transfer of information otherwise unknown.[23] The usefulness of NDEs as proof for any form of survival of the individual after bodily death rests on some combination of these three factors.

Many researchers of near-death phenomena have debated the universality of the experience. Carol Zaleski has argued through a comparison of modern and medieval accounts of near-death encounters that the culturally induced differences outweigh the similarities in their prominence.[24] Allan Kellehear goes even further in drawing upon a wide array of cultural sources to contrast NDE reports, again finding significant differences in the details of the experiences reported, though still maintaining the common characteristic of being experiences near-death.[25] From the preceding review of religious experiences, however, one can see that near-death experiences, as here defined, do not appear in every culture, and where they do appear there are often wide discrepancies in descriptions. For instance, Carl Becker, in his study of NDEs in the Pure Land Buddhist tradition, claims to find many of Moody's common features in the reports of Pure Land Buddhists. When one examines the actual reports of these so-called near-death experiences, the similarities quickly fade as it becomes obvious that they are highly culturally influenced and bear little resemblance to North American NDEs. To some degree, culturally determined interpretations of what seems to be similar experiences can be identified. S. Pasricha and Ian Stevenson came to the conclusion that the NDEs of Hindus were essentially the same as those of North Americans but for slight cultural variances, finding both similarities and differences, suggesting a common core of experience.[26] Karlis Osis and Erlendur Haraldsson also found this common core, arguing further that cultural expectations about the afterlife were ignored in the actual experiences, so neither purely Christian symbols nor Hindu ones were described by respective adherents.[27] Also, it has been shown that the experience is consistent enough, at least so far as the North American variant is concerned, to produce a prototypical NDE with specific delineated features. More recent research has increasingly narrowed the list of common factors, however, in an effort to establish some sort of common core to the NDE. Mark Fox recently went so far as to suggest that, in the end, the NDE may consist of nothing more than, "episodes of light and darkness."[28] While the search for the universality of the NDE continues, it is useful to bear in mind the following words of Michael Grosso:

> Obviously, the mere fact that a phenomenon is universal and consistent in itself need not impress us; drunkards of all cultures and personality types, for example, consistently have the same sort of experiences—say, delirium tremens. Consistency and universality here is no bar to seeing the drunkard's experience as delusory. But it is a different matter with near-death experiences, for we do not expect delusory experiences to produce momentous changes in personality or to involve extensions of normal human capabilities [such as, say, the acquisition of information through paranormal means].[29]

Certainly, in terms of the proof sought in the present study, Grosso's statement reveals that the first problem posed by the NDE in reference to the universality of the experience does not immediately concern this issue. It is not so much the present task to explain all aspects of the near-death experience, but primarily to seek to identify possible sources of proof for an afterlife. Therefore, as illustrated, it is to the other two aspects mentioned that one must turn in this instance.

Much is made in the literature of the dramatic changes survivors of an NDE undergo. The changes are truly profound and spiritual. People feel personally improved by the experience; they truly strive to love every person and try to create a life that is full of learning. The powerful impact of the NDE has forced many people to develop a strong belief in an afterlife based upon their experience. Many writers focus upon these life changes to various ends; some to promote their own religious beliefs, others to prevent suicide, still others to point to an underlying meaning to life. The impact this experience has on individuals is similar to the mystical experience of a total union with the absolute, or perhaps even a religious conversion as befell St. Paul on the road to Damascus. In fact, the NDE itself could easily be viewed as a subset of mystical experience and studied as such. Judith Cressy draws the connection between modern NDEs with Christian mysticism, emphasizing the life-changing aspects of both experiences.[30]

Regardless of the powerful effects the near-death experience has on the individual, the question remains as to whether this fact might provide any hard evidence for an afterlife. The answer to this question must be no. The following statement by Ring may seem obvious to some, but it deserves mention all the same: "Even those respondents . . . who recall nothing while they were close to death, report that afterward their lives were altered in significant and drastic ways by the sheer fact of approaching death."[31] One might expect that whether one has an actual near-death experience or "merely" comes close to actually dying without having an NDE, the individual might very well become a spiritually changed person simply through the fact of survival. While the NDE may well have relation to mystical experiences of transcendence, this fact bears little on the question of survival of bodily death. On the other hand, even those who experience the traumatic brush with death but do not experience an NDE might still be completely and fundamentally changed by their experience. Gaining no insight from this problem of the NDE, one must continue to seek further, turning now to the third of Grosso's problematic features of the NDE.

The final problem of the paranormal aspects of the NDE remains the last hope for evidence of survival then. In fact, there are two main areas that may prove to be most useful to that end; at least one of which is empirically testable. The apparitions of the dead and the out-of-body experience provide the most useful material in terms of deciding whether the NDE is actually an experience of the afterlife or whether it might be discounted as some form of hallucination.

Deathbed visions commonly include the appearance of deceased relatives and friends, though this might be expected, considering the psychological impact that being close to death might cause upon the mind of the dying. In the previous chapter devoted to apparitions in general, it was shown that such visions cannot be deemed more than hallucinations unless there is some veridical component to them that might lend them authenticity. Without some kind of empirical corroboration, visions of an apparition need not be seen as anything more than subjective experiences, which may or may not be anything more than mere fancy. R. W. K. Paterson describes the most imposing fact observed while studying these deathbed visions: "Possibly the most suggestive finding of our examination of the experiences of the dying is the huge preponderance of apparitions of the dead in deathbed visions, and the seemingly total absence of apparitions of the living in the recollections of those who have had near-death experiences."[32]

This coincidence need not be so astonishing when one realizes that, if these visions were no more than delusions, a person might be expected to imagine the apparitions of the dead as they, perhaps subconsciously, believe their own death to be imminent. If one believed they were dying, naturally the spirits of the dead would appear and not apparitions of the living. It may not be such a surprise then to consider that apparitions of the living, while relatively common among the regular population, are completely absent from NDE reports.

Lest these deathbed visions be cast aside, there are a few cases where some genuinely paranormal phenomena were reported. Sometimes, the dying person will see apparitions coming to take them away. Among these apparitions, they may see figures whom they thought to be alive and well. After the experience has been recounted, and the strange appearance of the spirit of a living person described, it is revealed that the person seen in the vision had in fact died before the experience took place, but the patient was not informed in order not to disturb their fragile state, or some such similar situation. That is to say, the apparition of an individual whom the percipient believed to be still alive turns out to be the apparition of a dead person instead. In this case, the percipient has somehow gained the information, through seemingly paranormal means, that the perceived individual was actually dead. It is true that these cases are rare, but they do exist in the literature. William Barrett, who undertook the first systematic examination of deathbed visions, records the following statement from the matron of the hospital tending to a young dying woman:

> I was present shortly before the death of Mrs. B., together with her husband and her mother. Her husband was leaning over her and speaking to her, when pushing him aside she said, "Oh, don't hide it; it's so beautiful." [referring to a beautiful golden light] Then turning away from him towards me, I being on the other side of the bed, Mrs. B. said, "Oh, why there's Vida," referring to a sister of whose death three weeks previously she had not been told. Afterwards the mother, who was present at the time, told me, as I have said, that Vida was the name of a dead sister of Mrs. B.'s, of whose illness and death she was quite ignorant, as they had carefully kept this news from Mrs. B. owing to her serious illness.[33]

A second important feature of the deathbed visions is the report of collectively seen apparitions. That is, the spirits that are seen to appear to the dying person are sometimes also seen by another person present at the time. Barrett again makes reference to several such cases, one of which is quoted here:

> In one case two women watching by their dying sister, Charlotte, saw a bright light and within it two young faces hovering over the bed, gazing intently at Charlotte; the elder sister recognized these faces as being two of her brothers, William and John, who had died when she was young. The two sisters continued to watch the faces till they gradually "faded away like a washed-out picture," and shortly afterwards their sister Charlotte died.[34]

Some of these cases involve witnesses not only seeing the apparitions that have appeared to take the dying patient away, but they also watch the patient's own spirit rise from their body and disappear with the others.[35]

Certainly, taken at face value, one would have to admit that these phenomena do seem to indicate that there is a spiritual component of the self that survives bodily death. Similar examples of both types have already been seen while reviewing the subject of apparitions earlier. Veridical apparitions, that is those bearing information not normally possible to attain, such as those of deceased individuals thought to be alive by the percipient, and collectively perceived apparitions were both discussed in the aforementioned chapter. The only difference here is that the apparitions are seen in the specific situation where an individual is close to the brink of their own physical extinction. The problem of deathbed visions can be compared to those of other apparitions, with all of the antecedent paradoxes that accompany them. Certainly, apparitions that appear bearing some form of verifiable information not otherwise known to the living, such as the appearance of the ghost of someone thought to be actually living, requires explanation.

There remains, then, only one aspect of the near-death experience left to discuss here, namely the out-of-body experience.[36] The sensation of leaving one's body is one that is certainly cross-cultural and has appeared throughout time. Readers will note that OBEs occurred in each of the religious traditions discussed in this text. Laboratory studies have sought to establish whether any part of a human self actually goes out of the body during an OBE. Certainly, ascertaining the capability of some part of a human being to leave the physical body would heavily urge us to accept the possibility that the human personality might survive bodily death. Indeed, such evidence would seriously damage a purely materialistic understanding of the universe.

Glen Gabbard and Stuart Twemlow defined the OBE as follows: "An altered state of consciousness in which the subject feels that his mind or self-awareness is separated from his physical body and that his sense of self-awareness is more vivid and more real than a dream."[37] One can easily see from this definition that the OBE is not strictly related to the near-death experience. Instead, OBEs remain a feature of some NDEs but occur far more often as a distinct phenomenon of their own in the population at large. Several studies have found the incidence of out-of-body experiences to range from anywhere from 11–12 percent to as high as 44–50 percent.[38] A comparison of the various studies warrants a figure closer to roughly 25 percent of the Western population. Considering the prevalence of OBE reports from other cultures, such as those of the major world's religions as well as shamanic and mystical traditions worldwide, it is safe to assume that the OBE is a fairly common, if as yet not wholly understood, experience. It is also worth noting that it seems that an OBE can occur to anyone. To quote Gabbard and Twemlow once more, "the 'typical profile' of the OBE subject is remarkably similar to the average, healthy American individual."[39] Once more, we will turn to an example to provide us with an idea of the aspects that define a typical out-of-body experience:

> Four or five times I have experienced, while lying in bed, the indescribable feeling of being apparently separated from my body. I then have the feeling that *I am hovering in the air, above my body, which I gaze upon, while fully conscious of my surroundings.* I then experience the glorious feeling of unlimited freedom, yet a slight effort on my part seems necessary to prolong it. After a few moments, a strange feeling comes over me, which causes me to think: "I must go back into my body again." I am convinced that I have succeeded in prolonging the *time* of freedom by my effort of will, but only by a few moments. Then something occurs within me which compels me gradually to re-enter the body.[40]

Among those who have experienced an OBE, most have reported only one such occurrence in their lifetime.[41] Once a subject has multiple OBEs, it is increasingly likely that they will have many more with each subsequent experience. Celia Green states that most "single" cases are caused by some form of stress, whether physical, mental, or emotional.[42] NDEs certainly involve a high degree of stress, which would therefore seem to be the trigger for the out-of-body experience in these particular instances. Once out of the body, the physical body itself may continue to move on its own accord. Often, the body is seen from the new vantage point simply lying in bed, as is most common in NDE cases; however, sometimes the body may be in the midst of performing some action, like driving, or maybe even having a perfectly normal conversation.[43]

When stress is not the issue, as in many of the cases where the body continues to walk or talk, the complete opposite seems to be the cause. A high level of relaxation may trigger an OBE as well. In fact, some forms of meditation aim specifically at attaining an out-of-body experience. With the even loftier goal of attaining transcendence and union with the absolute, as with some forms of yoga, these meditations often bring on an OBE, as well as other extraneous paranormal phenomena, or *siddhis*, along the path to the higher goal. Green found that over 80 percent of respondents (not including those who were unconscious at the time, as in an NDE) were in a position of repose, either sitting or lying down. The number leaps to over 90 percent when respondents who were unconscious at the time of the experience are included.[44] In addition to meditation, other forms of relaxation, from recreational drug use to hypnosis, have also induced out-of-body experiences. It has already been seen that the same kind of relaxed state, or altered state of consciousness, plays a part in both the subjects of mediumship and apparitions. In fact, Sylvan Muldoon and Hereward Carrington cite the case of a medium who describes his experiences with the spirit world in the terms of an out-of-body experience:

> I was talking to Mr. Britton, the materialization medium of Seattle, Washington, a few days ago, after a seance with him, at which time I asked him several questions, such as: "How do you feel when going into trance?" etc. To which he replied: "I hear the voices of the sitters growing dimmer and dimmer, as if moving far away from them, or as if the voices were moving away from me . . . when I come out of the trance, the past two hours seems but a few minutes . . . *When I first started sitting I often found myself moved outside my body and caught many glimpses of it sitting in the chair entrance* . . . There was a magnetic connection between the two bodies . . . I do not see myself from without any more . . . I am just unconscious of everything.[45]

Here again, with the case of OBEs, one finds yet another paranormal phenomenon with roots in a relaxed altered state of consciousness.

Of course, one can also look back to those cases of OBE resulting from a near-death experience and make one important observation. Where it has been observed that stress may be the cause of the OBE, this may not be entirely accurate. In analyzing the stages of NDE, Kenneth Ring found that the feelings of peace and quiet that are characteristic of NDEs generally supersede the OBE.[46] That is to say, it appears that rather than stress being the cause of the OBE, the stress causes some detached state of calm, which in turn triggers the OBE. When analyzed in this way, it becomes clear that a heightened state of relaxation, from whatever cause, developing into an altered state of consciousness can often result in an out-of-body experience.

During an OBE, one's senses seem to become clearer and thinking more precise. Much like in the percipience of apparitions, subjects with disabilities find themselves able to use their lost senses normally.[47] Green notes similarities between the statistics for sensory modality in OBE and those in cases of apparitions. That is, sight is primarily predominant, followed by hearing, with the other senses rarely reported. Additionally, the more often a subject had OBEs, the more common it becomes to discover multiple sensory perceptions appearing during the experience.

Also similar to the incidents of apparitions is the inability of the percipient to make physical contact with material objects. Rather, they seem to pass right through them harmlessly.[48] Again, distortions in reality similar to the types of things common in apparitional cases are reported.[49] For example, 360-degree vision is a common occurrence, which resonates with the story of the man who saw the ghost standing behind him, seemingly through the back of his head. Furthermore, scenes seen at night may be illuminated by some mysterious light, just as apparitions can be seen in the dark. It is these types of distortions that prompted Susan Blackmore to disavow the veridicality of OBEs and to assume a purely psychological interpretation of the phenomena. She herself had experienced OBEs resulting from her use of hashish. After feeling that she had left her body and flown about town, she later tried to verify whether what she had seen while astral traveling was in fact based in truth, but she instead found that her OBE perceptions did not match up to reality.[50]

Concerning the veridical nature of OBEs, however, there is something to be said despite Blackmore's condemnation. Michael Sabom and Sarah Kreutziger, in a medical study of the OBE in the near-death experience, found that:

> While "detached" from the physical body, the patient observed his or her own body in clear detail. Nearby objects (many out of "view" of the patient's body) could often be seen (cardiac monitor behind the patient's bed, etc.). In most patients, observation of the type and sequence of resuscitation measures occurred at the time *physiologic unconsciousness was most certain* (during a grand mal seizure, cardioversion of ventricular fibrillation, injection of intracardiac medications, etc.). [italics added][51]

Sabom further conducted a control experiment in which "seasoned" cardiology patients who had not had an NDE were asked to imagine watching the procedure from a corner of the room. Out of twenty-five responses, twenty contained a major error, namely the act of mouth-to-mouth resuscitation. This error was not present in NDE cases where the patient was able to describe the entire scene accurately.[52] From these studies, it is clear that information about the patient's environment is somehow being passed on to them despite the total lack of sensory stimulation, at least in those cases where "physiologic unconsciousness was most certain."

While there have been a number of experiments conducted within the laboratory setting using gifted individuals claiming to be capable of inducing an OBE at will, the findings have been contentious. These experiments have focused on the idea that if the subject can induce an OBE, then travel to another location, and accurately report some details from that remote location, the evidence would suggest that the subject must have actually left his or her body and traveled to said location. For example, in Sabom's studies the subjects have been capable of reporting accurately information they were not physically capable of perceiving. Other cases exist where the OBE percipient claims to travel over large distances and is able to accurately describe features from those locations, though as Blackmore points out, at least some of these experiences are more likely simply hallucinations than anything else. Laboratory tests proved somewhat successful in that certain individuals were able to identify targets hidden in a separate room as though seeing them from the given vantage point. However, errors were significant, forcing at least one investigator to conclude that accurate information could only be gained from a high-quality OBE, with lower quality OBEs providing at best nothing useful, at worst completely fictional information.[53] Charles Tart is responsible for what remains the most impressive study in terms of the success of its subject to accurately determine isolated targets while in an out-of-body state.[54] That his study has not been effectively repeated in four decades suggests that it may be an anomaly. Celia Green, though, reports certain cases of so-called extrasensory perception (ESP), including telepathy, clairvoyance, and even some very rare cases of psychokinesis, in which the subject is capable of directly influencing the surrounding physical environment.[55]

On the other hand, in much the same way that mediums have been found to sift out a fair amount of accurate information from their spirits' jumbled and misinformed chaff, individuals reporting OBEs also make inaccurate claims about their own experiences. A classic example of this is the nineteenth-century astral traveler, Helene Smith (pseudonym), studied by Théodore Flournoy. She claimed to make routine astral trips to Mars, and made detailed descriptions of what she found there on her trips.[56] Of course, modern space flight and the exploration of Mars proved her claims to be wildly false. Still, at the time of her experiences, she was convinced of their veracity, or at least claimed to be so convinced.

Blackmore may feel that these inaccuracies are enough to outweigh any correct information given during an OBE, but the matter should not be so easily closed. While it is true that the level of information gained during an OBE is quite poor, how is one to explain those instances where the subject of the OBE is so overwhelmingly correct, as in the Wilmot case outlined in the previous chapter on apparitions? What one may refer to at this juncture is Mrs. Wilmot's out-of-body experience, as opposed to her husband's, and his bunkmate's, perception of her, which began the whole story. Readers will recall that Mrs. Wilmot, in a state of physical relaxation, was having worrisome thoughts about her husband. She then had an OBE in which she traveled to the ship he was on and went directly to his room, having no idea where either of these things could have been. Once there, she accurately reported seeing her husband, the odd set-up of the bunks, as well as her husband's bunkmate staring at her. To make this case even more mystifying, there is the fact that she was actually seen by both her husband and the man in the bunk above.

As mentioned previously, there are cases in which witnesses in a dying patient's room claim to have seen the spiritual body of the patient rise up and leave the physical body behind. It has also been shown that a common type of apparition experienced by people is of other living people. If it is possible for others to perceive the figure of one having an OBE, would this not be proof that the individual really was present in some form or other, such as a spiritual body? The coincidence of one person having the sense of leaving one's body and traveling to another while at the same time the receiver of this spirit visitor should actually see the apparition of the traveler is simply too great to ignore. Again, if not for the inaccuracies and the paradoxical nature of many apparitions, one might be convinced of the spiritualist theory of survival of death.

Having now examined the most well-known of the areas here considered to provide possible sources for evidence of an afterlife, two factors appear most fruitful for the purposes of empirical evidence. The visions of the dying were seen to be remarkably similar to the apparitions already discussed, with the notable exception that dying people typically see apparitions only of the dead, whereas others sometimes also see apparitions of the living. This chapter then examined the out-of-body experience and found it to have much in common with other types of phenomena discussed earlier, namely mediumistic communications and apparitions. The information gained while in an out-of-body experience was seen to be of a similar quality to that of mediums, thus posing similar problems of interpretation. In addition, OBEs may provide the added possibility of actually detecting the so-called spiritual body while separated from the physical body. Again, the investigation of apparitions in a previous chapter dealt with the same issues. So, one is left once more with a number of unresolved questions. Is the near-death experience actually an afterlife experience, or even a brief glimpse thereof? Does anything actually leave the body during an out-of-body experience, or is it a hallucination? How does one explain the accrual of both verifiably correct information beyond the purview of the subject, and the fact that this is mixed in with so much falsity? And again, one is forced to wonder as to the true source of the apparitions encountered here of both the living and the dead.

Notes

1. Raymond Moody, *Life After Life* (Atlanta: Mockingbird, 1975), pp. 23–24.

2. Tom Harpur, *Life After Death* (Toronto: McClelland & Stewart, 1991), p. 47. Harpur himself is reporting figures from the International Association for Near-Death Studies, of which he is a member.

3. For full details of several studies into the pervasiveness of the NDE, see Craig R. Lundahl, ed. *A Collection of Near-Death Research Readings* (Chicago: Nelson-Hall Publishing, 1982).

4. Pim van Lommel, Ruud van Wees, Vincent Meyers, and Ingrid Elfferich, "Near-Death Experience in Survivors of Cardiac Arrest: A Prospective Study in the Netherlands," *The Lancet* 358:9298 (2001): 2039–2045.

5. Kenneth Ring, *Life at Death: A Scientific Investigation of the Near-Death Experience* (New York: Quill, 1982), pp. 36–37.

6. Moody, *Life After Life*, pp. 23–76.

7. William James, *The Varieties of Religious Experience* (London: Collier MacMillan, 1961), pp. 299–300.

8. Michael Sabom and Sarah Kreutziger, "Physicians Evaluate the Near-Death Experience," in Lundahl, *A Collection of Near-Death Research Readings*, p. 151.

9. Van Lommel et al., "Near-Death Experience."

10. Kenneth Ring, "Frequency and Stages of the Prototypic Near-Death Experience," in Lundahl, *A Collection of Near-Death Research Readings*, pp. 126–129.

11. Geena K. Athappily, Bruce Greyson, and Ian Stevenson, "Do Prevailing Societal Models Influence Reports of Near-Death Experiences? A Comparison of Accounts Reported Before and After 1975," *The Journal of Nervous and Mental Disease* 194:3 (2006): 218–222.

12. Celia Green, *Out-of-the-Body Experiences* (Oxford: Institute of Psychophysical Research, 1968).

13. Moody, *Life After Life*, pp. 43–44.

14. Karlis Osis, *Deathbed Observations by Physicians and Nurses* (New York: Parapsychology Foundation, 1961), pp. 29, 37.

15. Moody, *Life After Life*, p. 46.

16. Ring, "Frequency and Stages," p. 67.

17. Moody, *Life After Life*, p. 67.

18. David Lorimer, *Whole in One: Near-Death Experience and the Ethic of Interconnectedness* (London: Arkana, 1990), pp. 97–104.

19. Moody, *Life After Life*, p. 68.

20. Moody, *Life After Life*, p. 70.

21. Moody, *Life After Life*, p. 70.

22. Christopher Cherry, "Near-Death Experiences and the Problem of Evidence for Survival After Death," *Religious Studies* 22 (1987), 405.

23. Michael Grosso, "Toward an Explanation of Near-Death Phenomena," in Lundahl, *A Collection of Near-Death Research Readings*, p. 207.

24. Carol Zaleski, *Otherworld Journeys* (Oxford: Oxford University Press, 1988).

25. Allan Kellehear, *Experiences Near Death* (Oxford: Oxford University Press, 1996);

26. S. Pasricha and Ian Stevenson, "Near-Death Experiences in India: A Preliminary Report," *Journal of Nervous and Mental Disease* 174 (1986), 165–170.

27. Karlis Osis and Erlendur Haraldsson, *What They Saw . . . At The Hour of Death*, 3rd ed. (Norwalk, CT: Hastings House, 1997).

28. Mark Fox, *Religion, Spirituality and the Near-Death Experience* (London: Routledge, 2003), p. 139.

29. Grosso, "Toward an Explanation," p. 212.

30. Judith Cressy, *The Near-Death Experience: Mysticism or Madness* (Hanover, MA: The Christopher Publishing House, 1994), pp. 63–81.

31. Ring, "Frequency and Stages," p. 138.

32. R. W. K. Paterson, *Philosophy and the Belief in a Life After Death* (London: MacMillan, 1995), p. 149.

33. William Barrett, *Deathbed Visions* (London: Rider, 1926), chapter 2, online (2003), http://www.survivalafterdeath.org/books/barrett/dbv/chapter2.htm.

34. Frank Podmore, "Phantasms of the Dead From Another Point of View," *Proceedings of the Society for Psychical Research* 6 (1889–1890), p. 293, quoted by Barrett (1926), chapter 3, http://www.survivalafterdeath.org/books/barrett/dbv/chapter3.htm.

35. Again, a couple of such examples can be found in Barrett (1926), chapter 6, online, http://www.survivalafterdeath.org/books/barrett/dbv/chapter6.htm.

36. Some of the literature will also refer to this as an OOBE, astral projection, astral travel, exteriorisation, ecsomatic experience, bilocation, or traveling clairvoyance.

37. Glen O. Gabbard and Stuart W. Twemlow, *With the Eyes of the Mind: An Empirical Analysis of Out-of-Body States* (New York: Praeger, 1984), p. 5.

38. Gabbard and Twemlow, *With the Eyes*, pp. 8–13. This book covers the surveys of nine other psychical researchers who carried out their studies between 1954 and 1983.

39. Gabbard and Twemlow, *With the Eyes*, p. 40.

40. Sylvan Muldoon and Hereward Carrington, *The Phenomena of Astral Projection* (New York: Samuel Weiser, 1974), p. 206.

41. Green, *Out-of-the-Body Experiences*, p. 22.

42. Green, *Out-of-the-Body Experiences*, p. 25.

43. Green, *Out-of-the-Body Experiences*, pp. 62–66.

44. Green, *Out-of-the-Body Experiences*, p. 50.

45. Muldoon and Carrington, *The Phenomena of Astral Projection*, p. 207.

46. Ring, "Frequency and Stages," p. 40.

47. Green, *Out-of-the-Body Experiences*, p. 32. Ring reported similar findings for the NDE as a whole: Ring, "Frequency and Stages," p. 90.

48. Green, *Out-of-the-Body Experiences*, pp. 67–69.

49. Green, *Out-of-the-Body Experiences*, pp. 71–80.

50. Susan Blackmore, *Beyond the Body* (London: Heinemann, 1982).

51. Sabom and Kreutziger, "Physicians Evaluate," p. 150.

52. Michael Sabom, *Recollections of Death: A Medical Investigation* (New York: Simon & Schuster, 1982), pp. 84–86.

53. See Karlis Osis, "Out of Body Research at the ASPR," *ASPR Newsletter* (1974, Summer): 1–3 and Karlis Osis and Donna McCormick, "Kinetic Effects at the Ostensible Location of an Out of Body Projection During Perceptual Testing," *Journal of the American Society for Psychical Research* 74 (1980): 319–329.

54. Charles Tart, "Psychophysiological Study of Out-of-the-Body Experiences in a Selected Subject," *Journal of the American Society for Psychical Research* 62:1 (1968): 3–27.

55. Green, *Out-of-the-Body Experiences*, pp. 120–137.

56. Théodore Flournoy, *From India to the Planet Mars: A Study of a Case of Somnambulism, with Glossolalia*, trans. Daniel B. Vermilye (New York: Harper & Brothers, 1900).

CHAPTER ELEVEN

~

Past-Life Memories

The fourth, and final, area of research traditionally seen as a source of evidence for some form of a life after death to be examined in this book brings a radically different approach to the question. Mediumistic communication from the dead, apparitions, ghosts, and the subjective journeys of people out of their bodies and into a spiritual world beyond, all suggest that the individual can continue to exist in some form beyond the death of the physical body. Now we shall look at evidence that suggests the idea that each human may have already lived in a previous body and may yet again be reborn into another. Unlike the other areas of psychical research considered in the last three chapters, which might lend themselves to various interpretations, even when taken at face value, past-life memories demand a belief in reincarnation if taken at face value. Much of the literature dealing with these experiences assumes some acceptance of the idea of reincarnation when looking at the material. If memories of a past-life were factual, then they would, by default, support a belief in reincarnation.

Past-life memories are commonly discussed phenomena, especially popular in the entertainment media. Since the growing interest in Eastern religions in the West, many celebrities have espoused the notion that they have lived before, actress Shirley MacLaine being probably the best known among them. Stage psychics and palm readers commonly describe past-lives to their clients, usually with the kinds of exciting tales found in pulp literature. In these kinds of stories, inordinate numbers of people have led previous lives as Cleopatra, Julius Caesar, or any number of other famous or infamous individuals. And in the cases where they did not once incarnate the great figures themselves, clients are claimed to have at least figured as members of their courts or entourages. Psychiatrist Ian Stevenson, who devoted a lifetime to the study of past-life memories, reports having had nine separate past-life readings done by psychics. None of these past-lives corresponded to one another, while several even placed him in different countries at the same time.[1] Obviously, this is not the kind of evidence one can rely upon, unless one were prepared to accept one's being capable of being more than one person at a time. There are, however, a few instances of research that have made past-life memories a subject of serious consideration. Before moving on to these more promising areas, it is important to briefly mention some of the experiences that have often been popularly linked to the notion of reincarnation.

Déjà vu, or the experience of feeling a sense of familiarity, as if one has been in a certain location or situation before, is thought by some to suggest a past-life. This is a familiar experience to most people. Typically, one might be involved in a conversation and suddenly feel that they have heard it all before. One might have the feeling of knowing exactly what will be said an instant before it is said, though not being able to predict exactly—only realizing what they "knew" once it was said or done. While these experiences are often startling and sometimes quite impressive, they provide no objective proof of anything suggestive of a past-life. That one might feel they remember a specific instance in one's life would not be related to a notion of reincarnation unless such a belief implied the reliving of the exact same life over and over. Proponents of a reincarnationist interpretation would refer more successfully to déjà vu experiences involving the recognition of a specific location, the feeling that one has already been to a given place before. Even in these instances, though, the experience is never a full-blown memory but more a vague sense of familiarity. That is to say, the *present* stimulus is recognized rather than a past event remembered. Unless one can positively attribute a memory of some past location with a correspondence to the present, one is not actually referring to any kind of past-life recall. There can be no reason, then, to defend the leap from an experience of déjà vu to a belief in reincarnation.

Along similar lines, there are those who feel they have recognized individuals in their own lives who have shared a past-life with them. Basically, the subconscious dislikes or affinities that might influence who one's friends and foes might be are assumed to be indicative of a continuing relationship from one life to the next. Love at first sight is one aspect of such a belief, in which the lovers might be thought of as so-called "soul mates," sharing an intense emotional relationship spanning many lifetimes. Raynor C. Johnson provides a good case of this type in his book, *The Imprisoned Splendour*:

The lady had many psychic experiences by which she felt certain that none of her girlhood's boy friends would have any special significance for her, but that if she waited, her true mate would turn up. When she was in her middle thirties, she met her present husband at a public function, and both had an overwhelming and simultaneous conviction that, in an earlier life, they had been man and wife. They have now been happily married for over twenty-five years and both are convinced that this is their second incarnation. A year or two before meeting her husband, the lady had a vivid waking-dream of being in bed after the birth of a child whom she never saw. In the dream, her husband had to leave her in this distress to go on a forlorn and dangerous expedition on behalf of his king. The poignancy of parting was terrible, and in the waking dream—experienced, let me repeat, a year or so before she met her husband—the lady wept bitterly. When she met her husband, she knew that he was the father of this child and the hero of this dream.[2]

Many people report such experiences, however a deeper consideration shows that they have little, if any, evidential credence. To look at this example, one can discern three distinct elements. First, the woman had the impression that none of the boys she had ever known would ever be very significant. Presumably, this is why she never married any of them. Second, there was the mutual impression that their initial affinity for each other was due to the fact that they had been married in a past life. And finally, there was the dream, which she then associated with her husband once she had met him. There is nothing evidential in any of these statements. In fact, while the vague feeling of having been husband and wife in a previous life as the backdrop to some present attraction may bring a sense of romance to any relationship, there is nothing in these kinds of experiences which could be useful as objective, corroborative evidence. Déjà vu, love at first sight, and emotional dreams may all have considerable subjective impact, but for the purposes of the present inquiry they add nothing to the evidence of life after death, or in this case, life before birth.

However, two lines of investigation do lend some credence to the idea of reincarnation. Both lines remain quite controversial, even as compared to what has been discussed in previous chapters. Hypnotic age-regression has given way to the possibility of past-life regression, in which people under suggestion regress to a previous life and describe their experiences in great detail. There are also cases of spontaneous past-life recall in which spontaneous memories of a past-life leap to the mind of unsuspecting individuals. Most of the research on these has been done with the spontaneous memories of small children. Since this is the area in which the best evidence has been obtained, the greater part of this chapter will be spent dealing with it further.

Past-life regressions came into vogue in the 1950s with the publication of Morey Bernstein's *The Search for Bridey Murphy*, later released as a Hollywood movie of the same title.[3] This book brought the phenomenon of hypnotic regression to public attention, and is widely cited as one of the best examples. Bernstein regressed a friend of his, named Virginia, as a kind of experiment. He had been regressing her through her youth and wondered what would happen if he tried to go a little further back, to before she was born. What occurred was that the woman began to speak in an Irish brogue and referred to herself as a woman named Bridey Murphy. Over subsequent regressions, the identity of Bridey Murphy was flushed out in more and more detail with Bernstein asking specific questions about the identity of this alternate personality. Once the popular press got wind of the affair, investigations were made in Ireland and back in the United States to try to ascertain whether there ever lived an actual Bridey Murphy. The entire case has been surrounded by controversy since the beginning and there are some, like philosopher Paul Edwards, that simply see the case as worthless due to the media attention itself.[4] By far, the most comprehensive and coherent analysis of this case is presented by C. J. Ducasse, who concludes the following:

> the verifications summarized by Barker [William J. Barker, author of the first news reports on Bridey Murphy], of obscure points in Ireland mentioned in Bridey's six recorded conversations with Bernstein, do not prove that Virginia is a reincarnation of Bridey, nor do they establish a particularly strong case for it. They do, on the other hand, constitute fairly strong evidence that, in the hypnotic trance, *paranormal* knowledge of one or another of several possible kinds concerning the recondite facts of nineteenth century Ireland, became manifest.[5]

Ducasse bases his conclusion on the fact that *many*, though not all, of the facts described by the Bridey Murphy personality could be confirmed. The types of things confirmed relate to historical details and turns of phrase that could not have been normally known to anyone other than an expert on Irish history. On the other hand, some of these details were also found to be wrong. Perhaps most damning, in terms of ultimate authenticity, is the fact that many of the people described, including Bridey herself, could not be found in any historical records. The fact that no records of these people could be located does not necessarily mean that they did not exist, however, as record keeping has not always been an entirely accurate affair, especially in rural areas like that described by Bridey Murphy as her home. Still, if there had once existed such a person as Bridey Murphy, one might expect that other details of her life would be accurately remembered without significant errors.

Other past-life regressionists have uncovered similar cases to that of Bridey Murphy,[6] though no other has garnered the same degree of popular media attention. William Roll investigated many cases of past-life regression, "fruitlessly checking the identities of deceased personalities invented by hypnotized sub-jects,"[7] but concluded that they were nothing but fantasy. Jeffrey Iverson, after studying a past-life regressionist, observes : "Bloxham [himself a hypnotist prac-tising such regressions] believes that although a hypnotised person can be made to fantasise, it is possible, if the hypnotist remains neutral and unobtrusive, to secure a regression that is entirely the subject's own memory of a past life."[8]

The problem then becomes one of managing the subject's fantasy in such a way that the hypnotist has the most minor effect possible. Hypnosis, by its na-ture, is a guided practice, and so eliminating any effect by the hypnotist at all is impossible. Even Bernstein's book is full of leading questions to which the sub-ject dutifully answers. Ian Stevenson points out this same problem, though he has found that despite this there do still seem to be a very small minority of cases in which information appears to be attained through paranormal means, partic-ularly the appearance of xenoglossy, or the ability to speak in a language other-wise unknown to the subject.[9] Certainly, the extent to which such information can be determined to be factual and accurate will, as with cases in the preced-ing chapters, determine the legitimacy of past-life regression as anything more than fantasy.

In the case of Bridey Murphy, it has been shown that the information that was verified as accurate related more to historical details and geography than to the individual identity involved. This is typical of past-life regression memories. As was already noted, famous personalities are not normally encountered out-side of the prophecies of parlor psychics, thus making tracking down the pur-ported past-life identities a rather arduous task. Still, it is in tracking down just such central details that one might find the purest source for verification in the case of such hypnotic regressions.

> Contrary to the popular stereotype of past lives fostered by the tabloid press, the vast majority of past lives are *not* those of Egyptian princesses or wives of Henry VIII. Most of the lives that are reported are barely identifiable within the known framework of history. We encounter African tribesmen, nomadic hunters, name-less slaves, Middle Eastern traders, anonymous medieval peasants, and so on, from all times and places; often they can barely name their chieftain or lord, let alone place themselves upon some totally irrelevant time map of European or ancient history.[10]

One feature that has impressed many researchers is the ability of the subject to completely assume the role of the remembered identity. That is to say, as sub-jects remember their past-life under hypnosis, they begin to play the part. Bridey Murphy provides a minor example in assuming her Irish brogue. Other cases in-volve much more vivid displays in which, in the words of one therapist, "it was much more than just a retelling, a narration; *it was a reexperiencing.*"[11] There is a marked similarity here to the mediumistic cases where the mediums exhibited characteristic mannerisms recognizably similar to those of the deceased. However, it has been noted that it is not at all abnormal for a hypnotized subject to enact dramatic scenes.[12] While the reenactment of a past-life may seem remarkable to those watching, the fact that similar reenactments are common in hypnotic subjects not experiencing a past-life regression argues strongly that this not be included as evidence for a past-life. The most important element of the past-life regressions remains the accuracy of the information provided.

This leads one to a major problem with past-life regressions, namely that many of them contain glaring errors. Whatever veridical information can be gleaned from past-life regressions is generally surrounded by chaff. Again, a similarity can be noted here with mediumship. Factual inaccuracies must be sifted through in order to find some particle of truth. A possible explanation for this lack of consistency can be found once one takes into account the fact that memory itself is poorly understood, and is flawed even in everyday life. The observation has been made that past-life memories would logically be subject to the same kinds of errors as normal everyday memory.[13] As Roger Woolger puts it: "In both past and current life remembering our imagination will often fill the gaps and round out the story in all kinds of subtle little ways. Where the picture is not clear the unconscious mind may well touch it up for us."[14] This is particularly true when a subject is susceptible to suggestion, as is the case in hypnosis.

Before leaving the hypnotic regressions, there is one other interesting item to mention. There exist some very few cases of past-life regressions that have manifested xenoglossy, that is defined as the ability to speak a foreign language normally unknown to the subject. This is not to be confused with glossolalia, or speaking in tongues, which is a kind of gibberish said to be divinely inspired and which does not correspond to any known language. Such indistinct ramblings often occur during reported cases of demonic possession, and sometimes among certain religious groups, such as Pentecostal Christians. Again affinities with mediumship occur as it has been already noted that mediums sometimes communicate in languages they do not themselves know. Ian Stevenson has found a few cases of apparently veridical xenoglossy in hypnotized subjects during a past-life regression.[15] The cases he cites are of what he calls "responsive xenoglossy." That is, the subject is capable of entertaining a conversation in the previously unknown language, as opposed to merely spouting out a few stock phrases, which is the case in the more common "recitative xenoglossy." Certainly, truly responsive xenoglossy is an impressive phenomenon, but Stevenson's assertions that this is the strongest evidence in favor of reincarnation is somewhat premature given the relative rarity of such cases.

In the discussion of past-life regression, one finds one's self with very little to go on in terms of solid evidence for any form of survival of bodily death. As cited by Ducasse, there does exist compelling evidence for paranormal cognition in some cases where claimed memories correspond with certain details of an alleged historic past. The element of personation, while not unheard of during the regular process of hypnosis, does prove somewhat persuasive when combined with instances where information appears to be gained paranormally. Also, though more cases would be necessary to really bring this aspect to the fore, instances of xenoglossy can also be seen as strong evidence if they could be adequately substantiated as being of a high enough level of proficiency. Finally, the link between hypnotically induced past-life regression and the phenomena of trance mediumship ties these phenomena together in a manner that begs questions of the origins of both.

Ian Stevenson has found that the most reliable source for research into past-life memories is children, being less likely to be capable and interested in perpetrating complex frauds. He explains:

> The foregoing remarks will help readers to understand why I value so highly the spontaneous utterances about previous lives made by young children. With rare exceptions, these children speak of their own volition; no one has suggested to them that they should try to remember a previous life. And at the young age when they usually first speak about the previous lives their minds have not yet received through normal channels much information about deceased persons. Moreover, we can usually make a satisfactory appraisal of the likelihood that they have obtained normally whatever information they communicate about such persons.[16]

One can quickly see how the criteria Stevenson values in the cases of children helps to illuminate some of the problems with past-life memories that are often cited by skeptics who deny the possibility of such phenomena. There is no motivation, in general, for the children to lie, and it is highly unlikely that a small child could possibly coordinate the kinds of hoaxes that Stevenson's cases would require. Also, there is no suggestion, hypnotic or otherwise, for the child to try and remember anything that might lead to claims of a past-life. These children simply and spontaneously claim to have lived in a previous lifetime.

Stevenson was singly responsible for amassing as many as 2,500 cases, only a fraction of which have been published.[17] Stevenson has urged others to replicate his findings with studies of their own, and while there have been a couple of independent studies, Stevenson remains by far the primary and most reliable source of information. This has led critics to attack Stevenson himself in order to invalidate all of his findings in one stroke.[18] Stevenson points to impressive work done by others following his lead in this area, claiming that "In recent years the independent investigations of colleagues have increased my confidence in the authenticity of the cases of the children who claim to remember previous lives."[19] The criticisms of Stevenson and his methodology are not the most sound, and, in fact, most scholars who have taken the time to examine his case studies have found them to be quite solid methodologically even when they are not comfortable with the conclusions they suggest. As one reviewer stated the issue: "The problem lies less in the quality of the data Stevenson adduces to support his point than in the body of knowledge and theory which must be abandoned or radically modified in order to accept it."[20] Due to the fact that these experiences imply reincarnation from the outset, some, like Paul Edwards, attack Stevenson on the tenability of this belief from a philosophical point of view alone. Again, the arguments are typically weak, as Edwards himself demonstrates with the following conclusion relying on an ignorance of facts over alteration of one's own belief system:

> These assumptions [those inherent in reincarnation as an explanation] are surely fantastic if not indeed pure nonsense; and, *even in the absence of a demonstration of specific flaws*, a rational person will conclude either that Stevenson's reports are seriously defective or that his alleged facts can be explained without bringing in reincarnation. [Italics mine][21]

For those open minded enough to examine the evidence, the demonstration of flaws is required before one can properly judge something as pure nonsense. If this kind of hand-waving is the ultimate resource of the die-hard skeptic, then it can be accepted that the evidence stemming from this research into the memories of children claiming past lives might be of some value. Therefore, I will now turn to a consideration of Stevenson's work by summarizing the key features of his cases.

They are most easily found in Asian countries, or other reincarnation-friendly locales, thus implying that such experiences occur, or are at least reported, more readily within an atmosphere that fosters such beliefs. Western cases do exist, though these are extremely rare in comparison to those in areas where belief in reincarnation is predominant.

Mostly poor and uneducated families are involved, applying as readily to Western cases as Asian ones. While various reasons for this might be suggested, one outcome of this fact is the decrease in the likelihood that a complex fraud might be perpetrated against methodical scholars.

In some cultures, a person—usually elderly—predicts his own rebirth, even citing location and parents in some cases. The incidence of such reports is quite rare. Directly related to this, and just as rare, is the possibility that after death, someone else—perhaps not in his family—dreams of his return. Both of these characteristics are strongly influenced by the cultural context, appearing only in very specific cultures that foster such beliefs and expectations of such dreams.

More broadly speaking, the following features might appear in any of Stevenson's cases. Often, a baby is born bearing birthmarks corresponding to marks on the dead person, thus creating a physical coincidence between the two persons. Soon after beginning to speak, usually between the ages of two and four years, the child spontaneously reports memories of a previous life. Memories cluster about the last year, month, and days of life of the claimed incarnation. These memories typically begin to fade away from the child's mind between the ages of five and eight. Fully 61 percent of cases investigated involved the sudden and violent death of the claimed incarnation. The child is able to recognize people and places associated with the past-life. The child might be capable of identifying relatives and friends of the deceased by sight, or know his or her way about a given location known to the claimed incarnation but previously unvisited by the child. They also often describe associations and elements of their deaths with specific details that the child could not have known normally. The child might exhibit behaviors strange to his present family but later confirmed to relate to the habits of the ostensibly reincarnated individual.

It should be mentioned that the preceding list is a composite of the most common elements found in cases. The ideal case would include all of the features in the preceding paragraphs, though generally the strongest cases exhibit less of these features, while those that contain more of these features tend to be weaker. As noted, some features are also very culture specific while others can be found more widely, some occurring commonly enough to be considered almost universal, or at least forming a common core of such experiences. On the most common features, Stevenson states thus:

> The cases of children who claim to remember previous lives have four features that occur so regularly that I have presumed to call them "universal." These are: the early age of speaking about the previous life (between the ages of 2 and 4); the later age of ceasing to speak about the previous life (usually between the ages of 5 and 8); a high incidence of violent death in the previous life; and frequent mention of the mode of death in the previous life.[22]

In reviewing these features, an extremely important point to bear in mind is that most of Stevenson's cases come from Asian countries where reincarnation is an accepted part of life. The majority of these cases come from Northern India, in fact. This has led some to assume that the phenomena of past-life memories in these children can be explained by some form of cultural bias. The idea being that these children only remember alleged past lives because they are expected to within their culture's belief system. Still, such cultures do not actively

encourage widespread recollections of previous incarnations and the incidence
of these reports is relatively rare. In fact, the parents and others involved in such
cases generally tend to deny and subdue the memories at first as opposed to actually fostering such claims. From another angle, while they are relatively few,
there also exist cases from Western countries where a belief in reincarnation
would not normally be the culturally appropriate explanation for the phenomena. J. G. Matlock emphasizes this last point:

> The psychocultural hypothesis is also faced with explaining the occurrence of
> cases with similar features in places where reincarnation is a foreign concept, such
> as Europe and the United States. Certainly subcultures that believe in reincarna-
> tion can be found in the West, but the beliefs are likely to be related to adult
> memories, hypnotic age regressions, or past-life readings of sensitives—not to
> young children who, in addition to claiming memories of previous lives, behave
> in odd ways and bear strange birthmarks or other physical signs.[23]

Having put the notion of a purely cultural explanation for all cases aside,
one must then look at the features of the experiences themselves. The first to
consider still involves cultural expectations, but in a more specific way. The
features relating to a person's prediction of their own rebirth and the dream
foretelling of said birth are culture-specific features that appear in only a few
of the groups investigated by Stevenson. The problem with accepting these
features at face value is that it is not hard to imagine families, having had an
announcing dream or having heard the prediction of some recently deceased
person, somehow provoking the child to conform to the expectations. The
dream itself would be expected and thus can easily be explained through the
theory of cultural influence. Subsequently, children will be led, likely unin-
tentionally, into the role portrayed in the dream. Since Stevenson and other
investigators typically cannot arrive on the scene immediately, it is impossible to know how much influence the family may have exerted upon the child
before the arrival of investigators. One can easily imagine having an announcing dream and then seeking a resemblance in the newborn that might
correspond to the dream. One would then expect conversations to include reference to the fact that the baby is indeed the reincarnation of so-and-so, as
foretold in a dream. The child, hearing and absorbing all of this from birth,
may then simply behave in the way it thinks it is supposed to in order to live
up to the expectation that it is indeed the reincarnation of whom it is believed to be. Obviously, this problem may appear in other cases of past-life
memory in children, but the fact that there is an expectation on the part of
the families involved in some communities makes it more likely that such
contamination could interfere with the child's true memories.

As was said, however, these features only appear in some of the cultures considered. Those cases in which there is no specific expectation do not suffer from this criticism to the same degree because there is not the same level of motivation for contamination and there is no reason for the child to act out any presupposed role. Conversely, most parents would rather the child *not* admit to these memories. Not only can they be embarrassing, but they can also be hurtful and condescending to the birth parents, especially when the child refuses to eat food or wear clothes of a lesser quality than he or she was accustomed to in a previous incarnation.

Because of the problems inherent in these kinds of investigations, investigators look for sources of objective evidence. One such source is the appearance of birthmarks and birth defects that correspond to the claimed past life. Stevenson sees birthmarks as one of the most compelling pieces of evidence.[24] The most impressive cases involve the appearance of very unusual birthmarks, which correspond to the death-related injuries of the previous life. Most of the cases of this type unearthed by Stevenson suffer from the fact that the families were expecting the rebirth to occur. One argument here is that if the mother had foreknowledge that a specific person was to be reincarnated within her womb, she might unconsciously affect the development of the baby, thus producing the identifying birthmarks. While many might consider such an argument as farfetched as that of reincarnation, the idea is not as absurd as it may at first seem. It is known that individuals can influence their own bodies as demonstrated through biofeedback and the placebo effect. The extent to which this control extends is as yet not well understood, though the possibility does exist that such interaction might be possible, and even such a possibility must be considered before accepting the reincarnation hypothesis in such instances. Stevenson draws out the connection between purported cases of stigmata and such birthmark cases.[25] He also refers to so-called maternal impressions, in which the mother can somehow influence the development of her baby in utero. Stevenson examined 300 cases in medical journals, books, and other publications and found many cases where it seemed that the mother's having seen some shocking or disturbing condition wound up resulting in a baby with a corresponding birth defect. He uses the example of a woman who saw her brother after having his penis amputated for cancer. Later, her child was born with a congenital absence of penis, a condition found in only 1 in 30,000,000 of the population.[26] Still, of the cases of past-life memories associated with birthmarks, Stevenson cites twenty-five in which the mother had no knowledge of the deceased person's wounds, and thus argues that these ought to be considered evidential.[27]

It appears that in some cases birthmarks can be found that correspond to the injuries of the claimed previous life and for which coincidence (a normal explanation) is not immediately forthcoming. The truly good cases are very rare however, so the overall value of the birthmark cases in relation to the cases as a whole is not remarkably high. The majority of birthmark cases discovered are extremely vague or not well authenticated with supporting information derived from actual related memories. In fact, a more promising area for verifiable evidence seems to come from the actual memories themselves. Similarly to the verification of past-life regression cases, investigators of past-life memories of children seek to ascertain whether the memories are veridical or not. Other features such as the cross-cultural similarity of cases and the appearance of birthmarks or defects do not in themselves prove much, but might provide a useful addition when combined with veridical memories of past lives. The ideal case might then involve elements from all of these areas, though no case has yet exhibited strengths in more than one area at once.

Stevenson considers a case "solved" when he has been able to discover and verify the existence of the reported past-life and in which he has been able to conclude that various pieces of veridical information have been provided by the child without any possible normal explanation, either through contamination, fraud, or some other hypothetical alternative. Matlock notes, however, that even a case considered solved might exhibit some problems:

> The majority of Stevenson's Asian cases are solved, and although over 90 percent of recorded statements in these cases can be verified, the subject often makes errors of one sort or another. They are particularly likely to make errors in describing the way the previous person died. Sometimes they seem to merge or confuse memories of the previous life.[28]

While the subject may misremember some information, the vast majority of it can be shown to be accurate. Again, the general fallibility of memory might account for such errors. One might expect there to be some degree of inaccuracy in the memories of past lives simply by the very nature of memory itself. There is also some correspondence here between the amount of accurate information provided by mediums, though it would seem that reports of past-life memories are generally more accurate than mediums on the whole.

In discussing the actual memories, one must also consider what might be called behavioral memories, what Stephen Braude refers to as instances of "knowledge-how." Like hypnotized subjects, children who remember a past-life generally begin to adopt the behaviors suitable to the remembered identity. "The subjects may exhibit a wide range of behaviors, habits, aptitudes, skills, philias, and phobias related to the previous life, some of them quite specific to the persons they are talking about."[29] The child will react appropriately to people the past-life once knew. For example, a child might rush to hug a former wife, while recoiling in fear from the person's murderer. As mentioned briefly already, the child might behave as a member of the social level of the past-life, refusing to eat food deemed "unclean" or might begin to wear clothing of the opposite sex in cases where the child remembers a life as a member of the alternate gender. Phobias, generally related to the manner of death, occur in over a third of all Stevenson's cases, and may be evident before the child has even begun to speak.[30]

Perhaps the most striking ability demonstrated is that of communicating in a previously unknown and unlearnt language, called xenoglossy. With the child cases of spontaneous memory, the xenoglossy exhibited in some of them is of the recitative variety, in which the child can recite a few phrases or words but is unable to carry on a conversation of any length. While it is seldom difficult to ascertain whether or not a child has learned a language at all, it is not always as easy to know to what extent the child has been exposed to speakers of a given language. Cryptomnesia, or the forgetting of subliminally accrued information, is often used as an explanation for such recitative cases. This implies that the memories may stem from some forgotten contact, perhaps with someone who spoke the remembered phrases; the words are remembered but not the source. This is also the case when such recitative xenoglossy appears in hypnotized subjects as well as with cases of mediumship. Though a medium may not have learned French, for instance, it might be found that he or she has come across some French in reading works of fiction; having forgotten the source, this scant French remained. However, if the xenoglossy was determined to be of the responsive type one would find a stronger case for the surviving personality. Unfortunately, those cases that appear to involve responsive xenoglossy are all considered unsolved by Stevenson's standards, while xenoglossy that appears in solved cases is invariably of the recitative variety.[31] Basically, the best source for evidence appears only in the least verified cases, where those cases that have been adequately solved illustrate only lesser levels of evidence in terms of the present debate.

There are some additional problems to consider when looking at these phenomena. How does one explain the gradual loss of memory that occurs in most cases? Why is it that a child should lose the memories that once were vivid a few short years earlier? Matlock suggests that the loss of memory might be due to a kind of "layering over" of memories, in which the past-life memories gradually get buried under newer memories.[32] As the child reaches school age, other memories seem to become increasingly important. It should also be noted that few people can actually remember events from their early childhood, let alone any memories that might have existed about past lives. Still, given this analogy, one would still expect some memories of the past-life to survive, whereas they seem instead to completely fade.

The preceding observations notwithstanding, it is still important to bear in mind the sheer magnitude of cases that have been investigated to various levels of completion. Even the lesser quality cases contain at least some compelling evidence. What can be concluded from all of this is that there are many cases of purported past-life memories, and further research remains to be done in assessing them. Of those cases already investigated, there is a very small percentage containing enough evidential material to be suggestive of something, whether it be reincarnation or something else that as yet defies complete understanding. It does seem that some children are *remembering* the lives of deceased individuals and are actually experiencing these memories as if they were their own. It also seems that there may be some cases where this remembering, or reexperiencing, might extend into behavioral memory in which the children take on the distinctive personalities of the deceased, similar to the type of personation that might occur during hypnosis. It seems possible that some of these children may even be able to speak the language of the deceased, without having ever learned it before, though the evidence for this remains weak. And finally, there are some rare cases that show an impressive correspondence between birthmarks and birth defects in the child and the death-related injuries of the deceased. When all of these elements are combined, we find that there are some important questions that need answering. The spontaneous memories of children do seem more impressive than the hypnotically induced variety, though there are some definite similarities between them, as well as some real similarities between remembering past lives in general and the phenomena of trance mediumship. Louisa Rhine, in her review of Stevenson's initial book on this subject, concludes that Stevenson's evidence must remain as ambiguous as other survival evidence, and that a theory of reincarnation is "immature."[33] Stevenson, for his part, remains cautious in his conclusions, arguing simply that the evidence gathered leaves open the possibility for the conscientious thinker to rationally adopt reincarnation as a belief for the eventual fate of the soul after bodily death.

Notes

1. Ian Stevenson, *Children Who Remember Previous Lives* (Charlottesville: University Press of Virginia, 1987), p. 39.

2. Raynor C. Johnson, *The Imprisoned Splendour* (London: Hodder & Stoughton, 1953).

3. Morey Bernstein, *The Search for Bridey Murphy* (New York: Doubleday, 1965).

4. Paul Edwards, *Reincarnation: A Critical Examination* (New York: Prometheus, 1996).

5. C. J. Ducasse, *A Critical Examination of the Belief in a Life After Death* (Springfield, Ill: C. C. Thomas, 1961), p. 22. Relevant chapter also printed as Ducasse, "How the Case of *The Search for Bridey Murphy* Stands Today," *Journal of the American Society for Psychical Research* 54 (1960), pp. 3–22.

6. For examples see: Jeffrey Iverson, *More Lives Than One?: The Evidence of the Remarkable Bloxham Tapes* (London: Souvenir, 1976); D. Scott Rogo, *The Search for Yesterday* (Englewood Cliffs, NJ: Prentice-Hall, 1985), pp. 87–116.

7. William G. Roll, "Changing Perspectives on Life After Death," in *Advances in Parapsychological Research*, Vol. 3, ed. Stanley Krippner (New York: Plenum, 1982), p. 193.

8. Iverson, *More Lives Than One?* p. 16.

9. Stevenson, *Children Who Remember*, pp. 40–46.

10. Roger J. Woolger, *Other Lives, Other Selves: A Jungian Psychotherapist Discovers Past Lives* (New York: Doubleday, 1987), pp. 37–38.

11. Woolger, *Other Lives*, p. 32.

12. Edwards, *Reincarnation*, p. 68.

13. Iverson, *More Lives Than One?* p. 17; Stevenson, *Children Who Remember*, p. 46.

14. Woolger, *Other Lives*, pp. 31–32.

15. Ian Stevenson, *Xenoglossy* (Charlottesville: University Press of Virginia, 1974); Stevenson, *Unlearned Languages: New Studies in Xenoglossy* (Charlottesville: University Press of Virginia, 1984).

16. Stevenson, *Children Who Remember*, p. 59.

17. In chronological order, the main texts of his cases are: Stevenson, *Twenty Cases Suggestive of Reincarnation*, 2nd ed. (Charlottesville: University Press of Virginia, 1974); *Cases of the Reincarnation Type, Volume I. Ten Cases in India* (Charlottesville: University Press of Virginia, 1975); *Cases of the Reincarnation Type, Volume II. Ten Cases in Sri Lanka* (Charlottesville: University Press of Virginia, 1977); *Cases of the Reincarnation Type, Volume III. Twelve Cases in Lebanon and Turkey* (Charlottesville: University Press of Virginia, 1980); *Cases of the Reincarnation Type, Volume IV. Twelve Cases in Thailand and Burma* (Charlottesville: University Press of Virginia, 1983); *Where Reincarnation and Biology Intersect* (Westport, CT: Praeger, 1997); as well as those other texts already referred to. The last of this list is an abridgement of a four volume medical treatise on so-called birthmark cases, which will be discussed elsewhere.

18. See mainly Rogo, *The Search for Yesterday*; Edwards, *Reincarnation*.

19. Stevenson, *Where Reincarnation and Biology Intersect*, p. 110.

20. Eugene B. Brody, "Review of *Cases of the Reincarnation Type, Volume II. Ten Cases in Sri Lanka*," *Journal of the American Society for Psychical Research* 73 (1979), 73.

21. Edwards, *Reincarnation*, p. 255.

22. Stevenson, *Where Reincarnation and Biology Intersect*, p. 9.

23. J. G. Matlock, "Past Life Memory Case Studies," in *Advances in Parapsychology*, Vol. 6, ed. Stanley Krippner (Jefferson, NC: McFarland, 1990), p. 237.

24. Stevenson, *Where Reincarnation and Biology Intersect*.

25. Stevenson, *Where Reincarnation and Biology Intersect*, pp. 13–15.

26. Stevenson. *Where Reincarnation and Biology Intersect*, pp. 24–27.

27. Stevenson, *Where Reincarnation and Biology Intersect*, pp. 11–12.

28. Matlock, "Past Life Memory Case Studies," p. 200.

29. Matlock, "Past Life Memory Case Studies," p. 201.

30. Stevenson, *Where Reincarnation and Biology Intersect*, p. 7.

31. Matlock, "Past Life Memory Case Studies," p. 210.

32. Matlock, "Past Life Memory Case Studies," p. 200.

33. Louisa E. Rhine, "Review of *Twenty Cases of The Reincarnation Type*," *Journal of Parapsychology* 30 (1966), 263–272.

PART THREE

BELIEFS AND EXPERIENCES:
AN ATTEMPT AT A SYNTHESIS

CHAPTER TWELVE

~

Comparison of Beliefs

Throughout the preceding chapters, I have endeavored to show the evolution of beliefs in life after death from the world's major religious traditions, each receiving equal individual treatment. In so examining the various systems of thought and belief, it becomes fairly obvious that there are a number of interesting similarities as well as some radical differences. Huston Smith has likened the relationship between the world's religions "to a stained glass window whose sections divide the light of the sun into different colors."[1] While it is likely not surprising to most that there should be great variances in some details of belief, the more interesting matter is where the religions agree on certain points. Even the most casual reader will have observed some striking similarities from one tradition to the next. Through an in-depth analysis of the beliefs outlined, I will attempt to draw out the similarities, with reference to some important differences, that appear across these traditions. Through such a comparative analysis we might hope to arrive at a closer revelation of the truth that lies behind the veil of death, but at the very least, by sifting through various interpretations we might reach some consensus as to what *might* constitute truth. Certainly, the various traditions have not been idle speculation but represent centuries of careful thought and discussion of the fate of humankind. Such discussion has always involved a fair dose of personal experience, however strange these experiences may be, though the individual experiences and the orthodox beliefs do not often correspond perfectly. In any event, the experiences relating to the afterlife have influenced and encouraged discussion of what lies beyond death, sometimes hinting at answers, while other times opening up further questions. Even if the final answer to the question of life after death will have to wait until our personal experience of death itself, an analysis of centuries worth of philosophy can at least bring us closer to an understanding of the possibilities, perhaps leading to a best-guess scenario for what might be expected at the end of this life. Ernest Becker, who famously dealt with the denial of death in the modern age, says of this search for truth that ". . . each honest thinker who is basically an empiricist has to have some truth in his position, no matter how extremely he has formulated it. The problem is to find the truth underneath the exaggeration, to cut away the excess elaboration or distortion and include that truth where it fits."[2]

With this in mind, we must then turn to the comparison itself. In looking at the historical evolution of ideas, the first observation that can be made is that of a common understanding of the fate of the dead first appearing in the earliest records of human history in a number of different cultures, regardless of geography. In these ancient systems, upon death some spiritual aspect of every being is thought to continue its existence outside of the body. Typically, the spiritual side of human nature subdivides into several components, each responsible for different aspects of the human character. Examples of these aspects include the Egyptian *ba* and *ka*, the Greek *psyche, thymos,* and *noos,* and the Chinese *kuei* and *shen,* among others. In any event, there remains some connection between the recognizable aspects of the individual and his or her fate in the underworld. This spiritual aspect, however it is named, is considered to be but a mere shade of its former self, and is thought to wander among the nameless throngs of the dead in a subterranean underworld.

All of the traditions considered include the notion that the spirit of the dead might somehow be contacted at the gravesite, or some other threshold between the worlds of the living and the dead. During such contact, the spirit is seen to be a shadow, often lamenting its loss of individuality, especially in the Western traditions. Eastern traditions also include a similar notion in the evil spirits who demand sacrifices; without due respect, these spirits have a tortured shade-like existence, wandering in search of offerings to sate their hunger. In either case, the individual in death is seen, quite simply, as lacking the vibrancy of life. Certainly, in these beliefs there exists some element of Becker's empiricism in the myriad experiences of ghostly apparitions, hauntings, and related phenomena, a connection that will be examined in more detail in the following chapter.

Specific details of the domain of these early ghostly remains, the underworld itself, are generally lacking across cultures, though what little is said includes some correspondence from one culture to the next. The underworld of the Mesopotamians is seen as a dark and dreary place in which any joy is connected with the living legacy of the dead. The more progeny one leaves behind, the better off one is in death, which seems to indicate a common theme of ancestral cults seen elsewhere. Egyptian details are scant, as their earliest texts deal specifically with the unique fate of the pharaoh. Still, it would appear that the earliest conception of the afterlife of the average person is one not unlike that of the Mesopotamians in some respects; the dead would wander through a treacherous underworld with the goal of eventually merging into a collective Sun or else simply being annihilated. For the Egyptians, life was a bounteous pleasure and in death there was no greater boon than being a part of the Sun in its daily journey over the glorious Nile valley, and no greater fear than never having the opportunity to share in that experience again. The Homeric notion of Hades and the early Jewish concept of *Sheol* both describe an anonymous and depressive underworld, just as the Chinese describe the Yellow Springs. These places all share the characteristics of being dreary worlds existing below the ground and containing the multitude of dead, who form a kind of anonymous collective. Rare cases exist when specific individuals might be summoned from the underworld, or otherwise remembered or propitiated, but even then the images of the underworld share a gloomy veneer. The *Vedic* description of the afterlife differs from those previously described, though remains in a similar mold. The *paterloka*, or World of the Fathers, is described as a place of idyllic beauty, with flowing streams, singing birds, and beautiful maidens. On the other hand, the World of the Fathers is populated by the nameless throngs just as are the other underworlds described. Though the *Vedic* afterlife seems more like a kind of paradise, those who occupy it rely upon the graces of the living to continue the rituals necessary for their anonymous enjoyment. In all cases, the dead were thought to exist as spiritual beings that were not as whole as they were in life, literally lacking liveliness. In fact, most often the dead formed a kind of vague collective as part of some abstract otherworld.

The earliest religions all include some form of an ancestral cult in which the dead are propitiated with offerings, normally of food and drink. It was thought that the dead might return to cause harm to the living if not properly respected. The Mesopotamians, Egyptians, Greeks, pre-rabbinic Jews, *Vedic* Indians, and Chinese all followed rituals that aimed at providing for the spirits of the dead. Such practices also involved the possibility of contact between the living and the dead, including instances of apparitions and mediumship. In most cases, as religious society developed, the ancestral cults were controlled or subverted by the middle of the first millennium BCE. The Greeks appear to have continued sacrifices to the dead despite the growing influence of Platonic thought. The Jewish rabbis argued that ancestral offerings were a form of idolatry and were against God's will. This prohibition against ancestral rites carried over into Christianity and Islam, where the pre-Islamic Arabs had previously also revered the spirits of the dead. The *Upanishadic* understanding of karma took much of the power away from the ancestral rituals, though the rites were still permitted in a largely inclusive religious climate; the ritual system remained considered a path to *moksha*, the *karma marga*, while the new system insisted on higher ideals of wisdom and learning in the *jnana marga*. In the Chinese context, Confucius notably supported the ancestral cult originally as a means of honoring the ruling classes, and also as a means of demonstrating societal loyalties and communal bonds. Still, even Confucius did not condone the ancestral cult for the sake of the dead, but instead insisted on its use as a societal tool for the living. Popular culture and an official sanction of the rituals have kept the ancestral cult alive in China and neighboring cultures into the present; so entrenched has it become that not even Communist enforced atheism could stamp it out.

In many cases, the shade-like existence of the afterlife is balanced by a preoccupation with physical existence or even the cadaver after death. The Egyptians are famous for their carefully preserved mummies, as the continued existence of the spirit was predicated on the continued existence of the body. The Jewish concept of resurrection also stems from a similar belief that the soul and body are forever interconnected, certainly founded in the common-sense relation of life to the body. Care for the body was essential for the earliest Jews in order to prepare for the coming resurrection. The Mesopotamian and Chinese traditions illustrate the focus on the life of the body in their quests for personal immortality, though in both cases these are juxtaposed with the belief that death is natural and cannot be avoided. Reincarnation also appeared as another means of prolonging an earthly existence, though the ultimate goal was believed to be an eventual escape from it. As time went on, the preoccupation with bodily existence seems to have been transformed into two divergent ideas: on the one hand, a belief in the physical resurrection of the body that existed in the monotheistic Abrahamic tradition, while on the other hand, successive reincarnations, as described by Plato or the *Upanishads*, perpetuated bodily existence in another form.

Alongside the rather standard depiction of the dead as existing in a semi-anonymous state among all the other dead, there was special consideration given to the fate of leaders and other special individuals. In some cases, such as those of Utnapishtim from the *Epic of Gilgamesh*, Homer's Menelaus, or Judaism's Enoch, an especially revered individual of mythic proportions was brought into a personal paradise by divine will as reward for a particularly virtuous character. The examples given display men who served their particular god with extreme devotion and courage, setting the standard ideal for the average person. In the cases of Utnapishtim and Menelaus, both were sent to live on Isles of the Blessed, existing somewhere at the furthest reaches of the Earth, in eternal happiness. Enoch, whose fate is not given in detail, was simply taken up to be with God. In all cases, these men avoided the bleakness that their fellows faced. In addition, there are also cases where individuals have been awarded a special place in the underworld itself. The Greek King Minos was made a judge among the dead, sometimes interpreted later to be a judge *of* the dead as well. Similarly, the *Vedas* describe Yama, the god of the dead, as a deified hero from antiquity. Yama is said to have been the first mortal, though he overcame his fear of death through courage and devotion to the gods, thus becoming a god himself. In many cases, rulers and other powerful members of society were seen as somehow privileged in the afterlife. In the earliest Chinese tradition, the rulers would bypass the Yellow Springs to abide instead with the gods in heaven, from where they might continue to exert some influence. The pharaohs of Egypt were believed to become stars in the sky while the common people journeyed through the underworld by night and formed a part of the collective Sun during the day.

The notion of judgment in the afterlife became integral to concepts of life after death, appearing very early on in the development of the various systems under review here. The possibility that leaders and people of great courage or religious devotion should be able to escape the common underworld to live on in paradise opens the door for others to do so as well. For one thing, how does one set the bar for courage and religious devotion? Such a question demands the judgment of the dead be implemented somehow. The Egyptians were among the first to introduce the idea in their complex understanding of the afterlife. Those who could prove their devotion through a knowledge of certain mantras and rituals, combined with a virtuous heart, would be permitted to continue on with the eternal journey through the underworld and the sky with the Sun, while those who failed in either character or religious knowledge would be devoured by a monstrous alligator-god and obliterated for all time. Tibetan Buddhism incorporates a similar idea in adapting to the indigenous Bon religion in necessitating the knowledge of mantras to pass safely through the *bardo* state and into the next incarnation. Plato argued for a kind of judgment of the dead involving an intricate system of reincarnation depending upon the level of enlightenment one had achieved, with the more pure individuals being reborn in increasingly beneficial lives versus the terrible lives inflicted on the evil or ignorant. In the Indian context, the *Vedas* only reveal some inkling of judgment in the latest texts, and even then, these focus primarily on the treatment of the priestly classes, meting out punishment to those who have been disrespectful of the brahmin. The *Upanishads*, however, introduce the notion of reincarnation and reinterpret that of karma to institute a system of judgment, reward, and punishment. Where the *Vedic* concept of karma involved only the rituals needed to ensure the safekeeping of one's ancestors in the collective World of the Fathers, karma in the *Upanishads* is explained as a measure of one's deeds, good or bad, and thus determines the state into which one will be reborn after death. The *Upanishads* define good or bad action as being within the bounds of one's duty and class, expanding on the emphasis placed on ritual in the *Vedas*. With the appearance of Buddhism, karma came to incorporate an even more broad definition, propounding the belief that simply behaving in a morally good or bad way would determine one's future life, taking the emphasis away from the traditional religious power structures of India. For the Jews, the notion of judgment began as a direct relationship to nationality. The resurrection of the body was at first thought to be the right of all Jews, but later it was argued that only the good should be resurrected while the evil simply ceased to exist. Notions of heaven and hell appeared in the centuries just before the birth of Christ and it was thought by many that the soul would inhabit one of these two locales until the day of resurrection, though for the most part, souls would undergo some form of purgation in order to prepare every person for resurrection. Christianity and Islam later continued this notion of heaven, hell, and the in-between state of purgation before eventual resurrection. The Chinese traditions are unique in the context of the judgment of the dead as the complex bureaucracy of the afterlife was only concretely defined after the introduction of Buddhism in the era after Christ's death.

It can then be seen that judgment of the dead, while not originally a universal element of religious belief, entered into all of the major religions considered herein, perhaps due to an innate human need for justice or a growing sense of individual value. The Egyptians can be seen to have held the idea very early on, while the Greeks and Indians developed their own systems of divine retribution in the afterlife during the centuries before Christ. Greek ideas mingled with those of the Jews, and combined with political pressures, to integrate an idea of judgment into Judaism, and thereby also Christianity and Islam. Buddhism, growing out of Indian philosophical developments, spread throughout Asia, where the bureaucratic Chinese quickly embraced the concept of judgment.

Depictions of heaven and hell are fairly similar across traditions as well, with hellish symbolism generally emphasized over that of the heavenly realms, though Islam might be seen as one exception to this rule. Heaven is described in very pastoral scenes, featuring images such as radiant sunlight, flowing streams, singing birds, and refreshing breezes. Sometimes paradise is described in terms of splendid jewels and radiant gems. Sensual pleasures, like food and sex, are indicated in several traditions, including Judaism, Islam, and the Indian traditions. As time has gone by, however, all of the faiths considered have urged that the truest pleasure in heaven is one of transcendence, leaving worldly desires behind. In some instances, namely in the Judeo-Christian-Islamic tradition, this transcendence comes in the form of a personal nearness to God. In the Eastern traditions, especially those of a more mystical bent, the transcendence is generally seen as an overcoming of personal relationships in acquiescence to the greater whole. Obviously, there are ideas that cross over on both sides of this rather simplistic breakdown, as the mystical tradition exists across boundaries, and the idea of personal salvation appears in the East as well, especially in some forms of Mahayana Buddhism.

Hell appears in the Judeo-Christian-Islamic context originally as a place of smoke and fire. Sinners are burned, boiled, or otherwise tortured by intense heat. The *Vedas* include fire as a means of punishment, but the earliest references are directly linked with the worship of Agni, the god of fire. Fire becomes an important factor in later hellish scenes, however, but to these are added all manner of gruesome mutilation and torment, especially forcing the sinner to devour horrible and disgusting matter as food. Homer tells of similar torments tailor-made to exceptional sinners, like Tantalus and Sisyphus. Similarly, custom-designed hellish tortures are found only in later Jewish and Christian texts from the Middle Ages on.

While the overwhelming nature of hell is thought to be one of physical punishment, there is a strand of fairly recent thought passing through some traditions, most notably in the West but also on a global scale, that argues that all of these descriptions serve only to emphasize the spiritual pain of being prevented closeness with God or true transcendent enlightenment. To some extent, the Egyptian "second death" of total annihilation foreshadows this view of hell, and indeed, this is often a criticism made of modern materialism's nihilistic view of life and the universe. In many instances, the modern mind finds it offensive to conceive of a literal hell-state in which beings are tormented ruthlessly, regardless of the evils they may have committed in life.

Various opinions have been expressed as to the purpose of hellish tortures. All traditions seem to have looked to hell as a prod toward avoiding evil. The Greek notion of punishment was reserved for villains of mythic proportions, though by the Middle Ages, Christianity had evoked images of hell so widely that it was assumed that all but the most saintly should suffer in hell, if only temporarily. Originally, sins seemed to focus on respect for the priestly classes and the divine forces they represented. Murder, theft, and slander all became reason for torment, however, thus paving the way for the use of hell as a measure of justice to those who had avoided punishment for crimes in this life. Instances in both the East and West have seen the priestly classes taking advantage of the fear of such a fate, whether wittingly or not, as "offerings" to priests became common in order to gain favor with the divine and thus avoid hell, whether through forgiveness, karmic rewards, or something else. Rejection of this priestly control over salvation, combined with a modern distaste for eternal suffering, has resulted in the notion that hell-states are somehow less real than other states, even in Buddhism where no state is technically real at all. In some cases, hell is described as a wholly mental construct in that the individual creates his or her own hell through a denial of the divine will, thus taking the responsibility for punishment away from the divine, often conceived of as all good, especially in some modern Christian contexts.

Reincarnation has been posited in all of the major world's religions, though it has been accepted in some cultures more than in others. While the Egyptian pharaohs were conceived of as reincarnations of the sun god, Ra, there was no element of judgment in this early belief. The myth of the vegetation god, Osiris, who also became the god of the dead, does suggest the possibility of reincarnation on a broader scale, but details of any widespread belief in individual reincarnation do not exist outside of rebirth into a paradisiacal next life. The Greeks did incorporate different versions of a belief in reincarnation, from Pythagoras to Orpheus to Plato, which did involve some element of judgment. Later developments in Greek thought led to what might be called a mystical understanding of the afterlife in the form of Neoplatonism. In a seeming reversion to more ancient conceptions of the anonymity of the afterlife, the Neoplatonist position introduced the notion that every person would eventually unite with the divine; the individual is not entirely lost, but instead accentuated by this unity in becoming, as it were, more whole. Rabbinic Judaism wrestled with the ideas coming out of Greece, but opted to form a unique and independent system of belief involving an eventual resurrection and one lifetime before it. Neoplatonic ideas, and specifically that of reincarnation, entered into Judaism via the Kabbalah during the Middle Ages. By the time of Maimonides, the resurrection was beginning to be seen as a spiritual one and not a literally physical one. As time went by, the resurrection was seen as something abstract receding further and further into the distant future, leaving open the possibility that many lifetimes might be had between the present life and the resurrection. Alongside the kabbalists were other esoteric traditions, like the Gnostics in the Christian context that espoused a belief in reincarnation stemming directly from the ancient Greek concepts. In the Abrahamic context, these remained always at the extreme fringes of the faith, though they existed all the same.

Alternately, reincarnation entered the Indian mind with the *Upanishads* several centuries before Plato, predating even Pythagoras and the Orphic cults. This conception of reincarnation agrees with that of the Neoplatonists in arguing that the ultimate goal of successive lifetimes is to eventually achieve such a level of enlightenment (in this case measured by one's karma) that the eternal *atman* of each person should escape the cycle of death and rebirth and merge with the divine Brahman. Some Hindus, typically those of lower castes, did not, or could not, aim at the mystical goals of the *Upanishads* and sought instead simply to be reborn in a heavenly realm, or some other state that might be better than their present lot.

Buddhism appeared during a period in which rival philosophies grew in contrast to the seemingly elitist *Upanishadic* religion. The Buddha accepted the idea of reincarnation but changed it considerably within the context of his own revelations. Namely, where Hinduism posited an *atman* merging with Brahman, Buddhism rejected both as illusory. Rebirth was seen as a result of attachment to the illusion of life. To achieve release from the cycle of birth and death, *nirvana* in Buddhist jargon, one had to accept that the self did not exist and sever attachments to it and the apparent world around it. As in Hinduism, multiple worlds of varying qualities existed, but for the Buddhist, these were all seen as illusory. Later Buddhists, however, made the move toward a more personal idea of salvation, as did some Hindus. Mahayana Buddhism appealed to a wider audience in urging people to aim for immediate rewards in the next life with little concern for eventual *nirvana*. Pure Land Buddhism, which especially embodies such an outlook, spread the notion of rebirth into China, where it was embraced by the Chinese culture. The Taoist worldview wherein death and life were seen as naturally occurring flip-sides of the same coin easily incorporated the philosophy that suggested, in fact, the connection between life and death was so strong that it resulted in subsequent rebirths. Just as was the case in Hinduism where increasing numbers of the population turned to individual deities for personal salvation in the face of the rigors of a more mystical quest for *moksha*, or in this case *nirvana*, so too Buddhists turned to the saintly bodhisattvas for help in achieving a similar fate. With special devotion to specific divinities, so to speak, namely the bodhisattvas, one might hope to be reborn into a heavenly world where the thought of no-self was of little concern when compared to the sensual pleasures of paradise.

We can plainly see how the evolution of thought, across cultures, concerning the afterlife moved from a purely physical conception where the body itself was essential to continued life, toward a position of dualism in which the body is replaced instead by some spiritual body. The popular conception of the abode of this spiritual body is one of personal fulfillment, most often described in terms of sensual pleasures, but also seen as an *approchement* to the divine itself. Plato may be seen at the root of Western thought in this area, though dualism has now become widely accepted throughout Judaism, Christianity, and even Islam. In all three, the orthodox line remains one of eventual physical resurrection, but for the common adherent the main concern lies with the immediate state of the dead in the long interim before the Last Day. Similarly, though the goal of Hinduism is to achieve *moksha*, ultimately conceived of as a union with Brahman, many Hindus are content to be individually reborn into a paradisiacal world in what might be considered an alternate understanding of what *moksha* actually is. Similarly, in Buddhism, the older Theravadin conception of *nirvana* as a total renunciation of the illusory self is replaced by the Mahayana tradition allowing individuals to be reborn in some otherworldly paradise as the main goal for most people. The same can be said of the Chinese religions as well, where the search for physical immortality came to be replaced by the belief that the physical terminology is nothing but analogy for a spiritual immortality, in terms of the Taoist search for the elixir of life. Buddhism in the Chinese context gave the population a vast bureaucratic otherworld to look forward to, with little indication that *nirvana* might be behind the myriad levels of paradise and hell.

To summarize, then, there are a number of similarities that become apparent. First, the ancient propitiation of the dead in the ancestral cult is practically universal. The shade-like existence of the spirit world was questioned early on, and alternate theories were advanced as to the characteristics of the afterlife. Generally, some form of reward and punishment was conceived. This seems to have grown first from the special place awarded society leaders, but eventually demanded a wider inclusiveness. What was originally a political tool to coerce the population was eventually democratized so that heavenly rewards should be available to all, but this also entailed the element of punishment as well. Priestly classes in several traditions have been guilty of manipulating conceptions of the afterlife, and specifically hell-states, in order to exert power and influence. Generally, this has led to an increasingly personal conception of the afterlife, to the point where many modern people, of various faiths, have a choice of fates available to them. While many divide ideas of the afterlife along the lines of Eastern or Western, this delineation is seen to be not entirely useful. Superficially, the Western Abrahamic tradition is unique in its espousal of the resurrection of the flesh, while the Eastern traditions incorporate the idea of reincarnation or rebirth. Two things break down this dichotomy. First, the doctrine of reincarnation appears in the Western lineage, albeit as a fringe element, so this is not strictly an Eastern philosophy. Second, the doctrine of the resurrection has largely been relegated to some distant abstraction, with the immortality of the soul as it is judged and sent to heaven or hell upon death being seen as more important. In the same way, notions of *moksha* or *nirvana* have also been pushed back in favor of more immediate results. Further drawing the connection between East and West is the fact that hellish states have been all but cast aside, with reward the main idea of future fate; the grace of the various divinities is now perceived to be of too great a caliber to even permit any but the most horrible of sinners to suffer any kind of torture.

It might be easy to see this progression of thought as fulfilling the individual wishes of adherents, as the afterlife has become increasingly conceived of in individualistic terms, not to mention increasingly pleasant terms as well. Sigmund Freud argued that religious beliefs, and specifically those of a life after death, reflected deep-seated fears of loss.[3] Certainly, such an interpretation can be made when looking at the evolution of thought on the afterlife, which has moved from a decidedly anonymous and lifeless one to one filled with love and closeness to a divine savior. That the world has moved progressively toward an increasing emphasis on individual importance, it also makes sense that the view of the afterlife would similarly convey this same sense. If the individual is important in life, then it must also continue so after death. If I find meaning predominantly within myself, and within my own self-identity, then it only makes sense that to foresee the end of this self as inevitable would cast suspicion on the importance of the meaning that I find therein. Admittedly, not all adherents follow such a path, but it is a common one and one that exists across cultures. Still, it is too early to make any conclusive remarks, as there remains the examination of the various phenomena discussed throughout this text. Following Ernest Becker, if there be any truth to these theories of life after death, then they might appear more clearly with the empirical analysis. Turning now to the discussion of phenomena, we can then return to this comparison of beliefs in a new light.

Notes

1. Huston Smith, *The World's Religions* (San Francisco: HarperSanFrancisco, 1991), p. 386.

2. Ernest Becker, *The Denial of Death* (New York: Free Press, 1973), p. xi.

3. For instance, see Sigmund Freud, *Civilization And Its Discontents*, trans. Joan Riviere (London: Hogarth, 1930; Toronto: General, 1994), pp. 7, 52.

CHAPTER THIRTEEN

~

Comparison of Phenomena

The preceding chapters have covered a wide field of thought and experience. In the context of each religious tradition were those phenomena that are often taken by some to be suggestive of an afterlife of one kind or another. Alongside the historical analysis of religious thinking I have juxtaposed a phenomenological inquiry into strange experiences with the dead and the world thereof. For the sake of analysis, these phenomena were broken into four distinct categories of experience. I examined these four areas in order to evaluate their weight and effectiveness as potential evidence for an afterlife and justification of such beliefs. What remains to be accomplished here is the twofold business of both discussing the extent to which the various phenomena have appeared in the different traditions, and might thus be considered universal human experiences, and to draw some conclusions about what kind of afterlife such universal experience might then indicate. Those experiences that do not appear universally may be considered to be culturally determined. Thus, at issue is also the question of to what extent belief plays a role in actual experience. On the other hand, in the instances where experiences are found to be universal, the flip-side can be asked in terms of experience creating belief.

Mediumship

Certainly, of all the phenomena that I have covered in the present study, communication with the dead is as universal an experience as any, although its practice has long been discouraged in several religions. In fact, mediumistic contact with spirits of the dead can be found in all of the traditions we have examined. Certainly, in the earliest texts the details are scant, as with everything, but it is clear that the possibility was always thought to exist that the living could somehow reach out to communicate with the dead.

In the *Epic of Gilgamesh*, Gilgamesh is described as praying to the gods to allow the spirit of his dead friend, Enkidu, to return to him. Once the requisite prayers have been made to the appropriate god, Enkidu rises like a shade from the ground to speak with his dear friend. In the context of other traditions, it is likely that the act of praying performed by Gilgamesh is not an isolated incident and the fact that Gilgamesh should even have considered the action indicates the belief that such contact might be possible. The Egyptians, while sharing in the belief that some contact could be achieved between the living and the dead, do not exhibit the same kind of personal contact found in the Mesopotamian *Epic*. The Egyptians were seen to leave messages to the dead at the gravesite, sometimes speaking to them as well, though the dead did not answer. Egyptian magicians were thought to have certain powers over the spiritual realm, though there is little description of these practices in the very ancient writings.

The Greek tradition contains numerous references to mediumistic contact with the dead. Homer reveals the same kind of ritualistic raising of spirits as is suggested in the story of Gilgamesh and Enkidu. Odysseus learns of the necessary rites and libations from a witch, and performing them results in throngs of dead swarming up from the underworld to speak with him. Similar rites are reproduced in several of the Greek tragedies, and by the time of Plato professional mediums are reported. Greek mediums, like the Pythian oracle, could speak not only with spirits of the dead but with various divinities as well.

Mediumship appears in the Judeo-Christian traditions largely by way of its prohibition. The story of the Witch of En-dor, appearing in the first book of Samuel, forms a part of both religions. In an attempt to protect Judaism from religious pollution, the rabbis outlawed the otherwise common practice of communicating with the dead. Various interpretations of scripture notwithstanding, it is clear that the Witch of En-dor displays the abilities of a spiritualist medium in that she somehow summons forth what appears to be the spirit of Samuel. Necromantic practices such as these have been banned by the orthodox of both faiths, though mediumistic communication has continued to flourish in the Western cultures predominated by these faiths. Spiritualist churches have grown directly out of a Christian environment,[1] while Hasidic Jews, embracing the mysticism of the Kabbalah, are known to commune with the spiritual world in a number of ways. Aside from purposeful communication, there has also existed some belief in the ability of spiritual forces to possess the living, requiring elaborate exorcism rites to rid the victim of the invading entity. Normally, these beings are thought of as demons, though the line between demon and evil dead has often been blurred.

In Islam, which accepts the tale of the Witch of En-dor as part of its Abrahamic lineage, there is also a tradition of spiritual communication coming from the pre-Islamic Arabs. With a history of ancestral worship, the soothsayers of the pre-Islamic Arabs were capable of various magical feats, not the least among them the channeling of spiritual entities, including spirits of the dead. Like its Abrahamic cousins, Islam also condemned such activity. Ostensibly, this prohibition was due to the deceit and incorrectness of the soothsayers' messages in the face of the only true revelations being handed to Muhammad. From a humanist perspective, however, there must also have been some political motivation behind the decree, taking the authority away from the soothsayers as a whole. The Qur'an is explicit in its denial of any contact between the living and dead, and thus the explanation for the abilities of mediums like the soothsayers is that sinister *jinn* are masquerading as spirits of the dead in order to spread lies and confusion.

The spirit world is much more permeable in Indian thought than in the West. The ability to communicate with spirits is made apparent early in the *Vedic* Indian tradition with the god Soma incorporating certain shamanic abilities, including contact with the dead while in some ecstatic state. Thus has started a long history of mediumship in India, with specific professionals, usually a type of priest, possessing the ability to summon spirits for communicative purposes. Possession by human spirits, as well as by gods and demons, is also found in the *Vedas*, and continues to occur into the modern day, again requiring that exorcisms be performed to save the afflicted. Similarly, Buddhism also incorporates such widespread contact with spirits, especially in its Tibetan form. Tibetan shamans, growing out of the older Bon religion, commonly allow spirits and gods to enter their bodies to possess them and use them to communicate with the living. In this way, the shaman allows himself to be possessed in order to act as a medium.

Again, in the Chinese tradition there is a long history of mediumship. Ancestral worship remains integral to Chinese living, and mediums are one facet of the interplay between the living and the dead. Typically, Chinese mediums simply give messages of solace, assuring the living that their loved ones are well-placed in the postmortem bureaucracy, and this corresponds with the messages most often received through mediums elsewhere.

And so, mediumistic communication appears in each of the traditions discussed, though it has at times been suppressed or reinterpreted for doctrinal purposes. While such an observation points to the universal character of such experiences, it does little in terms of an argument for any given afterlife. Certainly, the great monotheisms originally rejected mediumship due to their reliance upon the physical body for any kind of afterlife and later, their particular belief in the impending resurrection. Also, many of those who were channeling spirits were also in contact with various divinities, conflicting with the Abrahamic notion of one God alone. The Eastern traditions, on the other hand, have remained much more open to mediumship, despite higher philosophical ideas within those same traditions that deny the legitimacy of the phenomena. Still, mediums form an active part of the culture even today. Ultimately, the universality of this human experience is such that mediumship thrives despite dogmatic rejection, whether from religion or modern science.

The present study has shown that mediumistic communications, while certainly anomalous, do not necessarily indicate the survival of any aspect of the human being. For one thing, descriptions of the afterlife coming from ostensible spirits are not uniform, whereas one would expect that if the communications were truly coming from the dead, depictions of the otherworld would bear some similarity. Instead, one finds a number of quite opposing views. Enkidu's description of the underworld paints a dark and gloomy picture. Chinese communications generally describe a bureaucratic realm, which serves as a middle ground before reincarnation. Modern Spiritualist mediums describe the spirit world in ever-widening spheres leading to eventual union with some spiritual absolute.[2]

A Hindu or Buddhist view, in which multiple worlds are accepted as possible destinations for the individual after death, might account for the fact that there are different descriptions coming from the "other side." The beings communicating do not always identify themselves as spirits of the dead, but might also, depending on the cultural environment, admit to being gods, demons, angels, jinn, Ascended Masters, aliens, or any number of other beings. The variance in identity is seen, however, to be entirely attributable to cultural influences, suggesting that other factors might be similarly so determined. Furthermore, the descriptions given seem to change with the present beliefs rather than it being the other way around. The belief in a bureaucratic afterlife did not enter the Chinese mind until the introduction of Buddhism, though mediumship had existed there before that time. Again, modern Spiritualist beliefs can be traced to a Western adaptation of a mixture of Eastern philosophies coming through organizations like Helena Blavatski's Theosophical Society.

Given these problems, it might be wise at this point to agree with William James, and accept that with mediumship there is definitely something very interesting happening, but still reserve judgment on its relation to the afterlife until more evidence is in.

Apparitions and Hauntings

Ghosts appear cross-culturally throughout recorded history, both in relation to mediumistic communications and on their own. Considering the widespread practice of communicating with the dead, it should come as no surprise that spirits might also be witnessed in one form or another by some from time to time. In many instances, spirits are not actually perceived but are inferred from other unexplained occurrences, which might include illness, accidents, or objects seemingly being lost or misplaced. In terms of evidential value, as discussed in previous chapters, those spirits that have been seen by multiple witnesses and that have disseminated some form of new information are seen to be the most useful. Still, the fact that ghosts appear across cultures indicates a universal human experience regardless of its evidentiality.

The early Greek and Mesopotamian epics depict scenes of wispy, shade-like phantoms rising up from the ground. The connection between the dead and a dwelling place in the ground or the grave itself is an early one appearing in other cultures as well. The Witch of En-dor caused the spirit of Samuel to actually rise up from the ground. Ghosts of the dead were also thought to remain, for a limited time, near the body in Egypt, Arabia, India, and China.

Likely connected to the belief that the spirit would abide near the body for a time is the notion that these spirits might haunt certain places. Notably, the themes identified as the causes of haunting are the same from one culture to the next. Murder, or other forms of unnatural death, and the desecration of the body or improper burial are the main reasons noted time and again. Also appearing in some traditions is the necessity for the living to continually propitiate the dead with offerings in order to sustain them in the afterlife; failure of these duties would result in serious repercussions. In all cases, the overriding element seems to be one of respect. If an individual has not received the respect he or she is due, whether in life or after death, then he or she might return to haunt the living as punishment. These themes remain common in reports of hauntings even today. In most cases, the source of the haunting remains anonymous, leaving them open to other interpretations. Demons are often blamed for causing similar problems to those attributed to haunting spirits, especially within those religions that deny any contact between the living and the dead. Alternately, "normal" explanations often suffice for such events as illness, storms, or accidents.

Apparitions are also known to appear in dreams. Nocturnal visitations are often seen as portentous and have been interpreted through the ages. Dream interpretation has been common among the Egyptians, Greeks, Jews, Muslims, Indians, and Chinese. In some cases, the beings encountered during sleep are not only spirits of the dead, but also angels, prophets, or other divine beings. Predating such experiences, shamans reported leaving the body to journey into the spirit world, and so dreaming was thought to be an extension of this ability. Herbert Spencer long ago theorized that "from dreams arises the idea of a wandering double; when follows the belief that the double, departing permanently at death, is then a ghost."[3] More sophisticated minds have realized that dreams are not real in the same way that physical reality is, and that they do not represent an objective spiritual reality but rather an inner, subjective one. Apparitions of the dead thus appearing in dreams should not be taken as suggestive of an afterlife any more than should dreaming of being a king should be taken to mean that one truly is royalty upon waking. Still, the emotional response to experiencing the presence of a lost loved one is often enough to lend such experiences personal authenticity.

Waking apparitions exist as well, however, and are potentially more impressive in terms of evidence for some spiritual existence. Some of these reports come from people on their deathbeds. Often, close to the moment of death, patients will report seeing visions of angels or spirits of the dead acting as *psychopomps*, coming to take them away from this life. Such stories have been related in the chapters on Judaism, Christianity, Islam, and Buddhism, most notably in the Pure Land School. Given the acceptance of spiritual elements, it is likely that similar experiences also occur within a Hindu context, though the present study has not included any examples. Certainly, a person close to death might be expected to imagine such visions, but that they should be seen across various cultures is interesting, to say the least.

Finally, apparitions also appear in normal waking states, seemingly of their own accord. Beginning with reports of so-called crisis-apparitions in ancient Greece, the phenomena also appear quite frequently in Christianity, Hinduism, Buddhism, and in the Chinese traditions. Christianity denies that spirits of the dead can actually appear to the living, though people have continued to have such experiences regardless. Orthodoxy interprets such experiences as the work of demons, or occasionally as the work of God himself for truly special purposes. On the other hand, both Judaism and Islam have similarly denied the possibility, with different results. In Islam, apparitions continue to appear, though they are always explained in terms of the *jinn*. The dead do sometimes appear legitimately in dreams, but similar visions while awake are thought to be the work of deceitful *jinn*. Judaism also accepts that spirits might sometimes appear in dreams, though it almost completely ignores the possibility in the waking state. Some Jewish tales exist from the Middle Ages of spirits actually appearing in person, but they are absent from modern Jewish discourse. Even the spiritually open Hasidic Jews do not report seeing ghosts, though they accept the existence of invisible entities. Given the almost universal appearance of spirits across other cultures, it is difficult to deal with this anomaly. Still, ghosts do appear to a wide audience, and they are accepted even where they are not physically perceived.

In fact, the descriptions of the actual spirits themselves vary from one tradition to the next. Horrible visions are most often reported in the Eastern traditions, versus the more common rather peaceful apparitions of Western experience. Indian and Chinese ghosts often appear bloodied, twisted, or monstrous in some way or another, likely reflecting the belief that wandering spirits of the dead can become evil, hungry ghosts. Certainly, a comparison can be made to Western horror stories. More common, however, is the appearance of spirits that come to console the living that they are still well in the next world. Despite the proliferation of monstrous visions in Eastern folklore, the same kind of consoling spirits appear to Eastern peoples as well.

Near-death and Out-of-Body Experiences

Deathbed visions of angels and departed loved ones represent a form of near-death experience in their simple proximity to death itself. Near-death experiences have come to form a phenomenological group of their own, however, with very specific parameters. Modern investigators have endeavored to show the universality of these experiences, but careful analysis shows that this simply is not the case. When broadly defined, as NDEs were by the earliest investigators from the 1970s on, one finds that most of the features of the experience are culturally determined.

The earliest reference often cited as an example of an NDE is the story of Er found in Plato's *Republic*. It is clear that the tale of Er does not correspond in any but the most vague way with the modern definitions of near-death experience. In fact, the only similarities are that Er has technically died, left his body, traveled to the afterlife, and returned to tell the tale. What he reports, in the words of Plato, is a place entirely unlike the paradise reported in the modern West. Similarly, reports from the Middle Ages abound from both Christian and Jewish sources, detailing various journeys to heaven, or hell, and back. In many of these cases, the subject of the experience is not even near death, but simply becomes privy to the experience by God's grace. Again, the details of the afterlife, and the journey there and back, are wholly unlike modern NDEs. Finally, though some scholars have found similarities to modern NDEs in reports from both Hindus and Pure Land Buddhists, these similarities are again of the most general type. In these, as in other cases, cultural variance results in widely different details of the experience.

If a common core of near-death experience can be found, it is only in the broadest of terms. It should go without saying that such experiences occur at or near the moment of apparent death. Such being the case, it is not surprising that those who wake from an NDE might report imaginings related to the state of moving from life to death. Being that there is no real agreement on the nature of the afterlife, one is left in a similar position as that regarding the depictions of the next world coming via spirit mediums. Again, it may be that these different experiences of the hereafter represent objectively different worlds, as in a Hindu conception of the possibilities. The fact that depictions bear striking similarities within a given tradition, but do not bear the same kind of resemblance to those of others, however, argues in favor of a wholly culture-based interpretation.

One key component of the NDE that does appear to be universal is the out-of-body experience (OBE). OBEs are actually more prevalent outside of near-death situations, though they are also an obvious part of any experience of visiting any form of afterlife. The feeling of leaving one's body is a fairly common one, and can be found in texts throughout history.

Shamanic cultures all intrinsically contain those who claim the ability to induce a spiritual aspect to leave the body and travel freely. The Eastern traditions include references to OBEs from the earliest times. The *Vedas* make reference to Soma, which is not only a god but also the name of a potion that could induce ecstasy. Shamanic voyages out of the body are also especially common in Tibetan Buddhism. There are also reports in the older Chinese texts of those who could travel in a spiritual form. On the Western side of the equation, OBEs are just as common. Beliefs commonly held include the idea that the spirit leaves the body during sleep and that dreams are thus the product of astral voyages of some kind. Mystics in all of the great monotheisms report OBEs.

It is easy to see how the experience of leaving the body and traveling to other parts might induce the belief that there was a spirit within the body that might leave upon death to carry on. For the person having the experience, the naturalness of the experience is enough to convince. Studies have shown, however, that many such experiences are no more than fantasy, acquiring information that is blatantly wrong, however real it may appear to the percipient. Most people would never have thought to test the veracity of their experiences, lending the OBE a particularly personal authenticity that is difficult to counter with objective reason.

Past-life Memories

Memories of a past-life necessarily go hand in hand with a belief in some form of reincarnation, rebirth, or metempsychosis. Given that some people do claim to remember past lives, the question remains as to whether these memories are elicited by a cultural belief in reincarnation or if the memories occur spontaneously, thus encouraging a belief in reincarnation.

The main studies in past-life memories have been carried out in India, where reincarnation has formed a part of the religious landscape for centuries. It might, then, go without saying that such memories are common in a Hindu and Buddhist context. Past-life memories also appear in other cultures, however, expanding the range considerably. The concept of reincarnation appears in some form in ancient Egypt, but sees its full development in post-Homeric Greece. Whereas Plato states that memories are forgotten from one life to the next, Pythagoras argued before him that remembering your past lives was key to improving your lot. Gautama Buddha and Pythagoras both claimed to be able to remember numerous past-lives, each deriving wisdom from the memories. Within the Abrahamic traditions, reincarnation beliefs have occupied only a fringe position. Typically, those who espouse the belief in reincarnation are those of a more esoteric or mystical bent. The Gnostics, only tangentially within the Christian tradition to begin with, maintained the Neoplatonic philosophy of life after death. Some modern Westerners now accept that reincarnation is a possibility; certainly, the ever-lengthening distance between the present and the Last Day leaves plenty of time. Hasidic Jews believe in the ability of some to recall the past-lives of others for them, while the Druze accept reincarnation as a doctrine, although it is considered heretical by orthodox Muslims.

Despite the appearance of such beliefs in various traditions, the study of past-life memories has remained focused in India, with smaller studies being carried out among other populations in which reincarnation is a majority belief. Reports of past-lives appear in the religious literature only sporadically, and it is difficult if not impossible to adjudicate the authenticity of these claims from the perspective of the temporally distant observer. The work being carried out primarily by Ian Stevenson and his colleagues is invaluable in terms of collecting and evaluating such claims. For all of Stevenson's efforts, the thousands of collected cases have yet to suggest strongly that reincarnation is the best answer to such experience, let alone conclusively prove that it should be so. The fact that almost all of the cases investigated come from areas where reincarnation is readily accepted does not help the cause, suggesting the possibility that the memories are culturally conditioned artifacts. Certainly, spontaneously occurring memories from cultures that are resistant to the idea would be impressive. Still, the historical texts do contain some references to memories of former lives, which lends credence to the notion of a potentially universal human experience.

All in all, when the various phenomena are taken together and analyzed in terms of the various religious traditions, many of them can be seen to be relatively universal across cultures. The ability of certain individuals to speak with beings purporting to be spirits of the dead is attested to in every religion discussed. The fact that many religions have attempted to prohibit the practice to no avail points to the tenacity of the experience. Apparitions of the dead appear cross-culturally, often in dreams, but occasionally in the waking state as well. Often, these same spirits are thought to become mischievous or malevolent, usually due to some form of disrespect. In some cases, mediums are used to communicate with the perceived angry spirit in order to determine, and correct, the slight caused to the spirit in the first place. That the spirits in question might truly be those of the dearly departed rather than mere hallucination is reinforced by the personal experience of leaving one's body in the common OBE. If nothing else, when taken at face value, the OBE points directly to the conclusion of dualism. Near-death experiences, though modern scholars have tried to argue for their universality, appear to be a modern construct, with the details of otherworldly journeys quite clearly culturally determined. The out-of-body experience is combined with visions of the next world that often correspond with some common assumptions in one's given culture. Finally, past-life memories appear in various traditions, though almost always hand in hand with a belief in reincarnation. These remembrances, if a universal human experience, seem to happen quite rarely. The historical reports of them are exceedingly uncommon, and they do not share the persistence of the other phenomena discussed. One would think that if past-life memories were as common as apparitions, OBEs, or mediumistic communications, they would force themselves into the cultural consciousness in the same way as these others have over the centuries. Additionally, while the collection of case studies has produced thousands of reports, the vast majority of these come from cultures that embrace the doctrine of reincarnation. It appears likely from the present evidence that past-life memories are culturally dependent, though the notion of reincarnation itself holds a certain appeal, especially for the more mystical schools of thought among the various religions.

Ultimately, when stripped of culturally determined differences in details of experiences, some universal common core experiences can be found. In so far as determining whether any such experiences might be useful as actual evidence for a genuine afterlife, specific elements emerge. Many of the experiences can be adequately explained by hallucination, even when cross-cultural; there should be no problem accepting the possibility that some types of hallucination are simply a part of the human condition. In some cases, certain experiences require further explanation, however, and it is these cases that lend themselves to a survivalist interpretation. The main elements of those experiences requiring further elucidation are objective physical manifestations and the accrual of information through means otherwise inexplicable.

Physical manifestations were discussed in relation to some forms of mediumship, the collective percipience of apparitions, and the appearance of coincidental birthmarks in past-life memory cases. Most often, such physical manifestations were found to be explicable by normal means such as coincidence or misinterpretation. Many physical mediums were discovered to be performing fraudulently, while the little modern research in the area remains controversial. Furthermore, many of the physical manifestations appearing during the typical séance do not force a spiritual conclusion upon the viewer, providing no definitive evidence for the spirit of a dead person given the vagaries of the manifestations themselves. Ian Stevenson believed that birthmarks provided the best possibility for objective evidence, but no good cases including birthmarks and other verifiable information have been recorded. Collectively perceived apparitions remain suggestive, though they are rare. Physical explanations, such as magnetic fields, can explain many such experiences but not necessarily all of them.

More confounding to normal explanation are those cases where information is obtained through nonnormal means. Such instances have been relatively common in contrast to those physical manifestations discussed. It was shown that information transfer resulted in the most suggestive evidence for the ongoing survival of a given human personality. Mediums prove they speak with a given individual by providing information known only by that individual and some few others. Apparitions illustrate themselves to be more than mere hallucination by importing some important information, such as the death of the appearing person. Similarly, OBEs, and relatedly NDEs, might be seen as other than hallucination only when the experience provides insight that would not otherwise be available to bodily form of the individual. Lastly, again, past-life memories can be seen as suggestive when they can be verified as relating to a real previous lifetime. Information, then, offers the most troubling component of all of these experiences. What remains is to explain from where such information might derive.

Notes

1. The following offers a good discussion of modern spiritualistic mediumship, or channeling: Michael F. Brown, *The Channeling Zone: American Spirituality in an Anxious Age* (Harvard, MA: Harvard University Press, 1997).

2. Brown, *The Channeling Zone*; A. R. Wallace, *Miracles and Modern Spiritualism* (1896; repr., New York: Arno, 1975).

3. Quoted in Walter H. Capps, *Religious Studies: The Making of a Discipline* (Minneapolis, MN: Fortress, 1995), p. 77.

CHAPTER FOURTEEN

~

Conclusions[1]

The great religions of the world have confronted the issue of death throughout recorded history. Mysticism has shared an uneasy partnership with religion since the beginning, and can be supposed to have predated even the establishment of the earliest religions. Elements of the mystical tradition have been pointed to in the chapters dealing with individual religious traditions. In this chapter I will attempt to demonstrate how this antediluvian wisdom can be applied to understanding what happens to us all after death, accounting also for those human experiences of death and the afterlife as studied by psychical research.

Normally, in discussing the variety of evidence for the survival of bodily death, there are two sides put forth—three if you include those who prefer to simply ignore the evidence altogether. Some take the evidence at face value and argue that some form of afterlife is proven by these experiences. The alternative is to look for other explanations for the transfer of information, which, in the absence of normal explanations, must turn to paranormal psychic faculties other than spirits of the dead. The weight of evidence tends to indicate that there is something strange going on, to say the least. To shrug the evidence aside smacks of dogmatism. In fact, it is not only the materialistic skeptics who are guilty of this ignorance, but mainstream religious institutions as well. Ancient prohibitions against communicating with the dead have seen all of the Abrahamic religions deny its possibility. Christians blame demons for appearing as the dead, Muslims blame the *jinn*, and Jews generally simply deny the phenomena in question when they don't agree with a demonic interpretation. Hindus and Buddhists, for their part, advise against necromancy as a distraction from ultimate enlightenment; the masses that incorporate these rituals into their religious life will simply have to get over their ignorance in future lifetimes. So, while all of these great traditions are forced to accept the facts of human experience, they all refuse to accept the common-sense assumptions that they tend to lead one toward. Each of the world's religions has its own take on what happens when we die, and human experience has little impact on dogma.

So, the question then becomes one of what exactly the afterlife might be like, based on these experiences. We can take the collection of evidence from psychical research and surmise from the various pieces just what kind of an afterlife they suggest. The philosopher H. H. Price most famously constructed a theory of the afterlife based upon a careful consideration of the evidence, though he wrote it before Ian Stevenson began accumulating his massive data on past-life memories.[2] Price suggests that the afterlife might be a mental realm, akin to the dream state. Certainly, such an idea would have been familiar in ancient times when dreams were thought to actually occur as the soul traveled in another plane of existence. The dreamlike qualities of OBEs and apparitions, that might suggest hallucination to some, are accounted for by this thesis. Price further argues that this mentally based afterlife frees the mind to more easily access psychic powers, thus enabling spirits to have the extreme powers of paranormal cognition that have been assumed according to the evidence. He further adds a moral element to his theory in positing that minds will exist in self-developed mental realities. For example, if a person was evil in life, his or her mental afterlife will be filled with images that accord with how he or she lived life, thus creating a kind of personal hell. His theory has some merit, especially in the emphasis on the dreamlike quality of the afterlife depicted by such phenomena as apparitions and mediumistic communications, but it relies too heavily on speculation without backing evidence. From an analysis of the raw experiences, however, the kind of afterlife we can look forward to is substantially different. OBEs and NDEs certainly lend support to the idea of dualism between the spirit and body and that the individual can exist apart from the physical form. From the evidence on apparitions and mediums, it would appear that the existence of a spirit in the afterlife is in a shade-like state of half-confused wanderings where the individual has very little ability for new thought, if any at all. Apparitions in haunting cases tend to repeat actions in an almost mindless way, sometimes for decades. Mediumistic communications have been found to contain a good deal of personal information known only to the deceased and some other person who recognizes the significance of the given statements beyond what the medium is capable of realizing. On the other hand, these messages tend to be filled with errors as well. Some of these can be explained as error on the part of the medium, or perhaps as some problem with the method of communication itself. The medium, Mrs. Holland channeled the purported spirit of Frederic Myers, who described his efforts to communicate from the other side saying, "I appear to be standing behind a sheet of frosted glass which blurs sight and deadens sounds—dictating feebly—to a reluctant and somewhat obtuse secretary."[3] Other cases, however, are inexplicable as the spirit insists on information that is blatantly incorrect. Furthermore, of all the great thinkers, poets, musicians, and so forth, none has succeeded in creating a masterpiece from beyond the grave.[4]

The existence thus depicted is dreary at best, though it does mesh closely with the afterlife conceived of by ancient civilizations from the Greeks to the Jews to the early Chinese. John Hick made the same observation in his study of death across cultures.[5] Before parting ways through a variety of philosophical and theological deliberations, all of these cultures held a similar view of the afterlife as a dismal, anonymous place. The Greeks called it *Hades*, the Jews *Sheol*, for the Chinese it was the *Yellow Springs*, and others held similar views. In these early days, people were familiar enough with their own experience to acknowledge the implications for the afterlife. I would imagine that just as the countless thinkers of more sophisticated times developed new and improved notions of the afterlife, so too modern philosophers like Price and others are not looking forward to such a bleak existence when they argue for survival after bodily death.

For what it is worth, both the evidence for past-life memories and NDEs offer some indication of a more hopeful existence. Past-life memories suggest that the dreariness of the spirit world would be only temporary, and the thought of eternally being alive in a body is comforting for some, especially Western materialists. It is worth noting that many of those from cultures that believe in reincarnation describe the prospect of limitless future lives as tiresome and frustrating, looking forward instead to the time when they can cease being reborn and finally "rest." Many NDEs depict a journey to an afterlife beyond this world that is blissful, beautiful, and full of love and loved ones. Given the cultural differences in these accounts, though, it is unreasonable to draw conclusions other than that these visions represent expectation more than reality. Of course, the possibility that there might be some kind of a life after death is at least more than nothing at all. Plus, such a possibility leaves the door open for another, even better existence lying beyond that spiritual one even if we accept the dreariness of its apparent being. The Hindu conception of multiple worlds can be seen to relate here.

This illustrates how some have taken the phenomena discussed at face value and see them thus as evidence for the ongoing survival of human consciousness. The alternate theory appears in a number of forms, all of which argue that paranormal explanations that do not involve spirits of the dead are more parsimonious. Such explanations as telepathy or other psychic faculties can be seen to account for the transfer of information that appears in the best cases, when normal means for acquiring such information have been ruled out. Stephen Braude has recently made a very good analysis of both sides of this debate.[6] Braude acknowledges that one of his main goals is to rectify the lack of a significant defense that has been brought to bear on this psychic hypothesis. While it is true that the theory had not received the kind of in-depth treatment that Braude provides, his argument fails from the outset. For one thing, Braude values Western notions of individual survival over Eastern ideas of a collective existence. This bias limits Braude's perspective on the issue as will be shown, and so weakens his conclusion overall.

Early in his argument, Braude discusses the meaning of survival beyond bodily death. Here, he briefly mentions the Eastern conception of the afterlife as a merging of the individual with some absolute in a kind of World Soul, or *anima mundi*. He quickly shrugs this conception of the afterlife aside:

> No doubt that would count as a kind of *life after death*, but it wouldn't be personally interesting, and it's certainly not the *survival of death* that has intrigued humankind for centuries and which many either anticipate or desire. Unlike merging with the infinite, personal postmortem survival would be a condition that *preserves* (rather than obliterates) who we are—or at least something we consider essential to who we are (many say it's our mind or soul).[7]

This is not the first time such an argument has been made to defend a certain approach to the evidence for an afterlife, but it remains a fallacious one. Michael F. Brown, in his study of New Age spirituality, echoes this line of reasoning in saying, "if the idea of oneness is pushed too far, the self would dissolve into the totality of everything. That might be acceptable to Buddhists, but it is unappealing to Americans convinced that each of us is unique in the universe."[8] The pragmatist, F. C. S. Schiller, found the notion of a World Soul to be, "the genuine and logical outcome of every dualistic view of the relations of body and soul," but then goes on to argue against it on the basis of personal satisfaction, as "it is pretty clear that the eternity of Universal Soul is not what men bargained for, nor anything that men desire, or perhaps ought to desire; it may or may not be an excellent doctrine philosophically, but it will hardly do duty instead of a personal immortality."[9] Whatever happens after our deaths surely happens without any correspondence to our desires, personal interests, or how appealing the outcome may or may not be. That some people, probably the vast majority of Westerners, feel that the afterlife must involve the continued existence of our individual selves in no way influences the reality of what actually happens after death. This simply illustrates a typically Western bias toward individualism.

Aside from this bias, there appears to be a serious misunderstanding of the Eastern view of the afterlife. Braude states that an acceptable form of afterlife would be one that preserves our individual identity, or the essential components thereof, as opposed to an Eastern view that he describes as the obliteration of the self. This is a common error made by Westerners approaching Eastern philosophy. In fact, when looking at the afterlife, there is no talk of destroying the self. It can more accurately be described as a realization of the true essence of the self. In eventually merging each self with a World Soul, the essential component of the self is preserved, it is only what we presently perceive of as the essential component of a self is actually mistaken. Ambrose Bierce's tongue-in-cheek spin on Descartes's old maxim is an appropriate syllogism for this idea: "I think that I think, therefore I think that I am."[10] According to these Eastern philosophies, our belief in ourselves as distinct individuals is the result of ignorance on our part, and through a succession of lifetimes, we might become sufficiently enlightened that we recognize this. Once this recognition is attained, then the dissolution of the illusory individual is achieved, and the essential components of the true, inner self are revealed in a union with everything and everyone.

All of this to point out that Braude, and others, erroneously ignore Eastern ideas of a communal afterlife because it goes against closely held Western notions of the importance of the individual as not "personally interesting." Certainly, the egocentric impulse is strong, particularly in an increasingly materialistic world where the instant gratification of individual desires is commonplace. However strong this impulse, though, it cannot be used as an argument for what will happen to each of us when we die. In fact, this Eastern worldview is actually much better suited to dealing with the evidence from psychical research than is the materialistic scientism of the West.

Mysticism runs across cultures and religions, though it is often closely associated in people's minds with the Eastern traditions. While it can be said that mysticism is often a major part of Eastern religion, especially Buddhism, mystics and mystical experience are important to all established religions. The great monotheisms of Christianity, Judaism, and Islam all contain streams of mystical thought that echo the Eastern philosophies. Mystical experience is, actually, as universal a human experience as the phenomena studied by psychical researchers. Such experiences might be described as a range of spiritual experiences that instill religious feelings while transcending all established religions and their doctrines. As a universal human experience, mysticism can be seen as a source for understanding the nature of our reality just as much as can the experiences directly relating to an afterlife discussed throughout this text. As such, the reality defined by mysticism bolsters the case for a kind of psychic hypothesis that does not fall victim to the criticisms leveled at it by Braude and others. So, we must understand more clearly what is meant by the term mystical experience if we are to understand how best to explain apparitions, mediums, OBEs, past-life memories, and what happens to us after we die.

Since the turn of the twentieth century, William James's *Varieties of Religious Experience* has garnered a lasting respect within the study of religion and religious experiences. In it, James sought to demonstrate the common elements of mystical states in order to better understand them. He delineated four characteristics, being the noetic quality, ineffability, transiency, and passivity.[11] The noetic quality refers to that aspect of the experience that implies a certainty of some knowledge learned through it, often to the point that the experience is seen as being even more real than everyday life. Confounding the explication of this knowledge is the second characteristic delineated by James, ineffability. Mystical experience defies words, forcing most mystics to resort to poetic and metaphorical language. The final two aspects describe how such experiences come upon individuals unexpectedly and without their control. While these four characteristics certainly appear in all mystical states, the core component of the experiences is what makes them truly unique. This element is best described as a unitive experience between the self and the absolute, the sense that all things are one and the same within infinitude and eternity. Walter Stace, in his *Mysticism and Philosophy*, identifies the unitive experience as what he calls a "common core" of all mystical experience.[12] If one reads through the theological interpretations which pervade mystics' accounts, one cannot fail to realize the same conclusion, what Ralph W. Hood calls the "unity thesis."[13] William James states it thus:

> This overcoming of all the usual barriers between the individual and the Absolute is the great mystic achievement. In mystic states we become one with the Absolute and we become aware of our oneness. This is the everlasting and triumphant mystical tradition hardly altered by differences of clime or creed. In Hinduism, in Neo-Platonism, in Sufism, in Christian mysticism, in Whitmanism, we find the same recurring note, so that there is about mystical utterances an eternal unanimity which ought to make the critic stop and think.[14]

Abraham Maslow takes this observation even further, emphasizing not only the cross-cultural importance of mystical experience to even atheistic religions, but also to humanity as a whole: "This private religious experience is shared by all the great world religions including the atheistic ones like Buddhism, Taoism,

Humanism, or Confucianism. As a matter of fact, I can go so far as to say that this intrinsic core-experience is a meeting ground for [every human being]."[15]

It must be pointed out that there is some debate on the universality of experience, namely from the likes of Stephen Katz.[16] His argument revolves around the idea that each mystic experiences his or her own personal mystical experience in culturally- and personally-bound ways, so that when a Buddhist experiences *nirvana*, the Buddhist actually experiences a oneness in Void, whereas when a Christian experiences a union with God, there is actually a union with God. The Void and God are, by definition different, and so the experiences cannot be the same. The problems with such a claim are many. For one thing, if one takes Katz's position to its logical end, one is left with no objective reality whatsoever, as each person's experience is identified as primarily subjective. Such a line of argument may be amusing, and perhaps even useful in some circles, but it does nothing to aid in the pursuit of an understanding of objective reality. It makes more sense to recognize the universal elements underlying the culturally and personally determined interpretive details.

One need not see the mystical experience as necessarily religious in the sense of pertaining to any specific established religion, but as an experience that is available to any human being, anywhere in the world, at any point in time. The unitive experience, then, is a common human experience in which individuals have had the sense of not only a personal union with some form of divinity, but have actually experienced a unity of all things in the cosmos. Within the context of mystical experience, it is important to keep in mind there remains a wide spectrum of actual experience, culminating in the total union of the individual with the absolute. Stace describes a range rising to the highest forms of mystical experience, what he calls introvertive and extrovertive. The former, which Stace argues to be the higher of the two, involves the actual experience of union, the latter involves the perception of everything as one, thus perceiving a separate self.[17] So, at the very basic level, a common out-of-body experience can be seen as the beginnings of mystical experience in its suggestion that our individuality is not as we normally perceive it in day-to-day life.

We can now speculate upon how such unitive mystical experience can account for the phenomena studied by psychical researchers. First, the reality depicted by mystical experience is one in which every human is in actuality united on some spiritual level with every other human. To go even further, this union transcends humanness to include the universe as a whole. Some branches of science, particularly quantum physics, tend to agree with this mystical worldview in describing the cosmos as an intermingling of indistinct particles and energy. For many, this quantum interconnectedness is seen as a solution to many of the problems posed by paranormal phenomena, from the instantaneous transfer of information to the influence of mind over matter. The evidence from psychical research does not necessitate a universe-wide interconnectedness, however, as the evidence from psychical research and parapsychology relates almost exclusively to phenomena revolving around our Earth. Any psychic claims relating to places more distant than our world cannot be verified, and those that have been made have been found to be wrong.[18] In terms of the experiences discussed in this book, the information that is transmitted and confirmed is such that relates not only to this Earth but is known to humans themselves. That is to say, whatever information might be gained by the medium or the perception of a ghost is information that comes from one person to another however one interprets the experience itself.

The interconnectedness proffered by mystical experience allows a theoretical conduit for the transfer of information. Whereas for many the main problem is to explain how information moves from one mind to the other, or from mind to matter, if all are one and the same then there is no more mystery to information transference between mind and mind as there is within an individual mind. That is to say, the problem of anomalous information transfer can be related to the problem of consciousness. An individual can access long forgotten memories spontaneously and without effort, though the process behind this act is not understood. If all minds are in fact mystically unified beyond the veil of physical reality, then it is no greater mystery if the same individual can access information from the mind of another individual, whether living or dead. The process in both cases will be the same, though in neither case has the problem of how the mind works been adequately explained.

William James discussed such possibilities at length, referring to the brain's function as being one of transmission rather than production, as materialism would have us believe. James talks of each individual consciousness separated from what he calls a "mother sea"—a vague notion of World Soul, Universal Mind, or Collective Consciousness—by the barrier of the brain. Within this mother sea exists the information that is spread from one mind to the next, so that each individual is in actuality connected one to another through this great sea of consciousness. James, in describing consciousness in this way, backs off from any claims to universal monism and the existence of a World Soul. His move is seemingly done, in part at least, for similar reasons to Schiller, Braude, and others who are uncomfortable either with the idea of a loss of individuality, or perhaps the public reaction to such a suggestion. In an attempt to salvage some possibility for individuality in the afterlife, James allows for the possibility of multiple transcendent minds existing within the mother sea.[19]

Specifically in the context of phenomena relating to life after death, the same process can be applied. The key evidence for survival of bodily death involves the transfer of information. The most common forms of such information are of what Braude refers to as the "knowledge-that" type. Knowledge-that is basically raw data appearing in the form of memories transferred ostensibly from the dead to the living, such as identifying information conveyed through a medium. The possibility that such information could be transferred between living minds has long been suggested, removing the dead from the equation. Various kinds of data have appeared that seem to tax the psychic hypothesis, such as the cross-correspondences, which are seen by some to suggest that multiple mediums would need to be operating unconsciously in unison in order to build the necessary framework of information. Further complicating matters are instances of "knowledge-how," in which someone, a medium for instance, gains knowledge of a skill that normally requires training versus simple data, such as the ability to speak a foreign language. The assumption is made that such skills could not simply be picked out like memories from the mind of another person since they require time, practice, and training to master.

In a unity of minds, the information from any given individual, whether alive or dead, need not travel from one specific mind to another, but instead simply exists within the Universal Mind, accessible to all transient minds that walk the Earth. Anyone, in this model, has access to all of the information ever known to any human being, though actually gaining that information is no easy task. There is a sense in the study of both mystical and paranormal experiences that effort does not necessarily lead to accomplishment. A Buddhist might spend a lifetime meditating and simply never achieve *nirvana*, while an atheist who has spent little time thinking about life's meaning might suddenly suffer the shock of a mystical experience when confronted by some numinous wonder. This is analogous to the functioning of memory, as anyone who has ever tried desperately to remember a phone number can attest to. Braude recognizes the importance of "passive volition,"[20] and argues that a psychological approach to case studies might be taken in order to discover the underlying needs being addressed by the phenomena at hand. In relation to a theory of a Universal Mind, passive volition makes sense in terms of giving one's self over to what might be deemed a transcendent agent. Without trying, the information that we need, whether we realize it or not, arrives.

Consider Raymond Moody's observations with his psychomanteum discussed in the chapter on apparitions. In conducting his study, he found a very high rate of success in inducing visions in his subjects. While all subjects were instructed to seek a specific deceased person, there were cases where a different, but no less familiar, apparition appeared. These instances lead Moody to conclude that witnesses often perceive the apparition that they personally need to at that moment in time, rather than the one they consciously wish to see. And the reason they need to, according to Moody, is the presence of unresolved emotions, which are dealt with by words of consolation from these visions.[21] If such non-veridical apparitions can be caused by unconscious needs, then surely the possibility must exist for similar needs being met through more complex phenomena. The experience occurs without any knowledge of the actual need's having even existed in the first place, and can run quite contrary to conscious effort and desire. This is not a point that is out of line with Braude's contention that underlying needs should be addressed, however it is not necessarily the case that such needs must come from the individual.

Several authors have correctly identified the need for meaning in the paranormal acquisition of information. For instance, questions about why a child might remember a given past-life over any other seem to imply some kind of specific need or meaning to explain. The survivalist would argue that the need comes from the dead themselves, while proponents of the traditionally conceived psychic hypothesis might argue that the need comes from the individual having the memories. The theory from mystical experience implies meaning and need on a far greater scale, transcending the boundaries of either the living or the dead. In any event, it is clear that the needs being discussed stem from the farthest reaches of the unconscious. It is ideological to limit meaning to the individual. In the face of mystical experience, it is likely that meaning transcends the individual and comes from without rather than from within. While this may sound like an odd proposition in this modern, secular age, the reality of transcendent meaning has been at the root of religious thought for millennia, and it is mystical experience that has lead humans to conclude the reality of implicit meaning in this world throughout time.

We then find that with mystical experience as a universal, cross-cultural human experience, we may have the answer to the problem of anomalous information transfer. All of us, as humans, are interconnected with everyone else. Jesus' commandment to "love thy neighbour as thyself"[22] could be no truer since my neighbor and myself are one and the same, despite outward appearances. Just as memories and thoughts percolate up from my unconscious mind for reasons unknown to me consciously, so too can memories, thoughts, and information in general surface from even deeper within the Universal Mind. Whether a medium communicates with spirits, a ghost appears to the living, a person has the sensation of leaving the body, or one remembers aspects of a past-life, information enters the subject's mind from what might be described as an unknown source. The survivalist notions that the information comes directly from spirits, from the actual separation of body and soul, or from verifiable memories have been shown to fail to account for many of the problematic features of these experiences. The alternative hypothesis, which argues that the information comes from the minds of other living beings combined with various other psychic faculties somehow working unconsciously, has likewise failed to account for some of the more complicated cases. The Universal Mind hypothesis might be said to take the middle path between the two, positing that the information comes to the individualized mind from within and from without at once, so to speak. By this theory, every mind is linked, facilitating the transfer of information among the minds of the living, as witnessed through apparent cases of telepathy. By extension, the minds of the dead are also linked, as they, having lived, remain a part of the *anima mundi* even in death.

Aniela Jaffé, one of Carl Jung's disciples, describes the analogy of consciousness as pyramids. The tips are the conscious minds of individuals, but as the bases widen, they eventually overlap one another, merging into a collective.[23] Extending this analogy for the context of a life after death, I might add that these pyramids should be imagined as stemming from a large piece of rubber, like a broken balloon. Pulling at the balloon will create a pyramid of sorts, the pinnacle of which is the individual mind. Any number of such pyramids can be formed by pulling at different parts of the balloon. When a person dies, however, the pinnacle might be released and the pyramid will thus snap back into the flat surface of the rubber. The individual is lost in terms of its individualized nature, but remains as a part of the whole. The pinnacle of the conscious self is only a very small part of the larger whole.

Jaffé describes apparitions as archetypal images of the unconscious appearing to reveal meanings of critical importance to the witness, or witnesses. Some need or meaning is being addressed by the unconscious of the observer, and the image of some spirit appears in order to best transmit this necessary idea. Similarly, all of the paranormal phenomena associated with life after death can be viewed in the light of unconscious meaning bubbling up in the form of archetypal images and symbols. In this way, verifiable information is conveyed by constantly occurring "meaningful coincidences," to borrow Jung's own term. Coincidences which strike us as somehow important can be analyzed for their implicit meaning, according to Jung's theory of synchronicity.[24]

Just as meaning can be found in dreams, so too can meaning be found in everyday experiences, from meaningful coincidences of a more mundane variety to legitimate paranormal experience. The hallucination of a deceased loved one might appear to correct some previous wrong. A medium may gain some insight ostensibly from the dead in order to help in the bereavement process. A child may remember the life of some person who lost their life unjustly in order to learn an important moral lesson, or perhaps to complete whatever tasks that previous person left unfinished. Evidence from psychical research invariably includes some element of meaning, and it is up to the individuals in each case to determine what the meanings of their own experiences are. Above all, such experiences convey the common message that death is not to be feared, while appearing to the average person in such a way so as not to fracture the carefully individualized personality working in the physical universe toward what end no one knows. In relation to experiences of the dying and those near-death, Jung was surprised at just this observation, noting: "On the whole, I was astonished to see how little ado the unconscious makes of death. It would seem as though death were something relatively unimportant, or perhaps our psyche does not bother about what happens to the individual."[25]

The reality described by mystical experience is one in which the individual that we each believe ourselves daily to be is, in fact, not as solid and independent a thing as we think. The transiency of our individuality becomes immediately apparent within the greater context of an infinite universe. The theosophist, Arthur Osborn puts it nicely in stating: "The question of survival . . . seems trivial when the timeless Self is known."[26] On the one hand, we are each of us temporary beings living apparently independent lives, while on the other hand we are also eternal in our oneness with everyone and everything else. Transcendent meaning seems to guide a forward evolution of some kind, with each transient individual playing an important, meaningful role. Mystics have been aware of this built-in meaning since the beginning of history, but it is clearly up to the individual to determine how it applies to his or her own life at any given moment. Paranormal phenomena can be seen as markers and indicators to this transcendent meaning. Evidence for survival is particularly effective in conveying meaning as it most often involves highly emotional subject matter. In this light, every experience must be considered individually for the implied meaning, for it is only through the manifestation of transcendent meaning that temporal life has any value. In considering the life after death, then, the mystic's message is that we must each focus upon this life and endeavor to live it appropriately, within the context of the meanings we can find from day to day. In the grand scheme of things, the individual that I am is no more than a drop in a bucket, with form for but a brief fall before merging back into the whole. But, rather than see this as a pessimistic state of affairs as most Westerners are wont to do, the truth of the matter is that each drop is essential, for without the constant drip there would be nothing but an empty, meaningless void. And a drop with no bucket to catch it is simply wasted.

Notes

1. This chapter is a slightly revised version of my "Mystical Experience and the Afterlife," which appeared in Lance Storm and Michael A. Thalbourne, eds. *The Survival of Human Con-*

sciousness: Essays on the Possibility of Life After Death (Jefferson, NC: McFarland and Co., 2006), pp. 31–46.

2. H. H. Price, "Survival and the Idea of Another World," *Proceedings of the Society for Psychical Research* 50 (1953).

3. Alice Johnson, "On the Automatic Writing of Mrs. Holland," *Proceedings of the Society for Psychical Research* 21 (1909) pp. 166–391.

4. The medium Rosemary Brown produced compositions claiming to come from a group of famous composers, though reviews of these compositions are mixed, and certainly none has achieved any notoriety. See: Rosemary Brown, *Unfinished Symphonies: Voices from the Beyond* (New York: William Morrow, 1971); _____, *Immortals by my Elbow* (London, Bachman & Turner, 1974).

5. John Hick, *Death and Eternal Life* (London: Collins, 1976), p. 141.

6. Stephen E. Braude, *Immortal Remains: The Evidence for Life after Death* (New York: Rowman & Littlefield, 2003).

7. Braude, *Immortal Remains*, p. 1.

8. Michael F. Brown, *The Channeling Zone: American Spirituality in an Anxious Age* (Harvard: Harvard University Press, 1997), p. 24.

9. F. C. S. Schiller, *Riddles of the Sphinx* (London: Swan Sonnenschein, 1910), pp. 377–378.

10. Ambrose Bierce, "Cartesian," in *The Devil's Dictionary* (1911; repr., Cleveland, OH: World, 1948).

11. William James, *The Varieties of Religious Experience* (Cambridge, Mass.: Harvard University Press, 1985). Originally published 1902 by Longmans, Green and Company, London.

12. Walter T. Stace, *Mysticism and Philosophy* (London: MacMillan, 1961).

13. Ralph W. Hood, "Mysticism, the Unity Thesis, and the Paranormal," in *Exploring the Paranormal: Perspectives on Belief and Experience*, eds. George K. Zollschan, John F. Schumaker, and Gregg F. Walsh (Dorset, UK: Prism Press, 1989), pp. 117–130.

14. James, *The Varieties of Religious Experiences*, p. 410.

15. Abraham H. Maslow, *Religions, Values, and Peak-Experiences* (New York: Penguin Books, 1964, 1976), p. 28.

16. Stephen T. Katz, ed. *Mysticism and Philosophical Analysis* (London: Oxford University Press, 1978).

17. Aside from the distinction outlined by Stace, other great minds have similarly seen layers of experience. Stace's extrovertive mysticism corresponds directly to Zaehner's nature mysticism as well as Otto's Unifying Vision and the spontaneous peak-experience described by Maslow. Introvertive experience finds its correspondence in Zaehner's monistic and theistic mysticisms combined, as well as Otto's mysticism of introspection and Maslow's more controlled plateau-experience. See: Maslow, *Religions, Values, and Peak-Experiences*; Rudolph Otto, *Mysticism East and West*, trans. B.L. Bracey and R.C. Payne (New York: Meridian Books, 1957); R.C. Zaehner, *Concordant Discord* (London: Oxford University Press, 1970); _____, *Mysticism Sacred and Profane* (London: Oxford University Press, 1967).

18. One will here recall the example from Flournoy mentioned in the chapter on mediumship. Théodore Flournoy, *From India to the Planet Mars: A Study of a Case of Somnambulism, with Glossolalia* trans. Daniel B. Vermilye (New York: Harper & Brothers, 1900).

19. William James, *The Will to Believe and Other Essays in Popular Philosophy: Human Immortality* (New York: Dover Publications, 1956).

20. Braude, *Immortal Remains*, p. 38.

21. Raymond Moody, *Reunions: Visionary Encounters With Departed Loved Ones* (New York: Ivy, 1993), p. 22.

22. Matt. 19:19.

23. Aniela Jaffé, *Apparitions: An Archetypal Approach to Death, Dreams and Ghosts* (Irving, TX: Spring, 1979), pp. 116–126.

24. Carl G. Jung, *Synchronicity: An Acausal Connecting Principle*, trans. R. F. C. Hull, (London: Routledge & Kegan Paul, 1955).

25. Carl G. Jung, "The Structure and Dynamics of the Psyche," *Collected Works*, vol. 8, trans., R. F. C. Hull (Princeton: Princeton University Press, 1960), pp. 410–411.

26. Arthur W. Osborn, *The Superphysical*, revised ed. (New York: Harper & Row, 1974), p. 316.

Bibliography

Aeschylus. *The Persae of Aeschylus*. Edited by H. D. Broadhead. Cambridge, UK: Cambridge University Press, 1960.

———. *Persians*. Translated by E. Hall. Warminster: Aris & Phillips, 1996.

Ahern, Emily M. *The Cult of the Dead in a Chinese Village*. Stanford: Stanford University Press, 1973.

Aldwinckle, Russell. *Death in the Secular City*. Grand Rapids: Eerdmans, 1972.

Algar, Hamid. *Sufism: Principles and Practice*. New York: Islamic Publications International, 1999.

Alger, William R. *The Destiny of the Soul: A Critical History of the Doctrine of a Future Life*. 10th ed. New York: Greenwood, 1968 [ca. 1878].

Al-Ghazali. *The Remembrance of Death and the Afterlife* (*Kitab dhikr al-mawt wa-maba'dahu*). Book XL of *The Revival of the Religious Sciences* (*Ihya `ulum al din*). Translated by T. J. Winter. Cambridge, UK: Islamic Texts Society, 1989.

al-Qadi, 'Abd ar-Rahim ibn Ahmad. *Islamic Book of the Dead: A Collection of Hadiths on the Fire & the Garden*. Norwich: Diwan, 1977.

Alster, B., ed. *Death in Mesopotamia: Papers Read at the XXVIe rencontre assyriologique internationale*. Copenhagen: Akademisk forlag, 1980.

Amergier, Paul. *La parole rêvée: essai sur la vie et l'oeuvre de Robert d'UZES O.P.* (*1263–1296*). Aix-en-Provence: Centre d'Études des Sociétées Méditerranéennes, 1982.

Angoff, Allan. *Eileen Garrett and the World Beyond the Senses*. New York: William Morrow, 1974.

Arcangel, Dianne. "Investigating the Relationship Between the Myers-Briggs Type Indicator and Facilitated Reunion Experiences." *Journal of the American Society for Psychical Research* 91 (1997): 80–95.

Aquinas, St. Thomas. *Basic Writings of Saint Thomas Aquinas*. Edited by Anton C. Pegis. New York: Random House, 1945.

Aristotle. *Metaphysics*. Translated and edited by John Warrington. London: J. M. Dent, 1956.

———. *De Anima (On the Soul)*. Translated by H. Lawson-Tancred. New York: Penguin, 1986.

Armstrong, A. H., ed. *The Cambridge History of Later Greek and Early Medieval Philosophy*. London: Cambridge University Press, 1967.

——, ed. *Classical Mediterranean Spirituality*. New York: Crossroad, 1986.

Athappily, Geena K., Bruce Greyson, and Ian Stevenson. "Do Prevailing Societal Models Influence Reports of Near-Death Experiences? A Comparison of Accounts Reported Before and After 1975." *The Journal of Nervous and Mental Disease* 194:3 (2006): 218–222.

Atharva-Veda-Samhita. 2nd ed. Translated by William Dwight Whitney. Delhi: Motilal Banarsidass, 1971.

Augustine, Saint. "The City of God." In *The Essential Augustine*. 2nd ed. Compiled by Vernon J. Bourke. Indianapolis: Hackett, 1978.

Badham, Paul. *Christian Beliefs About Life After Death*. London: MacMillan, 1976.

——. *The Contemporary Challenge of Modernist Theology*. Cardiff: University of Wales Press, 1998.

——, and Linda Badham, eds. *Death and Immortality in the Religions of the World*. New York: Paragon House, 1987.

Barrett, William. *Deathbed Visions*. London: Rider, 1926. http://www.survivalafterdeath.org/books/barrett/dbv/contents.htm (accessed January 28, 2008).

Becker, Carl B. "The Centrality of Near-Death Experiences in Chinese Pure Land Buddhism." *Anabiosis—The Journal for Near-Death Studies* 1 (1981): 154–171.

——. "The Pure Land Revisited: Sino-Japanese Meditations and Near Death Experiences of the Next World." *Anabiosis—The Journal for Near-Death Studies* 4 (1984): 51–68.

——. "Views From Tibet: NDEs and the *Book of the Dead*." *Anabiosis—The Journal for Near-Death Studies* 5 (1985): 3–20.

——. *Breaking the Circle: Death and the Afterlife in Buddhism*. Carbondale and Edwardsville, IL: Southern Illinois University Press, 1993.

Becker, Ernest. *The Denial of Death*. New York: Free Press, 1973.

Bell, Richard. *Introduction to the Qur'an*. Edinburgh: Edinburgh University Press, 1953.

Bender, Hans. *Verborgene Wirklichkeit: Parapsychologie und Grenzengebiete der Psychologie*. (Hidden Reality: Parapsychology and the Burden of Psychology.) Olten, Freiburg: Walter Verlag, 1973.

Benoit, Pierre, and Roland Murphy, eds. *Immortality and Resurrection*. New York: Herder and Herder, 1970.

Berg, Rabbi Phillip. *Wheels of a Soul*. New York: The Kabbalah Learning Center, 1995.

Berkouwer, G. C. *The Return of Christ*. Grand Rapids: Eerdmans, 1972.

Bernstein, Morey. *The Search for Bridey Murphy*. 2nd ed. With new material by William J. Barker. New York: Doubleday, 1965 [1956].

The Bible. King James Version.

Bierce, Ambrose. "Cartesian." In *The Devil's Dictionary*. 1911. Reprint, Cleveland, OH: World, 1948.

Billington, Ray. *Understanding Eastern Philosophy*. London: Routledge, 1997.

Blacker, Carmen. *The Catalpa Bow*. London: George Allen & Unwin, 1975.

Blackmore, Susan. *Beyond the Body*. London: Heinemann, 1982.

Blum, Mark Laurence. *The Origins and Development of Pure Land Buddhism: A Study and Translation of Gyonen's Jodo Homon Genrusho*. New York: Oxford University Press, 2002.

Bowker, John. *The Meanings of Death*. Cambridge: Cambridge University Press, 1991.

Braithwaite, Jason J. "Magnetic Variances Associated with 'Haunt-Type' Experiences: A Comparison Using Time-Synchronized Baseline Measurements." *European Journal of Parapsychology* 19 (2004): 3–28.

——, Katty Perez-Aquino, and Maurice Townsend. "In Search of Magnetic Anomalies Associated with Haunt-Type Experiences: Pulses and Patterns in Dual-Time Synchronized Measurements." *Journal of Parapsychology* 68:2 (2004): 255–288.

Braude, Stephen E. *Immortal Remains: The Evidence for Life after Death*. New York: Rowman & Littlefield, 2003.

Breen, John and Mark Teeuwen, eds. *Shinto in History*. Richmond, UK: Curzon, 2000.

Broad, C. D. *Religion, Philosophy, and Psychical Research*. New York: Harcourt, 1953.

Brody, Eugene B. "Review of *Cases of the Reincarnation Type, Volume II. Ten Cases in Sri Lanka*." *Journal of the American Society for Psychical Research* 73 (1979): 71–81.

Brown, Michael F. *The Channeling Zone: American Spirituality in an Anxious Age*. Harvard: Harvard University Press, 1997.

Brown, Rosemary. *Immortals by my Elbow*. London: Bachman & Turner, 1974.

———. *Unfinished Symphonies: Voices from the Beyond*. New York: William Morrow, 1971.

Brugioni, Dino A. *Photo Fakery: The History and Techniques of Photographic Deception and Manipulation*. Dulles, VA: Brassey's, 1999.

Buber, Martin. *Between Man and Man*. Translated by R. G. Smith. London: Kegan Paul, 1947.

Budge, E. A. W. *The Egyptian Book of the Dead*. 1895. Reprint, New York: Dover, 1967.

———. *Egyptian Religion: Egyptian Ideas of the Future Life*. 1899. Reprint, London: Routledge Kegan Paul, 1979.

Calvin, John. *Tracts & Treatises on the Reformation of the Church*. 3 vols. Edited by Thomas F. Torrance. Grand Rapids: Eerdmans, 1958.

Capps, Walter H. *Religious Studies: The Making of a Discipline*. Minneapolis, MN: Fortress, 1995.

Cardeña, Etzel. "Review of *The Survival of Human Consciousness: Essays in the Possibility of a Life After Death*." *Journal of Parapsychology* 70:1 (2006): 179–185.

Chakraborty, Chanda. *Common Life in the Rgveda and Atharvaveda*. Calcutta: Punthi Pustak, 1977.

Chapple, Christopher. Foreword to *The Bhagavad Gita*. Translated by Winthrop Sargeant. Albany: SUNYP, 1994.

Ch'en, Kenneth K. S. *Buddhism in China*. Princeton: Princeton University Press, 1964.

Cherry, Christopher. "Near-Death Experiences and the Problem of Evidence for Survival After Death." *Religious Studies* 22 (1987): 397–406.

Cheu, Hock Tong. *The Nine Emperor Gods: A Study of Chinese Spirit-Medium Cults*. Singapore: Times Books International, 1988.

CHOICE: Current Reviews for Academic Libraries. "Review of Hiroshi Obayashi, ed., *Death and Afterlife: Perspectives of World Religions*." http://www.greenwood.com/books/BookDetail.asp?sku=ODE/&imprinID=10 (accessed January 28, 2008).

Christopher, Milbourne. *ESP, Seers & Psychics*. New York: Thomas Y. Crowell, 1970.

Chuang Tzu. *The Complete Works of Chuang Tzu*. Translated by Burton Watson. New York: Columbia University Press, 1968.

Cohn-Sherbok, Dan, and Christopher Lewis, eds. *Beyond Death*. London: MacMillan, 1995.

Confucius. *Analects*. Translated by James Legge. 1893. New York: Globusz Publishing, n.d. http://www.globusz.com/ebooks/ConfucianAnalects/ (accessed February 11. 2008).

Conze, Edward, trans. *Buddhist Scriptures*. Harmondsworth, UK: Penguin, 1959.

Coward, Harold, ed. *Life After Death in World Religions*. New York: Orbis, 1997.

Cressy, Judith. *The Near-Death Experience: Mysticism or Madness*. Hanover, MA: The Christopher Publishing House, 1994.

Crooke, William. *Popular Religion and Folklore of Northern India*. 2 vols. 2nd ed. 1896. Reprint: Munshiram Manoharlal, 1968.

Crookes, William. *Researches into the Phenomena of Spiritualism*. 7th ed. London: Two Worlds, 1904.

Cross, Tom. "The Himalayas Case: Strong Survival Evidence Through Three Mediums." *Journal of the Society for Psychical Research* 62 (1998): 347–352.

David-Neel, Alexandra. *Magic and Mystery in Tibet*. New York: Dover, 1971.

Dawkins, Richard. "Viruses of the Mind." in *Dennett and His Critics: Demystifying Mind*. Edited by Bo Dalhbom. Cambridge, MA: Blackwell, 1993.

Davies, Jon. *Death, Burial and Rebirth in the Religions of Antiquity*. London: Routledge, 1999.

De Groot, J. J. M. *The Religious System of China*. 6 vols. Leyden: E. J. Brill, 1892–1910.

Dimmitt, Cornelia, and J. A. B. van Buitenen, eds. and trans. *Classical Hindu Mythology: A Reader in the Sanskrit Puranas*. Philadelphia: Temple University Press, 1978.

Dodds, E. R. *The Greeks and the Irrational*. Berkeley, CA: University of California Press, 1959.

———. *The Ancient Concept of Progress: And Other Essays on Greek Literature and Belief*. Oxford: Clarenden, 1973.

Donaldson, Bess Allen. *The Wild Rue*. 1938. Reprint, New York: Arno, 1973.

Ducasse, C. J. "How the Case of *The Search for Bridey Murphy* Stands Today." *Journal of the American Society for Psychical Research* 54 (1960): 3–22.

———. *A Critical Examination of the Belief in a Life After Death*. Springfield, IL: C. C. Thomas, 1961.

Ebrey, Patricia. "The Liturgies for Sacrifices to Ancestors in Successive Versions of the Family Rituals." In *Ritual and Scripture in Chinese Popular Religion*. Edited by David Johnson. Berkeley, CA: Chinese Popular Culture Project: Distributed by IEAS Publications, 1995.

Edwards, Paul. *Reincarnation: A Critical Examination*. New York: Prometheus, 1996.

Eklund, Ragnar. *Life Between Death and Resurrection According to Islam*. Uppsala: Almquist & Wiksells Boktryckeri, 1941.

Eliade, Mircea. *A History of Religious Ideas*. Vol. 1. Translated by W. R. Trask. Chicago: University of Chicago Press, 1978.

Ellis, David J. "Listening to the 'Raudive Voices.'" *Journal of the Society for Psychical Research* 48 (1975): 31–42.

———. *The Mediumship of the Tape Recorder: A Detailed Examination of the Raudive Voice Phenomenon of Voice Extras on Tape Recordings*. Pullborough, UK: D. J. Ellis, 1978.

Emmons, Charles F. *Chinese Ghosts and ESP*. Metuchen, NJ: Scarecrow, 1982.

Fadiman, James, and Robert Frager, eds. *Essential Sufism*. San Francisco: HarperSanFrancisco, 1997.

Fahd, Toufic. *La divination arabe*. Leiden: E. J. Brill, 1966.

Faulkner, R. O. *The Ancient Egyptian Book of the Dead*. London: The British Museum, 1985.

Felton, D. *Haunted Greece and Rome: Ghost Stories From Classical Antiquity*. Austin: University of Texas Press, 1999.

Flood, Gavin. *An Introduction to Hinduism*. Cambridge, UK: Cambridge University Press, 1998.

Flournoy, Théodore. *From India to the Planet Mars: A Study of a Case of Somnambulism, with Glossolalia*. Translated by Daniel B. Vermilye. New York: Harper & Brothers, 1900.

Foard, James, Michael Solomon, and Richard K. Payne, eds. *The Pure Land Tradition: History and Development*. Berkeley, CA: Regents of the University of California, 1996.

Fontana, David. *Is There and Afterlife? A Comprehensive Overview of the Evidence*. Deershot Lodge, UK: O Books, 2004.

Fowler, Merv. *Buddhism: Beliefs and Practices*. Brighton, UK: Sussex Academic Press, 1999.

Fox, Mark. *Religion, Spirituality and the Near-Death Experience*. London: Routledge, 2003.

Frankfort, H. *Ancient Egyptian Religion: An Interpretation*. New York: Harper &Row, 1961.

Frankl, Victor E. *Man's Search for Meaning*. 1959. Rev. and updated. New York: Washington Square, 1984.

Frawley, David. *The Myth of the Aryan Invasion of India*. New Delhi: Voice of India, 1994.

Freed, Ruth S., and Stanley A. Freed, *Ghosts: Life and Death in North India*. Seattle: University of Washington Press, 1993.

Freud, Sigmund. *Civilization And Its Discontents.* Translated by Joan Riviere. London: Hogarth, 1930; Toronto: General, 1994.

Gabbard, Glen O., and Stuart W. Twemlow. *With the Eyes of the Mind: An Empirical Analysis of Out-of-Body States.* New York: Praeger, 1984.

Gardner, John, and John Maier. *Gilgamesh.* New York: Vintage, 1985.

Gauld, Alan. *Mediumship and Survival.* London: Paladin, 1983.

Gibbs, Nancy, "Angels Among Us," *Time Magazine*, December 27, 1993.

Giles, Herbert A., trans. *Strange Stories from a Chinese Studio.* London: T. Werner Laurie, 1916.

Gillman, Neil. *The Death of Death.* Woodstock, VT: Jewish Lights, 1997.

Ginzberg, Louis. "Akiba ben Joseph." *Jewish Encyclopedia.* 1901–1906. http://www.jewishencyclopedia.com/view.jsp?artid=1033&letter=A#2666 (accessed January 25, 2008).

Goldfeld, Lee Naomi. *Moses Maimonides' Treatise on Resurrection.* New York: KTAV Publishing House, 1986.

Gombrich, Richard. *Theravada Buddhism.* London: Routledge & Kegan Paul, 1988.

Goodman, Lenn E. *Avicenna.* London: Routledge, 1992.

Goodrich, Anne Swann. *Chinese Hells.* St. Augustine, FL: Monumenta Serica, 1981.

Gopalacharya, Mahuli R. *The Heart of the Rig Veda.* New Delhi: Somaiya, 1971.

Green, Celia. *Out-of-the-Body Experiences.* Oxford: Institute of Psychophysical Research, 1968.

—— and Charles McCreery. *Apparitions.* London: Hamish Hamilton, 1975.

Greer, Rowan A., trans. *Origen.* New York: Paulist Press, 1979.

Guiley, Rosemary Ellen. *Encyclopedia of Mystical and Paranormal Experience.* San Francisco: HarperCollins, 1991.

Guillaume, Alfred. *The Traditions of Islam.* London: Oxford University Press, 1924.

Haldar, J. R. *Links Between Early and Later Buddhist Mythology.* Calcutta: Grantha Parikrama, 1972.

Hamilton, Margaret. *Is Survival a Fact?* London: Psychic Press, 1969.

Hamilton, T. Glen. *Intention and Survival.* Toronto: MacMillan, 1942.

Harpur, Tom. *Life After Death.* Toronto: McClelland & Stewart, 1991.

Head, J. and S. L. Cranston, eds. *Reincarnation: The Phoenix Fire Mystery.* New York: Julian Press/ Crown, 1977.

Herodotus. *The Histories.* Translated by A. de Selincourt. Harmondsworth, UK: Penguin, 1972.

Hesiod. "Theogony." In *Hesiod and Theognis.* Translated by Dorothea Walker. London: Penguin, 1973.

Hick, John. *Faith and Knowledge.* London: MacMillan, 1967.

——. *Death and Eternal Life.* London: MacMillan, 1985.

Himmelfarb, Martha. *Tours of Hell.* Philadelphia: University of Pennsylvania Press, 1983.

Hirsch, W. *Rabbinic Psychology: Beliefs about the Soul in Rabbinic Literature of the Talmudic Period.* London: Edward Goldston, 1947.

Hodgson, Richard. "A Record of Observations of Certain Phenomena of Trance." *Proceedings of the Society for Psychical Research* 8 (1892): 1–167.

——. "A Further Record of Observations of Certain Phenomena of Trance.*Proceedings of the Society for Psychical Research* 13 (1897–1898): 284–582.

Holck, Frederick H. *Death and Eastern Thought.* Nashville: Abingdon, 1974.

Holm, Jean, ed., with John Bowker. *Human Nature and Destiny.* London: Pinter, 1994.

Home, Daniel Dunglas. *Lights and Shadows of Spiritualism.* London: Virtue, 1877.

Homer. *Iliad.* Translated by R. Fagles. London: Penguin, 1990.

——. *The Odyssey.* Translated by Robert Fitzgerald. New York: Vintage Classics, 1990.

Hood, Ralph W. "Mysticism, the Unity Thesis, and the Paranormal." Pages 117–130 in *Exploring the Paranormal: Perspectives on Belief and Experience*, eds. George K. Zollschan, John F. Schumaker, and Gregg F. Walsh. Dorset, UK: Prism Press, 1989.

Hopkins, E. Washburn. *Epic Mythology*. 1915. Reprint, Delhi: Motilal Banarsidass, 1974.

Hori, Ichiro, ed. *Japanese Religion*. Tokyo: Kodansha International, 1972.

Hourani, Albert. *A History of the Arab Peoples*. Cambridge, MA: Belknap Press of Harvard University Press, 1991.

Hoyland, Robert G. *Arabia and the Arabs*. London: Routledge, 2001.

Hsu, Francis L. K. *Under the Ancestors' Shadow*. New York: Doubleday, 1967.

Hudson, Thomson Jay. *The Law of Psychic Phenomena*. Chicago: A. C. McClurg, 1902.

Hume, Robert Ernest, trans. *The Thirteen Principle Upanishads*. Delhi: Oxford University Press, 1921.

Hyman, Ray. "How Not to Test Mediums: Critiquing *The Afterlife Experiments*." *Skeptical Inquirer* 27:1 (2003): 20–30.

The Hymns of the Rgveda. Translated by Ralph T. H. Griffith. Edited by J. L. Shastri. Delhi: Motilal Banarsidass, 1973.

Ibn Hisham, 'Abdul-Malik. *The Life of Muhammad*. Lahore: Oxford University Press, 1968 [1955].

Ibn Taymeeyah. *Essay on the Jinn (Demons)*. Translated by Abu Ameenah Bilal Philips. Riyadh: Tahweed Publications, 1989.

Inada, Kenneth K. *Nagarjuna: A Translation of his Mulamadhyamakakarika with an Introductory Essay*. Tokyo: Hokuseido, 1970.

Irwin, Robert. *The Arabian Nights: A Companion*. London: Allen Lane, the Penguin Press, 1994.

Iverson, Jeffrey. *More Lives Than One?: The Evidence of the Remarkable Bloxham Tapes*. London: Souvenir, 1976.

Jaffé, Aniela. *Apparitions: An Archetypal Approach to Death, Dreams and Ghosts*. Irving, TX: Spring, 1979.

James, Edwin Oliver. *Myth and Ritual in the Ancient Near East*. London: Thames and Hudson, 1958.

James, William. *The Varieties of Religious Experience*. Cambridge, Mass.: Harvard University Press, 1985.

———. *William James on Psychical Research*. Compiled and edited by Gardner Murphy and Robert O. Ballou. London: Chatto and Windus, 1961.

———. *The Will to Believe and Other Essays in Popular Philosophy: Human Immortality*. New York: Dover Publications, 1956.

Jastrow, Morris. *The Civilization of Babylonia and Assyria*. 1915. Reprint, New York: Benjamin Blom, 1971.

Johnson, Alice. "On the Automatic Writing of Mrs. Holland." *Proceedings of the Society for Psychical Research* 21 (1909): 166–391.

Johnson, Raynor C. *The Imprisoned Splendour*. London: Hodder & Stoughton, 1953.

Johnston, Reginald Fleming. *Buddhist China*. 1913. Reprint, San Francisco: Chinese Materials Center, 1976.

Johnston, Sarah Iles. *Restless Dead: Encounters Between the Living and the Dead in Ancient Greece*. Berkeley, CA: University of California Press, 1999.

Jordan, David K. *Gods, Ghosts, and Ancestors*. Berkeley, CA: University of California Press, 1972.

Jung, Carl G. *Synchronicity: An Acausal Connecting Principle*. Translated by R. F. C. Hull. London: Routledge & Kegan Paul, 1955.

———. "The Structure and Dynamics of the Psyche." *Collected Works*. Vol. 8. Translated by R. F. C. Hull. Princeton: Princeton University Press, 1960.

———. *Memories, Dreams, Reflections*. Edited by Aniela Jaffé. London: Collins and Routledge & Kegan Paul, 1963.

———. *Jung on Alchemy*. Edited by Nathan Schwartz-Salant. Princeton: Princeton University Press, 1995.

Kaplan, Aryeh. *Immortality, Resurrection, and the Age of the Universe: A Kabbalistic View*. New Jersey: KTAV Publishing House, 1993.

Katz, Stephen T., ed. *Mysticism and Philosophical Analysis*. New York: Oxford University Press, 1978.

Keen, Montague, and Archie E. Roy. "Chance Coincidence in the Cross-Correspondences." *Journal of the Society for Psychical Research* 68:1 (2004): 57–60.

Keen, Montague, Arthur Ellison, and David Fontana. "The Scole Report." *Proceedings of the Society for Psychical Research* 58 (1999).

Kellehear, Allan. *Experiences Near Death*. Oxford: Oxford University Press, 1996.

Klass, Dennis. *The Spiritual Lives of Bereaved Parents*. Philadelphia, PA: Brunner/Mazel, 1999.

Knappert, Jan. *Islamic Legends*. 2 vols. Leiden: E. J. Brill, 1985.

The Qur'an. 2nd revised ed. Translated by N. J. Dawood. Harmondsworth, UK: Penguin, 1966.

Kübler-Ross, Elisabeth. *On Death and Dying*. New York: Touchstone, 1969.

Küng, Hans. *Eternal Life?* Translated by Edward Quinn. New York: Doubleday, 1984.

Laertius, Diogenes. *The Lives and Opinions of Eminent Philosophers*. Translated by C. D. Yonge. London: Henry G. Bohn, 1853.

Lai, T. C. *The Eight Immortals*. Hong Kong: Swindown, 1972.

Lamont, Corliss. *The Illusion of Immortality*. New York: Philosophical Library, 1959.

Lang, Andrew. *The Book of Dreams and Ghosts*. London: Longmans Green, 1899.

Lang, Graeme, and Lars Ragvald. *The Rise of a Refugee God*. Hong Kong: Oxford University Press, 1993.

Langdon, Stephen H. *Semitic Mythology*. New York: Cooper Square, 1964 [1931].

Lao Tzu. *Tao Te Ching*. Translated by Stephen Addiss and Stanley Lombardo. Indianapolis: Hackett, 1993.

The Last Days of the Buddha: The Maha-parinibbana Sutta (Digha Nikaya 16). Translated by Sister Vajira and Francis Story. Revised ed. Kandy: Buddhist Publication Society, 1998. http://www.accesstoinsight.org/ptf/sacca.html (accessed January 28, 2008).

Law, Bimala Charan. *Heaven and Hell in Buddhist Perspective*. 1925. Reprint, Sonarpura, Varanasi: Bhartiya, 1973.

Legge, James, trans. *The Texts of Taoism*. Sacred Books of the East. Vol. 39. 1891. Reprint, New York: Dover, 1962.

LeGoff, Jacques. *The Birth of Purgatory*. Translated by Arthur Goldhammer. London: Scolar, 1984.

Lewis, I. M. *Ecstatic Religion: A Study of Shamanism and Spirit Possession*. 2nd edition. London and NY: Routledge, 1989.

Li Chi (The Book of Rites). Translated by James Legge. Sacred Books of the East. Vol. 28. Oxford: Oxford University Press, 1885.

Lieberman, Saul. *Some Aspects of Afterlife in Early Rabbinic Literature*. Jerusalem: American Academy for Jewish Research, 1965.

Liebman, Joshua L. *Peace of Mind*. New York: Simon and Schuster, 1946.

Lorimer, David. *Whole in One: Near-Death Experience and the Ethic of Interconnectedness*. London: Arkana, 1990.

Lucretius. *On the Nature of the Universe*. Translated by R. E. Latham. London: Penguin, 1994.

Lundahl, Craig R., ed. *A Collection of Near-Death Research Readings*. Chicago: Nelson-Hall, 1982.

Luther, Martin. "Disputation of Doctor Martin Luther on the Power and Efficacy of Indulgences." Volume 1 of *Works of Martin Luther*. 6 volumes. Translated and edited by Adolph Spaeth, et al. Philadelphia: A. J. Holman, 1915. http://www.sacred-texts.com/chr/the9510.txt (accessed January 28, 2008).

MacGregor, Geddes. *Images of Afterlife: Beliefs from Antiquity to Modern Times*. New York: Paragon House, 1992.

MacKenzie, Andrew. *Apparitions and Ghosts*. London: Arthur Barker, 1971.

———. *Hauntings and Apparitions*. London: Granada, 1983.

Maimonides. *The Guide of the Perplexed*. Translated by M. Friedlander. New York: Hebrew Publishing, 1881.

Makarem, Sami Nasib. *The Druze Faith*. New York: Caravan, 1974.

Martyr, St. Justin. "Dialogue With Trypho." In *The Ante-Nicene Fathers*. Vol. 1. Edited and translated by Rev. Alexander Roberts and James Donaldson. New York: Christian Literature Publishing Co., 1885. www.newadvent.org/fathers/0128.htm (accessed January 28, 2008).

Marx, Karl, and Frederich Engels. *On Religion*. New York: Shocken, 1964.

Maslow, Abraham H. *Religions, Values, and Peak-Experiences*. New York: Penguin, 1964, 1976.

Maspero, Henri. *Taoism and Chinese Religion*. Translated by Frank A. Kierman, Jr. Amherst: University of Massachusetts Press, 1981.

Ma'Sumian, Farnaz. *Life After Death: A Study of the Afterlife in World Religions*. Oxford: Oneworld Publications, 1995.

Matlock, J. G. "Past Life Memory Case Studies." In *Advances in Parapsychology*. Vol. 6. Edited by Stanley Krippner. Jefferson, NC: McFarland, 1990.

McCagney, Nancy. *Nagarjuna and the Philosophy of Openness*. Oxford: Rowman & Littlefield, 1997.

McDermott, James Paul. *Development in the Early Buddhist Concept of Kamma/Karma*. New Delhi: Munshiram Manoharlal, 1984.

Mead, G. R. S. *Fragments of a Faith Forgotten*. New York: University Books, 1960.

Mehr, Farhang. *The Zoroastrian Tradition: An Introduction to the Ancient Wisdom of Zarathushtra*. Rockport, MA: Element, 1991.

Michaels, Axel. *Hinduism: Past and Present*. Translated by Barbara Harshav. Princeton, NJ: Princeton University Press, 2004 [1998].

Momen, Moojan. *An Introduction to Shi'i Islam*. New Haven: Yale University Press, 1985.

Moody, Raymond. *Life After Life*. Atlanta: Mockingbird, 1975.

———. "Family Reunions: Visionary Encounters with the Departed in a Modern Day Psychomanteum." *Journal of Near-Death Studies* 11:2 (1992): 83–121.

———. *Reunions: Visionary Encounters With Departed Loved Ones*. New York: Ivy, 1993.

Moore, C. H. *Ancient Beliefs in the Immortality of the Soul*. New York: Cooper Square, 1963.

Moreman, Christopher M. "Mystical Experience and the Afterlife." in *The Survival of Human Consciousness: Essays on the Possibility of a Life After Death*, eds. Lance Storm and Michael A. Thalbourne, 31–46 Jefferson, NC: McFarland and Co., 2006.

———. "Review of *Talking to the Dead: Kate and Maggie Fox and the Rise of Spiritualism*." *Journal of Parapsychology* 68:2 (2004): 436–438.

———. "Response to Keen and Roy re: Chance Coincidence in the Cross-Correspondences." *Journal of the Society for Psychical Research* 68:1 (2004): 60–62.

———. "A Re-Examination of the Possibility of Chance Coincidence as an Alternative Explanation for Mediumistic Communication in the Cross Correspondences." *Journal of the Society for Psychical Research* 67:4 (2003): 225–242.

Morewedge, Parviz, ed. *Islamic Philosophy and Mysticism*. New York: Caravan, 1981.

Mousselimis, Spiros G. *The Ancient Underworld and the Oracle for Necromancy at Ephyra*. Ioannina, Greece: n.p., 1989.

Muldoon, Sylvan, and Hereward Carrington. *The Phenomena of Astral Projection*. New York: Samuel Weiser, 1974.

Murata, Sachiko, and William C. Chittick. *The Vision of Islam*. St. Paul, MN: Paragon House, 1994.

Murty, K. Satchidananda. *Nagarjuna*. New Delhi: National Book Trust, 1971.

Myers, F. W. H. *Essays Classical*. London: MacMillan, 1883.

Myers, F. W. H., O. J. Lodge, W. Leaf, and W. James. "A Record of Observations of Certain Phenomena of Trance." *Proceedings of the Society for Psychical Research* 6 (1889–1890): 436–660.

Nasr, Seyyed Hossein, ed. *Islamic Spirituality*. New York: Crossroad, 1991.

Nebesky-Wojkowitz, Réne de. *Oracles and Demons of Tibet*. London: Oxford University Press, 1956.

Neufeldt, Ronald W., ed. *Karma and Rebirth: Post Classical Developments*. Delhi: Sri Satguru, 1986.

Nickelsburg, George W. E. *Resurrection, Immortality, and Eternal Life in Intertestamental Judaism*. Cambridge, MA: Harvard University Press, 1972.

Nigal, Gedalyah. *Magic, Mysticism, and Hasidism: The Supernatural in Jewish Thought*. Translated by Edward Levin. London: Jason Aronson, 1994.

Obayashi, Hiroshi, ed. *Death and Afterlife: Perspectives of World Religions*. New York: Greenwood, 1992.

O'Brien, D. *Empedocles' Cosmic Cycle*. Cambridge: Cambridge University Press, 1969.

Odell, Catherine M. *Those Who Saw Her: The Apparitions of Mary*. Huntington, IN: Our Sunday Visitor, 1986.

O'Flaherty, Wendy Doniger, ed. *Karma and Rebirth in Classical India*. Berkeley, CA: University of California Press, 1980.

Oldenberg, Hermann. *The Religion of the Veda*. Translated by Shridhar B. Shrotri. Delhi: Motilal Banarsidass, 1988.

Osborn, Arthur W. *The Superphysical*. Revised edition. NY: Harper & Row, 1974.

O'Shaughnessy, Thomas. *Muhammad's Thoughts on Death*. Leiden: E. J. Brill, 1969.

Osis, Karlis. "Out of Body Research at the ASPR." *ASPR Newsletter* (1974, Summer): 1–3.

———. *Deathbed Observations by Physicians and Nurses*. New York: Parapsychology Foundation, 1961.

Osis, Karlis, and Erlendur Haraldsson. *What They Saw…At The Hour of Death*. 3rd ed. Norwalk, CT: Hastings House, 1997.

Osis, Karlis, and Donna McCormick. "Kinetic Effects at the Ostensible Location of an Out of Body Projection During Perceptual Testing." *Journal of the American Society for Psychical Research* 74 (1980): 319–329.

Otto, Rudolph. *Mysticism East and West*. Translated by B. L. Bracey and R. C. Payne. New York: Meridian, 1957.

Pandey, Raj Bali. *Hindu Samskaras*. Delhi: Motilal Banarsidass, 1969.

Panikkar, Raimundo, ed. and trans. *The Vedic Experience: Mantramanjari*. Berkeley, CA: University of California Press, 1977.

Paper, Jordan. *The Spirits are Drunk*. New York: SUNYP, 1995.

Parente, Pascal P. *Beyond Space*. Rockford, IL: Tan, 1973.

Parry, Jonathan P. *Death in Banaras*. Cambridge, UK: Cambridge University Press, 1994.

Pasricha, S., and Ian Stevenson. "Near-Death Experiences in India: A Preliminary Report." *Journal of Nervous and Mental Disease* 174 (1986): 165–170.

Paterson, R. W. K. *Philosophy and the Belief in a Life After Death*. London: MacMillan, 1995.

Perry, Michael. *The Resurrection of Man*. Oxford: Mowbrays London and Oxford, 1975.

Persinger, Michael A., S. G. Tiller, and S. A. Koren. "Experimental Simulation of a Haunt Experience and Elicitation of Paroxysmal Electroencephalographic Activity by Transcerebral Complex Magnetic Fields: Induction of a Synthetic 'Ghost?'" *Journal of Perception and Motor Skills* 90:2 (2000): 659–674.

Pickthall, Mohammed Marmaduke. *The Meaning of the Glorious Qur'an: An Explanatory Translation*. New York: New American Library, 1953.

Pinch, Geraldine. *Magic in Ancient Egypt*. Austin: University of Texas, 1994.

Plato. *Phaedo*. Translated by D. Gallop. Oxford: Clarenden, 1975.

———. *Complete Works*. Edited by J. M. Cooper. Indianapolis: Hackett, 1997.

Pliny the Elder. *Natural History, Vol. II, Books III–VII*. Translated by H. Rackham. London: William Heinemann, 1947.

Plutarch. *Life of Kimon*. Translated by A. Blamire. London: Institute of Classical Studies, University of London, 1989.

Pocock, D. F. *Mind, Body and Wealth*. Oxford: Basil Blackwell, 1973.

Pope John Paul II. "General Audience." Wednesday, July 28th, 1999. http://www.vatican.va/holy_father/john_paul_ii/audiences/1999/documents/hf_jp-ii_aud_28071999_en.html (accessed January 28, 2008).

Prasad, Muni Narayana. *Karma and Reincarnation*. New Delhi: D. K. Printworld, 1994.

Prat, F. "Origen and Origenism." In *Catholic Encyclopedia*. Vol. 11. 1911. http://www.newadvent.org/cathen/11306b.htm (accessed January 28, 2008).

Price, H. H. "Survival and the Idea of Another World." *Proceedings of the Society for Psychical Research* 50 (1953).

Pye, Michael. *The Buddha*. London: Gerald Duckworth, 1979.

Radin, Dean, and J. Rebman. "Are Phantasms Fact or Fancy? A Preliminary Investigation of Apparitions Evoked in the Laboratory." *Proceedings of Presented Papers*. Parapsychological Association 38th Annual Convention, Durham, NC. Charlottesville, VA: Parapsychological Association, 1995: 342–365.

Rahner, Karl. *On the Theology of Death*. Translated by Charles H. Henkey. New York: Herder and Herder, 1961.

Rahul, Ram. *The Dalai Lama: The Institution*. New Delhi: Vikas Publishing House PVT, 1995.

Rahula, Walpola Sri. *What the Buddha Taught*. New York: Grove, 1974.

Ranade, R. D. *A Constructive Survey of Upanishadic Philosophy*. 2nd ed. Bombay: Bharatiya Vidya Bhavan, 1968.

Raphael, Simcha Paull. *Jewish Views of the Afterlife*. London: Jason Aronson, 1994.

Rappoport, Angelo S. *The Folklore of the Jews*. London: Soncino, 1937.

Ratzinger, Joseph. *Eschatology: Death and Eternal Life*. Translated by Michael Waldstein. Washington, D.C.: The Catholic University of America Press, 1977.

Raudive, Konstantin. *Breakthrough*. New York: Taplinger, 1971.

Rawson, Jessica, ed. *Mysteries of Ancient China*. New York: George Braziller, 1996.

Reader, Ian. *Religion in Contemporary Japan*. Honolulu: University of Hawaii Press, 1991.

Reat, N. Ross. *The Origins of Indian Psychology*. Berkeley, CA: Asian Humanities Press, 1990.

Report on Spiritualism of the Committee of the London Dialectical Society. London: Longmans, Green, Reader and Dyer, 1871.

Reynolds, Frank E., and Earle H. Waugh. *Religious Encounters with Death*. University Park, PA: Pennsylvania State University Press, 1977.

Rhine, Louisa E. "Review of *Twenty Cases of The Reincarnation Type*." *Journal of Parapsychology* 30 (1966): 263–272.

Rinbochay, Lati, and Jeffrey Hopkins. *Death, Intermediate State and Rebirth in Tibetan Buddhism.* London: Rider, 1979.

Ring, Kenneth. *Life at Death: A Scientific Investigation of the Near-Death Experience.* New York: Quill, 1982.

Robinson, Neal. *Discovering the Qur'an.* London: SCM, 1996.

Rogo, D. Scott. *The Search for Yesterday.* Englewood Cliffs, NJ: Prentice-Hall, 1985.

Roll, William G. *The Poltergeist.* Garden City, New York: Nelson Doubleday, 1972.

———. "Changing Perspectives on Life After Death." In *Advances in Parapsychological Research.* Vol. 3. Edited by Stanley Krippner. New York: Plenum, 1982.

———, and B. A. Braun. "Psychomanteum Research: A Pilot Study." *Proceedings of Presented Papers.* Parapsychological Association 38th Annual Convention, Durham. NC. Charlottesville, VA: Parapsychological Association, 1995: 438–443.

Sabom, Michael. *Recollections of Death: A Medical Investigation.* New York: Simon & Schuster, 1982.

Sahih Bukhari. Translated by M. Mushin Khan. http://www.usc.edu/dept/MSA/fundamentals/hadithsunnah/bukhari (accessed January 28, 2008).

Salter, William Henry. *Ghosts and Apparitions.* London: G. Bell & Sons, 1938.

Saltmarsh, Herbert Francis. *Evidence for Personal Survival From Cross Correspondences.* London: G. Bell & Sons, 1938.

Sargent, Epes. *The Proof Palpable of Immortality: An Account of the Materilization Phenomena of Modern Spiritualism.* Boston, MA: Colby and Rich, 1876.

Schiller, F. C. S. *Riddles of the Sphinx.* London: Swan Sonnenschein, 1910.

Schimmel, Annemarie. *Deciphering the Signs of God.* New York: SUNYP, 1994.

Schipper, Kristofer. *The Taoist Body.* Translated by Karen C. Duval. Berkeley, CA: University of California Press, 1993.

Schmitt, Jean-Claude. *Ghosts in the Middle Ages.* Translated by Teresa Lavender Fagan. Chicago: University of Chicago Press, 1998.

Scholem, Gershom. *Kabbalah.* New York: Quadrangle/The New York Times Book, 1974.

Schumann, H. Wolfgang. *Buddhism: An Outline of its Teachings and Schools.* Translated by Georg Fenerstein. London: Rider, 1973.

Schuon, Frithjof. *Dimensions of Islam.* Translated by P. N. Townsend. London: George Allen and Unwin, 1969.

Schwartz, Gary E. R., with William L. Simon. *The Afterlife Experiments: BreakthroughEvidence of Life After Death.* New York: Pocket Books, 2002.

Schwartz, Gary E. R., Linda G. Russek, and Christopher Barentsen. "Accuracy and Replicability of Anomalous Information Retrieval: Replication and Extension." *Journal of the Society for Psychical Research* 66:3 (2002): 144–156.

——— and Linda G. S. Russek. "Evidence of Anomalous Information Retrieval between Two Mediums: Telepathy, Network Memory Resonance, and Continuance of Consciousness." *Journal of the Society for Psychical Research* 65:4 (2001): 257–275.

———, Linda G. S. Russek, Lonnie A. Nelson, and Christopher Barentsen. "Accuracy and Replicability of Anomalous After-Death Communication Across Highly Skilled Mediums." *Journal of the Society for Psychical Research* 65:1 (2001): 1–25.

Segal, Alan F. *Life After Death: A History of the Afterlife in Western Religion.* New York: Doubleday, 2004.

Shahar, Meir, and Robert P. Weller. *Unruly Gods: Divinity and Society in China.* Honolulu: University of Hawaii Press, 1996.

Shakespeare, William. *The Complete Works.* Edited by Stanley Wells, et al. Oxford: Clarenden, 1988.

Sidgwick, H., A. Johnson, F. W. H. Myers, F. Podmore, and E. M. Sidgwick, "Report on Census of Hallucinations." *Proceedings of the Society for Psychical Research* 10 (1894): 25–422.

Smith, Huston. *The World's Religions.* Revised and updated ed. San Francisco: HarperSanFrancisco, 1991.

Smith, Jane Idleman, and Yvonne Yazbeck Haddad. *The Islamic Understanding of Death and Resurrection.* New York: SUNYP, 1981.

Smith, Margaret. *An Introduction to the History of Mysticism.* London: Sheldon, 1977.

Smith, Robert J. *Ancestor Worship in Contemporary Japan.* Stanford: Stanford University Press, 1974.

The Song Celestial or Bhagavad-Gita. Translated by Sir Edwin Arnold. London: Routledge & Kegan Paul, 1961.

Sonsino, Rifat, and Daniel B. Syme. *What Happens After I Die?: Jewish Views of Life After Death.* Northvale, NJ: Jason Aronson, 1994.

Stace, Walter T. *Mysticism and Philosophy.* London: MacMillan, 1961.

Stanton, H. U. Weitbrecht. *The Teaching of the Qur'an.* New York: Macmillan, 1919.

Stendahl, Krister, ed. *Immortality and Resurrection.* New York: MacMillan, 1965.

Stevenson, Ian. *Twenty Cases Suggestive of Reincarnation.* New York: American Society for Psychical Research, 1966.

———. *Twenty Cases Suggestive of Reincarnation.* 2nd ed. Charlottesville: University Press of Virginia, 1974.

———. *Xenoglossy.* Charlottesville: University Press of Virginia, 1974.

———. *Cases of the Reincarnation Type, Volume I. Ten Cases in India.* Charlottesville: University Press of Virginia, 1975.

———. *Cases of the Reincarnation Type, Volume II. Ten Cases in Sri Lanka.* Charlottesville: University Press of Virginia, 1977.

———. *Cases of the Reincarnation Type, Volume III. Twelve Cases in Lebanon and Turkey.* Charlottesville: University Press of Virginia, 1980.

———. *Cases of the Reincarnation Type, Volume IV. Twelve Cases in Thailand and Burma.* Charlottesville: University Press of Virginia, 1983.

———. *Unlearned Languages: New Studies in Xenoglossy.* Charlottesville: University Press of Virginia, 1984.

———. *Children Who Remember Previous Lives.* Charlottesville: University Press of Virginia, 1987.

———. *Where Reincarnation and Biology Intersect.* Westport, CT: Praeger, 1997.

Sullivan, Lawrence E., ed. *Death, Afterlife, and the Soul.* New York: MacMillan, 1989.

Swartz, Merlin L., ed. and trans. *Studies in Islam.* Oxford: Oxford University Press, 1981.

Tanakh. Philadelphia, PA: Jewish Publication Society, 1988.

Tart, Charles. "Psychophysiological Study of Out-of-the-Body Experiences in a Selected Subject." *Journal of the American Society for Psychical Research* 62:1 (1968): 3–27.

Teiser, Stephen F. *The Scripture of the Ten Kings.* Honolulu: University of Hawaii Press, 1994.

Thurston, Herbert. *Ghosts and Poltergeists.* London: Burns Oates, 1953.

The Tibetan Book of the Dead. Translated by Robert A. F. Thurman. New York: Bantam, 1994.

Tillich, Paul. *A Complete History of Christian Thought.* Edited by Carl E. Braaten. New York: Harper & Row, 1968.

Trachtenberg, Joshua. *Jewish Magic and Superstition.* New York: Meridian, 1961.

Trimingham, J. S. *The Sufi Orders in Islam.* Oxford: Oxford University Press, 1998.

Tyrrell, G. N. M. *Apparitions.* Revised ed. New York: Collier, 1970.

Underhill, Evelyn. *Mysticism.* 14th ed. London: Bracken, 1995.

Van Lommel, Pirn, Ruud van Wees, Vincent Meyers, and Ingrid Elfferich. "Near-Death Experience in Survivors of Cardiac Arrest: A Prospective Study in the Netherlands." *The Lancet* 358:9298 (2001): 2039–2045.

Vasubandhu. *Seven Works of Vasubandhu: the Buddhist Psychological Doctor.* Edited and translated by Stefan Anacker. Delhi: Motilal Banarsidass, 1998.

Walker, Benjamin. *Gnosticism: Its History and Influence.* Wellingborough, UK: The Aquarian Press, 1983.

Wallace, Alfred Russel *Miracles and Modern Spiritualism.* 1896. Reprint, New York: Arno, 1975.

Weatherhead, Leslie D. *The Resurrection of Christ: In the Light of Modern and Psychical Research.* London: Hodder & Stoughton, 1959.

Weinberger-Thomas, Catherine. *Ashes of Immortality: Widow-Burning in India.* Translated by Jeffrey Mehlman and David Gordon White. Chicago: University of Chicago Press, 1999.

Welch, Holmes. *Taoism: The Parting of the Way.* Boston: Beacon, 1965.

Westermarck, Edward. *Pagan Survivals in Mohammedan Civilization.* 1933. Reprint, Amsterdam: Philo, 1973.

Willoughby-Meade, G. *Chinese Ghouls and Goblins.* London: Constable, 1928.

Winklhofer, Alois. *The Coming of His Kingdom.* London: Nelson, 1962.

Wiseman, Richard, and Ciaran O'Keefe. "Accuracy and Replicability of Anomalous After-Death Communication Across Highly Skilled Mediums: A Critique." *The Paranormal Review* 19 (2001): 3–6.

Wolman, Benjamin B., ed. *Handbook of Parapsychology.* New York: Van Nostrand Reinhold, 1977.

Woolger, Roger J. *Other Lives, Other Selves: A Jungian Psychotherapist Discovers Past Lives.* New York: Doubleday, 1987.

Wylie, Turrell. "Ro-langs: The Tibetan Zombie." *History of Religions* 4 (1), (1964): 69–80.

Wyndham, Horace. *Mr. Sludge, the Medium: Being the Life and Adventures of Daniel Dunglas Home.* London: Geoffrey Bles, 1937.

Yao, Xinzhong. *An Introduction to Confucianism.* Cambridge, UK: Cambridge University Press, 2000.

Yuan Mei. *Censored by Confucius.* Edited and translated by Kam Louie and Louise Edwards. Armonk, NY: M. E. Sharpe, 1996.

Zaehner, R. C. *Hinduism.* London: Oxford University Press, 1962.

———. *Mysticism Sacred and Profane.* London: Oxford University Press, 1967.

———. *Concordant Discord.* London: Oxford University Press, 1970.

Zaleski, Carol. *Otherworld Journeys.* Oxford: Oxford University Press, 1988.

Zandee, Jan. *Death as an Enemy: According to Ancient Egyptian Conceptions.* Translated by W. F. Klasens. Leiden: E. J. Brill, 1960.

Index

~

About the Author

Christopher M. Moreman is assistant professor in the Department of Philosophy at California State University, East Bay. Specializing in comparative religion, he has taught courses in world religions; mysticism; death and the afterlife; and new religious movements. Dr. Moreman has published a number of articles dealing with aspects of death and the afterlife as well as religion and popular culture. He is also the founder and cochair of the American Academy of Religion's program unit, Death, Dying, and Beyond, and is the editor of the book *Teaching Death and Dying*.